MUHA

Karen Armstrong spent seven years as a Roman Catholic nun, an experience she recollected in her best-selling autobiography, *Through the Narrow Gate*. She is the author of the worldwide best-seller, *A History of God* (which has now appeared in more than thirty languages), the acclaimed *Islam: A Short History* and, most recently), *Buddha* in the Weidenfeld & Nicolson *Lives* series. She is a teacher at the Leo Baeck College for the Study of Judaism and, in 1999, she received the Muslim Public Affairs Council Media Award.

Also by Karen Armstrong

Buddha

Islam: A Short History

The Battle for God: Fundamentalism in Judaism, Christianity and Islam

In the Beginning: A New Interpretation of Genesis

A History of Jerusalem: One City, Three Faiths

Through the Narrow Gate

A History of God: The 4000-Year Quest of Judaism, Christianity and Islam

MUHAMMAD

A Biography of the Prophet

Karen Armstrong

PHOENIX

For Sally Cockburn, who also understands the pain and power of misrepresentation

A PHOENIX PRESS PAPERBACK

First published in Great Britain
by Victor Gollancz in 1991
This paperback edition published in 2009
by Phoenix Press,
a division of The Orion Publishing Group Ltd,
Orion House, 5 Upper St Martin's Lane,
London WC2H 9EA

An Hachette UK company

A CIP catalogue record for this book is available from the British Library.

Printed and bound in Great Britain by
Clays Ltd, St Ives plc

The Orion Publishing Group's policy is to use papers that are natural, renewable and recyclable products and made from wood grown in sustainable forests. The logging and manufacturing processes are expected to conform to the environmental regulations of the country of origin.

www.orionbooks.co.uk

Contents

Acknowledgements

My thanks to Liz Knights, my editor at Gollancz, and to Peter James, my copy-editor, for their careful work on the manuscript and their helpful suggestions. I am also greatly indebted to Rana Kabbani for her invaluable contribution.

INTRODUCTION TO THE OCTOBER 2001 EDITION

I wrote this biography of Muhammad just over ten years ago at the time of the Salman Rushdie crisis. For some time, I had been disturbed by the prejudice against Islam that I so frequently encountered, even in the most liberal and tolerant circles. After the horrific events of the twentieth century, it seemed to me that we simply could not afford to cultivate a distorted and inaccurate view of the religion followed by the 1.2 billion Muslims who make up a fifth of the world's population. When Ayatollah Khomeini issued his infamous *fatwah* against Rushdie and his publishers, this Western prejudice became even more blatant.

In 1990, when I was writing this book, nobody in Britain wanted to hear that almost exactly a month after the *fatwah,* at a meeting of the Islamic Congress, forty-four out of the forty-five member states condemned the Ayatollah's ruling as unIslamic – leaving Iran out in the cold. Very few Western people were interested to hear that the Sheikhs of Saudi Arabia, the Holy Land of Islam, and the prestigious al-Azhar *madrasah* in Cairo had also declared that the *fatwah* contravened Islamic law. Only a handful of people seemed prepared to listen sympathetically to the many Muslims in Britain who dissociated themselves from the Ayatollah, had no wish to see Rushdie killed, but who had felt profoundly distressed by what they regarded as the blasphemous portrait of the Prophet Muhammad in his novel. The Western intelligentsia seemed to want to believe that the entire Muslim world was clamoring for Rushdie's blood. Some of the leading writers, intellectuals and philosophers in Britain described Islam in a way that either showed astonishing ignorance or a quite horrifying indifference to the truth. As far as they were concerned, Islam was an inherently intolerant, fanatical faith, it deserved no respect; and the sensitivities of Muslims who felt hurt by Rushdie's portrait of their beloved Prophet in *The Satanic Verses* were of no importance.

I wrote the book because it seemed a pity that Rushdie's account of Muhammad was the only one that most Western people were likely to read. Even though I could understand what Rushdie was trying to do in his novel, it seemed important that the true story of the Prophet should also be available, because he was one of the most remarkable human beings who ever lived. It was quite difficult to find a publisher, since many assumed that Muslims would be outraged that an infidel woman like myself should have the audacity to write about their Prophet, and that if they published this book I would soon be joining Rushdie in hiding. But as it turned out, I was greatly moved by the warm and generous reception that Muslims gave my book in those difficult times. Indeed, Muslims and serious Islamists were the first people to take me seriously and to believe that I might be something more than a mere runaway nun, who liked to stir up trouble. And during the next ten years, it seemed that the endemic Islamophobia of the West was beginning to abate. The old prejudice would flare up from time to time, but increasingly people seemed more willing to give Muslims the benefit of the doubt.

Then came the shocking events of 11th September 2001, when Muslim extremists destroyed the World Trade Center in New York together with a wing of the Pentagon, killing over five thousand people. This hideous crime seemed to endorse all the negative Western notions of Islam as a fanatical faith that encourages murder and terror. I am writing this new introduction just over a month after the attack. It has been a strange time. The idea that Islam has a dangerous proclivity to violence is still alive and well. During the endless discussions that followed the tragedy, critics of Islam frequently quoted out of context the more ferocious passages of the Koran, arguing that these verses could easily inspire and endorse extremism. All too often they ignored the fact that both the Jewish and the Christian scriptures can be just as bellicose. In the Torah, the most sacred part of the Jewish Bible, the people of Israel are repeatedly urged to drive the Canaanites from the Promised Land, to destroy their sacred symbols, and to make no treaty with them. A tiny proportion of Jewish fundamentalists use these texts to justify violence against the Palestinians and a religious opposition to the Middle East peace process. But nearly everybody knows enough about Judaism to realize that these intransigent passages are not fully representative and that to use them in this way is illegitimate. Similarly, Jesus is usually presented as a pacifist, but in the gospels he frequently speaks and behaves quite aggressively. On one occasion, he even says that he has come to bring not peace but the sword. But nobody quoted these verses when Christian Serbs horribly slaughtered eight thousand Muslims in Srebreneca. Nobody accused Christianity of being an inherently dangerous and violent faith, because most people knew enough about this complex religion to understand that it would be quite inappropriate to make such an accusation. Most Western people have such an inadequate understanding of Islam that they are not equipped to judge it fairly or to discuss these matters in a useful way.

But even in these dark days, when it has sometimes seemed as though the effort to promote Muslim-Western understanding was now doomed to failure, there have been moments of light. First I was impressed by the way that President George W. Bush and Prime Minister Tony Blair went out of their way to make it clear that the terrorists did not represent the rich and complex tradition of Islam; they made it their business to visit mosques, to reassure Muslims that the war they were about to wage in Afghanistan was not against Islam, and stressed the fact that Islam was an essentially peaceful religion. This was something entirely new. No political leader had made this distinction at the time of the Rushdie crisis.

Then there was the heartening fact that many people seemed to realize that they could no longer remain ignorant about the Muslim faith. In the United States, the Koran was sold out in the bookstores; the sales of books on Islam, including some of my own, soared. Where very few people had been interested in learning the truth about the Muslim faith twelve years earlier, it seemed that people couldn't hear enough about Islam, the Koran, and the Prophet after the shock of September 11th. True, there was an anti-Muslim backlash in some Western countries. Men of Middle-Eastern appearance were killed, including one Sikh, one Coptic Christian and in London an Afghan taxi-driver, who was probably a refugee from the Taliban, was paralyzed from the neck down. Women were afraid to leave their homes wearing the *hijab.* Mosques were attacked. But there was also widespread concern about these horrible events and a determination to put a stop to them. All this is positive, and if the September atrocity leads to a new understanding and appreciation of Islam in the West, something good will have come out of this tragedy.

It was particularly painful to me that the terrorists believed that they were following in the footsteps of the Prophet Muhammad. Usama bin Laden, the chief suspect, followed a fundamentalist ideology based on Muhammad's prophetic career. According to this fundamentalist programme, first enunciated by Sayyid Qutb, an Egyptian intellectual who was executed by President Jamal Abd al-Nasser in 1966, the life of the Prophet was an epiphany, a divine programme, revealed by God; it was the only way to create a properly oriented society. The Prophet Muhammad had fought against what Muslims call the *jahiliyyah* (literally, the Age of Ignorance), the term used by Muslims to describe the corrupt barbarism of pre-Islamic Arabia. But every age, according to

Qutb, had its *jahiliyyah* and Muslims of the twentieth century must follow the example of the Prophet and extirpate this evil from their region. First, they must withdraw from mainstream *jahili* society and create a dedicated vanguard that would one day fight on behalf of the Muslim people, just as Muhammad had done when he first began to preach in Mecca. Eventually, like Muhammad, true Muslims would have to withdraw from the *jahiliyyah* altogether, and create a truly Islamic society, an enclave of pure faith, where they could prepare for the coming struggle. In the last stage of the programme, the Muslims would be forced to fight a *jihad*, a holy war, confident of their eventual success – just as Muhammad was when he conquered Mecca in 630 and united the whole of Arabia under Islamic rule.

Bin Laden clearly subscribed to this ideology. In the weeks following September 11th, he frequently used Qutb's terminology, and his training camps can be seen as those pious enclaves where his dedicated vanguard prepared for the *jihad*. The hijackers too had Muhammad in mind, when they boarded the doomed aircraft. 'Be optimistic,' they were told in the documents that were allegedly found in their luggage, 'the Prophet was always optimistic.'

But the very idea that Muhammad would have found anything to be optimistic about in the carnage committed in his name on September 11th is an obscenity, because, as I try to show in these pages, Muhammad spent most of his life trying to stop that kind of indiscriminate slaughter. The very word *islam*, which denotes the existential 'surrender' of their whole being to God which Muslims are required to make, is related to *salam*, 'peace.' And most importantly, Muhammad eventually abjured violence and pursued a daring, inspired policy of non-violence that was worthy of Gandhi. In imagining that the holy war was the culmination of his prophetic career, the fundamentalists have distorted the whole meaning of his life. Far from being the father of *jihad*, Muhammad was a peacemaker, who risked his life and nearly lost the loyalty of his closest companions, because he was so determined to effect a reconciliation with Mecca. Instead of fighting an intransigent war to the death, Muhammad was prepared to negotiate and to compromise. And this apparent humiliation and capitulation proved, in the words of the Koran, to be a great victory (*fat'h)*.

We need the Prophet's story at this dangerous time. Muslim extremists must not be allowed to hijack the biography of Muhammad and twist it to suit their own ends. Furthermore, there is much that we can learn from the Prophet about how we should conduct ourselves in our utterly changed world. Muhammad had no blueprint, no clear plan of action, when he began his mission. Any such plan would inevitably have been rooted in the old, violent world of attack, retaliation, and counter attack, which he knew must be superseded. Instead of forming a policy and sticking to it, Muhammad simply listened, with attention, intelligence and sensitivity to events as they unfolded, allowed their inner logic to speak to him, saw further than his contemporaries, and responded accordingly. Thus he was able to bring about a solution for war-torn Arabia that would have been utterly inconceivable at the outset. We too are grappling with fundamental change after the September tragedy. We must also realize that we cannot, for example, fight this new kind of warfare with the weapons and ideology of the Cold War. We need new solutions for our unprecedented situation, and can learn much from the Prophet's restraint. But above all, we can learn from Muhammad how to make peace. His whole career shows that the first priority must be to extirpate greed, hatred and contempt from our own hearts and to reform our own society. Only then is it possible to build a safe, stable world, where people can live together in harmony, and respect each other's differences.

In the West, we have never been able to cope with Islam; our ideas about this faith have been crude, dismissive and arrogant, but we have now learned that we cannot remain in an attitude of such ignorance and prejudice. At the end of this biography, I quoted the Canadian scholar Wilfred Cantwell Smith, whose work has been a constant inspiration to me. Writing in 1956, he pointed out that both the West and the Islamic world would have to make a major effort if they were not to fail the test of the twentieth century. Muslims would have to come to terms with Western society and Western success, because these were facts of life. But Western people too had to learn 'that they share the planet not with inferiors but with equals.' Until Western civilization and Christian theology could bring themselves 'to treat other men with fundamental respect, these two in their turn will have failed to come to terms with the actualities of the twentieth century.' The tragedy of September 11th showed that even though some progress may have been made, we have all – the West and the Islamic world alike – failed that test. If we are to do better in the twenty-first Christian century, Western people must learn to understand the Muslims with whom they share the planet. They must learn to respect and appreciate their faith, their needs, their anger, and their aspirations. And there can be no better place to start this essential process than with a more accurate knowledge of the life of the Prophet Muhammad, whose special genius and wisdom can illuminate these dark and frightening times.

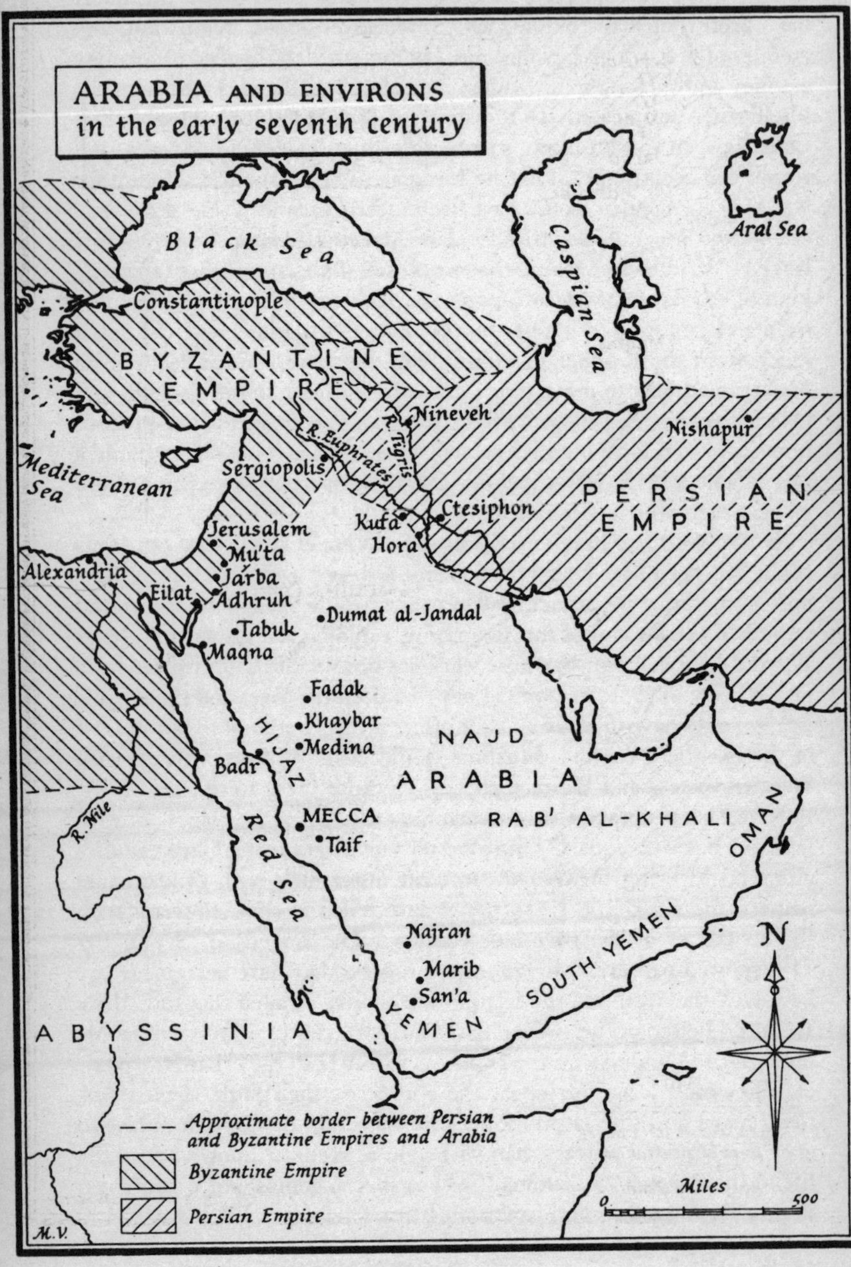
ARABIA AND ENVIRONS
in the early seventh century
Black Sea
Caspian Sea
Aral Sea
Constantinople
BYZANTINE EMPIRE
Nineveh
Nishapur
R. Euphrates
R. Tigris
Mediterranean Sea
Sergiopolis
PERSIAN EMPIRE
Ctesiphon
Kufa
Hora
Jerusalem
Mu'ta
Alexandria
Jarba
Eilat
Adhruh
Dumat al-Jandal
Tabuk
Maqna
Fadak
Khaybar
HIJAZ
NAJD
Medina
Badr
ARABIA
R. Nile
MECCA
RAB' AL-KHALI
OMAN
Taif
Red Sea
Najran
Marib
San'a
SOUTH YEMEN
YEMEN
N
ABYSSINIA
Approximate border between Persian and Byzantine Empires and Arabia
Byzantine Empire
Persian Empire
Miles
0
500
M.V.

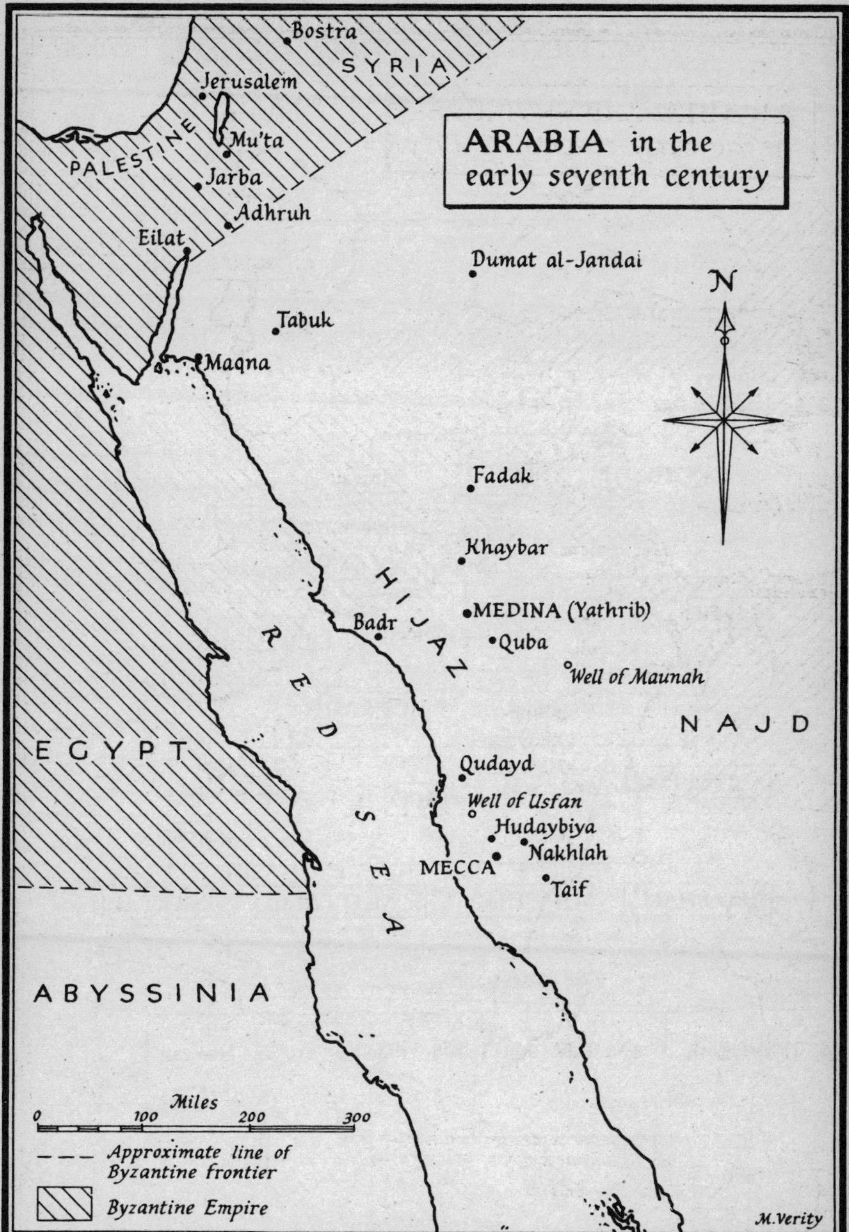
ARABIA in the early seventh century
Bostra
SYRIA
Jerusalem
PALESTINE
Mu'ta
Jarba
Adhruh
Eilat
Dumat al-Jandai
N
Tabuk
Maqna
Fadak
Khaybar
HIJAZ
MEDINA (Yathrib)
Badr
Quba
Well of Maunah
RED SEA
NAJD
EGYPT
Qudayd
Well of Usfan
Hudaybiya
Nakhlah
MECCA
Taif
ABYSSINIA
Miles
0
100
200
300
Approximate line of Byzantine frontier
Byzantine Empire
M.Verity

THE TRIBE OF THE QURAYSH OF THE HOLLOW, *CIRCA* FIFTH AND SIXTH CENTURIES

Founders of clans shown in Upper Case: e.g. TAYM

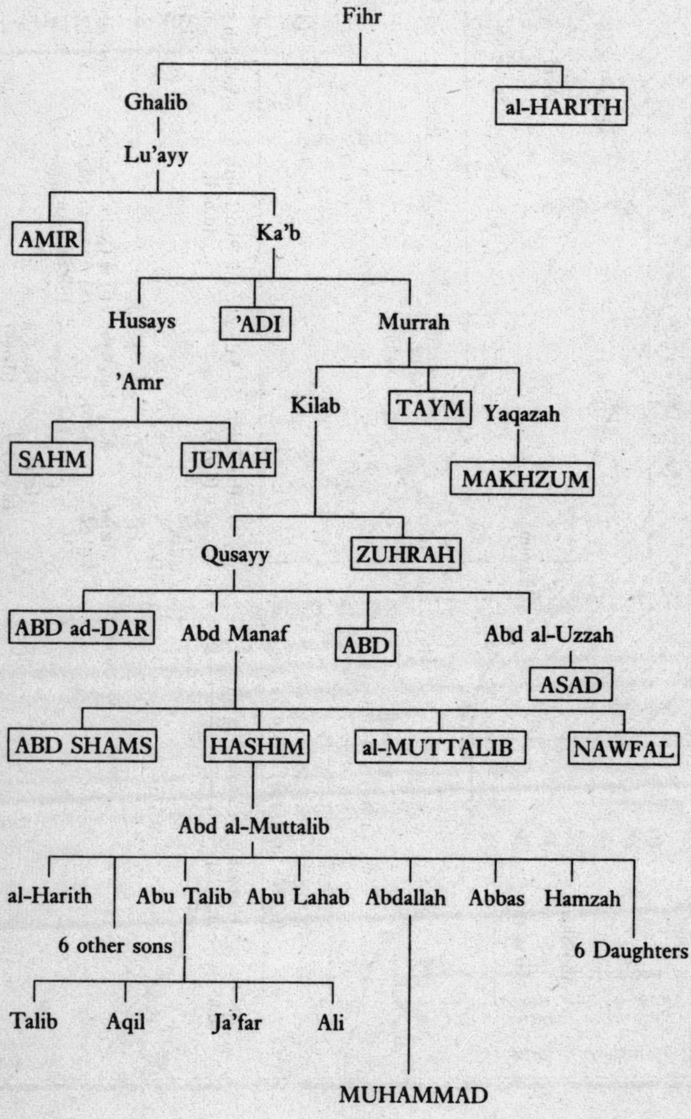

GENEALOGY OF MUHAMMAD AND RELATED FAMILIES

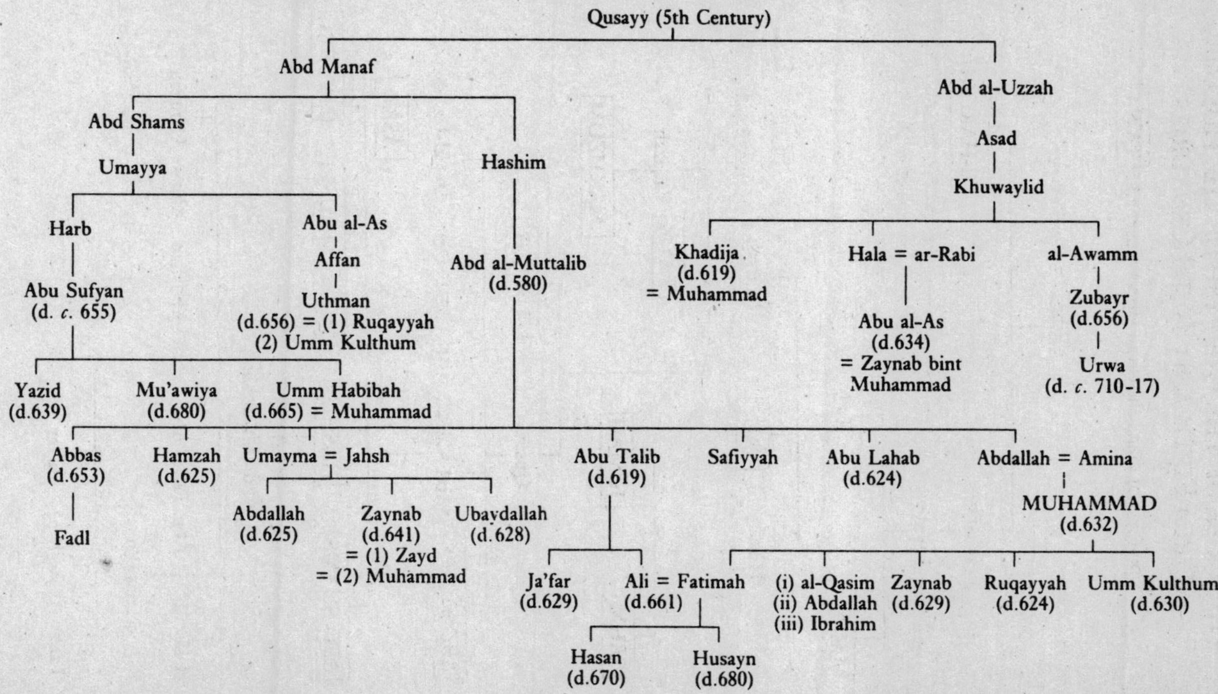

1 · Muhammad the Enemy

It has been difficult for Western people to understand the violent Muslim reaction to Salman Rushdie's fictional portrait of Muhammad in *The Satanic Verses*. It seemed incredible that a novel could inspire such murderous hatred, a reaction which was regarded as proof of the incurable intolerance of Islam. It was particularly disturbing for people in Britain to learn that the Muslim communities in their own cities lived according to different, apparently alien values and were ready to defend them to the death. But there were also uncomfortable reminders of the Western past in this tragic affair. When British people watched the Muslims of Bradford burning the novel, did they relate this to the bonfires of books that had blazed in Christian Europe over the centuries? In 1242, for example, King Louis IX of France, a canonised saint of the Roman Catholic Church, condemned the Jewish Talmud as a vicious attack on the person of Christ. The book was banned and copies were publicly burned in the presence of the King. Louis had no interest in discussing his differences with the Jewish communities of France in a peaceful, rational way. He once claimed that the only way to debate with a Jew was to kill him 'with a good thrust in the belly as far as the sword will go'.[1] It was Louis who called the first Inquisition to bring Christian heretics to justice and burned not merely their books but hundreds of men and women. He was also a Muslim-hater and led two crusades against the Islamic world. In Louis' day it was not Islam but the Christian West which found it impossible to coexist with others. Indeed, the bitter history of Muslim–Western relations can be said to have begun with an attack on Muhammad in Muslim Spain.

In 850 a monk called Perfectus went shopping in the *souk* of Cordova, capital of the Muslim state of al-Andalus. Here he was accosted by a group of Arabs who asked him whether Jesus or Muhammad was the greater prophet. Perfectus understood at once that it was a trick question, because it was a capital offence in the Islamic empire to insult Muhammad, and at first he responded cautiously. But suddenly he snapped and burst into a passionate stream of abuse, calling the Prophet of Islam a charlatan, a sexual pervert and Antichrist himself. He was immediately swept off to goal.

This incident was unusual for Cordova, where Christian–Muslim relations were normally good. Like the Jews, Christians were allowed full religious liberty within the Islamic empire and most Spaniards were proud to belong to such an advanced culture, light years ahead of the rest of Europe. They were often called 'Mozarabs' or 'Arabisers'.

> The Christians love to read the poems and romances of the Arabs; they study the Arab theologians and philosophers, not to refute them but to form a correct and elegant Arabic. Where is the layman who now reads the Latin commentaries on the Holy Scriptures, or who studies the Gospels, prophets or apostles? Alas! all talented young Christians read and study with enthusiasm the Arab books.[2]

Paul Alvaro, the Spanish layman who wrote this attack on the Mozarabs at about this time, saw the monk Perfectus as a cultural and religious hero. His denunciation of Muhammad had inspired a strange minority movement in Cordova whereby men and women presented themselves before the Qadi, the Islamic judge, and proved their Christian loyalty by a vitriolic and suicidal attack on the Prophet.

When Perfectus had arrived in gaol he had been extremely frightened, and the Qadi decided not to pass the death sentence because he judged that Perfectus had been unfairly provoked by the Muslims. But after a few days Perfectus cracked a second time and insulted Muhammad in such crude terms that the Qadi had no option but to apply the full rigour of the law. The monk was executed, and at once a group of Christians, who seem to have lived on the fringes of society, dismembered his body and began to revere relics of their 'martyr'. A few days later another monk called Ishaq appeared before the Qadi and attacked Muhammad and his religion with such passion that the Qadi, thinking him either drunk or deranged, slapped him to bring him to his senses. But Ishaq persisted in his abuse and the Qadi could not continue to permit this flagrant violation of the law.

Ninth-century Cordova was not like Bradford in 1988. The Muslims were powerful and confident. They seemed extremely reluctant to put these Christian fanatics to death, partly because they did not seem in control of their faculties but also because they realised that the last thing they needed was a martyr-cult. Muslims were not averse to hearing about other religions. Islam had been born in the religious pluralism of the Middle East, where the various faiths had coexisted for centuries. The Eastern Christian empire of Byzantium likewise permitted minority religious groups liberty to practise their faith and to manage their own religious affairs. There was no law against propaganda efforts by Christians in the Islamic empire, provided that they did not attack the beloved figure of the Prophet Muhammad. In some parts of the empire there was even an established tradition of scepticism and freethinking which was tolerated as long as it kept within the bounds of decency and was not too disrespectful. In Cordova the Qadi and the Amir, the prince, were both loath to put Perfectus and Ishaq to death but they could not allow this breach of the law. But a few days after Ishaq's execution, six other monks from his monastery arrived and delivered yet another venomous attack on Muhammad. That summer about fifty martyrs died in this way. They were denounced by the Bishop of Cordova and by the Mozarabs, who were all extremely alarmed by this aggressive cult of martyrdom. But the martyrs found two champions: a priest called Eulogio and Paul Alvaro both argued that the martyrs were 'soldiers of God' who were fighting bravely for their faith. They had mounted a complex moral assault against Islam which was difficult for the Muslim authorities to deal with because it seemed to put them in the wrong.

The martyrs came from all levels of society: they were men and women, monks, priests, laymen, simple folk and sophisticated scholars. But many seem to have been searching for a clear, distinct Western identity. Some appear to have come from mixed homes, with a Muslim and a Christian parent; others had been urged to assimilate too closely with Muslim culture – they had been given Arab names[3] or had been pushed into a career in the civil service – and felt disoriented and confused. The loss of cultural roots can be a profoundly disturbing experience and even in our own day it can produce an aggressive, defiant religiosity as a means of asserting the beleaguered self. Perhaps we should remember the martyrs of Cordova when we feel bewildered by the hostility and rage in some of the Muslim communities in the West and in other parts of the world where Western culture threatens traditional values. The martyr movement led by Alvaro and Eulogio was as bitterly opposed to the Christian Mozarabs as to the Muslims and accused them of being cultural defectors. Eulogio made a visit to Pamplona in neighbouring Christendom and came back with Western books: texts of the Latin Fathers of the Church and Roman classical works by Vergil and Juvenal. He wanted to resist the Arabisation of his fellow Spaniards and create a Latin renaissance which looked back with nostalgia to the Roman past of his country as a way of neutralising the influence of the dominant Muslim culture. The movement fizzled out when Eulogio himself was put to death by the Qadi, who begged him to save his life by making a token submission to Islam – nobody would check his subsequent religious behaviour – and not give in to this 'deplorable and fatal self-destruction' like the other 'fools and idiots'.[4] But Eulogio merely told him to sharpen his sword.

This curious incident was uncharacteristic of life in Muslim Spain. For the next 600 years members of the three religions of historical monotheism were able to live together in relative peace and harmony: the Jews, who were being hounded to death in the rest of Europe, were able to enjoy a rich cultural renaissance of their own. But the story of the martyrs of Cordova reveals an attitude that would become common in the West. At that time Islam was a great world power while Europe, overrun by barbarian tribes, had become a cultural backwater. Later the whole world would seem to be Islamic, rather as it seems Western today, and Islam was a continuous challenge to the West until the eighteenth century. Now it seems that the Cold War against the Soviet Union is about to be replaced by a Cold War against Islam.

Eulogio and Alvaro both believed that the rise of Islam was a preparation for the advent of Antichrist, the great pretender described in the New Testament, whose reign would herald the Last Days. The author of the Second Epistle to the Thessalonians had explained that Jesus would not return until the 'Great Apostasy' had taken place: a rebel would establish his rule in the Temple of Jerusalem and mislead many Christians with his plausible doctrines.[5] The Book of Revelation also spoke of a great Beast, marked with the mysterious number 666, who would crawl out of the abyss, enthrone himself on the Temple Mount and rule the world.[6] Islam seemed to fit these ancient prophecies perfectly. The Muslims had conquered Jerusalem in 638, had built two splendid mosques on the Temple Mount and did indeed seem to rule the world. Even though Muhammad had lived after Christ, when there was no need for a further revelation, he had set himself up as a prophet and many Christians had apostasised and joined the new religion. Eulogio and Alvaro had in their possession a brief life of Muhammad, which had taught them that he had died in the year 666 of the Era of Spain, which was thirty-eight years ahead of conventional reckoning. This late eighth century Western biography of Muhammad had been produced in the monastery of Leyre near Pamplona on the hinterland of the Christian world, which trembled before the mighty Islamic giant. Besides the political threat, the success of Islam raised a disturbing theological question: how had God allowed this impious faith to prosper? Could it be that he had deserted his own people?

The diatribes against Muhammad uttered by the Cordovan martyrs had been based on this apocalyptic biography. In this fear-ridden fantasy, Muhammad was an impostor and a charlatan, who had set himself up as a prophet to deceive the world; he was a lecher who had wallowed in disgusting debauchery and inspired his followers to do the same; he had forced people to convert to his faith at swordpoint. Islam was not an independent revelation, therefore, but a heresy, a failed form of Christianity; it was a violent religion of the sword that glorified war and slaughter. After the demise of the martyr movement in Cordova, a few people in other parts of Europe heard their story, but there was little reaction. Yet around 250 years later, when Europe was about to re-enter the international scene, Christian legends would reproduce this fantastic portrait of Muhammad with uncanny fidelity. Some serious scholars would attempt to achieve a more objective view of the Prophet and his religion, but this fictional portrait of 'Mahound' persisted at a popular level. He became the great enemy of the emerging Western identity, standing for everything that 'we' hoped we were not. Traces of the old fantasy survive to the present day. It is still common for Western people to take it for granted that Muhammad had simply 'used' religion as a way of achieving world conquest or to assert that Islam is a violent religion of the sword, even though there are many scholarly and objective studies of Islam and its Prophet that disprove this myth of Mahound.

By the end of the eleventh century, Europe was beginning to rise again under the Pope and was pushing back the frontiers of Islam. In 1061 the Normans had started to attack the Muslims in southern Italy and Sicily, conquering the area in 1091; the Christians of northern Spain had begun the Wars of Reconquest against the Muslims of al-Andalus and conquered Toledo in 1085; in 1095 Pope Urban II summoned the knights of Europe to liberate the tomb of Christ in Jerusalem in the expedition that would become known as the First Crusade. In 1099, after years of incredible hardship, the Crusaders managed to conquer Jerusalem and establish the first Western colonies in the Near East. This new Western success took the form of an out-and-out war against Islam, but at the start nobody in Europe had any particular hatred of the Muslim religion or its Prophet. They were more concerned with their own dreams of glory and the extension of papal Europe. The *Song of Roland*, which was composed at the time of the First Crusade, shows a revealing ignorance of the essential nature of the Islamic faith. The Muslim enemies of Charlemagne and Roland are depicted as idol-worshippers, bowing down before a trinity of the 'gods' Apollo, Tervagant and Mahomet, but they are valiant soldiers whom it was a pleasure to fight. When the armies of the First Crusade fought the Turks for the first time in Asia Minor, they were also full of respect and admiration for their courage:

What man, however experienced and learned, would dare to write of the skill and prowess and courage of the Turks, who thought that they would strike terror into the Franks as they had done into the Arabs and Saracens, Armenians, Syrians and Greeks, by the menace of their arrows? Yet, please God, their men will never be as good as ours. They have a saying that they are of common stock with the Franks and are naturally born to be knights. This is true and nobody can deny it, that if only they had stood firm in the faith of Christendom and been willing to accept One God in Three Persons. . . . you could not find stronger or braver or more skilful soldiers; and yet by God's grace they were beaten by our men.[7]

The Franks had felt kinship with the Muslim soldiers at the battle of Dorylaeum in 1097, but two years later when the Crusaders conquered Jerusalem they seemed unable to see the Muslims as human beings like themselves. They slaughtered the inhabitants of the city in cold blood in a massacre which shocked even their own contemporaries. After this, Muslims were regarded as vermin to be cleared away from the holy places: the official word for them in Crusading jargon is 'filth'.

Before 1100 there was practically no interest in Muhammad in Europe, but by 1120 everybody knew who he was. At about the same time as the myths of Charlemagne, King Arthur and Robin Hood were being evolved in the West, the myth of Mahound, the enemy and shadow-self of Christendom, was firmly established in the Western imagination. As R. W. Southern explains in his monograph *Western Views of Islam in the Middle Ages*:

There can be little doubt that at the moment of their formation these legends and fantasies were taken to represent a more or less truthful account of what they purported to describe. But as soon as they were produced they took on a literary life of their own. At the level of popular poetry, the picture of Mahomet and his Saracens changed very little from generation to generation. Like well-loved characters of fiction, they were expected to display certain characteristics, and authors faithfully reproduced them for hundreds of years.[8]

Mahound's fictional status in the West has perhaps made it even more difficult for people to see him as an historical character who deserves the same serious treatment as Napoleon or Alexander the Great. The fictional portrait of Mahound in *The Satanic Verses* resonates deeply with these established Western fantasies.

To explain Muhammad's success, the legends claimed that he had been a magician who had concocted false 'miracles' to take in the credulous Arabs and destroy the Church in Africa and the Middle East. One tale spoke of a white bull which had terrorised the population and which finally appeared with the Qu'ran, the scripture which Muhammad had brought to the Arabs, floating miraculously between its horns. Muhammad was also said to have trained a dove to peck peas from his ears so that it looked as though the Holy Spirit were whispering into them. His mystical experiences were explained away by the claim that he was an epileptic, which at that time was tantamount to saying that he was possessed by demons. His sexual life was dwelt on in prurient detail: he was credited with every perversion known to men and was said to have attracted people into his religion by encouraging them to indulge their basest instincts. There was nothing genuine in Muhammad's claims: he had been a cold-blooded impostor who had taken in nearly all his own people. Those of his followers who had seen through his preposterous ideas had kept quiet because of their own base ambition. The one way that Western Christians could explain Muhammad's compelling and successful religious vision was to deny its independent inspiration: Islam was a breakaway form of Christianity, the heresy of all heresies. It was said that one Sergius, an heretical monk, had been rightly forced to flee Christendom and had met Muhammad in Arabia, where he had coached him in his distorted version of Christianity. Without the sword, 'Muhammadanism' would never have flourished: Muslims were still forbidden to discuss religion freely in the Islamic empire. But Muhammad had come to a fitting end: during one of his demonic convulsions he had been torn apart by a herd of pigs.

Some details of this fantasy reflect Christian anxieties about their own emergent identity. Islam was stigmatised as the 'religion of the sword' during the Crusades, a period when Christians themselves must have had a buried worry about this aggressive form of their faith which bore no relation to the pacifist message of Jesus. At a time when the Church was imposing celibacy on a reluctant clergy, the astonishing accounts of Muhammad's sexual life reveal far more about the repressions of Christians than about the facts of the Prophet's own life. There is a definite note of ill-concealed envy in this depiction of 'Islam' as a self-indulgent and easygoing religion. Finally it was the West, not 'Islam', which forbade the open discussion of religious matters. At the time of the Crusades, Europe seemed obsessed by a craving for intellectual conformity and punished its deviants with a zeal that has been unique in the history of religion. The witch-hunts of the inquisitors and the persecution of Protestants by Catholics and *vice versa* were inspired by abstruse theological opinions which in both Judaism and Islam were seen as private and optional matters. Neither Judaism nor Islam share the Christian conception of heresy, which raises human ideas about the divine to an unacceptably high level and almost makes them a form of idolatry. The period of the Crusades, when the fictional Mahound was established, was also a time of great strain and denial in Europe. This is graphically expressed in the phobia about Islam.

It was becoming apparent that Western Christians were not going to be able to accommodate different religious communities and ideologies within their own systems as successfully as either the Muslims or the Byzantines. The only other alien religion on European soil was Judaism, and the First Crusaders had begun their journey to the Middle East by massacring the Jewish communities along the Rhine valley in the first mass pogroms of Europe. Anti-Semitism would become an incurable

European disease during the Crusading period and, at the same time as Christians evolved the myths about Mahound and the Saracens, they also evolved terrifying fantasies about the Jews. Jews were said to murder little children and mix their blood in the Passover bread, to desecrate the Eucharist and to be engaged in a vast international conspiracy for the overthrow of Christendom. There was nothing like these anti-Jewish myths in the Islamic world; they reveal in the Western psyche an unhealthy disturbance and disease. But the conquests in Spain, southern Italy and Sicily meant that there were now tens of thousands of Muslims within the borders of Christendom. The only way that the establishment seemed able to cope with these aliens was by imposing an official policy of apartheid, forbidding Christians to have any contact with their Muslim and Jewish neighbours. Special Church legislation linked the two together as a common foe in the Lateran Councils of 1179 and 1215. Christians were forbidden on pain of excommunication and the consequent confiscation of their property to take service in the houses of Muslims and Jews, to look after their children, to trade with Muslims and Jews or even to eat with them. In 1227 Pope Gregory IX added the following decrees: Muslims and Jews must wear distinctive clothing; they must not appear on the streets during Christian festivals or hold public office in Christian countries; and the muezzin was forbidden to offend Christian ears by summoning the Muslims to prayer in the traditional way.

Pope Clement V (1305–14) declared that the Islamic presence on Christian soil was an insult to God. Christians had already begun to expunge this obscenity. In 1301 Charles of Anjou, King of France, exterminated the last Muslims of Sicily and southern Italy in the reservation of Lucera, which he had described as 'a nest of pestilence . . . lurid in pollution . . . the stubborn plague and filthy infection of Apulia'.[9] In 1492 the final Islamic stronghold in Europe was destroyed when Ferdinand and Isabella conquered Granada: all over Europe church bells pealed joyfully at the Christian victory over the infidel. A few years later Spanish Muslims were given the choice of deportation or conversion. Many preferred to leave Europe but some did convert to Christianity, and they and their descendants were persecuted by the Spanish Inquisition for another 300 years. The spirit of the martyrs of Cordova had replaced the old tolerance, and Spanish Christians now seemed haunted by a fear of crypto-Muslims, living in their midst as the hidden enemies of society.

The unhealthy Western attitude to Islam was often revealed in a schizophrenic reaction. Thus the Holy Roman Emperor Frederick II was an Islamophile who was genuinely more at home in the Muslim world than in Christian Europe, but at the same time he systematically killed and deported the Muslims from his native Sicily. While Christians were butchering Muslims in the Near East, others were sitting at the feet of Muslim scholars in Spain. Christian, Jewish and Mozarabic scholars co-operated in a vast translation project, bringing the learning of the Islamic world to the West and restoring to Europe the classical and ancient wisdom that had been lost in the Dark Ages. The Muslim philosophers Ibn Sina and Ibn Rushd were venerated as intellectual luminaries, though it became increasingly difficult for people to accommodate the fact that they were both Muslims. The problem was graphically shown in Dante's *The Divine Comedy*. Ibn Sina and Ibn Rushd (known in Europe as Avicenna and Averroes) are in Limbo with the virtuous pagans who had founded the intellectual culture that they had helped the West to acquire: Euclid, Ptolemy, Socrates, Plato and Aristotle. Yet Muhammad himself is in the Eighth Circle of Hell, with the schismatics. He suffers a particularly disgusting punishment:

> No cask stove in by cant or middle ever
> So gaped as one I saw there, from the chin
> Down to the fart-hole split as by a cleaver.
>
> His tripes hung by his heels; the pluck and spleen
> Showed with the liver and the sordid sack
> That turns to dung the food it swallows in.[10]

Dante still cannot allow Muhammad an independent religious vision. He is a mere schismatic, who had broken away from the parent faith. The scatological imagery reveals the disgust that Islam inspired in the Christian breast, but it also depicts the split in the Western psyche, which sees 'Islam' as an image of everything in itself which it cannot digest. The fear and hatred, which is a complete denial of the loving message of Jesus, also represents a deep wound in the integrity of Western Christianity.

But others were trying to achieve a more objective vision. At a time when Jews and Muslims were being fused in the Christian imagination as the common enemy of civilisation, it is interesting that one of the first positive portraits of Muhammad in the West comes from Peter Alfonsi, a Spanish Jew who had converted to Christianity in 1106 and then lived in England as the doctor of Henry I. He was hostile to Islam, but presents it as a choice that a person who was uncommitted to the 'true' faith might reasonably make. In about 1120, when anti-Islamic hatred was at its height, William of Malmesbury was the first European to distinguish Islam from paganism: 'The Saracens and the Turks both worship God the Creator and venerate Muhammad not as God but as their prophet.'[11] It was an insight that many Westerners have been reluctant to accept: some people are still genuinely surprised to hear that Muslims worship the same God as Jews and Christians: they imagine that 'Allah' is an entirely different deity, like Jupiter in the Roman pantheon. Others tend to assume that 'Muhammadans' give the same kind of veneration to their Prophet as Christians to Christ.

The difficulty of separating fact from fiction is apparent in the *History of Charlemagne* by the Pseudo-Turpin, which was written some time before 1150. This romance depicts the idolatrous Saracens worshipping Mahomet alongside Apollo and Tervagant, in the usual manner of the *chansons de gestes.* But in the middle of it all, there is a rational debate between Roland and the Muslim giant Ferracutus which recognises that the Muslims worship the one God. At about the same time, the chronicler Otto of Freising denied the myth of Muslim idolatry:

> it is known that the whole body of Saracens worship one God and receive the Old Testament law and the rite of circumcision. Nor do they attack Christ or the Apostles. In this one thing alone they are far from salvation – in denying that Jesus Christ is God or the Son of God, and in venerating the seducer Mahomet as a great prophet of the supreme God.[12]

By the middle of the twelfth century, therefore, a more accurate view of Islam was beginning to be widespread, but this greater objectivity was not strong enough to oust the myths of hostility. Fact and fantasy lived quite happily side by side and, even when people were genuinely trying to be fair, the old hatred appears at some point. Muhammad is still the impostor and schismatic, even though Otto had a more rational view of his religion.

The most important of these twelfth-century attempts to find a more objective view of Islam was undertaken by Peter the Venerable, the humane Abbot of Cluny. In 1141 he had made a tour of the Benedictine monasteries in Christian Spain and commissioned a team of Christian and Muslim scholars, under the leadership of the Englishman Robert of Ketton, to translate some Islamic texts, a project that was completed in 1143. They produced the first Latin translation of the Qu'ran, a collection of Muslim legends, a Muslim history of the world, an explanation of Islamic teaching and a work of polemic called *The Apology of al-Kindi.* It was a remarkable feat; it gave people in the West the means to make a serious study of Islam for the first time. But it achieved little. By this period the Christians were beginning to suffer major military defeats in the Crusader states in the Near East. There was a new wave of anti-Muslim feeling, orchestrated by Bernard, Abbot of Clairvaux. It was not a good time to begin an objective study of the Qu'ran. Peter had written his own treatise, which addressed the Muslim world gently and with affection: 'I approach you, not as men often do, with arms but with words; not with force but with reason, not in hatred but in love. . . . I love you, loving you I write to you, writing to you I invite you to salvation.'[13] But the title of this treatise was *Summary of the Whole Heresy of the Diabolic Sect of the Saracens.* Few real Muslims, even if they were able to read the Abbot of Cluny's Latin text, would find such an approach sympathetic. Even the kindly Abbot, who demonstrated his opposition to the fanaticism of his time on other occasions, showed signs of the schizophrenic mentality of Europe vis-à-vis Islam. When King Louis VII of France led the Second Crusade to the Middle East in 1147, Peter wrote to him saying that he hoped he would kill as many Muslims as Moses (*sic*) and Joshua had killed Amorites and Canaanites.[14]

In the early thirteenth century, another saintly Christian made an attempt to reach out to the Muslim world in the context of a military crusade. During a lull in the disastrous Fifth Crusade (1218–19), Francis of Assisi appeared in the Christian camp in the Nile delta, crossed the enemy lines and asked to be taken to the Sultan al-Kamil. He is said to have spent three days with the Sultan, expounding the gospel message and urging al-Kamil to become a Christian. Because he did not insult the memory of the Prophet Muhammad, the Muslims were quite prepared to listen and seem to have been rather impressed by this ragged, dirty fellow. When he left, al-Kamil said: 'Pray for me, that God may deign to show me the law and the faith that are most pleasing to him.' He sent Francis back to the Christian camp 'with every mark of respect and in complete safety'.[15]

But before Francis had set off to the East, he had despatched a party of his Friars Minor to preach to the Muslims in Spain and Africa, and they approached the Islamic world in a very different spirit. Arriving at Seville, they resorted to the techniques of the martyrs of Cordova. First they tried to break into the mosque during the Friday prayers, and when they were driven away they screamed abuse at the Prophet Muhammad outside the palace of the Amir. There was no reaching out to the Saracens with compassion and love during this first major missionary venture to Islam. The Franciscans were not interested in converting the Muslims, but wanted to use them to gain the crown of martyrdom. They became so vociferous that the authorities, who were highly embarrassed by the incident, were forced to imprison them, and to avoid publicity they moved them from one prison to another. They were reluctant to pass the death sentence, but the local Mozarab Christians feared that these fanatics might endanger their own position and they begged the authorities to get rid of them. Eventually the Franciscans were deported to Ceuta in Morocco, where they went straight to the mosque and yet again abused Muhammad as the people assembled for the Friday prayers. Finally the authorities were forced to execute them. When Francis heard this, he is believed to have exclaimed joyfully: 'Now I know that I have five Friars Minor.'[16]

This attitude seems to have been characteristic of later Franciscan missions. In 1227 another group were executed at Ceuta; they had written home to say that the main object of their mission had been 'the death and damnation of the infidels'.[17] Others went to the Holy Land. James of Vitry, the Bishop of Acre, who disapproved of their methods, explained:

> The Saracens listen willingly to the Friars Minor when they speak of the faith of Christ and the teaching of the Gospels. But when their words openly contradict Muhammad, who appears in their sermons as a perfidious liar, they strike them without respect, and if God did not protect them marvellously, would almost murder them and drive them from their cities.[18]

Thus during the Middle Ages, even when people were trying to be fair and objective or approached the Muslim world with the Christian message, hostility erupted, sometimes in a particularly violent form. At the end of the thirteenth century, the Dominican scholar Riccoldo da Monte Croce travelled in Muslim countries and was impressed by the quality of the piety he saw: Muslims put Christians to shame, he wrote. But when he returned home to write the *Disputatio contra Saracenos et Alchoranum*, he simply repeated the old myths. The Western image of Islam was beginning to acquire an authority that was stronger than any contact with real Muslims, however positive. During the age of the Crusades, the West found its soul. Most of our characteristic passions and enthusiasms can be traced back to that period. As Umberto Eco points out in his essay 'Dreaming of the Middle Ages':

> In fact both Americans and Europeans are inheritors of the Western legacy, and all the problems of the Western world emerged in the Middle Ages: modern languages, merchant cities, capitalistic economy (along with banks, checks and prime rate) are inventions of medieval society. In the Middle Ages we witness the rise of modern armies, of the modern concept of the nation state, as well as the idea of a supernatural federation (under the banner of a German Emperor elected by a Diet that functioned like an electoral convention); the struggle between the poor and the rich, the concept of heresy or ideological deviation, even our contemporary notion of love as a devastating unhappy happiness. I could add the conflict between church and state, trade unions (albeit in a corporative mode), the technological transformation of labour.[19]

He could also have added: the problem of Islam. After the Middle Ages people in the West continued many of the old medieval mythologies. Many more attempts were made to gain a more positive and objective perspective, but alongside the growing scholarly consensus that 'Islam' and its Prophet were not the monstrous phenomena that people imagined, the traditional prejudice remained.

The apocalyptic view of Islam promoted by the martyrs of Cordova had continued during the Crusading period, though it was not a major theme. In 1191, when Richard the Lionheart had been travelling to the Holy Land with the Third Crusade, he had met the celebrated Italian mystic Joachim of Fiori at Messina in Sicily. Joachim had told Richard that he would certainly defeat Saladin. He was wrong, but he made some other interesting observations. He believed that the end of the world was at hand and that resurgent Islam was one of the chief instruments of Antichrist, but he added that Antichrist himself was already alive in Rome and was destined to become the Pope. As people in Europe became more critical of their society, Islam became associated with the enemy within. The reformers made the same identification between the faithless papacy (their own arch enemy) and Islam. Thus in the later writings of the fourteenth-century English reformer John Wycliffe, the main faults of 'Islam' were exactly the same as the faults of the Western Church in his own day: pride, greed, violence and the lust for power and possession. 'We Western Mahomets,' he wrote, referring to the Western Church as a whole, 'though we are only a few among the whole body of the Church, think that the whole world will be regulated by our judgement and tremble at our command.'[20] Until the Church returned to the true spirit of the Gospels and to evangelical poverty, this 'Islamic' spirit would grow in the West as well as in the East. This was a subtle transmutation of the old habit of making 'Islam' and its Prophet the opposite of everything that 'we' hoped (or feared) that we were.

Wycliffe had to rely on much unreliable information, but he had read the Qu'ran in translation and thought that he had found important points of comparison between Muhammad and the Church of Rome. Like the Church, he argued, Muhammad had been very cavalier with the Bible, picking out what suited him and discarding the rest. Like the religious orders, Muhammad had made innovations which laid an extra burden on the faithful. Above all, like the Church Muhammad had forbidden any free discussion of religion. Wycliffe had read the old medieval prejudice into certain passages of the Qu'ran, which does not forbid religious discussion *per se* but points out that some kinds of theological debate had been divisive in both of the older religions of the one God and had divided them into warring sects. Some ideas about God could only be speculative guesswork: nobody, for example, could prove the doctrine of the Incarnation, which appeared to Muhammad to have been added by some Christians to the pristine message of the Prophet Jesus. Wycliffe, however, compared this so-called Islamic intolerance to the attitude of the Church over problematic doctrines like the Eucharist, telling Christians to believe blindly the things that they could not understand.

Luther and the other Protestant reformers continued this habit. At the end of his life, faced with the frightening encroachments of the Ottoman Turks into Europe, Luther shared the nightmare of the martyrs of Cordova and believed that Christendom could be entirely engulfed by Islam. In 1542 he published his own translation of Riccoldo da Monte Croce's *Disputatio*. In his preface, he mentions that he had read it years earlier but had found it impossible to accept that people could believe such a manifest tissue of lies. He had wanted to read the Qu'ran but could not find a Latin translation – as R. W. Southern points out, this is a telling indication of the low state of Islamic studies in the sixteenth century – but recently a copy had come into his hands and he had realised that Riccoldo had spoken the truth. He asked whether Muhammad and the Muslims were the Antichrist and replied that 'Islam' was too gross to fulfil this terrible destiny. The real enemy was the Pope and the Catholic Church and, as long as Europe clung to this internal enemy, it laid itself open to the danger of defeat at the hands of the 'Muhammadans'. Zwingli and some of the other reformers put forward similar ideas, seeing Rome as the 'head' of Antichrist and 'Muhammadanism' as its body. This Protestant development shows that 'Islam' had been interiorised by many people in Europe and had become a symbol of absolute evil in their emotional landscape. As Norman Daniel explains in his perceptive study *The Arabs and Medieval Europe*, it was no longer an exterior historical reality that could be examined critically like any other. The reformers had 'introduced the idea of Islam as an interior state which may be imputed to the enemies of pure doctrine (however the writer may define it). In so doing they in effect admitted the interiorization of Islam as the "enemy" (undifferentiated) which it had been for so long in the European imagination.'[21] Daniel gives the example of Catholics and Protestants comparing their Christian opponents with 'Islam' but with little understanding of what the comparison really entailed. The seventeenth-century Catholic missionary M. Lefebvre saw Muslims as 'Muhammadan Protestants' who believe in justification by faith: 'they hope for the remission of all their sins, provided they believe in Mahomet'. But the eighteenth-century Protestant travel writer L. Rauwolff saw Muslims as 'Muhammadan Catholics': 'they go after their own invented devotion to good works, alms, prayers, fasting, redeeming of captives etc., to make satisfaction to God'.[22] In the Middle Ages, Christians had been able to see Islam only as a failed version of Christianity, and had created myths to show that Muhammad had been instructed by a heretic. Later, in the light of fresh internal divisions in Christendom, Westerners continued to see

Muhammad and his religion in essentially Christian terms; they seemed unconcerned with the objective historical truth, nor does it seem to have occurred to them that Muslims had their own independent enthusiasms that could not adequately be defined with reference to Christian practice.

But during the Renaissance other Western people were trying to acquire a more objective understanding of the Islamic world. They were carrying on the tradition and aspiration of Peter the Venerable, which had been continued in the fifteenth century by scholars like John of Segovia and Nicholas of Cusa. In 1453, just after the Turks had conquered the Christian empire of Byzantium and brought Islam to the threshold of Europe, John of Segovia pointed out that a new way of coping with the Islamic menace had to be found. It would never be defeated by war or conventional missionary activity. He began work on a new translation of the Qu'ran, collaborating with a Muslim jurist from Salamanca. He also proposed the idea of an international conference, at which there could be an informed exchange of views between Muslims and Christians. John died in 1458, before either of his projects had been brought to fruition, but his friend Nicholas of Cusa had been enthusiastic about this new approach. In 1460 he had written the *Cribratio Alchoran* (The Sieve of the Qu'ran), which was not conducted on the usual polemical lines but attempted the systematic literary, historical and philological examination of the text that John of Segovia had considered essential. During the Renaissance, Arabic studies were instituted and this cosmopolitan and encyclopaedic approach led some scholars to a more realistic assessment of the Muslim world and to an abandonment of cruder Crusading attitudes. But, as in the Middle Ages, the growing appreciation of the facts was not enough to neutralise the old images of hatred, which had such a powerful hold on the Western imagination.

This is very clear in the year 1697, when, at the very beginning of the Enlightenment, two influential works were published. The first was the *Bibliothèque orientale* of Barthélmy d'Herbelot, which remained the most important and authoritative source of reference in Islamic and Oriental studies in England and Europe until the beginning of the nineteenth century. It has been described as the first *Encyclopaedia of Islam*. D'Herbelot had used Arabic, Turkish and Persian sources and had made a real effort to break out of the blinkered Christian approach: he had, for example, given alternative accounts of the creation myths current in the East. This approach could only be positive and was a sign of a healthier spirit. But under the heading 'Mahomet' we find this sadly familiar entry:

> This is the famous impostor Mahomet, Author and Founder of a heresy, which has taken on the name of religion, which we call Mohammadan. See entry under *Islam*.

The interpreters of the Alcoran and other Doctors of Muslim or Mohammadan Law have applied to this false prophet all the praises which the Arians, Paulicians, or Paulianists, and other Heretics have attributed to Jesus Christ, while stripping him of his Divinity. . . .[23]

Even though d'Herbelot was aware of the proper name of the religion, he continued to call it 'Mohammadan' because that was the name that 'we' use; similarly the Christian world could still see the Prophet only in its own distorted way as an inferior version of 'us'.

The same year the English Orientalist Humphry Prideaux published his important *Mahomet: The True Nature of Imposture.* The title alone shows that he had swallowed the old medieval prejudice – indeed, he cites Riccoldo da Monte Croce as his major source – even though he was claiming to have achieved a more rational and enlightened view of religion than had been possible in the benighted and superstitious Middle Ages. As a man of reason, Prideaux argued that not only was Islam a mere imitation of Christianity but it was a clear example of the idiocy to which all religions, Christianity included, could sink if they were not based firmly on the rock of reason. The Age of Reason had supposedly liberated people from the crippling religious prejudice of the Crusading period, but Prideaux repeats all the old irrational obsessions of the past. He wrote of Muhammad:

For the first Part of his Life he led a very wicked and licentious Course, much delighting in Rapine, Plunder, and Blood-shed, according to the Usage of the *Arabs*, who mostly followed this kind of Life, being almost continually in Arms one Tribe against another, to plunder and take from each other all they could. . . .

His two predominant Passions were *Ambition* and *Lust*. The Course which he took to gain Empire, abundantly shews the former; and the multitude of Women which he had to do with, proves the latter. And indeed these two run through the whole Frame of his *Religion*, there being scarce a Chapter in his *Alcoran*, which doth not lay down some Law of War and Blood-shed for the promoting of the one; or else give some Liberty for the use of Women here, or some Promise for the enjoyment of them hereafter, to the gratifying of the other.[24]

But during the eighteenth century people were trying to promote a more accurate understanding of Islam. Thus in 1708 Simon Ockley produced the first volume of his *History of the Saracens*, which upset many of his readers because he did not reflexively present Islam as the religion of the sword, but tried to see the seventh-century *jihad* from the Muslim point of view. In 1734 George Sale had published a remarkable English translation of the Qu'ran which is still regarded as accurate, though it is a trifle dull. In 1751, François Voltaire published *Les Moeurs et l'esprit des nations* in which he defended Muhammad as a profound political thinker and founder of a rational religion; he pointed out that Muslim polity had always been more tolerant than the Christian tradition. The Dutch Orientalist Johann Jakob Reiske (d.1774) was an incomparable scholar of Arabic who could see a quality of the divine in Muhammad's life and the creation of Islam (but was hounded by some of his colleagues for his pains). During the eighteenth century, a myth was developing that presented Muhammad as a wise, rational lawgiver of the Enlightenment. Henri, Comte de Boulainvilliers, published his *Vie de Mahomed* (Paris, 1730; London, 1731), which portrayed the Prophet as a forerunner of the Age of Reason. Boulainvilliers agreed with the medievals that Muhammad had made up his religion in order to become the master of the world, but turned the whole tradition on its head. Unlike Christianity, Islam was a natural, not a revealed, tradition and that was what was so admirable about it. Muhammad was a great military hero like Julius Caesar and Alexander the Great. This was another fantasy, because Muhammad was certainly no Deist, but it was at least an attempt to see the Prophet in a positive light. At the end of the century, Edward Gibbon in the fiftieth chapter of *The Decline and Fall of the Roman Empire* praised the lofty monotheism of Islam and showed that the Muslim venture deserved a place in the history of world civilisation.

But so entrenched was the old prejudice that many of these writers could not resist giving the Prophet a gratuitous swipe occasionally, demonstrating that the traditional image was not dead. Thus Simon Ockley described Muhammad as 'a very subtle and crafty man, who put on the appearance only of those good qualities, while the principles of his soul were ambition and lust'.[25] George Sale agreed in the introduction to his translation that 'It is certainly one of the most convincing proofs that Mohammadanism was no other than a human invention, that it owes its progress and establishment almost entirely to the sword.'[26] At the end of the essay *Les Moeurs*, Voltaire concluded his positive description of Islam with the observation that Muhammad had been 'regarded as a great man even by those who knew that he was an impostor and revered as a prophet by all the rest'.[27] In 1741 in his drama *Mahomet or Fanaticism*, Voltaire had been able to take advantage of the current prejudice to use Muhammad as an example of all the charlatans who have enslaved their people to religion by means of trickery and lies: finding some of the old legends insufficiently scurrilous, he had blithely made up some of his own. Even Gibbon had little time for Muhammad himself, arguing that he had lured the Arabs to follow him with the bait of loot and sex. As for the Muslim belief in the divine inspiration of the Qu'ran, Gibbon loftily declared it an impossible position for the truly civilised man:

> This argument is most powerfully addressed to a devout Arabian whose mind is attuned to faith and rapture, whose ear is delighted by the music of sounds, and

> whose ignorance is incapable of comparing the productions of human genius. The harmony and copiousness of style will not reach, in a version, the European infidel; he will peruse with impatience the endless incoherent rhapsody of fable and precept and declamation, which seldom excites a sentiment or an idea, which sometimes crawls in the dust, and is sometimes lost in the clouds.[28]

This shows a new Western confidence. No longer are Europeans cowering before the Islamic threat; instead they regard the Muslim religion with amused condescension, assuming that, if 'we' do not understand the Qu'ran, it must mean that there is nothing in it. In 1841, Thomas Carlyle would also dismiss the Qu'ran with contempt in his lecture on Muhammad, 'The Hero as Prophet'. This was, however, a passionate plea for Muhammad and a denial of the old medieval fantasy. For almost the first time, somebody in Europe was trying to see Muhammad as a genuinely religious man. But the Qu'ran was condemned as the most boring book in the world: 'a wearisome, confused jumble, crude, incondite; endless iterations, long-windedness, entanglement; most crude, incondite, insupportible stupidity in short'.[29]

At the very end of the eighteenth century, a telling incident showed the direction in which the new European confidence was tending. In 1798 Napoleon sailed to Egypt, accompanied by scores of Orientalists from his Institut d'Égypte. He intended to use all this new scholarship and understanding to subjugate the Islamic world and challenge the British hegemony of India. As soon as they landed, Napoleon sent the scholars off on what we should call a fact-finding mission, giving his officers strict instructions to follow their advice. They had obviously done their homework well. Napoleon had cynically addressed the Egyptian crowd at Alexandria with the claim: 'Nous sommes les vrais musulmans.' Then he had sixty sheikhs of al-Azhar, the great mosque in Cairo, brought with full military honours into his quarters. He carefully praised the Prophet, discussed with them Voltaire's *Mahomet* and seems to have held his own with the learned *ulema*. Nobody took Napoleon very seriously as a Muslim, but his sympathetic understanding of Islam did allay the hostility of the people to a degree. Napoleon's expedition came to nothing: he was defeated by the British and Turkish armies and sailed back to Europe.

The nineteenth century was characterised by the colonial spirit, which was giving Europeans the unhealthy belief that they were superior to other races: it was up to them to redeem the barbarous world of Asia and Africa in a *mission civilisatrice*. This inevitably affected the Western view of Islam, as the French and the British looked covetously towards the declining Ottoman empire. In the French Christian apologist François René de Chateaubriand, for example, we find a revival of the Crusading ideal which had been adapted to meet the new conditions. He had been impressed by Napoleon's expedition, seeing him as a Crusader–pilgrim. The Crusaders had tried to bring Christianity to the East, he argued. Of all religions, Christianity was the one 'most favourable to freedom', but in the Crusading venture it had clashed with 'Islam': 'a cult that was civilization's enemy, systematically favourable to ignorance, to despotism and to slavery'.[30] In the heady days after the French Revolution, 'Islam' had once again become the opposite of 'us'. During the hierarchically minded Middle Ages, some critics of Islam had blamed Muhammad for giving too much power to menials, like slaves and women. This stereotype had now been reversed, not because people necessarily had a fuller knowledge of Islam but because it suited 'our' needs and was as always a foil against which we could measure our achievements.

In his bestseller *Journey from Paris to Jerusalem and from Jerusalem to Paris* (1810–11), Chateaubriand applied his Crusading fantasy to the situation in Palestine. The Arabs, he wrote, 'have the air of soldiers without a leader, citizens without legislators, and a family without a father'. They were an example of 'civilised man fallen again into a savage state'.[31] Therefore they were crying out for the control of the West, because it was impossible for them to take charge of their own affairs. In the Qu'ran there was 'neither a principle for civilisation nor a mandate that can elevate character'. Unlike Christianity, 'Islam' preaches 'neither hatred of tyranny nor love of liberty'.[32]

The influential French philologist Ernest Renan attempted a scientific explanation for these new racial and imperialist myths. He argued that Hebrew and Arabic were degraded languages, deviations from the Aryan tradition, which had become irredeemably flawed. These Semitic tongues could be studied only as an example of arrested development and lacked the progressive character of 'our' linguistic systems. That was why Jews and Arabs were both 'une combinaison inférieure de la nature humaine'.

> One sees that in all things the Semitic race appears to us to be an incomplete race by virtue of its simplicity. This race – if I dare use the analogy – is to the Indo-European family what a pencil sketch is to a painting; it lacks that variety, that amplitude, that abundance of life which is the condition of perfectibility. Like those individuals who possess so little fecundity that, after a gracious childhood, they attain only the most mediocre virility, the Semitic nations experienced their fullest flowering in their first age and have never been able to achieve true maturity.[33]

Yet again, Jews and Arabs had been fused in a single image which provides a flattering description of 'our' superior virtues. The new racism would, of course, have disastrous consequences for European Jewry.

Hitler drew upon the old Christian patterns of hatred in his secular crusade against the Jews, unable to bear the presence of an alien race on pure European and Aryan soil.

There were no Muslims left in Europe, but during the nineteenth century the British and the French began to invade their lands. In 1830 the French colonised Algiers, and in 1839 the British colonised Aden; between them they took over Tunisia (1881), Egypt (1882), the Sudan (1898) and Libya and Morocco (1912). In 1920, even though they had made pledges to the Arab countries that they would have their independence after the defeat of the Turkish empire, Britain and France carved up the Middle East between them into mandates and protectorates.

Today the Muslim world associates Western imperialism and Christian missionary work with the Crusades. They are not wrong to do so. When General Allenby arrived in Jerusalem in 1917, he announced that the Crusades had been completed, and when the French arrived in Damascus their Commander marched up to Saladin's tomb in the Great Mosque and cried: '*Nous revenons, Saladin!*' The Christian missionary effort supported the colonialists, attempting to undermine traditional Muslim culture in the conquered countries, and local Christian groups, like the Maronites of Lebanon, were given a disproportionate role in the running of the protectorate. The colonialists would have argued that they were bringing progress and enlightenment, but the effort was informed with violence and contempt. The pacification of Algeria, for example, took many years and any resistance was brutally put down in reprisal raids. The contemporary French historian M. Baudricourt gives us an idea of what one of those raids was like:

> Our soldiers returning from the expedition were themselves ashamed. . . . about 18,000 trees had been burnt; women, children and old men had been killed. The unfortunate women particularly excited cupidity by the habit of wearing silver ear-rings, leg-rings and arm-rings. These rings have no catch like French bracelets. Fastened in youth to the limbs of girls they cannot be removed when they are grown up. To get them off our soldiers used to cut off their limbs and leave them alive in a mutilated condition.[34]

The colonialists displayed their basic contempt for Islam. In Egypt, Lord Cromer decried the attempt of the liberal intellectual Muhammad Abduh (d.1905) to rethink some traditional Islamic ideas. Islam, he declared, could not reform itself, and the Arabs were incapable of regenerating their own society. As he explained in his magisterial two-volume work *Modern Egypt*, the 'Oriental' was irredeemably childish and the diametrical opposite of 'us':

Sir Alfred Lyall once said to me: 'Accuracy is abhorrent to the Oriental mind. Every Anglo-Indian should always remember that maxim.' Want of accuracy, which easily degenerates into untruthfulness, is in fact the main characteristic of the Oriental mind.

The European is a close reasoner; his statements of fact are devoid of any ambiguity; he is a natural logician, albeit he may not have studied logic; he is by nature sceptical and requires proof before he can accept the truth of any proposition; his trained intelligence works like a piece of mechanism. The mind of the Oriental, on the other hand, like his picturesque streets, is eminently wanting in symmetry. His reasoning is of the most slipshod description. Although the ancient Arabs acquired in a somewhat higher degree the science of dialectics, their descendants are singularly deficient in the logical faculty. They are often incapable of drawing the most obvious conclusions from any simple premises of which they may admit the truth.[35]

Even though Western scholars continued to attempt a more objective picture of the Arab and Muslim world, this colonial superiority made many people believe that 'Islam' was beneath their serious attention.

Certainly this offensive Western attitude has succeeded in alienating the Muslim world. Today anti-Western feeling seems rife in Islam, but that is an entirely new development. The West may have harboured fantasies of Muhammad as its enemy, but in fact most Muslims remained unaware of the West until just over 200 years ago. The Crusades were crucial in the history of Europe and had a formative influence on the Western identity, as I have argued elsewhere.[36] But, though they obviously deeply affected the lives of Muslims in the Near East, the Crusades had little impact on the rest of the Islamic world, where they were simply remote border incidents. The heartlands of the Islamic empire in the Iraq and Iran remained entirely unaffected by this medieval Western assault. They had, therefore, no concept of the West as their enemy. When Muslims thought of the Christian world, they did not think of the West but of Byzantium; at that time Western Europe seemed a barbarous, pagan wilderness, which was indeed far behind the rest of the civilised world.

But Europe caught up and the Muslim world, which was occupied with its own concerns, failed to notice what was happening. Napoleon's expedition to Egypt was an eye-opener for many thoughtful people in the Near East, who were much impressed by the easy, confident bearing of the French soldiers in this post-revolutionary army. Muslims had always responded to the ideas of other cultures, and many were drawn to the radical, modernising ideas of the West. At the turn of this century, nearly every leading intellectual in the Islamic world was a liberal and a Westerniser. These liberals may have hated Western imperialism, but they imagined that liberals in Europe would be on their side and would oppose people like Lord Cromer. They admired the quality of the Western way of life, which seemed to have enshrined many ideals that were central to the Islamic tradition. In the last fifty years, however, we have lost this goodwill. One reason for the alienation of the Muslim world has been its gradual discovery of the hostility and contempt for their Prophet and their religion which is so deeply embedded in Western culture and which they consider still affects its policy towards Muslim countries even in the post-colonial period.

As the Syrian writer Rana Kabbani points out in *Letter to Christendom*:

> Is the Western conscience not selective? The West feels sympathy for the Afghan Mujahedin, propped up by American intelligence just as the Nicaraguan Contras were, but feels no sympathy for militant Muslims who are not fighting its Cold War battles but have political concerns of their own. As I write, Palestinians are dying every day in the Occupied Territories – nearly 600 dead at the latest count, over 30,000 wounded and 20,000 in detention without trial . . . yet Israel remains a democracy in Western eyes, an outpost of Western civilization. What is one to think of such double standards?[37]

The West must bear some measure of responsibility for the development of the new radical form of Islam, which in some hideous sense comes close to our ancient fantasies. Today many people in the Islamic world reject the West as ungodly, unjust and decadent. Some Western scholars like Maxime Rodinson, Roy Mottahedeh, Nikki R. Keddie and Gilles Kepel are trying to understand the meaning of this new Islamic mood. But, as usual, these attempts to attain a more objective and sympathetic comprehension of the present crisis in the Muslim world are the concern of a minority. Other more aggressive voices show little desire to understand but promote the old tradition of hatred.

The new radical Islam is not simply inspired by hatred of the West, however. Nor is it in any sense a homogenous movement. Radical Muslims are primarily concerned to put their own house in order and to address the cultural dislocation that many have experienced in the modern period. It is really impossible to generalise about the rise of this more extreme form of the religion. It not only differs from country to country, but from town to town and from village to village. People feel cut off from their roots: Western culture has invaded the interstices of their lives. Even the furniture of their homes has undergone major change and becomes a disturbing sign of domination and cultural loss. In turning to religion, many are attempting to return to their roots and recover an identity which is profoundly threatened. But in each area, the type of Islam is entirely different and idiosyncratic and is deeply affected by local traditions and conditions that are not specifically religious. In his classic book *Recognizing Islam, Religion and Society in the Middle East*, Michael Gilsenan has argued that the differences are so great from one district to another that the term 'Islam' or 'fundamentalism' is simply not useful in defining the current attempt to articulate the experience of people in the Middle East during the post-colonial period. The phenomenon is certainly far more complex than the media tends to suggest. Many Muslims in the area may well be experiencing rather the same sense of dread and loss of identity as that felt by the martyrs of Cordova, who felt that their culture and traditional values were being eroded by an alien power.

We constantly produce new stereotypes to express our apparently ingrained hatred of 'Islam'. In the 1970s we were haunted by the image of the immensely rich oil sheikh; in the 1980s by the fanatical ayatollah; since the Salman Rushdie affair, 'Islam' has become a religion that spells death to creativity and artistic freedom. But none of these images reflects the reality, which is infinitely more complex. Yet this does not stop people from making sweeping and inaccurate judgements. Rana Kabbani cites two hostile remarks by Fay Weldon and Conor Cruise O'Brien. In *Sacred Cows*, her contribution to the Rushdie debate, Weldon writes:

> The Koran is food for no-thought. It is not a poem on which a society can be safely or sensibly based. It gives weapons and strength to the thought-police – and the thought-police are easily set marching, and they frighten . . . I see it as a limited and limiting text when it comes to the comprehension of what I define as God.[38]

I can only say that this remark does not cohere with my own experience of studying the Qu'ran and the history of Islam. But Conor Cruise O'Brien, reverting to the tradition that makes any respect for Islam a cultural defection, would call me a hypocrite. Muslim society, he writes,

> looks profoundly repulsive . . . It looks repulsive because it is repulsive . . . A Westerner who claims to admire Muslim society, while still adhering to Western values, is either a hypocrite or an ignoramus or a bit of both.

He concluded: 'Arab society is sick, and has been sick for a long time. In the last century, the Arab [*sic*] thinker Jamal al-Afghani wrote: "Every Muslim is sick, and his only remedy is in the Koran." Unfortunately the sickness gets worse the more the remedy is taken.'[39]

But not all critics take this Crusading line. Many scholars in our own century have tried to enlarge the Western understanding of Islam: Louis Massignon, H. A. R. Gibb, Henri Corbin, Annemarie Schimmel, Marshall G. S. Hodgson and Wilfred Cantwell Smith. They have followed in the footsteps of people like Peter the Venerable and John of Segovia and have used scholarship to challenge the prejudice of their time. Religion has for centuries enabled members of a given society to cultivate serious understanding. People may not always succeed in expressing their religious ideals as they should, but they have helped notions of justice, benevolence, respect and compassion for others to provide a standard against which we can measure our behaviour. A serious study of Islam shows that for 1,400 years the ideals of the Qu'ran have contributed in large measure to the spiritual welfare of Muslims. Some scholars, like the outstanding Canadian scholar Wilfred Cantwell Smith, would go so far as to say that 'the Muslim segment of human society can only flourish if Islam is strong and vital, is pure and creative and sound.'[40] Part of the Western problem is that for centuries Muhammad has been seen as the antithesis of the religious spirit and as the enemy of decent civilisation. Instead, perhaps, we should try to see him as a man of the spirit, who managed to bring peace and civilisation to his people.

2 · Muhammad the Man of al-Llah

During the month of Ramadan in about the year 610, an Arab merchant of the city of Mecca in the Hijaz had an experience that would ultimately change the history of the world. Each year Muhammad ibn Abdallah retired with his wife and family to a cave on Mount Hira in the Meccan valley to make a spiritual retreat. This was quite common practice in the Arabian peninsula at that time: Muhammad would have spent the month in prayer and would have distributed alms and food to the poor who came to visit him during this sacred period. From the jagged mountain-top the thriving city of Mecca was clearly visible in the plain below. Like all Meccans, Muhammad was very proud of his city, which had become a centre of finance and the most powerful settlement in Arabia. The Meccan merchants had become wealthier than any other Arabs in the Hijaz and enjoyed a security that would have been inconceivable two generations earlier, when they would have been living the grim nomadic life of the Arabian steppes. Above all, the Meccans were fiercely proud of the Ka'aba, the ancient cube-shaped shrine in the centre of the city which, many believed, was really the Temple of al-Llah, the High God of the Arabs. It was the most important shrine in Arabia and each year pilgrims came from all parts of the peninsula to make the *hajj* pilgrimage. The tribe of Quraysh, Muhammad's tribe, had been responsible for the commercial success of Mecca and they knew that a great deal of their prestige among the other Arab tribes was due to the fact that they had the great privilege of guarding the huge granite shrine and ensuring that its sanctities were preserved.

Some of the Arabs believed that al-Llah, whose name simply meant 'the God', was the deity who was also worshipped by the Jews and the Christians.[1] But unlike the 'people of the scriptures', as the Arabs called these two venerable faiths, the Arabs were painfully aware that He had never sent them a revelation or a scripture of their own, even though they had had His shrine in their midst from time immemorial. Those Arabs who came into contact with the Jews and Christians felt an acute sense of inferiority: it seemed as though God had left the Arabs out of His divine plan. But that changed on the seventeenth night of Ramadan when Muhammad was torn from sleep in his mountain cave and felt himself overwhelmed by a devastating divine presence. Later he explained this ineffable experience by saying that an angel had enveloped him in a terrifying embrace so that it felt as though the breath was being forced from his body. The angel gave him the curt command: '*iqra!*' 'Recite!' Muhammad protested in vain that he could not recite; he was not a *kahin*, one of the ecstatic prophets of Arabia. But, he said, the angel simply embraced him again until, just as he thought he had reached the end of his endurance, he found the divinely inspired words of a new scripture pouring from his mouth. The Word of God had been spoken for the first time in Arabia and God had finally revealed Himself to the Arabs in their own language. The holy book would be called the Qu'ran: the Recitation.

The consequences of this strange experience were immense. When Muhammad began to preach the Word in Mecca, the whole of Arabia was in a state of chronic disunity. Each of the numerous Bedouin tribes of the peninsula was a law unto itself and in a state of constant warfare with other tribal groups. It seemed impossible for the Arabs to unite and that meant that they were unable to found a civilisation and polity that would allow them to take their place in the world. The Hijaz seemed doomed to savage barbarism and existed beyond the pale of civilisation. Twenty-three years later, when Muhammad died on 8 June 632, he had managed to bring nearly all the tribes into his new Muslim community. True, this was a precarious state of affairs. Many of the Bedouin, as Muhammad well knew, clung in secret to the old paganism. But, against all the odds, this Arab unity was preserved. Muhammad had political gifts of a very high order: he had entirely transformed the conditions of his people, rescued them from fruitless violence and disintegration and given them a proud new identity. They were now ready to found their own unique culture and Muhammad's teaching had unlocked such reserves of power that within 100 years, the Arabs' empire stretched from Gibraltar to the Himalayas.

If this political feat had been Muhammad's sole achievement, he would have a claim to our admiration. But his success depended upon the religious vision that he communicated to the Arabs and which was adopted with alacrity by the subject people of the empire, clearly fulfilling a deep spiritual need. Muhammad and his first Muslims did not achieve their triumph easily, as is sometimes imagined. They were engaged in a grim, desperate struggle and unless the religion had come first with the Prophet and his closest companions, they would not have survived. Throughout these years of danger, Muhammad believed that he received direct inspirations from God but he also had to use every natural talent he possessed. Muslims were aware of their Prophet's exceptional ability and were conscious that he had changed the course of history. Four major historians wrote about his life in the classical Islamic period. Muhammad ibn Ishaq (d. *c.* 767). Muhammad ibn Sa'd (d. 845), Abu Jafar at-Tabari (d. 923) and Muhammad ibn Umar al-Waqidi (d. *c.* 820), who concentrated on the Prophet's military campaigns. These are vital sources for any life of Muhammad and I shall constantly refer to them. These historians were not relying simply on their own ideas but were attempting a serious historical reconstruction. They include earlier documents in their narratives, trace oral traditions back to their original source and, though they revere Muhammad as a man of God, they are not writing uncritical hagiography. Thus Tabari records the now notorious affair of the Satanic Verses, which seems to show Muhammad making a mistake. Ibn Sa'd and Ibn Ishaq both include traditions and stories that are not wholly flattering: in particular Muhammad's wife Aisha was an outspoken woman and her sharp comments about her husband are scrupulously recorded. From these biographies, which are confident enough about the quality of their subject not to indulge in whitewash, we get a compelling and realistic portrait of this extraordinary man.

Naturally these early biographers were not writing in the same mode as modern Western historians. They were men of their time and often include stories of a miraculous nature which we would interpret differently today. But they are aware of the complexity of their material and of the elusive nature of truth. We shall see that the Muslim spirit is deeply egalitarian. In Islamic art, the arabesque, with its continuously repeated motifs, does not give greater prominence to any one item by means of perspective or foregrounding. The effect is created by the pattern as a whole and by the intricate relationship that exists between the equal parts. We find much the same spirit in our four historians. They do not usually promote one theory or interpretation of events at the expense of others. Sometimes they put two quite different versions of an incident side by side and make no attempt to explain the discrepancy away. We shall see, for example, that Tabari gives two quite separate accounts of the story of the Satanic Verses and that Ibn Ishaq puts two mutually exclusive versions of the conversion of Umar ibn al-Khattab next to one another without even commenting on the apparent contradiction. In each case the historian lists his sources conscientiously, even though this 'chain' of authorities (*silsilah*) would not meet modern requirements. To the best of their ability they try to give equal weight to each account of events. They will not always agree with all the traditions they include. This in itself shows that, despite their obvious reverence for the Prophet, these early historians were trying to tell his story as honestly and as truthfully as they possibly could.

There are lacunae in their accounts. We know practically nothing about Muhammad's early life before he began to receive the revelations at the age of forty. Inevitably pious legends developed about Muhammad's birth, childhood and youth and these are duly recorded, but there is nothing more solid to go on. Again, there is very little material about Muhammad's early prophetic career in Mecca. At that time, when he was a relatively obscure figure, nobody thought it worthwhile to make a note of his mission. But during the last ten years of his life, after the emigration to Medina, the Muslims were aware that history was being made before their astonished eyes and incidents are recorded in much more detail.

The historians were drawing on oral traditions which had been passed on by the Prophet's first companions to later generations. In the ninth century, scholars such as Muhammad ibn Ismai'il al-Bukhari and Muslim ibn al-Hijjaj al-Qushayri carefully examined the pedigree of each tradition (*hadith*) to make sure it was reliably attested. Any tradition for which the chain of authorities was unreliable, either because there were worrying gaps or because the authorities had a dubious religious reputation, were ruthlessly discarded in their great collections of traditions (*ahadith*), no matter how edifying or flattering they might seem to the Prophet and the early Muslims. As we shall see, the *ahadith* became a major source of the Shari'ah, the Islamic Holy Law, and the editing of the traditions shows that Muslims were able to adopt a critical attitude to their early history. This objectivity is also apparent in the work of the early historians and neither they nor later generations of Muslims have regarded all the preserved traditions as equally valid or authoritative.

Our principal source of information is the Qu'ran itself. This, of course, is not an account of Muhammad's life: it reveals the Creator rather than His Messenger. But it does indirectly provide us with invaluable material about the early history of the Islamic community. Western people find the Qu'ran a difficult book. I shall discuss it in more detail in later chapters, but it is perhaps important to explain what this revealed scripture is at the outset and how we should regard it. Muhammad claimed that for twenty-three years he received direct messages from God, which were collected into the book now called the Qu'ran. The Qu'ran did not descend from heaven all at once, like the Torah or the Law which, according to the Biblical account, was revealed to Moses in one session on Mount Sinai. The Qu'ran came to Muhammad line by line, verse by verse, chapter by chapter. Sometimes the messages dealt with a particular situation in Mecca or Medina. In the Qu'ran, God seems to answer some of Muhammad's critics; He explains the deeper significance of a battle or of a conflict within the Muslim community. As each new message was revealed to Muhammad (who, like many Arabs of the Hijaz, was said to be illiterate) he recited it aloud, the Muslims learned it by heart and those who could wrote it down. The Arabs found the Qu'ran quite astonishing: it was unlike any other literature they had encountered before. Some, as we shall see, were converted immediately, believing that divine inspiration alone could account for this extraordinary language. Those who refused to convert were bewildered and did not know what to make of this disturbing revelation. Muslims still find the Qu'ran profoundly moving. They say that when they listen to it they feel enveloped in a divine dimension of sound, rather like Muhammad on Mount Hira when he experienced the embrace of the angel or when, later, he saw this supernatural being filling the entire sky whichever way he looked.

Western people find this very difficult to understand. We have seen that even the likes of Gibbon and Carlyle, who were reasonably sympathetic to Islam, were baffled by the Qu'ran. This, of course, is not particularly surprising. It is always difficult to appreciate holy books of other cultures. There is a well-known story of some Japanese tourists visiting the West for the first time. Their English was reasonably good and, as they always liked to know something about the religion of countries they visited, they dutifully sat down and started to read the Bible. They were utterly bemused by it and when they arrived in the United States they took their difficulties to a notable scholar. They had really tried to persevere with this book, they explained, but could not for the life of them find any religion in it! The scholar, highly amused, agreed that unless one approached these scriptures in a particular frame of mind, it was indeed difficult to find anything religious or transcendent in its account of the history of the ancient Jewish people.

In the case of the Qu'ran there is also the problem of translation. The most beautiful lines of Shakespeare frequently sound banal in another language because little of the poetry can be conveyed in a foreign idiom; and Arabic is a language that is especially difficult to translate. Arabs point out that they find translations of poems or stories they have enjoyed in the original Arabic unrecognisable in another tongue. There is something about Arabic which is incommunicable in another idiom: even the speeches of Arab politicians sound stilted, artificial and alien in an English translation. If this is true of ordinary Arabic, of mundane utterance or conventional literature, it is doubly true of the Qu'ran which is written in highly complex, dense and allusive language. Even Arabs who speak English fluently have said that when they read the Qu'ran in an English translation, they feel that they are reading an entirely different book. I shall frequently quote from the Qu'ran, but the reader must not expect to be as overwhelmed by the words as were the first Muslims.

This does not mean that we should dismiss the Qu'ran arrogantly. It is not meant to be read like other books. If approached in the right way, believers claim, it yields a sense of divine presence. This is difficult for somebody who has been brought up in the Christian tradition to understand because Christians do not have a sacred language, as Sanskrit, Hebrew and Arabic are sacred to Hindus, Jews and Muslims. It is Jesus himself, not the scriptural texts, who constitutes the Christian revelation and there is nothing holy about the New Testament Greek. Jews will understand this Muslim spirituality more easily, because they revere the Torah (the first five books of what Christians call 'The Old Testament') in a similar way. When they study the Torah, Jews do not simply pass their eyes over the page to acquire information. They say the words aloud, savouring the language that God himself used when He revealed Himself to Moses, until they have learned them by heart (a revealing phrase). Frequently they sway backwards and forwards while they recite, as though they were blown by the breath of God's spirit. Obviously, therefore, when Jews read Torah in this way they are experiencing quite a different book from Christians, who often find that most of the Pentateuch is an extremely dull collection of obscure laws. Muslims also encounter a sense of *barakah* (blessing) in the holy words of God in the Qu'ran. Like the Eucharist, it represents a Real Presence of the divine Word in our midst; in it God has expressed Himself in human form. The power of the Qu'ran can be seen from the fact that many peoples within the Islamic empire abandoned their own languages in order to adopt the sacred tongue of the holy book.

As it stands, the Qu'ran does not present the various suras in the order in which they were uttered by Muhammad. When the first official compilation of the Qu'ran was made in about 650, some twenty years after Muhammad's death, the editors put the longer suras at the beginning and the shortest, which include those revealed earliest to the Prophet, at the end. This is not as arbitrary as it might appear, because the Qu'ran does not present a narrative or an argument that needs a sequential order. Instead we have pronouncements and reflections on various themes, like God's presence in nature, the lives of the prophets, and the Last Judgement. Western people tend to find the Qu'ran tediously repetitive, because it seems to go over the same ground again and again, but the book was not designed for private perusal but for liturgical recitation. When Muslims listen to a sura in the mosque, they are reminded of the central tenets of their faith in a single recitation. Non-Muslims, however, will find the Qu'ran a valuable source of information about Muhammad. Even though it was not officially compiled until after his death, it can be regarded as authentic. Modern scholars, who have been able to date the various suras with reasonable accuracy, point out that, for example, the earliest parts of the Qu'ran refer to the special problems that Muhammad encountered while his religion was still a struggling little sect and that these would have been forgotten later, when Islam was an established and triumphant religion. In the Qu'ran, therefore, we have a contemporaneous commentary on Muhammad's career that is unique in the history of religion: it enables us to see the peculiar difficulties he had to contend with, and how his vision evolved to become more profound and universal in scope.

In contrast, we know very little about Jesus. The earliest Christian writer was St Paul, who dispatched his first epistle some twenty years after Jesus' death. Paul, however, had no interest in Christ's earthly life but concentrated almost entirely on the spiritual meaning of his death and resurrection. Later, in the gospels, the evangelists drew on the oral tradition which dwelt more than he on Jesus' life in Palestine and recorded his words. Mark, the first, wrote about forty years after Jesus' death in the seventies; Matthew and Luke wrote during the eighties and John in about 100 CE. But these gospel accounts are quite different from the early biographies of Muhammad by the Arab historians. They are more concerned with the religious meaning of Jesus' life than with the historical facts and frequently express the needs, the preoccupations and beliefs of the early churches rather than the original events. New Testament scholars, for example, point out that the gospel accounts of Jesus' passion and death are hopelessly confused; facts have been changed. The Christians at this time were anxious to dissociate themselves from the Jews and so they blame them and not the Romans for Jesus' death. Very few of the actual words of Christ have been recorded. This does not mean that the gospels are untrue, however. They express an important religious truth. Jesus had promised to send his disciples his Spirit, so that their deepest inspirations were in some sense his.

Muhammad comes over very differently from the idealised, numinous person of Christ in the gospels. Muslims have evolved a symbolic devotion to Muhammad, as I shall explain in Chapter 10, but they have never claimed that he is divine. Indeed, he is a very human figure in the early histories. He does not even bear much resemblance to a Christian saint – though, of course, once one penetrates the veil of hagiography, the saints themselves become all too human. Muhammad is more like the colourful figures of the Jewish scriptures – Moses, David, Solomon, Elijah or Isaiah – who were passionately religious men but not paragons. It is a painful struggle to incarnate the transcendent, ineffable reality which some call 'God' in the flawed and tragic conditions of human life. Muhammad was no plaster saint. He lived in a violent and dangerous society and sometimes adopted methods which those of us who have been fortunate enough to live in a safer world will find disturbing. But if we can lay aside our Christian expectations of sanctity, we will find a passionate and complex human being. Muhammad had great spiritual as well as political gifts – the two do not always go together – and he was convinced that all religious people have a responsibility to create a good and just society. He could become darkly angry and implacable, but he could also be tender, compassionate, vulnerable and immensely kind. We never read of Jesus laughing, but we often find Muhammad smiling and teasing the people who were closest to him. We will see him playing with children, having trouble with his wives, weeping bitterly when a friend dies and showing off his new baby son like any besotted father.

If we could view Muhammad as we do any other important historical figure we would surely consider him to be one of the greatest geniuses the world has known. To create a literary masterpiece, to found a major religion and a new world power are not ordinary achievements. But to appreciate his genius to the full, we must examine the society into which he was born and the forces with which he contended. When he descended from Mount Hira to bring the Word of God to the Arabs, Muhammad was about to attempt the impossible. A few Arabs of the peninsula were moving towards monotheism, but they had not fully explored the implications of this belief in only one God. This is hardly surprising. It had taken the Jews centuries to believe that Yahweh was the *only* God. The ancient Israelites probably practised monolatry: that is, they had agreed that they would worship Yahweh alone, but they believed that the other gods existed. Even Moses may not have been a thorough-going monotheist. The Ten Commandments which he brought to his people take the existence of other gods for granted: 'Thou shalt not have strange gods before me.' About 700 years elapsed between the Exodus from Egypt under the leadership of Moses (*c.* 1250 BCE) and the unequivocal monotheism of the prophet, usually known as Second Isaiah, who lived with the Jewish exiles in Babylon in about 550 BCE. Yet Muhammad set out to make the Arabs achieve this major change in a mere twenty-three years! We shall see that some of the Arabs begged him to adopt a monolatrous solution and to accept the cult of other gods, while he and his followers worshipped al-Llah alone; but Muhammad absolutely refused to compromise.

To proclaim belief in only one God was not a mere notional, cerebral assent. It demanded a change of consciousness. The Bible shows that the ancient Israelites found the lure of paganism irresistible and we shall see that the Arabs found the prospect of losing their ancestral gods and goddesses extraordinarily painful. It is perhaps not surprising that it was during their exile to the Babylonian empire that the Jews finally abandoned paganism for ever. Like all the major world religions, monotheism is in one sense a product of civilisation. In a world empire, people acquired a wider perspective and an entirely new view of the world, which made the local gods seem petty and inadequate. The ancient empires provided the public order and security that was necessary for civilisation to flourish, and people began to see that the universe itself was an ordered place and might be under a unified command. In the great cities, cultural change accelerated and the individual conscience was born as people became aware that their own actions could affect the fate of future generations. But in a more primitive society, like seventh-century Arabia, such a perspective was well-nigh impossible. It was almost impossible to believe in an omnipotent, and benevolent deity, when life was dangerous and fate seemed arbitrary, when there was communalism instead of individualism and when there was precious little social security. In a primitive, pagan world the various deities represented sources of power and influence and it seemed simply perverse to turn one's back on a potential source of help by opting for only one God. It is true that some Arabs, like the people of Mecca, were living in cities, but the desert was a very recent memory and the desperate tribal ethos remained predominant.

One of the most remarkable aspects of Muhammad's achievement was his isolation. He knew about Judaism and Christianity, but his knowledge was very limited. Unlike the prophets of Israel, Muhammad was not working towards the difficult monotheistic solution with the support of an established tradition which had its own momentum and insight and could provide ethical guidance that had been hammered out over centuries. Jesus and St Paul were both embedded in Judaism and the first Christians came from the Jews and their supporters, the Godfearers, in the synagogues. Christianity took root in the Roman empire where Jewish communities had paved the way and prepared the minds of the pagans. But Muhammad had to start virtually from scratch and work his way towards the radical monotheistic spirituality on his own. When he began his mission, a dispassionate observer would not have given him a chance. The Arabs, he might have objected, were just not ready for monotheism: they were not sufficiently developed for this sophisticated vision. In fact, to attempt to introduce it on a large scale in this violent, terrifying society could be extremely dangerous and Muhammad would be lucky to escape with his life.

Indeed, Muhammad was frequently in deadly peril and his survival was a near-miracle. But he did succeed. By the end of his life he had laid an axe to the root of the chronic cycle of tribal violence that afflicted the region and paganism was no longer a going concern. The Arabs were ready to embark on a new phase of their history. To appreciate this unique achievement, we must understand conditions in Arabia before the coming of Islam – a period which Muslims call the *jahiliyah*, the time of ignorance.

3 · *Jahiliyah*

the time of ignorance

Today Arabia is one of the richest regions in the world and the major powers anxiously protect their oil interests there. But when Muhammad was born in the city of Mecca in about 570, neither of the great powers of the region gave Arabia a thought. Persia and Byzantium were both locked in a debilitating struggle with one another, which ended shortly before Muhammad's death. Both were anxious to cultivate the Arabs in the south of the Peninsula, in what is now Yemen. The Kingdom of Southern Arabia was quite different from the rest of the region: it had the benefit of the monsoon rains, so it was rich, fertile and had an ancient and sophisticated culture. But the intractable steppes of Arabia were a terrifying wilderness, inhabited by a wild race of men to whom the Greeks had given the name 'Sarakenoi', the people who dwell in tents. Neither Persia nor Byzantium considered invading this desolate region and nobody would have dreamed that it was about to give birth to a new world religion, which would soon become a major world power.

Indeed, Arabia was considered a God-less region and none of the more advanced religions, which were associated with modernity and progress, had managed to penetrate the area. It is true that there were a few Jewish tribes of doubtful provenance in the agricultural settlements of Yathrib (which later became the city of Medina), Khaybar and Fadak, but these Jews were practically indistinguishable from their Arab pagan neighbours and their religion was of a somewhat rudimentary nature. In the civilised lands, many of the Arabs had converted to Christianity and in the fourth century had formed their own distinctive Syriac Church. But in general the Bedouin Arabs of Arabia Deserta were suspicious of both Judaism and Christianity, even though they realised that these religions were more sophisticated than their own. They knew that the great powers of Persia and Byzantium were ready to use both faiths as a means of imperial control. This had become tragically apparent in the Kingdom of Southern Arabia, which had lost its independence for ever in 570, the year of Muhammad's birth. The Christian Empire of Byzantium had made Abyssinia, the modern Ethiopia, a client state when it had converted to an heretical form of Christianity known as Monophysitism, which held that Christ had only one, divine nature. Byzantium may have persecuted heretics at home but it was quite happy to use them to further imperialistic ambitions abroad. Having affiliated Abyssinia, Byzantium encouraged its ruler, the Negus, to infiltrate the Yemen to bring it under the suzerainty of Constantinople. Instead of standing on their own feet, the Southern Arabians had appealed to Persia for help against this Abyssinian threat and the Persian Sassanids were only too happy to oblige. The Persians also used religion as an ideological weapon in this struggle for empire, favouring Judaism against the Christianity of Byzantium. In 510 Yusuf As'ai, the King of South Arabia, converted to Judaism and became known as Dhu Nuwas, He of the Hanging Locks. But this bid for Persian patronage failed when the Jewish Kingdom fell to Abyssinia in 525: the handsome young king, it is said, had ridden his horse out to sea in despair, until horse and rider disappeared beneath the waves. South Arabia had become a mere province of Abyssinia and its people constantly appealed to Persia for help. Eventually King Khusrua did invade the region in 570 and the proud kingdom of the South became a mere colony of Persia. This time the Christian heresy of Nestorianism (which held that Christ had two natures, human and divine and which was also favoured by Persia) became the official religion. The Bedouin Arabs of the Hijaz and Najd regions had been intensely proud of their southern Arab neighbours and saw their fall as a catastrophe. Inevitably Judaism and Christianity became tinged with suspicion.

Their distrust of the two advanced religions had been compounded by events in the north, where both of the great powers had been anxious to secure their borders against each other and against the wild Saracens, who periodically invaded the settled lands during years of especially bad drought. Both made use of Arab tribes in the north, which had converted to heretical forms of Christianity. Byzantium had encouraged the Arabs in the borderlands to convert to the true faith by building monasteries and cult centres there. Eventually the tribe of Ghassan, which wintered on the Byzantine border, converted to Monophysite Christianity and became confederates of the Byzantines. They built their southern winter camp outside Rusafa at Sergiopolis, which had a splendid hall for their chief in the Byzantine style, the remains of which can still be seen today. The Ghassanids formed a Byzantine buffer state which was supposed to defend the Christian empire from the Zoroastrian empire of Persia.[1] But Persia was able to retaliate. The Lachmid Arabs of eastern Syria became Nestorians, a faith also favoured by Arabs in the Mesopotamian regions of the Persian empire. The Sassanids accordingly appointed the Lachmid Arabs rulers of a buffer state to guard their own borders, with its capital at Hira. But Persia and Byzantium both withdrew from these Arab states: the Byzantine Emperor Heraclius stopped his subsidies to the

Ghassanids as an economy measure during the war against Persia in about 584 and King Khusrua put an end to the Lachmid regime in about 602 and installed Persian rulers in place of the Arabs. When the Muslim armies invaded these regions after Muhammad's death some thirty years later, they found the Arabs there highly resentful of the great powers and ready to throw in their lot with Islam.

But that was in the future. At the beginning of the seventh century, the Arabs of central Arabia were surrounded by deviant forms of Christianity: the majestic Christian church at Najran in the south was a source of wonder to the Bedouin, but they retained their distrust of these religious systems and were determined to remain independent of the great powers. At the same time there was a sense of dissatisfaction. The Arabs felt inferior, both religiously and politically. Until they managed to create a united Bedouin state and take their destiny into their own hands, they would still be vulnerable to exploitation and could even lose their independence, like the Arabs of the South. But there seemed little chance of a united Bedouin state. For centuries the Arabs of the Hijaz and Najd had lived as nomads in tribal groups which were constantly at war. Over the years they had evolved a highly specialised way of life that had become normative in the peninsula by the sixth century CE. Even the Arabs who lived in the cities and the settled areas organised their life according to the old pastoral ethos: they still kept camels and thought of themselves as sons of the desert.

The tribal ethic demanded certain technical and social skills as well as personal qualities which were carefully cultivated. The Arabs of the peninsula had not always been nomads. The camel, which made their life possible, had only been domesticated about two thousand years before our own era. This animal, with its unique capacity to store water, had the ability to travel long distances in the desert at exceptional speed. Originally the Arabs had been farmers in the more civilised lands of the Fertile Crescent. After long experience of breeding animals for transport, some of the more daring spirits had taken to the arid, inhospitable steppes during the periodic times of drought and desiccation.[2] To attempt to wrest a livelihood in these difficult circumstances had been a gesture of defiance and rebellion against a cruel fate, demonstrating, perhaps, a determination to prove that Arabs could survive in these well-nigh impossible circumstances. Gradually they would have moved out into the more desert regions, putting some distance between themselves and the centres of civilisation. In summer they grazed their camels beside the wells that each tribe appropriated for itself and during the winter they wandered in the steppes, which had been covered with a rich vegetation that was a paradise for their animals after the rains. They lived on camels' milk and the flesh of beasts killed by their hunters. But the nomads could not survive alone: they needed the support of agriculturalists, who would provide them with the wheat and dates that were essential to supplement their meagre diet. As the nomads gradually penetrated the desert regions of the Fertile Crescent and the Arabian peninsula, they would have been followed step by step by pioneering farmers, who settled in the oases, irrigated the surrounding area and, to an extent, made the desert bloom. In their turn, the agriculturalists depended on the nomads' greater mobility, which provided them with goods and merchandise from abroad. As the nomads were usually more skilful warriors, they would provide the settled Arabs with protection in return for a portion of the harvest.

Life in the steppes was desperately precarious. The nomads were nearly always hungry and suffering from malnutrition; they were also in fierce competition with one another for the necessities of life. The only way to survive was in a closely-knit group; an individual on his own stood no chance at all. The nomads had consequently formed themselves into autonomous groups, on the basis of blood and kinship. They were united by a real or mythical common ancestry and called themselves, for example, the *Bani* Kalb or the *Bani* Asad (the sons of Kalb and Asad). These groups then allied themselves with others in larger and more tenuous associations; in the West we usually call the small groups 'clans' and the larger groups 'tribes'. The Arabs, however, did not usually make this distinction and used the word *qawm* (people) for both the larger and smaller groups. In order to avoid the tribes becoming too big and unmanageable, the groups were constantly reconfigurating. It was essential to cultivate a fierce and absolute loyalty to the *qawm* and to all its related allies. Only the tribe could ensure the personal survival of its members, but that meant that there was no room for individualism in our sense of the word nor the rights and duties associated with it. Everything had to be subordinated to the interests of the group. To cultivate this communal spirit, the Arabs evolved an ideology called *muruwah*, which Western scholars usually translate as 'manliness' but which has a far more complex and extensive meaning. *Muruwah* meant courage in battle, patience and endurance in suffering, and a dedication to the chivalrous duties of avenging wrong done to the tribe, protecting its weaker members and defying the strong. Each tribe prided itself on its own special brand of *muruwah*, which was believed to be inherited by blood. To preserve the *muruwah* of the group, each member had to be ready to leap to the defence of a fellow-tribesman and obey his chief without question. Outside the tribe, obligation ceased and there was no notion of a universal, natural law at this stage of Arab development.

Muruwah fulfilled many of the functions of religion, giving the Arabs an ideology and a vision which enabled them to find meaning in their perilous existence. It was a religion, however, which was entirely earth-centred. The tribe was its sacred value; Arabs had no notion of an after-life and an individual had no unique or eternal destiny. The only immortality that a man or woman could achieve was in the tribe and the continuation of its spirit. Each had a duty to cultivate *muruwah* to ensure that the tribe would survive. Thus the tribe looked after its own. Its chief was expected to take care of the weaker members of his group and to distribute its possessions and goods equally. Largesse was an important virtue: a chief could demonstrate his power and confidence (and hence the power of his tribe) by means of lavish and generous hospitality to his tribesmen and to his friendly confederates in other tribal groups. Hospitality and generosity are still supreme Arab virtues. It had a pragmatic aspect, of course. A tribe which was rich today could easily become destitute tomorrow and if you had been niggardly in good fortune, who would help you in your hour of need? But the cultivation of largesse also helped Arabs to rise above the grim struggle for existence by taking no heed for the morrow. It encouraged an indifference to material goods which was essential in a region where there were not enough of the basic necessities to go round. This approach also informed the deep fatalism of *muruwah*: *dahr* (Time or Fate) was a hard fact of life and had to be accepted with dignity. Life would be impossible if people did not accept some disasters as inevitable. Arabs, therefore, firmly believed that there was nothing that could be done to prolong the term (*ajal*) of a man's life or to ensure a sufficient 'provision' (*rizq*) of food and sustenance.

To protect the tribe and its members a chief had to be prepared to avenge each and every injury. Where there was no common law that could be enforced by a central authority, the only way of preserving a modicum of social security was by means of the blood-feud or vendetta. Life was cheap and there was nothing immoral about killing *per se*: it was only wrong to kill your own tribesmen or their allies. Each tribe had to avenge the death of a single one of its members by killing somebody in the murderer's tribe. This was the only way a chief could provide protection to his tribesmen: if he failed to retaliate, nobody would respect his *qawm* and would feel free to kill tribal members with impunity. Since it was so easy for an individual to disappear without trace in Arabia there was no duty to punish the killer himself. Instead, the offending tribe would be weakened by the loss of an equivalent number of its own men. It is here that we see the communal mentality most clearly: one member of a tribe was much the same as another for such purposes. Having long outgrown this type of social organisation we now find the vendetta principle unacceptable, but in the absence of a modern police force it was the only way of ensuring a minimum of public order. The system also ensured a reasonable balance of power since a loss in one caused the offending tribe to be comparably weakened. While this meant that no one group could easily gain precedence over the others, it also made it impossible for the Arabs to unite. Instead of pooling their meagre resources, the Arabs seemed caught up in a cycle of violence, where one vendetta bred another if a tribe felt that revenge had been disproportionate.

Another time-honoured way of preserving the balance of power was the *ghazu* or raid, which was a constant occupation and almost a national sport. In times of hardship, members of one tribe would raid the territory of one of its enemies in the hope of carrying off camels, cattle or other goods. Bloodshed was avoided whenever possible, because this would lead to a vendetta. Again, robbery was not considered immoral unless you stole the goods of kinsmen or confederates. The *ghazu* ensured a reasonable turn-over of wealth and meant that what food and goods were available were, in a rough and ready way, shared between the groups which were competing for them.

Brutal as it undoubtedly was, *muruwah* had many strengths and some of these would become important values in Islam. Knowing no other means of social organisation, Muhammad would organise the Muslim community on tribal lines. Despite the new individualism that Islam helped the Muslims to cultivate, the ideal of community and brotherhood remained crucial. Also vital in the Muslim vision was equality since there was no room for a privileged elite in the tribal system. There was no such thing as an aristocracy or inherited office. A chief did not hand on his position to his son because the tribe needed the best man available for the job, regardless of parentage or privilege. This deep and strong egalitarianism would characterise the Islamic spirit and inform its religious, political and even its artistic and literary institutions.

But it remained a savage ethic. Only the strong would survive and that meant that the weak were eliminated and could be grievously exploited. Infanticide was the normal means of population control: female babies survived infancy more frequently than boys and, since no tribe could support more than a certain number of women, female babies were killed without regret. Indeed women, like slaves, had no human or legal rights but were considered mere chattels. They were cruelly treated and could expect no amelioration of their lot. Men could take as many wives as they wanted. Since descent was often reckoned through the female line, officially property was inherited by women, but this gave them no power or influence. Men sometimes married women simply to appropriate their rightful inheritance.

Not surprisingly, the Arabs had little time for religion in the more conventional sense of the term. They could not afford to support a caste of priests or shamans responsible for evolving the mythological tribal traditions. Instead the poet sang the glories of the tribe, the supreme Arab value, and immortalised it in verse. Rather than recounting stories of the gods and their cosmic struggles or exploring the complex paths of the spirit in their legends and tales, poets described the battles and achievements of the tribe, lamented its disasters and helped its members to appreciate the special qualities of *muruwah*. Poetry was a highly important skill, much valued by the Arabs. As illiteracy was the rule in the peninsula, poets would recite their verses aloud. They felt possessed by a *jinni*, one of the sprites that were thought to haunt the landscape and, indeed, poetry was not only considered superhuman but was also believed to have magical qualities. The curse of an inspired poet could have a disastrous effect on an enemy. The sense of being taken over by an alien power is common to inspirational experiences and in Arabia the poet fulfilled many of the functions of a priest or prophet in other communities. He opened himself to the unconscious hopes and desires of his tribe and when the people heard his words they therefore recognised them as profoundly their own. Poets were thus of crucial importance in the political and social life of Arabia. It has been said that they fulfilled the function of the responsible press in our own society, disseminated information and fed other tribes with an interpretation of events that could be a powerful influence in the propaganda war.

There were, however, other possessed individuals who were not respected so greatly in Muhammad's time. The *kahins* or ecstatic prophets were similar to the peripatetic seers in the early books of the Bible. They were not prophets in the later exalted sense but were more like soothsayers, consulted if someone lost a camel or wanted his fortune told. The *kahin* often had to cloak his ignorance in ambiguity, so his 'oracles' were usually delivered in an incoherent or unintelligible doggerel. Muhammad, as we shall see, had no time at all for the *kahins*, finding their 'prophecies' trivial, mischievous and meaningless.

But the Arabs did have a spiritual life, one which meant a great deal to them. Various places were felt to be holy and were the site of shrines which had their own ancient rituals centring round a particular deity. The most important of all these shrines was the Ka'aba, which was situated by the sacred spring of Zamzam in Mecca. The granite boxlike shrine seems to be extremely ancient and was similar to other shrines and sanctuaries which have not survived. Embedded in its eastern corner was the sacred Black Stone, which may have been a meteorite that had once hurtled brilliantly from the sky, linking heaven and earth. At the time of Muhammad, the Ka'aba was officially dedicated to the god Hubal, a deity who had been imported into Arabia from the kingdom of the Nabateans in what is now Jordan. But the pre-eminence of the shrine as well as the common belief in Mecca seems to suggest that it may have been dedicated originally to al-Llah, the High God of the Arabs. Around the Ka'aba was a circular area where pilgrims gathered to perform the ceremony of *tawwaf*, seven ritual circumambulations of the shrine following the direction of the sun. The shrine was also surrounded by 360 idols, or effigies of the gods, that may have been the totems of all the different tribes that came to worship there during the appointed month. The land around Mecca (on a twenty-mile radius from the Ka'aba at its centre) was a sacred area, a sanctuary where all violence and fighting was forbidden.

This sounds strange to people brought up in a more secular society, but shrines like the Ka'aba and its attendant rituals seem to have answered an important spiritual and psychological need in Arabia. We shall see that Muhammad felt the mysterious attraction of the Ka'aba all his life and that the ritual circumambulations, which sound so arbitrary and tedious to an outsider, were extremely important in the life of the people of Mecca. It was not a dreary duty which people grudgingly and mindlessly performed. They seemed to enjoy doing it and made it part of their daily lives. They liked to round off a pleasant day's hunting by performing the circumambulations before returning to their homes; they might go along to the nearby market place to drink wine with some boon companions and then decide to spend the evening making the circumambulations instead, when their drinking companions failed to turn up. What was so compulsive about this rite and what did people think they would achieve?

It seems that the shrine itself was common in the Semitic world. The circle, the four corners (representing the four corners of the world) and the 360 symbols around it seem to have come from the old Sumerian religion. The Sumerian year consisted of 360 days and five extra holy days, which were spent 'outside time' as it were, performing special ceremonies that linked heaven and earth. In Arabian terms, these five special days might have been represented by the *hajj* pilgrimage, which took place once a year and was attended by Arabs from all over the peninsula. The *hajj* would start at the Ka'aba and then proceed to various shrines outside Mecca, all of which seem to have been dedicated to other gods. The *hajj* originally took place during the autumn and it has been suggested that the various ceremonies may have been a way of persecuting the dying sun in order to bring on the winter rains. Pilgrims would rush in a body to the hollow of Muzdalifa, the abode of the Thunder God; make an all-night vigil on the plain around Mount Arafat, which was about sixteen miles outside Mecca; hurl pebbles at the three sacred pillars of Mina and finally offer an animal sacrifice. Nobody today really understands what these rites meant and, by Muhammad's time, the Arabs themselves had probably forgotten their original significance, but they remained fiercely attached to the Ka'aba and the other shrines of Arabia and performed their ritual devoutly.

We all need a private place in our lives where we can take some time out: it helps us to centre ourselves and to become more creative. In Arabia where the whole of life was such a struggle the Sanctuary must have been a necessity. There the Arabs could meet in relaxed circumstances, knowing that the rules of a tribal vendetta would be null and void for the duration. In practical terms it meant that they could trade with one another, without fearing an attack by an enemy tribe, and shrines like Mecca were usually important markets which held an annual fair. But the Sanctuary and its ritual probably also provided an essential spiritual respite. The *tawwaf* seems to have been recreative, helping the Arabs to centre themselves and discover in symbolic gesture an eternal dimension to their lives.

The shrine itself probably represented the world, with its four corners radiating from a central point. The circle seems to be an archetype, found in nearly all cultures as a symbol of eternity, of the world and the psyche. It represents, in both temporal and spatial terms, a totality: tracing a circle or circumambulating – a common religious practice in many traditions – means that you are constantly coming back to where you started: you discover that in your end is your beginning. At the centre of the circle, the still, small point of the turning world, is eternity, the ultimate ineffable meaning, and circling round and round it the pilgrim learned to reorient himself and find his own centre vis-à-vis the world. The circumambulation would become a form of meditation: it seems to have been performed in a kind of 'trot', perhaps not dissimilar to the *pas gymnastique*. It required physical concentration which was perhaps boring but which therefore enabled the mind to take off. Most holy places in all traditions are somehow believed to stand at the centre of the world, and to have been the first place created by the gods. For the pilgrim they were invested with the glamour of beginnings and he felt that he was somehow approaching the centre of power.

We all need ritual in our lives to help us to create an inner attitude: the rites of courtesy, for example, help us to cultivate a habit of respect for others. In our more secular society many people no longer take part in this type of symbolic activity, so it seems arbitrary or even deranged. In our world, it is the artist who creates our meaningful symbols for us to help us to discover another dimension to life. In such rites as the *tawwaf* or the rituals of the *hajj*, the Arabs were creating a type of practical artistry, through which they discovered a meaning or significance that could not easily be put into words. They were probably aware, at a deep if inarticulate level, of the symbolic, figurative nature of what they were doing – a state of mind which many of us in the West have lost. It is perhaps particularly difficult for people brought up in the Protestant world to appreciate, because some forms of Protestantism regard ritual with a profound – almost a superstitious – suspicion and hostility.

The Ka'aba was the most important shrine, but there were others. Circumambulation and the kind of standing worship practised during the pre-Islamic *hajj* at Mount Arafat were essential cult elements everywhere in the peninsula. So too was the piece of land (*hima*) removed from profane use with the right of asylum for all living beings. None of the other shrines have survived, but we know of other temples like the Ka'aba at Najran in the Yemen and at al-Abalat, to the south of Mecca. But of crucial importance for our story were the three shrines close to Mecca that were dedicated to the three daughters of al-Llah (*banat al-Llah*). In the walled city of Taif was the shrine of al-Lat, whose name simply means 'the Goddess', which was tended by the tribe of Thaqif. They also liked to call her al-Rabba, the Sovereign. At Nakhlah was the shrine of al-Uzzah, the most popular of the three, whose name meant 'the Mighty One', and at her seaside shrine at Qud^yd was Manat, goddess of fate. These goddesses were not like the goddesses in the Graeco-Roman pantheon. They were not characters like Juno or Pallas Athena, with their own story, mythology and personality, and they had no special sphere of influence, like love or war. The Arabs had developed no mythology to explain the symbolic importance of these divine beings, and even though they were called the 'daughters of God' this does not mean that they were part of a fully developed pantheon. The Arabs often used kinship words to denote an abstract relationship, so that, for example, *banat al-dahr* (literally 'the daughters of time/fate') simply meant misfortunes or vicissitudes. The *banat al-Llah* may well simply have been 'divine beings'. They were represented in their shrines not by a personalised statue or portrait but by large standing stones, rather like the fertility symbols used by the Canaanites which are so often described in the Bible. When the Arabs venerated these stones they were not worshipping them in any crude, simplistic way but were seeing them as a focus of divinity. It has also been suggested that these three goddesses were related to the Semitic fertility goddesses Anat and Ishtar, so their cultus may have begun before the Arabs adopted the nomadic life, while they were still farmers and living on the land.[3]

The Arabs may not have worshipped al-Lat, al-Uzza and Manat in a personalised way, but we shall see that they felt very passionate about them. Their cultus was confined to their shrines, so people did not worship them in their own homes as the Greeks and Romans had worshipped their gods and goddesses.[4] But they were an essential part of the spiritual landscape of the Bedouin of the Hijaz, who all saw Nakhlah, Taif and Qudayd as holy places and sanctuaries where the Arabs could find their centre. The antiquity of the goddesses was another reason for their cult. When they worshipped them at their shrines the Arabs felt in touch with their forefathers, who had also venerated the *banat al-Llah* there, and this provided a sense of healing continuity. Their shrines were not considered to be as important as the Ka'aba, but like the other holy places of Arabia they were an imaginative way of claiming the landscape and giving the harsh steppes of Arabia a spiritual relevance. They were built in to the fundamental identity of many of the Arabs and they would feel deeply threatened by any denigration of this ancient cult.

But other Arabs were becoming dissatisfied with the old religion and during the last phase of the *jahiliyah* there seems to have been a spiritual restlessness and malaise in Arabia. The tribal system and the old paganism had served the Bedouin well for centuries, but during the sixth century life had changed. Even though most of the Arabian peninsula was outside the mainstream of civilisation, the Arabs were beginning to be aware of some of its ideas and motivation. Some seem to have heard about the religious idea of the afterlife, for example, which made the eternal fate of the individual a supreme value. How did this square with the old communal ideal of tribalism? The Arabs who had begun to engage in trade with the civilised countries brought back impressive stories and poets described the marvels of Syria and Persia. But it seemed that the Arabs could not hope for such power and splendour. The tribal system made it impossible for them to pool their meagre resources and face the world as the united people they were dimly aware of being. The tribes seemed caught up in an endless cycle of wars and vendettas: one blood-feud led inevitably to another, at the same time as the new intimations of individualism were obscurely undermining the communal ethos.

But the Arabs who felt most disoriented were those who had taken to the settled life. During the sixth century a tribe had emigrated from the troubled region of South Arabia to the oasis at Yathrib and settled beside the Jewish tribes there. They made a success of this agricultural venture, yet found that the tribal system simply did not work when the Arabs were no longer roaming vast territories but living together in close proximity. By the beginning of the seventh century the whole oasis seemed in the grip of a chronic cycle of violence and warfare. But in Mecca the tribe of Quraysh, into which Muhammad had been born in about 570, and which had become the most powerful tribe in Arabia, was experiencing a more obscure type of malaise as they also found that the old ideology had not equipped them for city life.

The Quraysh had settled in Mecca towards the end of the fifth century. Their ancestor Qusayy, his brother Zuhrah and his uncle Taym had settled in the Meccan valley beside the Sanctuary. Makhzum, the son of another uncle, and his cousins Jumah and Sahm settled there with Qusayy and they and the clans named after them became known as the Quraysh of the Hollow.[5] Qusayy's more remote kinsmen settled in the surrounding countryside and were known as the Quraysh of the Outskirts. Legend has it that Qusayy had travelled in Syria and brought the three goddesses al-Lat, al-Uzza and Manat to the Hijaz and enthroned the Nabatean god Hubal in the Ka'aba. In a campaign that combined trickery and force, the Quraysh managed to take control of Mecca and expel the Khuza'ah, its guardian tribe who were considered to have failed their sacred trust. After Qusayy's death, his sons Abd ad-Dar and Abd Manaf apparently quarrelled, and the effects of this conflict continued among their descendants and affected the internal politics of Mecca right up to Muhammad's time. Abd ad-Dar had been Qusayy's favourite son and he was supported by Makhzum, Sahm, Jumah, their uncle Adi and their families. They became known as the Ahlaf, the Confederates. Abd Manaf, Qusayy's younger son, contested his inheritance and he was supported by his nephew Asad, Zuhrah, Taym and the venerable al-Harith ibn Fihr. They sealed their pact by bathing their hands in a bowl of perfume at the Ka'aba and became known as the Mutayyabun, the Scented Ones. But neither side wanted a full-scale conflict and a compromise was achieved whereby Abd ad-Dar and the Confederates retained nominal privileges while the real power resided with Abd Manaf and the Scented Ones. Their descendants in the clans named after them tended to keep this old alliance.

The Quraysh started to engage in trading, combining this mercantile activity with the traditional stock-breeding. Mecca was ideally situated for long-term business ventures. The prestige of the Ka'aba brought many Arabs on the *hajj* to the city each year and the Sanctuary created a climate that was favourable to trade. Mecca stood conveniently at the crossroads of the two major trade routes of Arabia: the Hijaz Road, which ran along the eastern coast of the Red Sea and linked the Yemen with Syria, Palestine and the Transjordan, and the Najd Road, which linked the Yemen with the Iraq. The Quraysh became highly successful. They ensured the security of the city by building alliances with the Bedouin in the area. The nomads were better soldiers than the Quraysh and, in return for military help, they had shares in the various Meccan companies. Cultivating a shrewd, calculating statesmanship, known as *hilm*, the Quraysh had become the greatest power in Arabia during the sixth century.

They realised that they must not allow themselves to be exploited by the great powers, so in order to avoid the fate of the kingdom of the South they remained strictly neutral in the struggle between Persia and Byzantium. But relations with the Byzantines deteriorated sharply in about 560,[6] when South Arabia was still a province of Abyssinia, the client state of Byzantium. Abraha, the Abyssinian Governor of South Arabia, seems to have become jealous of Mecca's commercial success and attempted to invade the city. The incident has been embellished by legend, but it appears that Abraha had realised that the Ka'aba was crucial to the success of the Quraysh. To deflect pilgrims to South Arabia and hence attract more trade, he had built a magnificent Christian temple in Sana'a of striped marble, and, it is said, when he camped outside Mecca with his army his avowed intention was to destroy the Ka'aba. But at the very gates of the city it seems that his army was stricken by plague and was forced to beat an ignominious retreat. This dramatic deliverance naturally struck the Quraysh as miraculous. The Abyssinians had brought an elephant with them and the Meccans had been fascinated by this huge, peculiar beast. Later it was said that when it had arrived at the sacred area outside the city, the elephant had fallen to its knees and refused to budge; next God had sent a flock of birds from the coast, which dropped poisonous pebbles on the Abyssinians, bringing them out in horrible boils. The Year of the Elephant became extremely important to the Quraysh. As Muhammad ibn Ishaq (d. *c.* 767), Muhammad's first biographer, explains, after this miracle the Bedouin greatly respected the Quraysh, saying, 'They are the people of God; God fought for them and thwarted the attack of their enemies.'[7] Muhammad himself was moved by the story of the elephant, which is recounted in Sura 105 of the Qu'ran.

After this the Quraysh became very careful to preserve their independence and by the beginning of the seventh century they had become rich beyond their wildest dreams in the old nomadic days. Naturally they saw wealth and capitalism as their salvation, which seemed to have rescued them from a life of poverty and danger and given them an almost godlike security. They were no longer hungry, no longer plagued by enemy tribes. Money began to acquire a quasi-religious value, as we shall see. But aggressive capitalism was not really compatible with the old communal tribal ethic. It naturally encouraged a rampant greed and individualism. The various clans were engaged in fierce competition and by the time Muhammad was a young boy had divided into three major parties. Some of the weaker clans, including the clan of Hashim into which Muhammad was born, had not done as well as the others and felt that they were being pushed to the wall. Instead of sharing their wealth equally, according to the old tribal ethic, individuals were building up personal fortunes. They were exploiting the rights of orphans and widows, absorbing their inheritance into their own estates, and were not looking after the weaker, poorer members of the tribe as the old ethos had required. Their new prosperity had severed their links with traditional values and many of the less successful Quraysh felt obscurely disoriented and lost. Naturally the most successful merchants, bankers and financiers were delighted with the new system. They aggressively accumulated more capital with near-religious zeal. Only two generations away from the penury of the nomadic life, they believed that money and material goods could save them and they wanted as many of these things as they could get. But some of the younger generation were growing disenchanted and seemed to be searching for a new spiritual and political solution to the malaise and disquiet in the city.

It is often said that Islam is a religion of the desert, but this is not true. The old tribal ethic affected the Qu'ranic message, but the new religion was first received by the Arabs of Mecca in an atmosphere of cut-throat capitalism and high finance. Like all the great confessional religions and the philosophical rationalism of Greece, Islam was a product of the city. This seems odd to those of us who have been brought up to consider the unworldly Jesus of Nazareth as the epitome of the religious spirit. We would not expect a prophet to arise in the City of London or in Wall Street. But Hinduism, Buddhism, Jainism and Confucianism all sprang up in the market-place. The Greek philosophers taught in the *agora* and the great prophets of Israel preached in the cities at a time when the Israelites were beginning to leave the nomadic life behind them. These world religions had all developed in the commercial atmosphere of city life, at a time when merchants were beginning to wrest some of the power which had once been solely in the hands of the kings and the aristocratic and priestly castes. The new prosperity drew people's attention to the disparity between rich and poor and made them deeply concerned with problems of social justice. All the great religious leaders and prophets had addressed themselves to these issues and provided their own distinctive solutions. At the beginning of the seventh century, when the Quraysh and some of the other Arabs were leaving the old nomadic life behind and were becoming aware of the social problems of the settled life, the Prophet of Islam brought a new religious message to the Arabs.

People were already groping towards a monotheistic religion and some were ready to listen to Muhammad's message that there was only one God. By the time he began to preach in Mecca, it seems to have been generally acknowledged that the Ka'aba was dedicated to al-Llah, the

High God of the pagan Arabs, despite the presiding effigy of Hubal. By the beginning of the seventh century, al-Llah had become more important than before in the religious lives of many of the Arabs. Many primitive religions develop a belief in a High God, who is sometimes called the Sky God. He is believed to have created the heavens and the earth and then seems to have retired, as though exhausted by the effort. The people lost interest in this transcendent being, who disappeared from view, and his place was taken by more attractive and accessible deities. Fertility goddesses in particular affected the lives of men and women more immediately once they had settled down and started to farm the land. We see this in the Jewish scriptures. The ancient Israelites began to worship Baal, Anat and Ashtaroth when they settled in Canaan, alongside their High God Yahweh. It seemed stupid to neglect these ancient deities, who knew the land much better than they did. But in times of trouble, they called once more upon the name of Yahweh.

During the nomadic years, the old fertility functions of the Arabian goddesses had probably been forgotten, so al-Llah, the High God, became more important. The Qu'ran makes it clear that the Quraysh all believed that al-Llah had created the heavens and the earth. It was a fact that was taken for granted:

> If thou askest them [that is, the Quraysh]
> 'Who created the heavens and the earth
> and subjected the sun and the moon?'
> they will certainly say al-Llah. . . .[8]

But they also carried on worshipping the other gods, who remained deeply important to them. Like the ancient Israelites, the Arabs turned to al-Lat, al-Uzza and Manat when times were easy, but in a crisis turned instinctively to al-Llah, who alone had the power to help them in times of great danger. The Qu'ran shows that when they went on a sea voyage, which the Arabs seemed to have found a risky business, they frequently called upon al-Llah until the danger was past, but when they were safe on dry land again they turned to the other deities.[9]

But it seems that some were ready to go further than this. By the beginning of the seventh century, most of the Arabs had come to believe that al-Llah, their High God, was the same as the God who was worshipped by the Jews and the Christians. Arabs who had converted to Christianity also called their God 'al-Llah' and seem to have made the *hajj* to his shrine alongside the pagans. But Arabs were becoming increasingly aware that al-Llah had given them no scriptures of their own. We can see from the early biographies of Muhammad that the pagan Arabs felt a great respect for 'the people of the scriptures', who had knowledge that they had not. Some of them decided to look for an authentic religion that was not associated with the great powers or tainted by its connection with imperialism and foreign control. As early as the fifth century, Sozomenus, a Palestinian Christian historian, tells us that some of the Arabs had rediscovered the old religion of Abraham and had continued to practise it in his own day. Abraham had, strictly speaking, been neither a Jew nor a Christian. He had lived before Moses had brought the Torah to the people of Israel. In Arabia at the time when Muhammad was receiving his revelations, we shall find some Arabs who were trying to practise the religion of Abraham.

In his biography, Ibn Ishaq tells us that shortly before Muhammad began his mission four of the Quraysh decided to withdraw from the pagan worship at the Ka'aba and look for the true religion. They entered a secret pact and told their fellow tribesmen that they:

> had corrupted the religion of their father Abraham, and that the stone they went round was of no account; it could neither hear, nor see, nor hurt, nor help: 'Find yourselves a religion,' they said, 'for by God, you have none.' So they went their ways in the lands, seeking the *Hanifiyyah*, the religion of Abraham.[10]

Some Western scholars have argued that the little *Hanifiyyah* sect is a pious legend, symbolising the spiritual restlessness that characterised the last phase of the *jahiliyah*, rather than an historical fact. But it must have some factual basis. Three of its four members figured in the life of Muhammad and his early companions, and the fourth, Uthman ibn al-Huwayrith, had been an important character in Mecca when Muhammad was a young man in his twenties. A Qurayshi merchant, he had converted to Christianity and tried to persuade his fellow tribesmen to accept him as their king. He promised that he would get them better trading terms with the Byzantines, who probably wanted to make Mecca a client state. His proposal was rejected out of hand: like all Arabs, the Quraysh were deeply opposed to the idea of kingship.

The other three *hanifs* were well known to the early Muslim community. Ubaydallah ibn Jahsh was Muhammad's cousin. He became a Muslim but eventually converted to Christianity. In the next chapter we shall find that Waraqa ibn Naufal, who also became a Christian, was cousin to Muhammad's first wife and gave him important encouragement when he began to receive the revelations that he believed came from God. But the last member of this possibly legendary sect remained a seeker all his life and never converted to an officially established religion. Zayd ibn 'Amr not only withdrew from the worship at the Ka'aba but was said to have been an outspoken critic of the pagan religion. His half-brother Khattab ibn Nufayl was a devout pagan and was so scandalised by Zayd's apostasy and disrespect for the goddesses that he eventually drove him out of the city. He is said to have organised a young band of pagan zealots to patrol the hills outside Mecca where Zayd was in hiding and prevent him from entering the Sanctuary. So Zayd left the Hijaz and travelled in the civilised countries in search of the true faith. He got as far as Mosul in the Iraq and then travelled to Syria, questioning any monk or rabbi he met about the pure religion of Abraham. Eventually he met a monk who told him that a prophet was about to arise in Mecca who would preach the religion he was looking for, so Zayd set off home, but was attacked and killed on the southern border of Syria and never made contact with Muhammad. His son Sa'id, however, became one of Muhammad's most trusted companions.

The story is instructive. It eloquently expresses the questing spirit of some of the Arabs at this time. But it also shows the opposition that anybody who threatened the pagan religion could expect to face. There were many Quraysh like Khattab ibn Nufayl who were devoted to the faith of their fathers and could not bear to hear a word against the old gods and goddesses. They did not feel that there was any need for change: the religion of the Ka'aba made perfect sense and was a focus for the unity of the Quraysh in their city. We shall see that Khattab's son Umar passionately shared his father's love of the old faith. But the longing for an alternative religion remained. There is a story that one day before he had been forced to leave Mecca, Zayd had been standing by the Ka'aba, leaning against the shrine and telling the Quraysh who were making the circumambulations: 'O Quraysh, By Him in whose hand is the soul of Zayd, not one of you follows the religion of Abraham but I.' But then he added: 'O God, if I knew how you wished to be worshipped I would so worship you; but I do not know.'[11] Soon, however, the Arab's prayer was to be answered.

4 · Revelation

We know very little about Muhammad's early life. The Qu'ran gives us the most authoritative account of his experience before he received his prophetic vocation when he was forty years old:

> Did he not find thee an orphan and shelter thee?
> Did he not find thee erring and guide thee?
> Did he not find thee needy and suffice thee?[1]

Later Muslim tradition embellished these bare facts with legendary details, rather as the Gospels of Matthew and Luke added legendary stories about Jesus' birth, infancy and childhood which are poetic versions of theological truths: they reflect upon the nature of Christ's mission and indicate that he had been marked out for greatness in his mother's womb. Both Jesus and Muhammad became heroes, almost in the classical sense. Both penetrated to new realms of experience, confronted situations of great peril and brought back to their people a gift which transformed their lives, as Prometheus had stolen fire from the gods and brought it down to earth to illuminate the lives of men. Stories about the childhood of such heroes often show them being prepared for their exceptional fate by powers that lie beyond our ken. Jesus became a charismatic healer, and the miraculous was a notable element of his adult life. Muhammad, on the other hand, did not work miracles: he always claimed that the revelation of the Qu'ran was a miracle in itself and a sufficient sign of its divine origin. He insisted that he was simply 'a man like other men' and the Qu'ran confirmed this: in the verse just quoted it points out that Muhammad had been 'erring' when God revealed Himself.[2] The miraculous stories of his mother's pregnancy and his childhood are not characteristic of the rest of his life, therefore, but they are poetic reflections upon the nature of his prophecy and reveal the Muslims' later conviction that he was 'the desired of the nations': even Jews and Christians were eagerly awaiting his coming.

A Christian monk had been said to have prophesied the coming of the Arabian prophet to Zayd ibn 'Amr, the *hanif.* This is a constant motif in the early life of Muhammad and the Muslim community. In fact the Arabs of the Hijaz had very few contacts with Christians and knew next to nothing about Christianity. It was not until after Muhammad's death that the Muslims came up against flourishing and fully functioning Churches in Syria and Palestine; the Qu'ran has a very limited understanding of the Christian faith but was not antagonistic towards the religion of Jesus. It saw the revelation to Muhammad as a continuation and confirmation of the earlier faith. Some Arab Christians in the Syriac Church had translated one passage of the Gospels in such a way as to indicate that they were expecting Muhammad's message. Jesus had said that after his death he would send his disciples a Comforter (the Paraclete), who would remind them of everything he had taught them and help them to understand it.[3] In the Syriac lectionary, 'Paraclete' had been translated by the word *munahhema*, which, after the event, seemed very close to 'Muhammad'. Other Arab Christians had read *periklytos* instead of 'Paraclete', which can be translated by the Arabic '*Ahmad*'. This was a common name in Arabia and, like 'Muhammad', it means 'the praised one'. Muhammad had obviously been made aware of this translation because the Qu'ran refers to the belief that Jesus had foretold that another prophet, called 'Ahmad', would come after him and confirm his message.[4]

The Jews of Arabia in the agricultural settlements in the north were also believed to have expected a prophet to arise in the peninsula. It could be that there was an upsurge of messianic belief, which translated into traditional Jewish terms the restlessness in Arabia at the end of the *jahiliyah*. A rabbi of great piety had actually emigrated to Yathrib from Syria. When people asked him why he had left that gentle, fertile country for 'a land of hardship and hunger', he had replied that he had wanted to be in the Hijaz when the 'Prophet' arrived. 'His time has come,' he said to the Jewish tribes of Yathrib, 'and don't let anyone get to him before you, O Jews, for he will be sent to shed blood and to take captive the women and children of those who oppose him. Let not that keep you back from him.'[5] This messianic ferment made a great impression on the pagan Arabs of Yathrib, who felt that their religion was inferior and inadequate compared with the revelation which the Jews possessed in their scriptures. Later one of them recalled the tension that existed between the Jewish and Arab tribes in the oasis:

> We were polytheists worshipping idols, while they [the Jews] were people of the scriptures with knowledge which we did not possess. There was continual enmity between us, and when we got the better of them and excited their hate, they said: 'The time of a prophet who is to be sent has now come. We will kill you with his aid as Ad and Iram perished.' We often used to hear them say this.[6]

In Chapter 7 we shall see that this prepared the Arabs of Yathrib for Muhammad and that when they came across him they instantly recognised him as the one that was to come. The Gospels also speak of a sense of heightened expectation in Palestine, where there seems to have been a similar messianic mood. The prophet who speaks on behalf of God is also in a profound sense the spokesman of his people, voicing their hopes and fears. He will share the unrest and disturbance of his time but will be able to address them at a deeper level. The stories of Jewish and Christian expectation reflect the spiritual dis-ease in Arabia at the beginning of the seventh century but they also show the powerful effect that a prophetic hero like Jesus or Muhammad had on his own and later generations: what they achieved was so remarkable and so perfectly attuned to the needs of the day that it seemed foreordained in some mysterious way and to have fulfilled the religious aspirations of the past.

Muhammad was acutely aware of the malaise that afflicted Meccan society, despite its spectacular recent success. He had been born into the clan of Hashim in about 570, which had declined in power and felt at a disadvantage. Hashim ibn Abd Manaf, the grandson of Qusayy, had been an important figure in Mecca during his lifetime. It was he who had first equipped the two caravans that went each year from Mecca to Syria and the Yemen and was said to have been on good terms with the Negus of Abyssinia and the Emperor of Byzantium. At first, the clan that he had founded continued to be successful. Hashim's son, Abd al-Muttalib, was a charismatic figure who was believed to have rediscovered the sacred spring of Zamzam, which had been covered up by the impious predecessors of the Quraysh in Mecca. So the clan of Hashim had the privilege of giving water from Zamzam to the pilgrims when they came to make the *hajj*. Abd al-Muttalib was also a wealthy merchant, whose large herd of camels suggests that he continued some of the old nomadic pursuits. He had ten sons and six daughters, each more handsome and beautiful than the last. The historian Muhammad ibn Sa'd recalled the impression made by the sons of Abd al-Muttalib on the people of Mecca: 'Among the Arabs there were no more prominent and stately men, none of more noble profile. Their noses were so large that the nose drank before the lips.'[7] The youngest son Abdallah was particularly dear to Abd al-Muttalib and was said to have been even more handsome than his brothers: Abdallah was Muhammad's father.

But these were crucial years for the Quraysh, and the fortunes of its clans were in constant flux. During Muhammad's childhood a telling incident revived the old conflict between the Ahlaf (the Confederates) and the Mutayyabun (the Scented Ones) and showed how dramatically the fortunes of Hashim had plummeted when Abd al-Muttalib was an old man. A Yemeni merchant had sold some goods to one of the most important men in the clan of Sahm, which had been one of the Confederates. But he refused to pay for them and the Yemeni appealed to the tribe of the Quraysh as a whole to see that justice was done. The chief of the clan of Taym, one of the Scented Ones, called a meeting to which he invited anybody who cared about justice and right dealing. The clans of Hashim, al-Muttalib, Asad and Zuhrah – who were all in the Scented party – responded and made a pact which was later known as the Hilf al-Fudul, the League of the Virtuous.[8] They all went to the Ka'aba and swore that they would always take the side of the wronged and the oppressed. The boy Muhammad was said to have been present at this ceremony and to have spoken warmly and approvingly of this chivalric association. But the Hilf probably also had a commercial objective. The clans who joined this league were now in a weaker position than the Confederate clans, who were gaining a monopoly of Meccan trade and pushing the others to the wall. The Hilf may well have banded together to fight the monopolists in order to guard their own corner.

The circumstances of Muhammad's childhood show that his family had fallen on harder times. When it was time for the young Abdallah to take a wife, Abd al-Muttalib decided to take a new wife himself to forge an alliance with the clan of Zuhrah. He engaged himself and his youngest son to Hala bint Wuhayb and Amina bint Wahb, Muhammad's mother, who were both related to a leading merchant of Zuhrah. A legend about the conception of Muhammad is in striking contrast to the conception of Jesus, as related by Matthew and Luke. Islam has never had much time for celibacy and there was no virgin birth for its Prophet. Abd al-Muttalib and his son Abdallah were walking through the streets of Mecca together to visit their new wives when a woman rushed out and invited Abdallah into her bed. Arabs seem to have been able to have any number of women in the pre-Islamic period and even though he was on the way to his wedding Abdallah does not appear to have found the suggestion in bad taste. He simply replied that he had to stay with his father, but fully intended to visit the lady on his way home in the morning. When he arrived at the house of Amina's father, he consummated his marriage immediately and Muhammad was conceived. But the next morning when he looked up the woman who had propositioned him she was no longer interested. Yesterday there had been a blaze of bright light between Abdallah's eyes, she said, which showed that he was about to produce the Prophet of his people. Today the light had gone and another woman had conceived the Messenger of God.

Abdallah died while Amina was still pregnant and the family was now in such straitened circumstances that he was able to leave her only five camels and a young slave girl called Bahira. Amina is said to have experienced no discomfort while she was carrying Muhammad. Instead she heard a voice which told her that she was carrying the lord of the

Arabs, and she saw a light issuing from her belly in which were visible the castles of Basra in Syria, later recipient of the light of Islam. Muhammad was born on 12 Rabi'u al-awwal, and immediately Amina sent for Abd al-Muttalib and told him that the baby would one day be a great man. In joy and thanksgiving the old man carried his new grandson to the Ka'aba. He himself was said to have been told of the great future ahead of Muhammad: a *kahin* had prophesied that one of his descendants would rule the world, and one night he had a dream in which he saw a tree growing out of the child's back; its top reached the sky and its branches stretched east and west. From this tree came a light, which was worshipped by the Arabs and the Persians who later accepted Islam.

Children were often given out to foster-parents in the desert, because it was believed to be healthier for them than in the city. Bedouin women were willing to take a Qurayshi baby to foster because they could expect presents and help from the family, but because Amina was obviously so poor nobody was very interested in Muhammad. It had been a particularly bad year in Arabia and many of the tribes had suffered from severe famine. The tribe of Bani Sa'd were desperate and Halima bint Abu Dhuayb, a member of one of its poorest families, decided to take Muhammad anyway because she had not been able to find another suckling. But Halima was so hungry herself that she had no milk to give her own baby, the milk of her camel had dried up and even the donkey on which she had ridden to Mecca was on its last legs. But this is what happened as soon as she took the baby Muhammad:

I took him back to my baggage, and as soon as I put him in my bosom, my breasts overflowed with milk which he drank until he was satisfied, as also did his foster-brother. Then both of them slept, whereas before this we could not sleep with him. My husband got up and went to the old she-camel and lo, her udders were full; he milked it and he and I drank of her milk until we were completely satisfied, and we passed a happy night. In the morning my husband said: 'Do you know, Halima, you have taken a blessed creature!' I said, 'By al-Llah, I hope so.' Then we set out and I was riding my she-ass and carrying him with me, and she went at such a pace that the other donkeys could not keep up so that my companions said to me, 'Confound you! stop and wait for us. Isn't this the donkey on which you started?' 'Certainly it is,' I said. They replied, 'By al-Llah, something extraordinary has happened.' Then we came to our dwellings in the Bani Sa'd country and I do not know a country more desolate than that.

When we had him with us my flock used to yield milk in abundance. We milked them and drank while other people had not a drop, nor could they find anything in their camels' udders, so that our people were saying to their shepherds, 'Woe to you! send your flock to graze where the daughter of Abu Dhuayb's shepherd goes.' Even so, their flocks came back hungry, not yielding a drop of milk, while mine had milk in abundance.[9]

Not surprisingly Halima was reluctant to lose Muhammad and begged Amina to let him stay with them a little longer. Then a frightening but portentous incident made her change her mind.

The story goes that one day Muhammad's foster-brothers had rushed to their parents, crying in terror that two men in white had seized Muhammad and had seemed to slit his belly open. Halima had rushed to the scene to find the little boy lying weakly on the ground: later he explained that the men had taken his heart from his body and washed it with snow; then they had lifted him on to a pair of scales and declared that he was heavier than all the rest of the Arabs put together. Finally, one of the men kissed him on the forehead, saying gently: 'O beloved of God, verily you will never be frightened, and if you knew what good has been prepared for you you would be very happy.'[10] This story is similar to legends in other cultures describing an initiation: it symbolises the purity that is necessary if the initiate is to receive an experience of the divine without tainting the sacred message. Some Muslim writers placed this incident just before the Night Journey (the supreme mystical experience of Muhammad's life which we shall discuss in Chapter 7), which shows that they were well aware of its true significance.

But poor Halima and her husband al-Harith knew nothing of all this and were understandably terrified. Fearing that Muhammad had had a stroke they took him back to Mecca immediately, before the damage should become apparent. But Amina calmed them down, made them tell her the whole story and reassured them: this was an exceptional child and a great future had been foretold for him. She decided to keep Muhammad with her in Mecca, but when he was six years old Amina died and Muhammad had been orphaned twice over. He went to live in the house of his grandfather Abd al-Muttalib, who seems to have made quite a favourite of him. He had had two sons by his own late marriage and Muhammad was brought up with his two uncles Abbas and the cheerful Hamzah, who were about his own age. Abd al-Muttalib was now very old, however, and close to death. He liked to have his bedding carried out to the Ka'aba, where he could lie in the shade of the shrine surrounded by all his elder sons. Muhammad used to jump boldly on to the bed beside him and his grandfather would sit watching him fondly, stroking the child's back. He died when Muhammad was about eight, so the boy went to live in the household of his uncle Abu Talib, who had become the chief of Hashim, and had the companionship of his cousins Talib and Aqil.

Abu Talib was a good man, much respected in Mecca despite the declining fortunes of his clan. He was always kind to his orphaned nephew, even though his financial position was increasingly difficult. One year he decided to let Muhammad accompany him on a business trip to

Syria, and, to the surprise of the Quraysh, when they reached Basra the local monk Bahira rushed out of his cell to invite them to a meal. He usually ignored the caravan but this year he had seen that it was overshadowed by a bright cloud, which told him that the long-awaited Prophet must be present. This is the Muslim equivalent of the gospel story of the child Jesus lost in the Temple, but the early accounts show how ignorant these early sources still were about Christianity: the monk's name Bahira has been confused with the Syriac *bhira*, the title 'reverend'. Christians would claim that it was Bahira who had coached Muhammad in the heresy that they called 'Muhammadanism'.

Because Muhammad was the youngest, he was left outside to guard the merchandise while the Quraysh responded to Bahira's invitation. During the meal the monk studied the merchants carefully but none of them answered the descriptions of the Prophet that he had found in his books. Was there anybody else with them? The Quraysh suddenly felt ashamed that they had left the grandson of the great Abd al-Muttalib sitting outside like a slave, so they brought him in and the monk watched him attentively. After the meal, Bahira took Muhammad to one side and asked him to swear by al-Lat and al-Uzza, the goddesses of his people, that he would answer him truthfully. 'Do not ask me by al-Lat and al-Uzza,' Muhammad protested, 'for by al-Llah nothing is more hateful to me than those two.' Instead he swore by al-Llah alone, and answered Bahira's questions about his life. Then the monk examined his body and found the special mark of prophecy between his shoulder-blades. 'Take your nephew back to his country and guard him carefully against the Jews,' Bahira advised Abu Talib, 'for by al-Llah! if they see him and know about him what I know, they will do him evil; a great future lies before this nephew of yours, so take him home quickly.'[11]

But until Muhammad was about twenty-five there was little sign of this greatness, even though he grew up to be a very able young man. In Mecca he was known as al-Amin, the reliable one: all his life he had the ability to inspire confidence in others. He had grown up to be good-looking, with a compact, solid body of about average height. His hair and beard were thick and curly and he had a luminous expression which was particularly striking and is mentioned in all the sources. He had a decisive and whole-hearted character, which made him give his full attention to whatever he was doing, and this was also expressed in his physical bearing. Thus he never looked over his shoulder, even if his mantle were caught on a thorny bush; in later years his attendants could talk and laugh freely behind him, certain that he would not look round and see them. If he turned to speak to somebody, he never inclined partially towards them but would turn his whole body and address him full face. When he shook hands, he was never the one to withdraw his own first. His uncles had made sure that he had a good military training and he became a skilled archer and competent swordsman and wrestler. He would never be as spectacular on the battlefield as his young uncle Hamzah, however, who had grown into a giant of prodigious physical strength. His uncle Abbas became a banker and Muhammad became a merchant whose job it was to lead the caravans to Syria and Mesopotamia. In the West, he was frequently called a camel-driver, a derogatory description for this responsible administrative task. Some recent Western scholars, however, have questioned his profession, claiming that he showed no first-hand knowledge of Syria and the other civilised lands and that the Qu-ran never refers to the spectacular and attractive processions and practices of Syriac Christianity, which inspired other contemporary poets of the peninsula.[12] But it seems rather perverse to question the traditional view of Muhammad's early career as a merchant, because it is difficult to see why anybody should have invented it.

Despite his ability, his orphaned status held him back. This must have been painful and we shall see that throughout his life he remained concerned about the plight and treatment of orphans. His lowly position made it difficult for him to find a wife. At one point he wanted to marry Fakhita, a daughter of Abu Talib who was about his own age. But Abu Talib had to point out to him that he was not yet in a position to marry and made a more advantageous match for her in the aristocratic clan of Makhzum. However kind and tactful Abu Talib had been, this must have been deeply distressing. Muhammad was a man who loved and needed women. In this he differed from many of his contemporaries. Later, some of his closest companions, who clearly believed that women should be kept in their place, noted that in the pre-Islamic period most Meccans thought little of the female sex. We have seen that women had no status during the *jahiliyah* and even some of the most prominent Muslims treated their wives and daughters harshly. But Muhammad seems genuinely to have enjoyed women's company and to have needed affection and intimacy. In later years, his gentleness and apparent leniency with the women in his life perplexed some of his closest companions. Muhammad was not the perverse lecher of Western legend: he needed a woman as a beloved friend as well as a lover.

In about 595, however, his luck changed dramatically. A distant relative, Khadija bint Khuwaylid asked him to take some merchandise to Syria for her. City life often gives certain women a chance to flourish in business and commerce: in Europe during the twelfth century a significant number of women bankers, merchants and shopkeepers became extremely successful and it seems that this was also the case in Mecca.

Khadija had been married twice and had borne a number of children; she came from the clan of Asad, which was more powerful than Hashim by the beginning of the seventh century, and she was able to make a very good living as a merchant. Muhammad agreed to take her commission and set off on a decisive trip. One Maysara, who accompanied him, saw many strange things, which he duly reported back to Khadija. A monk, he claimed, had taken him aside and told him that Muhammad was the prophet whose coming was so eagerly awaited in Arabia. Later and to his astonishment, he said, he had seen two angels shading Muhammad from the fierce sun. When Khadija heard these stories, she went straight to consult her cousin Waraqa ibn Naufal, the *hanif*, who had become a Christian and had studied the scriptures. Waraqa was also eagerly awaiting the Arabian prophet, however, and when he heard Khadija's news he exclaimed: 'If this is true, Khadija, verily Muhammad is the prophet of this people!'[13]

Khadija proposed marriage to Muhammad. She was not solely motivated by Waraqa's enthusiasm but was impressed by the personal qualities of her young kinsman. Despite the disparity in their ages, she needed a new husband and Muhammad was an appropriate choice. 'I like you because of our relationship,' she told him, 'and your high reputation among your people, your trustworthiness, and good character and truthfulness.'[14] Tradition has it that Khadija was forty at this time, but, as she went on to bear Muhammad at least six children, she was probably somewhat younger, though still significantly older than her new husband. It has been common in the West for people to sneer at this marriage to the elderly, wealthy widow. It has been implied that Muhammad agreed to the match for cynical reasons. Even Maxime Rodinson, in his sympathetic biography, suggests that Muhammad must have found the marriage sexually and emotionally frustrating. But the opposite seems to have been true. In the early years of his prophetic mission, he could not have managed without her support and her spiritual counsel. Khadija was a remarkable woman. She was, says Ibn Ishaq, 'determined, noble and intelligent.' Whenever Muhammad was attacked by his enemies or shaken by the power of his mystical experience, he always went straight to his wife for comfort and for the rest of her life Khadija, the first person to recognise her husband's exceptional ability, 'strengthened him, lightened his burden, proclaimed his truth.'[15] Muhammad was a passionate man but he never took another, younger wife while he was married to Khadija – a fact that should be noted by those who criticise him for his polygamy in later years. Indeed, after her death, Muhammad used to infuriate the women he married by endlessly singing Khadija's praises and on one occasion turned white with grief when he thought he had heard her voice.

This was no marriage of convenience: Muhammad gave a large proportion of the family income to the poor and made his own family live very frugally.

Despite its austerity, it seems to have been a happy household. Khadija bore Muhammad at least six children. Their two sons – al-Qasim and Abdallah – both died in infancy, but there were four daughters: Zaynab, Ruqayyah, Umm Kulthum and Fatimah. Muhammad loved children: all his life he would hug and kiss them and join in their games. He was always devoted to his daughters. It was customary for the Arabs to take an honorary title, known as the *kunya*, when their first son was born and henceforth Muhammad was often called Abu al-Qasim (the father of Qasim), a name that always gave him particular pleasure. Khadija would have been called Umm al-Qasim, Qasim's mother.[16] But to some extent, Muhammad was able to compensate for the loss of his sons. On his wedding day, Khadija had presented him with a young slave boy from the northern Arab tribe of Kalb. Zayd ibn Harith became so attached to his master that when his family eventually traced him and came to Mecca with the money to ransom him, he begged to stay with Muhammad. In return, Muhammad gave him his freedom and Zayd became his foster son. A few years later, when his youngest daughter Fatimah was about four years old, there was another addition to the family. Abu Talib was by this time in financial trouble and in that year of particularly severe famine, his fortunes had deteriorated still further. To lighten his burden, Abbas took his younger brother Ja'far into his household and Muhammad took Abu Talib's youngest son, the five year old Ali. Muhammad, an orphan himself, took the foster relationship very seriously. Whenever his own Bedouin foster parents came to visit him, he gave them a gift of food or sheep. Both Zayd and Ali prospered under his care; they became remarkable leaders in the early Muslim community and Ali, in particular, seemed to possess the power of inspiring a deep devotion in his friends.

In these uneventful years before Muhammad received his call, his position in Mecca had improved. He was known in particular for his kindness to the poor and to slaves. One incident seems with hindsight to be prophetic. In 605, when Muhammad was about thirty-five years old, the Quraysh had decided to rebuild the Ka'aba: several stones had become loose, it needed a new roof and had recently been vandalised by thieves. But the sanctity of the building made this a risky, delicate job. In most traditional societies holy things are taboo and have to be handled with great care. The Quraysh would have been extremely nervous of demolishing this great shrine; nevertheless they pressed on with the project. Walid ibn al-Mughira, chief of Makhzum, who was one of the most influential men in Mecca, approached it warily with his pickaxe, saying: 'O God, do not be afraid, O God, we intend only what is best.' The work was allowed to commence and each clan took responsibility for a particular section to make sure that it was a communal effort of the whole tribe. When they reached the foundations, however, it was said that the whole city shook, and the Quraysh decided to leave them intact.

The new walls rose but a heated quarrel developed when it was time to put the Black Stone back in position, because each clan wanted the honour. After five days the dispute was still raging, a telling sign of the fierce competitiveness that was destroying tribal unity in Mecca. Eventually, in despair of reaching a satisfactory compromise, the clans decided to accept the judgement of the first person who came on the scene. This happened to be Muhammad, who had just returned from a business trip and had, as usual, gone straight to the Ka'aba to perform the circumambulations on his arrival. He was hailed with relief: 'Here is al-Amin,' everybody cried, 'we are satisfied.'[17] Muhammad asked them to bring a cloak, to lay the sacred stone in the centre, and then made a representative from each clan take hold of the edge of the garment so that they could lift it back into place together. Muhammad would rebuild the Ka'aba in a more fundamental way when he made it the centre of the Muslim world; he was also destined to repair the unity of the Quraysh around the sacred shrine of al-Llah.

As we have seen, when Muhammad was about forty years old he had begun to make a regular spiritual retreat. His later wife Aisha says that he began to spend more time in solitude, devoting himself to the worship of God. He began to have dreams which seemed radiant with promise and hope, 'like the dawn of the morning.' During these solitary periods he practised the spiritual exercises, which the Arabs called *tahannuth* and distributed food to the poor: prayer and almsgiving both became essential practices of his religion of al-Llah. He probably spent much time in anxious thought. We know from his later career that he had diagnosed the malaise in Mecca very accurately. He must have felt deeply frustrated: nobody in Mecca would have taken his ideas seriously and the poor position of his clan prevented him from taking a leading role in city life. Yet he must also have been instinctively aware that he had exceptional qualities that were not being used. The Qu'ran often reflects on the fact that God had never sent a prophet to the Quraysh, even though he had sent prophets to every other people on the face of the earth. Muhammad probably believed that only a messenger from God could heal the problems of his city, but we know from the Qu'ran that He had never imagined for one moment that *he* was going to be that Prophet.[18] At all events, like Moses, he climbed his mountain and on the mountain top met his God on the seventeenth night of Ramadan, 610.

We do not know much about *tahannuth* but it probably consisted of the disciplined exercises that have appeared in most religious traditions to help adepts transcend the limitations of their ordinary experience. Later Muhammad would express this experience of the ineffable by saying that he had been visited by an angel, who had appeared beside him in the cave and given him orders to 'Recite!' Like some of the Hebrew prophets, who were also deeply reluctant to utter the Word of God, Muhammad refused. 'I am not a reciter!' he insisted, thinking that the angel had mistaken him for one of the disreputable *kahins*, the soothsayers of Arabia. But the angel simply 'whelmed me in his embrace until he had reached the limits of my endurance,'[19] and eventually Muhammad found himself speaking the very first words of the Qu'ran:

> Recite in the name of thy Lord who created!
> He createth man from a clot of blood.
> Recite: and thy Lord is the Most Bountiful
> He who hath taught by the pen,
> taught man what he knew not.[20]

Muhammad came to himself in a state of terror and revulsion. The idea that he had, against his will, probably become a *jinn*-possessed *kahin* filled him with such despair, says the historian Tabari, that he no longer wanted to go on living. Rushing from the cave, he began to climb to the summit of the mountain to fling himself to his death. But on the mountainside he had another vision of a being which, later, he identified with Gabriel:

> When I was midway on the mountain, I heard a voice from heaven saying: 'O Muhammad! thou art the apostle of God and I am Gabriel.' I raised my head towards heaven to see who was speaking, and lo, Gabriel in the form of a man with feet astride the horizon. . . . I stood gazing at him, moving neither backward or forward; then I began to turn my face away from him, but towards whatever region of the sky I looked, I saw him as before.[21]

This angel was no pretty, naturalistic being such as sometimes appears in Christian art. In Islam, Gabriel is the Spirit of Truth, the means by which God reveals Himself to man. This was an overwhelming, towering experience of a Presence which filled the entire horizon and from which escape was impossible. Muhammad had had that overpowering apprehension of numinous reality which has devastated prophets and seers in most traditions. In Christianity it has been described as the *mysterium terribile et fascinans* and in Judaism it has been called *kaddosh*, 'holiness', the terrifying otherness of God.

The various traditions give conflicting accounts of Muhammad's original vision; some say that it consisted only of the vision in the cave; others mention only the vision of the angel on the horizon. But all emphasise Muhammad's fear and horror. The Hebrew prophets had also cried out against the vision of holiness, fearing that they were close to death: 'What a wretched state I am in!' Isaiah had cried when he saw his vision of God in the Temple, 'I am lost!' Even the angels shielded themselves with their wings from the divine presence but he had looked on the Lord of Hosts with his own impure eyes.[22] Jeremiah had experienced God as an agonising pain that filled his every limb; like Muhammad in the embrace of the Angel, he experienced revelation as a sort of divine rape.[23] It invaded his being with fearful force, doing violence to his natural self which was not built for such a divine impact. What all these prophets had experienced was transcendence, a reality that lay beyond concepts and which the monotheistic faiths call 'God'. The experience was *terribile* because it had taken each prophet into an uncharted realm, far from the consolations of normality, where everything was a profound shock. But it was also *fascinans*, exerting an irresistible attraction because it was somehow a reminder of something already known, intricately bound up with the deepest self. But unlike Isaiah and Jeremiah, Muhammad had none of the consolations of an established religion to support him and help him to interpret his experience. It seemed to have come upon him entirely unsought and left him feeling suicidal and despairing. He had been propelled into a sphere that he had never imagined and had somehow to explain it to himself. In his isolation and terror, he turned instinctively to his wife.

Crawling on his hands and knees, the whole upper part of his body shaking convulsively, Muhammad flung himself into her lap. 'Cover me! cover me!' he cried, begging her to shield him from this terrifying presence. Despite his contempt for the *kahins*, who always covered themselves with a cloak when delivering an oracle, Muhammad had instinctively adopted the same posture. Trembling, he waited for the terror to abate, and Khadija held him in her arms, soothing him and trying to take his fear away. All the sources emphasise Muhammad's profound dependence upon Khadija during this crisis. Later he would have other visions on the mountainside and each time he would go straight to Khadija and beg her to cradle him and wrap him in his cloak. But Khadija was not just a consoling mother figure; she was also Muhammad's spiritual adviser. It was she who was able to provide the support that other seers and prophets have found in an established religion. When the fear receded on that first occasion, Muhammad asked her if he had become a *kahin*; it was the only form of inspiration that was familiar to him and despite its towering holiness it also seemed disturbingly similar to the experience of the *jinn*-possessed people of Arabia. Thus Hassan ibn Thabit, the poet of Yathrib who later became a Muslim, says that when he received his poetic vocation, his *jinni* had appeared to him, thrown him to the ground and forced the inspired words from his mouth.[24] Muhammad had little respect for the *jinn*, who could be capricious and make mistakes. If this was how al-Llah had rewarded him for his devotion, he did not want to live. Throughout his life, the Qu'ran shows how sensitive Muhammad was to any suggestion that he might simply be *majnun*, possessed by a *jinni*, and carefully distinguishes the verses of the Qu'ran from conventional Arabic poetry.

Khadija hastened to reassure him. God did not act in such a cruel and arbitrary way. Muhammad had tried honestly to live in the way that God required and in return God would never allow him to fail: 'You are kind and considerate toward your kin. You help the poor and forlorn and bear their burdens. You are striving to restore the high moral qualities that your people have lost. You honour the guest and go to the assistance of those in distress. This cannot be, my dear.'[25] To reassure him further, she suggested that they consult her cousin Waraqa, who was learned in the scriptures and could give them more expert advice. Waraqa had no doubts at all. 'Holy! holy!' he cried at once: 'If you have spoken the truth to me, O Khadija, there has come to him the greatest *namus* who came to Moses aforetime, and lo, he is the prophet of his people.'[26] The next time he met Muhammad at the Ka'aba, the Christian hurried over to the new prophet of the one God and kissed him on the forehead.

We must pause for a while to consider the nature of this experience. We no longer automatically dismiss all such vision or intuition as hysteria or bad faith. In all cultures, inspiration has been seen as a form of benign possession, in artistic as well as in religious terms. The poem or the message seems to talk to its creator with imperative force and seems also to declare itself. Frequently, a truly creative thinker also feels that he has been inspired in this way: he has in some sense touched or dis-covered an uncreated reality, that has independent existence. The most famous example is that of Archimedes, who leapt from his bath when he discovered his famous principle, crying 'Eureka! I have found it!' While he had been relaxed, he was in a receptive frame of mind and the solution seemed to have entered unbidden as if it had an existence independent of his own mind. All truly creative thought is in some sense intuitive; it demands a leap forward into the dark world of uncreated reality. Seen in this way, intuition is not the abdication of reason but rather reason speeded up, encapsulated in an instant, so that a solution appears without the usual laborious logical preparations. A creative genius comes back from this undiscovered country like one of the heroes of antiquity, who has wrested something back from the gods and brought it to mankind. It is possible, perhaps, to see religious inspiration in a similar way.

The poet who 'listens to' the poem which seems to be outside himself is, of course, listening to the unconscious. He has become the carrier of a message or gift from what has been called the muses or the gods. In a small society like Mecca, the unconscious minds of the people had much in common. In purely secular terms, Muhammad had reached down to a deeper level of the problem facing his contemporaries and had brought them something that a few of them were ready to listen to. We shall see that as he brought the Qu'ran to light, verse by verse, sura by sura, and recited it to the people, many of them recognised it at a profound level. It was able to break through their prejudices, anxieties and ideological objections to an imaginative, spiritual and social solution that nobody had thought of before but which answered their deepest longings and aspirations. In every religion, the idea of God or the Ultimate Reality is culturally conditioned. The Arabs of the Hijaz seem to have been seeking a new religious solution that was right for their own particular needs. They did not want the Christian idea of God, for example, which had become coloured with the rationalistic philosophy and ideals of ancient Greece. Muhammad had instinctively cut back into the Semitic religious experience of the great Hebrew prophets, which was better suited to the people of the Middle East. It is tempting to see the popularity of Islam among the people of Syria, Mesopotamia, Iran and North Africa as a rejection of a Greek-inspired idea of God which was alien to their needs and a return to a more Semitic vision.

But Muhammad never had any idea that he was founding a new world religion. This was to be a religion for the Arabs, who seem to have been left out of the divine plan. God had sent the Jews and the Christians a scripture – in the Qu'ran they were called the *ahl al-kitab*, the People of the Book – but no special revelation to the Arabs. The revelation that Muhammad had started to recite under divine inspiration on Mount Hira was an Arabic Qu'ran. It was a message that answered the Arabs' deeper needs: Muhammad had somehow broken through to a new level of consciousness, where he could recognise what had gone wrong in his society, and was little by little providing the Arabs with their own special solution.

We often use the word 'revelation' to describe an entirely original thought or vision. But the etymology of the word shows that it is something that has been 'unveiled', 'dis-covered'. Of its nature, no religious vision or concept can be original, because it claims to point to the fundamental, pre-existent reality. Muhammad understood and expressed this truth more clearly than many other religious leaders. There was nothing new about the revelation on Mount Hira. This was simply the old religion of God, which had been revealed over and over again, but which Muhammad had been entrusted to bring to the Arabs. The religion of al-Llah that Muhammad would shortly begin to preach in Mecca had begun not on Mount Hira but on the day of Creation. God had made Adam his *kalipha* or vice-gerent on earth and after that time He had sent one prophet after another to every people on the face of the earth.[27] The message had always been the same, so all religions were essentially one. The Qu'ran never claimed to cancel out previous revelations, but in principle one cult, one tradition, one scripture was as good as another.[28] What mattered was the quality of one's surrender to God, not to any mere human expression of His will. People had no business to 'desire another religion than God's.'[29] The prophets had all confirmed and continued God's unfolding revelation of Himself. Thus, referring to the belief that Jesus had prophesied the coming of a 'Paraclete' (which as we have seen some Arabs had translated as Ahmad, a variant on Muhammad's own name), the Qu'ran says:

> Jesus son of
> Mary said, 'Children of
> Israel, I am indeed the
> Messenger of God to you,
> confirming the Torah
> that is before me, and
> giving good tidings of
> a Messenger who shall
> come after me, whose
> name shall be Ahmad.'[30]

The only thing that made Muhammad's revelation different was that for the first time God had sent a messenger to the Quraysh and a scripture in their own language.

There is, therefore, a casual attitude towards the historical forms of revelation. It is worth emphasising this point, because tolerance is not something which people in the West today are likely to associate with Islam. But as the next chapter indicates, the intolerance of Islam springs not from the kind of doctrinal differences that have divided Christians from one another but from quite a different source. After Muhammad's death, Jews and Christians were never required to convert to Islam but were allowed to practise their religion freely in the Islamic empire. Later Zoroastrians, Hindus, Buddhists and Sikhs were also counted among the People of the Book. It has never been a problem for Muslims to coexist with people of other religions. The Islamic empire was able to play host to Christians and Jews for centuries; but Western Europe has found it almost impossible to tolerate Muslims and Jews in Christian territory.

The revelation on Mount Hira in 610 was obviously an important event in Islamic history, but it was only a beginning. The miracle of the Qu'ran, according to many Muslims today, was not the manner of its original revelation to Muhammad on Mount Hira, in Mecca and, later, in Medina, but its continuing ability to give millions of men and women all over the world faith in the ultimate meaning and value of life. The religion of Islam has had to be continuously inventive and creative in its application of the original vision to the changing world: in each generation it has had to respond to modernity like any other faith.

In the Qu'ran, Muhammad is often called the *ummî* prophet, the unlettered prophet, and the doctrine of his illiteracy stresses the miraculous nature of his inspiration. Some Western scholars, however, have claimed that the title *ummî* should not be interpreted as illiterate and that, as a merchant, Muhammad probably would have mastered the rudiments of writing. They believe that he was claiming to be a prophet for the 'unlettered' people who had not received a scripture from God. In other words, *ummî* means the Prophet to the gentiles. Other writers have proceeded from this position to the incorrect assertion that *ummî* is related to the word *umma*, community, and that the title thus means 'the prophet of the people'. In fact, however, *ummî* and *umma* have no relation to one another and Muslims find this interpretation insulting. We have seen that for nearly a thousand years, Westerners have been unable to believe that Muhammad had a genuine prophetic vocation. This appears as another attempt to explain it away. In fact, it seems perverse to challenge the traditional Muslim interpretation of *ummî*. There is no mention in the early sources of Muhammad reading or writing. When he needed to send a letter he would dictate it to somebody like Ali, who was literate. To have concealed his ability to read and write all his life would have been a major deception. Apart from being uncharacteristic, this fraud would have been very difficult to sustain, given how closely he lived among his own people. The interpretation of *ummî* as illiterate is very early indeed: it is also of great importance to Muslims. It has rather the same symbolic significance as the notion of the Virgin Birth in Christianity, emphasising the purity required of a man or woman who brings the Word of God to mankind: the revelation must not be qualified by purely human input.

Nevertheless, it would be a mistake to imagine Muhammad acting passively as a sort of telephone between God and man. Like other prophets, he sometimes had to struggle to make sense of the revelations, which did not always come to him in a clear, verbal form. Sometimes they came as visions rather than words.[31] As we have seen, Muhammad's later wife Aisha claimed that Muhammad's earliest revelations were visual.

They consisted of a vaguer, richer intimation of overwhelming and transfiguring meaning: 'the first sign of prophethood vouchsafed to the apostle was true visions, resembling the brightness of daybreak [*falaq as-subh*]'.[32] The phrase expresses the sudden transformation of the world when the sun breaks through the darkness in these eastern lands where there is no twilight. What Muhammad experienced was a startling vision of hope rather than an explicit message.

Muslim tradition shows that putting this message into words was never easy. Muhammad once said: 'Never once did I receive a revelation without thinking that my soul had been torn away from me.'[33] It was a process of creation that was agonising. Sometimes, he said, the verbal content was clear enough: he seemed to see the angel in the form of a man and heard his words. But at other times it was more painful and incoherent: 'Sometimes it comes unto me like the reverberations of a bell, and that is the hardest upon me; the reverberations abate when I am aware of their message.'[34] We shall see him turning inwards and searching his own soul for a solution to a problem, rather as a poet listens to the poem that he is gradually hauling to light. The Qu'ran warns him to listen to the inarticulate meaning carefully and with what Wordsworth would call a 'wise passiveness'. He must not rush to put it into words before these had emerged in their own good time:

> Move not thy tongue with it
> to hasten it;
> Ours it is to gather it, and to recite it.
> So, when We recite it, follow thou its recitation.
> Then Ours it is to explain it.[35]

The Divine Voice was not booming a message from heaven; God was no clearly definable reality 'out there'. He was to be heard by looking within. Later the Sufis, the mystics of Islam, would develop this notion of God as the ground of our being. Some would hear the divine voice telling them: 'There is no god but thou.'

Again, we do not know how many revelations Muhammad received in those very early days. But we do know that Muhammad, Khadija and Waraqa kept quiet about them. He was not at all the eager self-publicist described by his Western enemies. After the first few revelations, however, Muhammad experienced a period of silence for about two years. It was a time of great desolation, and some Muslim writers have attributed his suicidal despair to this period. Had he been deluded after all? Or had God found him wanting as the bearer of revelation and abandoned him? The silence seemed catastrophic, but then came Sura 93 – the Sura of Morning – with a burst of luminous reassurance:

By the white forenoon
and the brooding night!
Thy Lord has neither forsaken thee nor hates thee
and the Last shall be better for thee than the First.
Thy Lord shall give thee, and thou shalt be satisfied.

Did He not find thee an orphan, and shelter thee?
Did He not find thee erring, and guide thee?
Did He not find thee needy, and suffice thee?

As for the orphan, do not oppress him,
and as for the beggar, scold him not;
and as for thy Lord's blessing, exalt it.[36]

Muhammad was now about to begin his mission. He had learned to have faith in his experiences and he now believed that they came directly from God. He was no deluded *kahin*. This act of faith demanded courage, but now he had resolved to take a step which would demand even more resolution. He had decided to accept Waraqa's interpretation of his experience: he had been called to be the Prophet of the Quraysh. Now he would have to present himself to his people. Waraqa warned him that this would not be easy. He was an old man and not likely to live long, he told Muhammad, but he wished he could still be alive to help Muhammad when his people cast him out. Muhammad was horrified to hear this. Would they really cast him out, he asked in dismay. Waraqa sadly told him that a prophet is always without honour in his own country. As we shall see, Muhammad was very cautious when he began to spread the word. He knew that his claim was likely to be ridiculed. People might think that he was an agent for the Byzantines, like the Christian *hanif* Uthman ibn al-Huwayrith, or they might accuse him of treachery and impiety to the traditional religion. Nevertheless, Muhammad was ready to accept his dangerous mission. It would lead him in a direction that he had never imagined.

5 · The Warner

Muhammad had grappled with a terrifying but ultimately illuminating experience on Mount Hira, rather as Jacob had wrestled with his angel. Now he had to bring his people the message that he had wrested from the divine realm. The Sura of Morning issued a clear social command: men and women must look after the disadvantaged people of the tribe. There was nothing new about this. It had been crucial to the old ideal of *muruwah*, but the Quraysh seemed to have lost sight of it. The Qu'ran says that this message had been central to the revelations of every one of the previous prophets throughout the world. Muslim tradition claims that there had been 124,000 such prophets, a symbolic number suggesting infinitude. God had not left mankind without knowledge of the correct way to live, even though people had usually obstinately ignored the divine message. But now God had finally sent a prophet to the Quraysh, who had never had such an envoy before. In 612, at the start of his mission, Muhammad had a modest conception of his role. He was no saviour or messiah; he had no universal mission – at this date he did not even feel that he should preach to the other Arabs of the peninsula. He was simply to deliver a message to Mecca and its environs, as the latest in the long line of prophets.[1] He should have no political function.[2] He was just the *nadhir*, the Warner. Muhammad's conception of his vocation would change, but when he began he simply believed that he had been sent to warn the Quraysh of the dangers of the course they had recently adopted:

O thou shrouded in thy mantle
arise and warn!
thy Lord magnify
thy robes purify
and defilement flee![3]

But this did not mean that Muhammad started with a message of doom. The Last Judgement was only mentioned briefly in the earliest suras, or chapters, of the Qu'ran but the early message was essentially joyful. He wanted every man and woman of Mecca to become aware of God's goodness, which they could see in the natural world. He had created them, guided them and preserved the whole order of the universe for their benefit. By contemplating the 'signs' (*ayat*) of al-Llah's activity in the world which all the Quraysh acknowledged He had created, they would begin to sense His abundant generosity and their own perverse ingratitude:

Perish Man! How unthankful he is!
Of what did He create him?
Of a sperm-drop
He created him, and determined him,
then the way eased for him,
then makes him to die, and buries him,
then, when He wills, He raises him.
No indeed! Man has not accomplished His bidding.

Let man consider his nourishment.
We poured out the rains abundantly,
then we split the earth into fissures
and therein made the grains to grow
and vines and reeds
and olives and palms,
and dense-tree'd gardens,
and fruits and pastures,
an enjoyment for you and your flocks.[4]

But still men refused to live in the way that God had intended.

Muhammad did not issue a long list of requirements, however. In the main he was content to reform the old Arab code of honour with which the Quraysh were familiar. All that the Qu'ran requires is that men and women strive to create a just society, where the vulnerable are treated decently. This was the bedrock of the Qu'ranic message. If Muslims seem intolerant to us today, we should realise that they are not always intolerant of rival visions of reality, as Western Christianity has been. Instead they are intolerant of injustice, whether this is committed by one of their own rulers, like Shah Muhammad Reza Pahlavi of Iran and President Anwar al-Sadat of Egypt, or by the powerful Western countries. The early message of the Qu'ran is simple: it is wrong to stockpile wealth to build a personal fortune, but good to give alms and distribute the wealth of society.

Western scholars tell us that it is mistaken to see Muhammad as a socialist. They point out that he never criticised capitalism, which had, after all, done great things for the Quraysh, and that he did not attempt to abolish poverty altogether, which would have been an impossible task in seventh-century Arabia. Muhammad may not have conformed to all the recent concepts of socialism, as it has evolved in the West, but in a deeper sense he was certainly socialist and this has left an indelible impression on the ethos of Islam. True, he did not condemn wealth and possessions as Jesus did: Muslims were not commanded to give away everything that they had. Instead, they must be generous with their wealth and give a regular proportion of their income to the poor. Almsgiving (*zakat*) would become one of the five essential 'pillars' (*rukn*) of Islam.[5] Some kind of almsgiving was required in the earliest Islamic ethic.[6] Muslims must not hoard their money or develop a compulsive rivalry to acquire more than anybody else.[7] They must look after the poor and should not swindle orphans of their inheritance when they administer their property, as so many of the Quraysh were doing.[8] This ethos prevailed, even when the Muslims became a major world power and when many were extremely wealthy. The egalitarianism of Islam meant that the Holy Law gradually deprived the Caliph of any real political power and he became mainly a symbol of unity. The court may have been wealthy, but pious Muslims in all areas of religious life in the Islamic empire – jurists as well as mystics – claimed that such ostentatious wealth was unIslamic. When a local ruler wanted to prove his Muslim credentials, one of the first things he had to do was to show that he lived frugally and conformed to the egalitarian ideal. Thus at the time of the Crusades, Nur ad-Din and Saladin, who organised the Muslim riposte, both gave the bulk of their estate to the poor and lived simple, austere lives, alongside their companions. In this way they appealed to the people, proving that they were better Muslims than any other rulers in the Near East. They built empires that relied on this popular acclaim and the people considered them as authentic because their lives were so similar to the Prophet's.

Muhammad himself always lived a simple and frugal life, even when he became the most powerful *sayyid* in Arabia. He hated luxury and there was often nothing to eat in his household. He never had more than one set of clothes at a time and when some of his Companions urged him to wear a richer ceremonial dress, he always refused, preferring the thick, coarse cloth worn by most of the people. When he received gifts or booty, he gave it away to the poor and, like Jesus, he used to tell the Muslims that the poor would enter the Kingdom of Heaven before the rich. It was no accident that many of his first converts were among the disadvantaged people of Mecca: slaves and women both recognised that this religion offered them a message of hope. As we shall see, he did attract converts from the richer clans, but most of the powerful and aristocratic Quraysh held aloof: when the Muslims gathered together at the Ka'aba, they scoffed at the riff-raff with whom the grandson of the great Abd al-Muttalib was pleased to associate. When Islam became more powerful, it was not the wealthier Muslims of the upper-class who were his closest companions but the more plebeian converts from the poorer clans of Quraysh. None of this was simply a matter of personal preference. Muhammad knew that he had to set an example to the first Muslims and that al-Llah hated injustice and exploitation. A decent society, that reflected God's will, must cultivate a strictly egalitarian way of life.

So, a modern secularist may ask, why did he bother with God at all? Instead of going through all those harrowing experiences on Mount Hira, why did Muhammad not simply begin a campaign for social reform? He knew that the problem had a deeper source and that such reforms would be merely cosmetic. They would remain ineffectual unless the Quraysh placed another, transcendent value at the centre of their lives. He had realised, at a more profound level than any of his peers, that at the root of the Meccan malaise was an unhealthy and unrealistic attitude of presumption (*yatqa*) and self-sufficiency (*istaqa*).[9] In former days, when the tribe had come first, the Arabs had of necessity realised that all its members depended upon one another. In the Arabian steppes they had always faced the possibility of extinction, but their success had cushioned them from the dangers that were facts of normal Arabian life. Consequently they had, understandably enough, made a new religion of money. They believed that they were the masters of their own fate. The Qu'ran hints that some even believed that money could give them a certain immortality,[10] which in the old days had been provided only by the tribe. Their society had, however, been based on a communal ideal. Now clans fought other clans and some, like Hashim, felt that their very survival was threatened. The old unity of the tribe was breaking down and that meant that it was bound to disintegrate. Muhammad's own career would justify this insight. Eventually, some twenty years later, he would defeat the Quraysh not merely because of his own skill – though that was considerable – but because they had been unable to oppose him with a united front. When Muhammad began his mission a cruel individualism was usurping the old communal ethic: the Qu'ran depicts this in the chilling example of the person who would be willing to sacrifice all his nearest relatives to save himself at the Last Judgement[11] – a phenomenon which would once have been unthinkable when the ties of blood were considered sacred.

In order to correct these abuses the Quraysh would have to create a new spirit within themselves. Most new political solutions at this time were religious. When Muhammad asked the Quraysh to consider the implications of their belief in al-Llah, Creator of heaven and earth, he was not proposing anything new. Atheism in our modern sense seems to have been psychologically impossible before the eighteenth century and that only in the West. All the Quraysh would have believed implicitly in the existence of their High God. Many of them had come to believe that al-Llah was the God worshipped by the Jews and the Christians. Now Muhammad was making them think out the consequences of such faith.

He did not have to prove al-Llah's existence but pointed out that, if the Quraysh really believed the things they said, they would have some thinking to do. The Jews and Christians believed that God would raise men up at the Last Day – an idea which the old Arab fatalism had denied but which had drastic consequences for each individual soul: even the weakest members of their tribe had an eternal destiny and hence a sacred importance. If the Quraysh were serious in their belief that al-Llah had created the world, perhaps they should look at His creation with new eyes.

In the early years of his mission, when Muhammad was preaching only to carefully selected people, he reminded the Quraysh of many precious beliefs that he asked them to reconsider and apply to the current situation. How did the new cult of self-sufficiency cohere with their proud memories of the Year of the Elephant, when God had saved the city from destruction by a dramatic miracle and immeasurably increased their own prestige? This was yet another 'sign' which they should consider carefully:

> Hast thou not seen how thy Lord did with the Men of the Elephant?
> Did He not make their guile to go astray?
> And He loosed upon them birds in flights,
> hurling against them stones of baked clay
> and He made them like green blades devoured.[12]

The Quraysh had confessed by their boasting about this event that they had not achieved their power and success simply by means of their own efforts.

The Qu'ran was not revealing anything novel: it claimed to be a 'Reminder'[13] of things that everybody knew already. It was simply making the old facts clear, throwing them into more lucid relief. Frequently the Qu'ran introduces a new topic with words like 'Hast thou not seen?' or 'Have you not considered?' The Word of God was not thundering commands arbitrarily from on high but was inviting the Quraysh to enter into a dialogue, was issuing a challenge which did not destroy the past but built on the old Arab insights and traditions. For example, the Qu'ran reminded the Quraysh that the Ka'aba, of which they were so fiercely proud, was the House of al-Llah and one of the main reasons for their success. This had been the cause of the Abyssinian invasion during the Year of the Elephant. Without their Sanctuary, which al-Llah had provided, they would not have been able to establish such a successful market, their city would be constantly threatened by attack from other tribes and they would not have freed themselves from the Arab disease of hunger:

> For the composing of Quraysh,
> their composing for the winter and summer caravan!

So let them serve the Lord of this House
Who has fed them against hunger
and secured them from fear.[14]

The Qu'ran was not urging them to sit back and leave everything to God – quite the contrary, as we shall see. But it was asking them to reconsider some of their most fundamental beliefs in the light of their present position. The Quraysh loved to make the sacred circumambulations around the House of al-Llah, but when they put themselves and their own material success into the centre of their world they seemed to have forgotten the meaning of the old rites. The 'composing' (*ilaf*), the unity of the Quraysh around this sacred place, had been thrown into jeopardy because they were splitting up the old communal ideal and giving no consideration to the weaker clans, the orphans, the poor, the elderly and the vulnerable. If they continued to act in this manner they would lose all sense of their real position in the world.

At this early stage the Qu'ran was trying to make the Meccans see how many things they still owed to al-Llah, despite their recent success and apparent security. They should look at the signs of His goodness and power that were evident wherever they looked in the natural world. If they failed to reproduce this benevolence in their own society they would be putting themselves outside the real nature of things:

The All-merciful has taught the Qu'ran.
He created man
and He has taught him the Explanation.

The sun and the moon to a reckoning,
and the stars and the trees bow themselves;
and the heaven – He raised it up, and set
the Balance.
(Transgress not in the Balance,
and weigh with justice, and skimp not in the Balance.)
And earth – He set it down for all beings,
therein fruits, and palm-trees with sheaths,
and grain in the blade, and fragrant herbs.
O which of your Lord's bounties will you and you deny?[15]

All the other creatures acknowledge God and bow before Him, recognising Him as their first cause, the source of their being without which they could not continue. God is the essential force or energy that informs all things and keeps them functioning and powerful. He had created the balance that keeps all things in their correct relationship to one another, and unless the Quraysh recreated that balance in their own society, giving due weight and just measure in all their dealings with one another, they would be out of step with the nature of things. To help his first converts to acquire this attitude of responsible acknowledgement of God, Muhammad demanded that they bow towards Him in ritual prayer twice a day, like the stars and the trees. This prayer (*salat*) became another of the five pillars of Islam. The external gesture would help Muslims to cultivate the internal posture and reorient their lives at a fundamental level.

Eventually Muhammad's religion of al-Llah was known as *islām*, the act of existential surrender that each convert was expected to make to God: a *muslīm* is 'one who surrenders' his or her whole being to the Creator. At first, however, the believers called their religion *tazaqqa*. This is an obscure word, which is not easy to translate. By cultivating *tazaqqa*, Muhammad's converts were to cloak themselves in the virtues of compassion and generosity; they were to use their intelligence to cultivate a caring and responsible spirit, which made them want to give graciously of what they had to all God's creatures. By pondering the mysteries of creation intelligently Muslims would learn to behave kindly and this generous attitude would mean that they acquired a spiritual refinement. Al-Llah was the great exemplar. Muslims were urged to contemplate His 'signs' in order to appreciate His graciousness to the whole of the natural world. As a consequence of his generous intelligence, there was order and fruitfulness instead of chaos and selfish barbarism. If they submitted to His edicts, they would find that their own lives could be transfigured by a similar refinement.

All other creatures are natural *muslīms* who cannot choose but do God's will and surrender to the divine plan.[16] Man alone has the freedom to make a voluntary act of *islām* and conform his life to the source and sustainer of his being. He is submitting not to an arbitrary tyrant, but to the essential laws that govern the universe.

But what about the cruelty of nature, the natural disasters that we call 'acts of God' in legal parlance? The Qu'ran does not ignore these. The verses that I have just quoted continue:

> And a sign for them is that We carried their seed
> in the laden ship,
> and We have created for them the like of it
> whereon they ride;
> and if We will, We drown them,
> then none have they to cry to,
> neither are they delivered,
> save as a mercy from Us, and enjoyment
> for a while.[17]

Nobody knew the harshness of the natural world better than the Arabs. In paganism and in the Oriental religious tradition, the various gods are merely manifestations of a primal force, the *rerum natura*, which is supreme, inscrutable and quite impersonal. Some of these deities symbolised its benevolent characteristics and personified love, fertility, law or wisdom, but others expressed the darker aspects of life that men and women experienced in the world. They were gods of war or violence and sometimes had malign characteristics. The Hindu tradition would say that evil is one of the masks of the transcendent, impersonal reality of God. The pagan vision, with its warring gods and goddesses, was a tragic but courageously truthful expression of the conflict that everyone feels in the world and in his inmost being. In paganism the conflict has no conceivable resolution. In Arabia the original symbolic significance of the old gods had been lost during the nomadic period and Arab religion had no developed mythology to express this pagan insight. But it is possible to see elements of this insight in the Qu'ran, where the 'signs' of God in the world express the inscrutable mystery of God which had been symbolised by the gods in other systems.

In the Qu'ran, al-Llah is far more impersonal than Yahweh in the Jewish scriptures or the Father who is incarnated in Jesus Christ. In the early tribal religion of the Hebrews, Yahweh had inflicted disasters or conferred benefits on men and women as an expression – sometimes rather arbitrary – of His good pleasure. But when al-Llah somehow causes people to drown, for example, He is inspired by no *personal* animus. He is closer both to the *rerum natura* and to the sublime God of the later Hebrew prophets, who utterly transcends all purely human concepts of good and evil, right and wrong:

> My thoughts are not your thoughts
> my ways not your ways – it is Yahweh who speaks.
> Yes, the heavens are as high above the earth
> as my ways are above your ways,
> my thoughts above your thoughts.[18]

One can only marvel at the spiritual genius of Muhammad, who had practically no contact with practising Jews or Christians and whose actual knowledge of these earlier revelations was inevitably rudimentary, but who managed to get to the heart of the monotheistic experience. The Qu'ran emphasises that God eludes our human thoughts and that we can speak about Him only in signs and symbols, which half reveal and half conceal His ineffable nature. The whole mode of the Qu'ranic discourse is symbolic; it constantly speaks of the great 'similitudes' that it offers for the consideration of the Muslims. There are no doctrines about God, defining what He is, but mere 'signs' of a sacramental nature where something of Him can be experienced.

Western people often misunderstand the metaphorical nature of the Qu'ranic theology, because we tend nowadays to read a book for information. But in the Middle Ages Christians developed a wholly symbolic method of reading their scriptures, which is not dissimilar from the way that Muslims approach the Qu'ran. Even some of the events it describes – in the lives of the prophets or the approaching Last Judgement – are essentially symbolic representations of divine truths and should not be understood as literal facts. As Buddhists see the various gods and goddesses as aspects of themselves, so too Muslims have always spoken of the 'Moses of one's soul' or the 'Joseph of the heart', seeing the conflict between good and evil, so frequently described in the Qu'ran, as a spiritual drama endlessly enacted within themselves. When Muslims recite the Qu'ran, therefore, they become aware of the history of their own being, rather than an objective history of salvation. They make the imaginative effort to create their own inner experience of the struggle to return to the Source of creation and to fight the evil in themselves.

From the earliest days, the Qu'ran encouraged men and women to acquire this imaginative, symbolic attitude. This is especially apparent in the great descriptions of the 'signs' of nature. In Christianity, there is sometimes a rather pessimistic view of the natural world, which is believed to have lapsed from its original perfection because of man's sin. But, like Judaism, Islam does not believe in the Fall of man and Original Sin in the Christian sense: death, pain and sorrow were not punishments for a primordial failure on the part of men, but were always a part of the inscrutable divine plan. The physical world is not fallen but is an epiphany, revealing an experience of the sublime which normal human language or modes of thought cannot contain. To see *through* this fragmentary world to the full power of original being has always been a function of the imagination, of art and of religion. The Qu'ran would urge Muslims to make the imaginative and intellectual effort to look at the world around them in a symbolic way:

> Surely in the creation of the heavens and the earth
> and the alternation of night and day
> and the ship that runs in the sea with profit
> to men, and the water God sends down from heaven
> therewith reviving the earth again after it is dead
> and His scattering abroad in it all manner of
> crawling things, and the turning about of the winds
> and the clouds compelled between heaven and earth –
> surely these are signs for a people having understanding.[19]

Muslim tradition has stressed the importance of the imagination: the great Sufi philosopher Muid ad-Din al-Arabi (d. 1240) speaks of the imagination as the God-given faculty of creating a personal theophany, or manifestation of God, in the world around us. This extraordinary human capacity enables men and women to survive the shocks and tragedy that flesh is heir to. But the Qu'ran does not ask Muslims to abdicate their reason. The signs are 'for a people having *understanding*', 'for a people who *know*': Muslims are urged to '*look upon*' signs in the natural world and examine them carefully.[20] This attitude also helped to cultivate that habit of intelligent curiosity which enabled Muslims to develop an outstanding tradition of natural science and mathematics. There has never been a conflict between rational scientific inquiry and religion in the Islamic tradition, such as became apparent in the nineteenth century when Christians felt that the discoveries of Lyell and Darwin irrevocably undermined the faith. In fact some mystics in the radical Shiite sects have used science and mathematics as a prelude to contemplation.

Thus when Muhammad asked the Quraysh to accept his revelation as coming from God, he did not demand that they assent to a creed or to a set of theological opinions. As in Judaism, there is no cult of orthodoxy in Islam, where ideas and concepts about God are essentially private matters. In fact the Qu'ran is highly suspicious of theological speculation, which it sees as mere human projection and wish-fulfilment. Such doctrinal thinking, applied to the transcendent reality of al-Llah, can only be 'guesswork' (*zanna*): this habit of idle conjecture about ineffable matters had divided the People of the Book into warring sects.[21] Instead of promoting orthodoxy or right teaching, Islam and Judaism both insist upon orthopraxy, a common customal observance. In the Qu'ran, therefore, a 'believer' is not one who has made an assent to a list of propositions, like the various Creeds or the Thirty-Nine Articles. He had acquired an immediate, heart-shaking apprehension of the divine reality to which he had surrendered, expressing his *islām* in the twin practices of prayer (*salat*) and almsgiving:

> Those only are believers who, when God
> is mentioned, their hearts quake, and
> when his signs are recited to them, it
> increases them in faith, and in the Lord
> they put their trust,
> those who perform the prayer, and expend
> of what we have provided them,
> those in truth are the believers.[22]

By contrast the 'unbeliever' (*kafir bi na'mat al-Llah*) is not a person who refuses to believe in the existence of al-Llah or who has adopted the wrong theology, but 'one who is ungrateful to God'. The Qu'ran makes it clear in its use of the root *KFR* that this attitude was one of deliberate perversity: the *kafirs* of Mecca knew in their hearts what the 'signs' meant but arrogantly opposed God rather than reorder their lives.[23]

Although in the early years Muhammad went out of his way to appeal to basic Qurayshi enthusiasms like the Ka'aba, he knew instinctively that his message would arouse a deep antagonism. He was very cautious indeed about the people he approached. For the first three years of his mission, he exercised a strictly private ministry and the word spread on the grapevine. But he did manage to build up a small group of fervent believers, who instantly recognised the importance of what he was saying. The little group met for ritual prayer each morning and evening and it seems that the *salat* inspired a deep revulsion among the Quraysh: it seemed appalling that Arabs, with centuries of fierce Bedouin independence behind them, should be ready to grovel on the ground like slaves. This instant reaction showed that Muhammad had put his finger unerringly on a sensitive spot: the deep obeisance challenged the new Qurayshi pride and haughty self-sufficiency so strongly that it became impossible for the Muslims to perform the *salat* in public and they had to retire into the glens surrounding the city. They also seemed to have practised a form of almsgiving, which was seen as a moral purification, and rose during the night to make vigils, during which they recited the Qu'ran.

This practice probably derived from the night vigils made by the Christian monks of the Syrian desert, who used to rise in the small hours to recite the psalms. This had affected the Arab idea of what a scripture was meant to be: it was not a book for private perusal but a text to be chanted aloud in liturgical worship. Though Muslims obviously do study it privately today, they still claim that its full impact is experienced only when it is recited aloud to a special chant. The sound has its own mysterious meaning and makes the language of the Qu'ran aspire to the condition of music, which gives a more powerful and complete experience of the transcendent than any other art. It was the Qu'ran which prevented al-Llah from being entirely a remote God 'out there'. The early biographers constantly describe somebody's conversion by saying that Islam 'entered his heart'. I shall examine the role of the Qu'ran and the experience of the first Muslims who were converted by it in more detail in the following chapter. But it seems that the extraordinary beauty of the recited Arabic touched something deeply buried and resonated with the unconscious longings and aspirations of those who heard it. We have all had a similar experience when a poem or a piece of music seems to lift us for a while beyond ourselves and gives us intimations of a larger reality. The uttering of this Word was no easy experience for Muhammad. Revelations continued to come down while he was in the midst of ordinary activities. He used to swoon and perspire heavily, even on a cold day. Other authorities say that he felt a great heaviness, an emotion like grief and that while listening to the divine words, he would lower his head between his knees.

Who were the first Muslims? Khadija had accepted the truth of the revelations from the start and the rest of Muhammad's household followed her: Ali, Zayd and the Prophet's four daughters. But to Muhammad's intense disappointment his uncles Abu Talib, Abbas and Hamzah were not interested. Abu Talib told him that he could not find it in himself to abandon the religion of his fathers, expressing a reservation that many of the other Quraysh would feel. Muhammad was aware that, despite its roots in the old pagan tradition, his revelation from al-Llah would threaten the more conservative Quraysh, which was one reason why he kept a low profile for the first three years of his mission. But Abu Talib had great respect for Muhammad personally and, even when it became difficult to do so, he continued to act as his official protector. As chief of Hashim, Abu Talib's support was crucial for Muhammad: the old tribal ethos may have been breaking down but it was still impossible for an individual to survive unless he was protected by his clan.

But other members of Muhammad's family did accept him as their prophet, including Abu Talib's other son Ja'far, his special friend and cousin Abdallah ibn Jahsh and his sister Zaynab, and his brother Ubaydallah. Ubaydallah was one of the *hanifs* who had been looking for an alternative form of monotheism. The wives of both Abbas and Hamzah had no patience with their husbands' timidity, however: Umm Fadl and Salamah both became Muslims, as did Ja'far's wife Asma, and Muhammad's aunt Safiyah bint Abd al-Muttalib. Umm Ayman, Muhammad's freedwoman, also joined the sect: she had been the little slave girl that Abdallah, Muhammad's father, had left to Amina with the five camels. Muhammad once said of her: 'He that would marry a woman of the people of Paradise, let him marry Umm Ayman.'[24] When Zayd heard this he was greatly impressed and asked Muhammad for her hand, even though she was years older than he. Umm Ayman agreed and the couple bore Usamah, Muhammad's first grandchild and one of the first children to be born into Islam.

But in the very early days Muhammad made a crucial convert outside the family when his friend Attiq ibn Uthman, who is always known by his *kunya* Abu Bakr, entered Islam. In later years Muhammad is believed to have said: 'I have never invited anyone to accept Islam but he has shown signs of reluctance, suspicion, and hesitation, except Abu Bakr. When I told him of it he did not hold back or hesitate.'[25] Few of the other converts had much influence in Mecca but, as Ibn Ishaq says, Abu Bakr:

> was a man whose society was desired, well liked and of easy manners. He knew more about the genealogy of Quraysh than anyone else and of their faults and merits. He was a merchant of high character and kindliness. His people used to come to him and discuss many matters with him because of his wide knowledge,

his experience in commerce and his sociable nature. He began to call to God and to Islam all whom he trusted of those who came to him and sat with him.[26]

Abu Bakr brought many of the younger men of Mecca into the religion of al-Llah, including some from the more powerful clans. He was known for his skilful interpretation of dreams, and one day Khalid ibn Sa'id, son of an important financier in Abd Shams, came to him in great distress. He had dreamed that he was standing on the brink of a vast pit filled with fire and found to his horror that his father was trying to push him in. Then he became aware of two hands on his waist pulling him to safety. At the moment of waking he had turned to see that his saviour was none other than Muhammad. The dream, as it has come down to us, demonstrates the obscure but urgent sense of personal peril which many of the younger generation experienced. The hardship of the desert was a more distant reality to them and they seem to have been less enamoured of the new capitalism than their fathers, with whom there was unspoken but deep conflict. Muhammad was touching raw and buried emotions in those young people, who felt the malaise in Mecca most acutely. Khalid became a Muslim but kept his religion secret from his father for as long as he could.

Another conversion-dream illustrates the more positive aspect of the Qu'ranic impact. The young and aristocratic merchant Uthman ibn Affan, who was also a member of Abd Shams, was returning from a business trip to Syria when he heard in a dream a voice crying aloud in the wilderness: 'Sleepers awake! for verily Ahmad has come forth in Mecca!'[27] Uthman was impressed but bewildered by this voice, which appealed to something within him even though he had no notion what the words meant: the experience of *islām* frequently made Muslims feel that they had woken up after a long period of torpor. The following day, however, Uthman was joined on the road by another young merchant, Talhah ibn Ubaydallah of Taym, who was Abu Bakr's cousin. Talhah was also returning from Syria and he told Uthman that he had met a monk there who had told him about the Prophet Ahmad who would soon arise in the Hijaz, but added the astonishing news that 'Ahmad' was really Muhammad ibn Abdallah of Hashim. The young men hurried back to Mecca as fast as they could and went immediately to Abu Bakr.

The Meccan historian Ibn Shihan al-Zuhri, who was born about forty years after Muhammad's death and devoted his life to researching the early Muslim period, tells us that Muhammad soon became quite successful:

The Messenger of God (God bless and preserve him) summoned to Islam secretly and openly, and there responded to God whom He would of the young men [*ar-dath ar-rijal*] and weak people [*du'afar ar-nas*] so that those who believed in him were numerous, and the unbelieving Quraysh did not criticise what he said. When he passed by them, as they sat in groups, they would point to him, 'There is the youth of the clan of Abd al-Muttalib who speaks things from heaven.'[28]

Ibn Ishaq also confirms this early success,[29] but al-Zuhri makes it clear that the early converts came from two particular groups: the young and the 'weak'. There were some extremely disadvantaged people in the new sect, who would naturally have been attracted by its social teaching and who became important personages in Islam. These included Abdallah ibn Ma'sud, a shepherd who had a particular talent for memorising the new revelations as they came down and so became one of the most authoritative of the early Qu'ran reciters; Khabbab ibn al-Aratt, a smith and maker of swords; the two freedmen Suhayb ibn Sinan and Ammar ibn Yasir, who had been adopted as confederates by the powerful clan of Makhzum; and a group of slaves – men and women – the most famous of whom was the Abyssinian Bilal, who became the first muezzin to call the faithful to prayer.

But not all the 'weak' were down-and-outs. This was a technical tribal term which referred to the status of the various clans. By the time Muhammad began his mission, the clans of the Quraysh were divided into three main groups, which W. Montgomery Watt has listed as follows:

A	B	C
Hashim	Abd Shams	Makhzum
al-Muttalib	Nawfal	Sahm
Zuhrah	Asad	Jumah
Taym	Amir	Abd ad-Dar
al-Harith ibn Fihr		
Adi		

The clans in Group A had all belonged to the old Hilf al-Fudul and were the weaker clans in the city. The exceptions were Adi, whose position had declined recently, and Asad (Khadija's clan), which had grown stronger. It was from Group A that most of Muhammad's early converts came. Abu Bakr and Talhah, for example, were both members of Taym; the promising young merchant Abd al Ka'aba (whose name was changed to Abd al-Rahman) was a member of Zuhrah. The members of these 'weak' clans might well be personally successful – Abu Bakr, for example, was a wealthy man – but the reduced power of their clans gave them a marginal place in the city. Most of Muhammad's most dedicated enemies, as we shall see, came from the more powerful clans in Groups B and C: they were more than happy with the status quo. But some of Muhammad's converts from the important clans – like Khalid and Uthman – may have felt that there was no place for them at the top and have become aware of the gap that was opening up between the most successful and those of the second rank. Such hierarchies, inequities and divisions were alien to the Arab spirit and they welcomed Muhammad's message. At the beginning, therefore, Islam was a movement of young men and people who felt that they were being pushed into a marginal place in the city of Mecca.

This meant that there was bound to be a conflict and it soon became clear that Islam was beginning to split families right down the middle. Instead of healing the disunity of the Quraysh, it seemed to be making matters worse. This became dramatically clear as soon as Muhammad began to preach more openly and publicly. In 615, some three years after he had started his mission, he received a revelation commanding him to declare himself openly to his whole clan and invite them to enter Islam.[30] At first he felt that the task was beyond his strength, but he went ahead and invited the forty leading men of Hashim to a modest meal. The meagre repast was a message in itself: Muhammad had become very critical of the ostentatious hospitality that had become traditional among the Arabs as a display of power and confidence: he felt that it smacked of the old presumption.[31] Years later, Ali, who served at the meal, makes it sound like the miracle of the five loaves and fishes: even though there was really only enough for one person, everybody had more than he could eat.

At the end of the meal, Muhammad expounded the principles of his revelation, during which Abu Lahab, Abu Talib's half-brother, interrupted Muhammad rudely and eventually broke up the gathering. Muhammad had to invite them all back on the following day. Again, he explained Islam to them and at the end he begged them to join him:

> O sons of Abd al-Muttalib, I know of no Arab who has come to his people with a nobler message than mine. I have brought you the best of this world and the next. God has ordered me to call you to Him. So which of you will co-operate with me in this venture, my brother, my executor, and my successor being among you?

There was an awkward silence: not even Abu Talib or Muhammad's contemporaries Abbas or Hamzah said a word. Eventually Ali could bear it no longer and, gawky adolescent though he was, spoke out before them all:

> I, though the youngest, most rheumy-eyed, fattest in body and thinnest in legs, said: 'O prophet of God, I will be your helper in this matter.' He laid his hand on the back of my neck and said, 'This is my brother, my executor and my successor among you. Hearken to him and obey him.'

This was too much. The men got up to go, crying jovially to Abu Talib: 'He has ordered you to listen to your son and obey him!'[32]

Even though people were well disposed towards Muhammad in general, he was dividing families. Khadija's nephew Abu al-As ibn Rabi of the clan of Abd Shams had married Muhammad's eldest daughter Zaynab, but he had not converted to Islam and his clan were trying to persuade him to divorce her. But Abu al-As and Zaynab loved one another and Abu al-As told his clansmen firmly that he had no intention of repudiating her even though he could not follow her into the new faith. In Khadija's family, Islam was beginning to make other bitter divisions: her half-brother Nawfal ibn Khuwaylid seemed bitterly opposed to Islam, but his son Aswad became a Muslim; her nephew Hakim ibn Hizam retained his affection for Khadija but would not convert to Islam, though his brother Khalid did. Abu Bakr had similar problems. His wife Umm Ruman had followed him into the religion of al-Llah with his two children Abdallah and Asma, but their son Abd al-Ka'aba was vehemently opposed to it. Like Jesus, Muhammad seemed to be turning father against son, brother against brother, and undermining the essential bonds, duties and hierarchy of family life. Soon this problem would become even more acute.

What did people find objectionable in Muhammad's message in these first years? Nobody seems to have criticised his social teaching, even though the more successful clans did oppose his message: it was one thing to *be* selfish and money-grubbing, but another to defend selfishness and materialism. From the Qu'ran it appears that most of the early criticisms centred round the notion of the Last Judgement, which Muhammad had taken from the Jewish–Christian tradition. It was gradually assuming a more central place in the revelations and stressed the eternal fate of the individual, whose actions have crucial significance. The symbolism of the Judgement reinforced the notion of individual as opposed to merely communal responsibility, giving the Arabs a motive and incentive to acquire and foster the new spirit. The Qu'ran warns the Quraysh that on the Last Day their wealth and the power of their clan, on which many people relied, would be of no help to them. Instead every single one of them would be asked why he or she had not taken care of the orphans or attended to the wants of the poor. Why had they selfishly accumulated personal fortunes and not shared their wealth with the more vulnerable members of the tribe? This was obviously a threatening idea to the rich Quraysh, who had no intention of taking this egalitarian ideology too seriously, even though they may have been uncomfortably aware at a subconscious level that their behaviour violated the traditions of their forefathers. It was easier to scoff at the whole idea of the Judgement: these were simply 'fairy-tales of the ancients'[33] or a mere trick.[34] How could bodies that had rotted away in the earth come to life again? Was Muhammad seriously suggesting that their long-dead ancestors would also rise from the grave?[35] They clung to the old Arab belief that there was no afterlife, but the Qu'ran points out that they cannot prove this: it is mere human speculation (*zanna*).[36]

The Qu'ran also points out that these objections are inspired by guilt and by materialism, which has blunted people's perceptions. The people who deny the reality of the Judgement are those who know that their social behaviour is wrong.[37] It seems that many of the passages describing the 'signs' were intended to answer some of these objections: if God could create a human being out of a drop of semen – a marvel that the Qu'ran can never praise too often – and all the other wonders of the world, why could He not raise a dead body?

> Has not man regarded how that We created him
> of a sperm-drop?
> Then lo, he is a manifest adversary.
> And he has struck for Us a similitude
> and forgotten his creation;
> he says, 'Who shall quicken the bones
> when they are decayed?'
> Say: 'He shall quicken them, who originated them
> the first time; He knows all creation,
> who has made for you out of the green tree
> fire and lo, from it you kindle.'
> Is not He, who created the heavens and earth,
> able to create the like of them? Yes, indeed;
> He is the All-creator, the All-knowing.
> His command, when He desires a thing, is to say to it
> 'Be,' and it is.
> So glory be to Him, in whose hand is the dominion
> of everything
> and unto whom you shall be returned.[38]

The Last Judgement itself became a powerful image of the final Return, which all beings must eventually make to God, their creator, sustainer and source.

But despite these objections, Muhammad seems to have been quite successful in the early years of his mission. At one point it seemed as though he was about to win all the people of his tribe to the reformed religion of al-Llah. But in the year 616 there was a crisis. Up to this point, Muhammad had made no official mention of the other Arabian deities. Many of the Quraysh probably assumed that they could go on venerating al-Lat, al-Uzza and Manat in the traditional way. Muhammad does not appear to have stressed the monotheistic element of his revelation. But eventually he was forced to speak out. When he forbade his converts to worship the *banat al-Llah*, he discovered that he lost most of his supporters overnight and that the Qu'ran was about to split the tribe of Quraysh.

6 · The Satanic Verses

The first sign of trouble erupted out of the blue. Some of the Quraysh followed a group of Muslims to the glens of Mecca and attacked them during the *salat* they were performing there. The Muslims fought back, shedding the first blood for Islam when Muhammad's cousin, Sa'd ibn Abu Waqqas, wounded one of his assailants with the jawbone of a camel. The incident probably shocked everybody in Mecca. The Quraysh were generally a tolerant people, but as soon as Muhammad forbade the cult of the old deities of Arabia a gulf of suspicion and hatred suddenly opened between the Qurayshi majority and the Muslim community. As Ibn Ishaq says:

When the apostle openly displayed Islam as God ordered him, his people did not withdraw or turn against him, so far as I have heard, until he spoke disparagingly of their gods. When he did that they took great offence and resolved unanimously to treat him as an enemy, except those whom God had protected by Islam from such evil, but they were a despised minority.[1]

But why were the Quraysh so upset? Some had already moved towards the monotheistic vision by regarding Judaism and Christianity as superior to the old Arab paganism. The cult of the Daughters of God (*banat al-Llah*) was mainly confined to shrines at Taif, Nakhlah and Qudayd and must have been marginal to the religious life of Mecca. It is true that some of the Quraysh were wary of offending the Bedouin tribes, who had already driven guardian tribes of the Ka'aba out of Mecca for impiety, but the problem went deeper than this. The Qu'ran shows that all the leading men of the city instinctively banded together against Muhammad and declared him an enemy of the people. The idea that there was only *one* God was an extraordinary innovation, they exclaimed; the worship of the *banat al-Llah* was a sacred duty, binding upon all the people of Arabia.[2]

When Muhammad had invited Abu Talib to become a Muslim, Abu Talib had said that he could not abandon the faith of his fathers. Such instinctive devotion to the past is difficult for us to appreciate because our modern society has institutionalised change and we expect continual progress. We prize originality and would not be upset – as Muhammad was – if accused of innovation.[3] But in more traditional societies, continuity with the past is a sacred value. The kind of change that we take for granted demands a constant revision of the infrastructure that no society before our own could afford. Religion often has the character of a treaty obligation in certain pre-modern societies. Civilisation and culture have been seen as precarious achievements which must not be wantonly threatened by insulting the patronal gods. Innovation is usually confined to a small elite, therefore: the fate of Socrates, who was sentenced to death in Athens in 399 BCE, shows that it could be dangerous to unleash a questing spirit among the people. He was accused of blasphemy and the corruption of youth. Muhammad would have to face the same charges and would narrowly escape death.

When he demanded that the people of Mecca worship al-Llah alone and abandon the worship of other gods, Muhammad was asking them to adopt an entirely new religious attitude that many of his fellow-tribesmen were not ready to accept. We have seen that the monotheistic creed did not merely require an intellectual assent but a change of consciousness. The Prophet's demand inspired deep fear because it threatened sanctities on which the very survival of society was believed to depend. The early Christians had had a similar experience in the Roman empire, where 'progress' was not seen as a fearless march forward into the future but as a return to an idealised past. The pagan gods of Rome were regarded as the guardians of the state: if their cult were neglected, the gods would withdraw their protection. This does not mean that Roman paganism was an inherently intolerant faith: as long as new gods did not claim to replace the ancestral deities of the Romans, their worshippers were allowed full religious liberty. There was always room for a new cult and people often belonged to a number of different sects. A radical conversion to one religion and a rejection of all the rest was unheard of. True, the Jews worshipped only one God and condemned idolatry but everybody knew that Judaism was an ancient and therefore an esteemed religion. As long as Christians were thought to be members of the synagogue they enjoyed the same toleration as the Jews, but when they made it clear that they did not observe the old Jewish Law, they were accused of impiety – disrespect for the parent faith – and atheism, because they refused to worship the gods of Rome. In refusing to give these pagan deities their due, the Christians had violated a taboo: people believed that they would cause a catastrophe, and to ward it off successive Emperors ordered that they be persecuted. The horrible sufferings of the martyrs showed how deeply they threatened the Roman spirit; their mangled bodies were a sacrifice to the gods to prove that the people as a whole did not approve of this 'atheism'.

If this had been the case in the powerful Roman empire, it is easy to see that the Quraysh would feel deeply disturbed by the 'atheism' of

Muhammad, once he had refused to give the ancient goddesses their due. Nomadic life had been conservative precisely because it was precarious. Nobody, for example, would have dreamed of striking out traditional ways to find a new route to the ancestral wells. The Quraysh were only two generations from the steppes and must have felt that their mercantile achievement was fragile, despite their vaunted cult of self-sufficiency. Like the Romans, they valued their continuity with the past and believed that their success depended on a pious regard for the traditions of their fathers. In the Qu'ran and the early sources, therefore, Muhammad is constantly accused by his enemies of being a danger to society, of neglecting the religion of the fathers and of atheism; it was much the same complex of emotion that had filled the crowds in the Roman stadiums with rage and dread.

Some of the early Christian apologists had tried to reach out to the pagans to show that their religion was not a blasphemous innovation: Justin, the celebrated theologian of Palestine, wrote two *apologiae* (*c.* 150 and 155) to prove that the Christians were following in the footsteps of Plato and other revered philosophers who had believed in only one God. The Qu'ran also refers to a moment when, it seems, Muhammad had tried to reach out to the Quraysh to still their fears and in the hope of re-establishing friendly relations. God reminds Muhammad:

> Indeed, they were near to seducing thee
> from that We revealed to thee, that thou
> mightest forge against Us another, and
> then they would surely have taken thee
> as a friend.
> And had we not confirmed thee, surely
> thou wert near to inclining unto them
> a very little.[4]

In the West, some scholars have assumed that this refers to the now notorious incident of the so-called 'Satanic Verses' when, they say, Muhammad had made a temporary concession to polytheism.

The story, as it appears in the histories of Ibn Sa'd and Tabari, says that on one occasion Satan interfered with Muhammad's reception of the divine Word. While Sura 53 was being revealed, this tradition has it, Muhammad felt inspired to utter two verses which declared that the three goddesses al-Lat, al-Uzza and Manat could be revered as intermediaries between God and man. But since the Quraysh considered the *banat al-Llah* divine beings, they wrongly believed that the Qu'ran had placed them on the same level as God Himself. Thinking that Muhammad had accepted their goddesses as having equal status to al-Llah, the pagan Qu'raysh bowed down to make the *salat* with the Muslims and the bitter dispute seemed at an end. Because the Qu'ran appeared to have endorsed the piety of their fathers and to have abandoned its monotheistic message, they no longer saw Islam as a sacrilegious threat that could bring a catastrophe on the people of Mecca. The story goes on, however, that Muhammad later received another revelation which indicated that his apparent acceptance of the cult of the *banat al-Llah* had been inspired by 'Satan'. Consequently, the two verses were expunged from the Qu'ran and replaced by others which declared that the three goddesses were figments of the Arabs' imagination and deserved no worship at all.

We have to be clear here that many Muslims believe this story to be apocryphal. They point out that there is no clear reference to it in the Qu'ran, that it is not mentioned by Ibn Ishaq in the earliest and most reliable account of Muhammad's life, nor in the great collections of traditions (*ahadith*) about Muhammad which were compiled in the ninth century by Bukhari and Muslim. Muslims do not reject traditions simply because they could be interpreted critically, but because they are insufficiently attested. Western enemies of 'Islam', however, have seized upon it to illustrate Muhammad's manifest insincerity: how could a man who changed the divine Word to suit himself be a true prophet? Surely any genuine prophet would be able to distinguish between a divine and a satanic inspiration? Would a man of God tamper with his revelation merely to attract more converts? Recently, however, scholars like Maxime Rodinson and W. Montgomery Watt have attempted to show that even as the story stands it does not necessarily bear such a negative interpretation. Nevertheless, the incident remained far more important in the Western than in the Islamic world; at least until 1988.

Since the conflict occasioned by Salman Rushdie's novel *The Satanic Verses*, which was published that year, the story has acquired a new significance. Muslims have protested that the novel presents a parody of Muhammad's life: it repeats all the old Western myths about the Prophet and makes him out to be an impostor, with purely political ambitions, a lecher who used his revelations as a licence to take as many women as he wanted, and indicates that his first companions were worthless, inhumane people. Most painfully, Muslims claim, the book denigrates the integrity of the Qu'ran. They feel that the incident of the Satanic Verses, from which the novel takes its title, is used to show that the sacred book of the Muslims is unable to distinguish good from evil and that, as Western critics have always maintained, it claims that purely human or even wicked inspirations are the will of God.

Many of Rushdie's most eloquent supporters declared that 'Islam' was a religion which vetoed scholarship and artistic freedom, even though the early Muslims founded a major civilisation of great beauty and established a rationalistic philosophic tradition which was an inspiration to scholars in the medieval West. Rushdie's fantastic portraits of the Prophet and his early companions were not, of course, presented as fact but as the dream visions of one of the characters who is suffering a psychotic breakdown. Gibreel Farishta, an Indian film star who has become deracinated and lost his cultural roots, has interiorised and made his own the imagery of hatred and contempt that for nearly a thousand years has been fostered by the West, with which he has tried to compromise.

Because this recent conflict between the West and the Muslim world has reopened old wounds, it is important to be clear what the incident of the Satanic Verses really involved; if, that is, it actually happened. Was Muhammad ready to compromise his monotheistic message to attract more converts? Was the Qu'ran even momentarily tainted by the influence of absolute evil? In context, we can see that, as Rodinson and Watt have both argued, the story does not present Muhammad as a cynical impostor. When we turn to Tabari, who gives two different versions of the story in his history and in his commentary on the Qu'ran, we see him considering the circumstances of Muhammad's final rupture with the Quraysh. Like Ibn Ishaq, he says that at first the Quraysh had been ready to accept Muhammad's message. He quotes an early tradition of one Urwah ibn al-Zubayr, a distant relative of Muhammad who wrote about seventy years after his death, which emphasises Muhammad's initial success. At first, Urwah says, the Quraysh did not withdraw from Muhammad 'but almost hearkened to him'. As long as he preached the cult of al-Llah, with its concern for the poor and needy, everybody in Mecca had been ready to accommodate this reformed cult of the old High God. But once he affirmed that the worship of al-Llah must preclude the worship of all the other ancestral gods, Urwah says, the Quraysh 'rebutted him with vehemence, not approving what he said, and aroused against him those who had followed him, except those whom God kept safe and they were few in number'. Overnight, Islam became a despised minority sect. Urwah adds one interesting detail: he tells us that the first Quraysh to agitate against Muhammad were those who had property in Taif, the city of al-Lat.[5]

Many of the Quraysh liked to escape to Taif from the broiling heat of Mecca and they had summer houses in the city of al-Lat which was in a cooler and more fertile part of the Hijaz. The shrine of the goddess would have been important to them, because they would perform her rites there during their absence from the Ka'aba. When Muhammad forbade his tribe to worship al-Lat, they would have been distressed and fearful that he had jeopardised their own position in Taif. Tabari quotes the tradition of one Abu al-Aliyah to suggest that the Quraysh were disturbed enough to attempt to make a deal with Muhammad: if he promised to make some conciliatory remarks about the three *banat al-Llah*, this tradition has it, the Quraysh would admit him to the inner circles of Meccan power. Accordingly, it is said that Muhammad recited the two verses praising al-Lat, al-Uzza and Manat as valid intercessors, only to realise later that the words had been inspired by 'Satan'.[6] But this story is in conflict with other traditions and with the Qu'ran itself. We must remember that a Muslim historian like Tabari does not necessarily endorse all the traditions he records: he expects the reader to compare them with others and to make up his or her own mind about their validity. At this very early stage of his prophetic career, Muhammad was not interested in political power. So this story, as told by Abu al-Aliyah, is not very likely. The Qu'ran, as we have seen, denies that Muhammad should have a political function in Mecca at this point, and later the Prophet would turn down similar deals with leading Quraysh without a second's thought.

In his history Tabari also preserves a tradition which gives a very different version of the story. Here Muhammad is shown searching his soul to find a solution to the distressing conflict with the Quraysh. He was not simply slipping in a flattering reference to the *banat al-Llàh* in order to gain material advantage, as the other version of the story suggests. Tabari shows that Muhammad was listening for a genuinely creative solution that would reconcile the Quraysh to his monotheistic message:

> When the apostle saw that his people had turned their backs on him and he was pained by their estrangement from what he brought them from God, he longed that there should come to him from God a message that would reconcile his people to him. Because of his love for his people and his anxiety over them it would delight him if the obstacle that made his task so difficult could be removed; so he meditated on the project and longed for it and it was dear to him.[7]

One day, Tabari says, while he was meditating in the Ka'aba, the answer seemed to come in a revelation that gave a place to the three 'goddesses' without compromising his monotheistic vision. Many of the Quraysh were sitting at the Ka'aba when Sura 53 was revealed. They would all have sat up and listened intently when Muhammad began to recite these words:

> Have you considered al-Lat and al-Uzza
> and Manat, the third, the other?[8]

Anything that Muhammad had to say about the *banat al-Llah* could have far-reaching consequences. Was he about to show that the Qu'ran utterly rejected their cult or would he utter a more positive message about them? It was at this point, Tabari says, that 'Satan' put something like these two verses on his lips:

these are the exalted birds [*gharaniq*]
whose intercession is approved.

According to this version of the story, the Quraysh were delighted with the new revelation. The *gharaniq* were probably Numidian cranes which were thought to fly higher than any other bird. Muhammad, who may have believed in the existence of the *banat al-Llah* as he believed in the existence of angels and *jinn*, was giving the 'goddesses' a delicate compliment, without compromising his message. The *gharaniq* were not on the same level as al-Llah – not that anybody had suggested that they were – but, hovering as it were between heaven and earth, they could be valid intermediaries between God and man, like the angels, whose intercession is approved in the very next section of Sura 53.[9] The Quraysh spread the good news throughout the city: 'Muhammad has spoken of our gods in splendid fashion. He alleged in what he recited that they are the exalted *gharaniq* whose intercession is approved.'[10]

People who have been brought up in the Christian world are likely to misunderstand the word 'Satan' as it is referred to in this incident. In the Christian world, Satan became a figure of monstrous evil, but in the Qu'ran – as in the Jewish scriptures – he is a much more manageable character. In its account of his fall from grace, the Qu'ran says that when God had created mankind he commanded all the angels to bow before Adam but the Shaitan (or Iblis, as he is often called, in an Arabisation of the Greek *diabolos*), refused and was cast out from the divine presence. The Qu'ran does not see this as the primal, absolute sin but indicates instead that Satan will be forgiven on the Last Day.[11] Some Sufis even came to claim that Satan had loved God more than the other angels, because he had refused to honour a mere creature with an obeisance that was due to God alone. The controversial incident of the 'Satanic Verses', therefore, does not imply that the Qu'ran was even momentarily tainted by actual evil. Islam does not subscribe to the doctrine of the Fall in the Christian sense. It tells us that Adam did succumb to Satan's temptation but this exercise of free will was seen by Muslims, as by most Jews, as a necessary stage of human development. Despite his sin, Adam became the first of the great prophets, even though he was guilty of a 'satanic' slip and the Shaitan never became the destroyer of mankind. We should bear this linguistic distinction in mind when we hear some Muslims today refer to America as 'the Great Satan'. In popular Shiism, the Shaitan is considered a poor, trivial creature who was satisfied with idle trumpery instead of true gifts of the spirit. At the time of the Shah, many Iranians saw America as 'The Great Trivialiser', trying to tempt their people astray with decadent materialism.[12]

Later we shall see the Quraysh asking Muhammad to make a monolatrous compromise: he could worship al-Llah alone and they would worship their ancestral deities as well as the High God. But Muhammad always refused. In the story as it has been preserved by Tabari, he substituted the so-called 'Satanic Verses' with an outright denial that these goddesses even existed. The tradition says that one night Gabriel came to the Prophet and asked: 'What have you done, Muhammad? You have recited to those people something I did not bring you from God and you have said what He did not say to you.'[13] New verses were sent down which dismissed the *banat al-Llah* as 'mere names'. The goddesses were human fabrications and there was no revelation from God about them:

> They are naught but names yourselves
> have named, and your fathers; God has
> sent down no authority touching them.
> They follow only surmise (*zanna*) and what their
> whims desire.[14]

This is the most radical of all the Qu'ranic denigrations of the goddesses and after this verse had been included in the Qu'ran, there could be no further question of a compromise with the Quraysh.

Even as it stands in Tabari's history the story of the Satanic Verses does not suggest that Muhammad was making a cynical compromise. The tradition says that when Muhammad heard that the verses he had uttered had been inspired by the Shaitan, he was devastated. But, Tabari says, God had immediately comforted him by sending down a revelation which told him that all the previous prophets had made similar 'Satanic mistakes'. This was not a disaster, because God always improved matters by sending down replacement verses which were far superior to the ones that had to be discarded. Here the Qu'ran acknowledges the risks involved in the concept of 'revelation':

> We sent not ever any Messenger
> or Prophet before thee, but that Satan
> cast into his fancy, when he was fancying:
> but God annuls what Satan casts, then
> God confirms his signs.[15]

Adam, the first prophet, had, as we have seen, yielded to a suggestion of Satan and later messengers had also included Satanic Verses when they had delivered the word of God to their people. This did not mean that their scriptures had been contaminated by evil influences. The Arabs frequently used the word *shaitan* to allude to a purely human tempter. We have seen how difficult it could be for Muhammad to interpret the revelations correctly: it was all too easy to mistake the deeper under-current of the inspiration with an idea of one's own or to express it in the wrong words. But this, of course, did not give Muhammad leave to tinker with the Qu'ran to suit himself. The Qu'ran makes it clear that no mere mortal can change the divine words and that if Muhammad ever took such an initiative the consequences would be fatal.[16] During the time it was being revealed to a particular prophet, God could amend the scriptures. In a human sense, we can say that Muhammad felt continually inspired while he was bringing the Qu'ran to the Arabs. This was a progressive revelation and Muhammad sometimes saw new implications in his message that qualified certain previous insights.

At this point a new emphasis developed in Muhammad's message, stressing the Divine Unity as the most important part of the revelation. From this point he became a jealous monotheist.

We have recently begun to appreciate the beauty of traditional paganism with its many deities and the truthful and courageous way it faces up to tragedy and suffering, refusing the luxury of a final solution. By contrast, monotheism can seem monolithic and to have caused all kinds of philosophical problems. Where the pagan pantheon had demonstrated that there were a variety of ways to the ultimate, the monotheistic insistence that there is only *one* God seems intolerant and to make no allowances for human difference. But it seems that polytheism belongs to a stage in the evolution of the human race when consciousness has not been fully unified and when the world and the cosmos seem to contain a number of different elements which are not always in perfect harmony. When men and women begin to see that they themselves are each an indissoluble unity and when the universe seems to have become a single entity, governed by a common force, people start to turn to the monotheistic solution. The old gods become merely aspects of the ultimate being or reality or – in traditional theistic terms – mere attributes of God.

We can see this in the period of late antiquity in the Roman empire. The experience of living within a giant political entity had helped people to see the known world as a single whole: local gods and cults tied to a particular area now seemed inadequate. More and more people had begun to see that God was somehow One, as the great Greek philosophers had taught. But, as we have seen, it was a painful transition. Some people were inevitably more ready for the radical change to a monotheistic religion than others, and paganism flourished for a long time after Christianity became the official state religion of the Roman empire in the early fourth century. The particular solution of monotheism meant that people had to put the sacred past firmly to one side, and some found the break in continuity profoundly disturbing. In Arabia in the early seventh century, there was a similar crisis. The political scene had affected the spiritual and personal psychology of the Arabs. They were surrounded by great empires and were aware of a unified world outside Arabia Deserta. They were beginning to see themselves as individuals, with inalienable rights and responsibilities. That meant that consciousness was beginning to be experienced as a unity perspicacious to itself. The old tribal system – which had meant that each tribe went its own way – was beginning to appear disastrously inadequate to the conditions of modernity. The story of the *hanifs* demonstrates a readiness on the part of some of the Arabs for monotheism, but others were not yet ready to make the radical break with the past and lose that continuity which had been central to their old spirituality.

If it is true that Muhammad's sense of his own vocation was just starting to expand, he must have been even more aware of the need for the Arabs to find a common focus. Monotheism is essentially inimical to tribalism: it demands that a people unite in a single community. Ultimately Muhammad would see Arab unity as an important ideal but in 616, when there was a serious rupture with the Quraysh, he was more aware of the religious need to find a single transcendent reality behind the multifarious signs of nature. The verses that had replaced the Satanic Verses had indicated that the old deities were mere human projections, not on the same level as the sublime and transcendent al-Llah who surpassed the limited conceptions of men. But most of the Qu'ranic polemic against al-Llah's 'partners' or associates stresses the ineffectiveness of the pagan gods in rather the same way as some of the Jewish scriptures. It is no use making them the centre of your world because they can do nothing for you. They cannot provide their devotees with food and sustenance,[17] and they are even hopeless intercessors: at the Last Judgement they will be unable to help the men and women who had put their trust in them.[18] The gods were mere creatures, like men, women, angels and *jinn*, who could give no radical help. Here the Qu'ran sounds very like some of the Hebrew psalms, which Muhammad would not have read but which employed the same arguments:

> Those on whom you call
> apart from God, are
> servants the likes of you;
> call them and let them answer you, if you speak truly.
> What, have they feet
> wherewith they walk,
> or have they hands wherewith they lay hold,
> or have they eyes
> wherewith they see,
> or have they ears wherewith they give ear?
> Say: 'Call you then

to your associates [*shuruka*];
then try your guile on me, and give me no respite.
My protector is al-Llah
who sent down the Book,
and He takes into His protection the righteous.
And those on whom you
call, apart from God,
have no power to help you, neither they help themselves.'[19]

The Qu'ran conceives this transcendent God in essentially Arab terms: he is described in the terms of tribalism as an effective chief, who can give protection (*awliya*) and help (*nasr*), while the old goddesses were like dangerously weak chiefs, who could not take adequate care of their tribesmen.

The divine unity would become the basis of Muslim spirituality, which becomes an attempt to realise this unity in one's own life and in society. It was a constant effort to achieve a personal integration, which would give intimations of the one God in this experience of finding a single centre and goal in the truly integrated self. The first part of the *shahada*, the Muslim profession of faith, sums up the personal intent of each Muslim: 'I bear witness that there is no god but al-Llah.' Ultimately this would forbid Muslims not only to venerate – in however limited a form – other deities like al-Lat, al-Uzza and Manat, but to allow other apparent goods to distract them from their commitment to al-Llah. Human ideologies, aspirations or enthusiasms might promise a sort of salvation but ultimately they would be bound to disappoint. This obviously applied to money, success or material luxury, but it also applied to other secular enthusiasms that seem attractive but cannot assuage that basic human restlessness and dissatisfaction that impels so many human beings to the consolations of art and religion. In our own day, when some Muslims have turned with enthusiasm to foreign ideologies like nationalism or socialism, reformers warn them that these will not bring the satisfactions they promise. They are not wicked but inadequate, and can give no final 'protection', 'help' or satisfaction either on an individual or on a social or political level. The sin of *shirk* (associating mere creatures with al-Llah, the supreme good) thus warns Muslims not to make merely human ideals – however good in themselves – of supreme importance so that they become an idolatry.

Just after the final break with the Quraysh, Sura 112 – the Sura of Sincerity – was revealed. It is used frequently by Muslims in the daily prayers at the mosque and reminds them of the divine unity which they must try to experience in their own lives by integrating their personalities, gathering together their scattered forces and finding their deepest priority:

Say: 'He is God, One
God, the Everlasting Refuge,
who has not begotten, and has not been begotten,
and equal to Him is not anyone.

But not many of the Quraysh were ready to make this radical break with the past and let the old sanctities go. Many of Muhammad's converts seem to have defected and some of the most powerful Quraysh began a campaign to get rid of him. They regarded him as an apostate, an 'atheist' who was an enemy of the most sacred, inviolable values of their society. A delegation approached Abu Talib, the chief of Muhammad's clan, and asked him to withdraw his protection (*awliya*) from Muhammad. Without a protector, nobody could survive in Arabia: the tribal system may have declined but the tribe or the clan was the basic unit of society, and life outside such a group was literally impossible. An unprotected man could be killed with impunity. But the delegation reminded Abu Talib of his duty to the whole tribe of the Quraysh: 'O Abu Talib, your nephew has cursed our gods, insulted our religion, mocked our way of life and accused our forefathers of error; either you must stop him or you must let us get at him . . . and we will rid you of him.'[20] The situation was extremely delicate. Abu Talib loved Muhammad, but he certainly did not want to incur the enmity of all the other clans. He was not a Muslim and he was also uneasy about Muhammad's condemnation of the old religion, but if he simply handed his nephew over to be killed he would have failed as a chief because he had not provided adequate protection. This would be a great blow to the prestige of Hashim, which had already fallen upon hard times. For the time being, Abu Talib refused to commit himself. He made an evasive answer to the chiefs and Muhammad went on preaching under his protection.

But after a while the Quraysh returned to Abu Talib with a threat. 'By God, we cannot endure that our fathers should be reviled, our customs mocked and our gods insulted,' they cried. 'Until you rid us of him we will fight the pair of you until one side perishes.' The Quraysh felt that they were fighting for their whole way of life, which was being daily undermined. They had already realised that there was no possibility of compromise and that only one side could win. Abu Talib was dismayed. He called Muhammad to him. 'Spare me and yourself,' he begged. 'Do not put on me a burden greater than I can bear.' Thinking that Abu Talib was going to give him up, Muhammad replied, with tears in his eyes, that he was ready to die: 'O my uncle, by God if they put the sun in my right hand and the moon in my left on condition that I abandon this course, until God has made it victorious, or I perish therein, I would not abandon it.' He then broke down, and left the room weeping bitterly. But at once Abu Talib called him back: 'Go and say what you please, for by God I will never give you up on any account.'[21] For the time being Muhammad was safe. As long as Abu Talib was his protector and could make this protection effective nobody in Mecca would be able to touch him.

Abu Talib was one of the most gifted poets in Mecca and he now wrote passionate verses denouncing all the clans which had traditionally been allies of Hashim but were now joining forces against them because of Muhammad. The clan of al-Muttalib responded by declaring their solidarity with Hashim, with whom they were closely related, but this good news was followed by a sad defection. Abu Lahab had been hostile to Muhammad from the start, but to try to mend relations with his nephew he had betrothed two of his sons to Muhammad's two daughters Ruqayyah and Umm Kulthum. But after Muhammad had finally refused to acknowledge the *banat al-Llah* he decided to ally himself more closely with Abd Shams, the clan of his wife, and he forced his sons to repudiate the two women. The young, elegant Muslim convert Uthman ibn Affan, however, had long admired Ruqayyah, who was the most beautiful of Muhammad's daughters, and was now able to ask for her hand.

Abu Lahab would now work as closely as he could with Muhammad's main enemies. The chief of these was Abu al-Hakam, the nephew of Walid, the old chief of Makhzum. He became the leader of the opposition to Muhammad, and Muslims renamed him 'Abu Jahl': the Father of Ignorance. He was personally ambitious and may have been jealous of Muhammad's political ability but he also seems to have been profoundly disturbed by Muhammad's religious message. Other important chiefs joined him, including Abu Sufyan, the chief of Abd Shams, who was an extremely intelligent man and had once been a personal friend of Muhammad. His father-in-law Utba ibn Rab'ia and his brother Shayba were also both in the forefront of opposition, as was Ummayah ibn Khalaf, the corpulent, elderly chief of Jumah. They would ultimately be joined by Suhayl ibn Amr, chief of Amir – a devout pagan who had been accustomed, like Muhammad, to make spiritual retreats. But as yet Suhayl was undecided: he may have recognised certain religious themes in Muhammad's message. They were also supported by some of the younger generation: Amr ibn al-As, an energetic and able warrior and diplomat, Khalid ibn al-Walid, and Safwan ibn Ummayah. But the most zealous of all these younger enemies of Muhammad was Umar ibn al-Khattab, who was about twenty-six years old at the time of Muhammad's break with the Quraysh. Umar was the son of the ardent pagan Khattab, who had driven his own half-brother Zayd the *hanif* out of the city when he had denigrated the old religion. Umar was a chip off the old block and while the others urged caution, with typical Qurayshi cunning, Umar was ready for violent action.

All these men had lost relatives who had gone over to the Muslim camp. The Qu'ran was continuing to divide families bitterly. Suhayl ibn Amr, for example, had lost his eldest son Abdallah, two of his daughters and their husbands, three of his brothers and his cousin and sister-in-law Sawdah. It seemed almost as though Muhammad was forming a new kind of clan composed in the main of young dissidents who had thrown aside their old family loyalties. His opponents probably saw the political implications of Muhammad's message before he did himself. The Qu'ran had continued to insist that Muhammad had no political function in Mecca, but how long would a man who claimed to be receiving messages from al-Llah be content to accept the leadership of more ordinary mortals like themselves? Some of his more extreme enemies also seemed to believe that there was no hope of a compromise. Only one side could win in this crucial battle, and men like Abu Jahl and young Umar, who happened to be his nephew, could see no possibility of a peaceful solution.

But as yet there was little they could do. As long as Muhammad had the support of Abu Talib nobody could kill him without bringing the whole clan of Hashim and al-Muttalib out in a vendetta which would injure his own family. At first, therefore, the opposition tried sanctions and ridicule. They could attack the slaves and the weaker Muslims with impunity, but were forced to use subtler methods with those like Muhammad who had adequate protection. Ibn Ishaq tells us Abu Jahl's general policy:

> When he heard that a man had become a Muslim, if he was a man of social importance and had relatives to defend him, he reprimanded him and poured scorn on him, saying, 'You have forsaken the religion of your father, who was a better man than you. We will declare you a blockhead and brand you as a fool, and destroy your reputation.' If he was a merchant, he said, 'We will boycott your goods and reduce you to beggary.' If he was a person of no social importance, he beat him and incited the people against him.[22]

The people who suffered most were the slaves, who had no clan protection. Ummayah, chief of Jumah, used to take his Abyssinian Muslim slave Bilal outside in the hottest part of the day, tie him up and leave him exposed to the sun with a great stone on his chest. Bilal remained undaunted, proclaiming the divine unity and shouting 'One! One!', his extraordinarily powerful voice echoing through the district. Abu Bakr, who lived near by, could not bear to watch Bilal's suffering and bought him from Ummayah, granting his freedom. He is said to have freed about seven other slaves in this way. But some of the well-born Muslims suffered at the hands of their own families: Khalid ibn Sa'id, the young man who had been converted by the dream of the fiery pit, was locked up by his father and deprived of food and water. The clan of Makhzum treated the family of the freedman Ammar ibn Yasir so badly that his mother eventually died.

Muhammad decided to find a safe home for the Muslims who were exposed to the worst suffering and asked the Negus of Christian Abyssinia to take them in. Even though the Quraysh had been the enemies of Mecca since the Year of the Elephant, the Negus agreed and in 616 about eighty-three Muslims left Mecca with their families. They were led by Uthman ibn Ma'zum, who had been a monotheist and an ascetic before his conversion. Some of Muhammad's own family went too, including Ja'far, Abu Talib's son, and Muhammad's daughter Ruqayyah with her husband Uthman ibn Affan. Modern Western scholars have suggested that there may have been other reasons for this exodus than the attempt to seek asylum. Muhammad may have been trying to establish an independent trade route to the south for those Muslims who were suffering from Abu Jahl's trade sanctions. It has also been suggested that the list of emigrants shows that there might have been some disagreement in the Muslim community. Some of the emigrants like Uthman ibn Ma'zum and Ubaydallah ibn Jahsh had made their own way to monotheism and may have been jealous of the influence that a relative newcomer like Abu Bakr had with Muhammad. But if these disagreements were a motive for some they cannot have been serious: Ubaydallah converted to Christianity while he was in Abyssinia, but Uthman returned to Mecca as soon as it was safe to do so and continued to be loyal to Muhammad and Abu Bakr.

The Quraysh sent two delegates to the Negus shortly after the Muslims had arrived there to ask him to send them back home: this mass departure was threatening in all sorts of ways. The delegates told the Negus that the Muslims had blasphemed against the faith of the people of Mecca and had disrupted society. They were therefore extremely dangerous and should not be trusted. The Negus summoned the Muslim emigrants and asked them what they had to say for themselves. Ja'far explained that Muhammad was a prophet of the true God, who confirmed His revelation to Jesus. To prove his point, he began to recite the Qu'ranic account of the virginal conception of Christ in the womb of Mary:

> And mention in the Book Mary
> when she withdrew from her people
>   to an eastern place,
> and she took a veil apart from them;
> then we sent unto her Our Spirit
> that presented himself to her
>   as a man without fault.

She said, 'I take refuge in
the All-merciful from thee!
If thou fearest God.'
He said, 'I am but a messenger
come from thy Lord, to give thee
a boy most pure.'
She said, 'How shall I have a son
whom no mortal has touched, neither
have I been unchaste?'
He said: 'Even so my Lord has said;
"Easy is that for Me; and that We
may appoint him a sign [*aya*] unto men
and a mercy from Us, it is
a thing decreed."'[23]

When Ja'far had finished, the beauty of the Qu'ran had done its work. The Negus was weeping so hard that his beard was wet, and the tears poured down the cheeks of his bishops and advisers so copiously that their scrolls were soaked.

The delegates tried to make trouble by pointing out to the Negus that the Qu'ran did not accept the divinity of Christ, but he still refused to deport the Muslims and send them back to Mecca. The Christians of Abyssinia were upset by the Negus' support of people who were obviously heretical and he had to resort to some shady dealings to justify this. But the Muslims were able to practise their religion freely as long as they chose to remain in Abyssinia. As it has come down to us, however, the story of the Abyssinian enterprise is incomplete: Muhammad may have had an economic or political plan that did not work out so that, by the time historians like Ibn Ishaq started to write, these plans had been forgotten. The delegation from Mecca may have shown the Negus that the Muslims were not as powerful a group as he had imagined when he had taken them in, and henceforth he may not have given them the support they had hoped for.

Meanwhile, back in Mecca, Abu Jahl and his colleagues continued to harass the Prophet and his Companions. They found new objections: why had al-Llah decided to choose Muhammad and not a more important man like al-Walid? Why did Muhammad not work miracles? Why was al-Llah sending down the Qu'ran bit by bit instead of in one impressive revelation such as Moses received on Mount Sinai? Why had God not sent an angel as his messenger instead of using an ordinary human being? Some of the Quraysh thought that Muhammad was being coached by a Jew or a Christian instead of receiving revelations from al-Llah Himself. But the Quraysh could do little more than complain. The persecution was mainly confined to trade sanctions and verbal abuse once the most vulnerable Muslims had gone to Abyssinia. Muhammad himself came in for a certain amount of harsh treatment. Thus Amr ibn al-As, who had been one of the two delegates sent by the Quraysh to the Negus and who, as we shall see, did not become a Muslim until much later, recalled an occasion when Muhammad was insulted at the Ka'aba. While he was making the circumambulations, the leaders of the Quraysh were sitting nearby complaining about him: 'They said that they had never known anything like the trouble they had endured from this fellow; he had declared their mode of life foolish, insulted their forefathers, reviled their religion, divided the community, and cursed their gods. What they had borne was past all bearing, or words to that effect.' By the time Muhammad had made the third circuit, to the accompaniment of this chorus, his face was as black as thunder. Then he stopped in his tracks, faced his critics and said: 'Will you listen to me, O Quraysh? By Him who holds my life in His hand I bring you slaughter [*dhabh*].' This last word shocked the bystanders and they were struck dumb, but the next day they had recovered their nerve. They leaped on Muhammad when he appeared at the Ka'aba, encircled him menacingly and started to pull him about by his robe. At that point Abu Bakr intervened, weeping, and said: 'Would you kill a man for saying al-Llah is my Lord?' Then they left him alone. 'That', Amr concluded, 'is the worst that I ever saw Quraysh do to him.'[24] It must have been distressing and annoying, but this harassment was obviously not severe. The Quraysh were easily abashed and the violence was contained.

Indeed this kind of behaviour was proving to be counter-productive as it moved some people to join Muhammad. One day, for example, Abu Jahl was particularly insulting to Muhammad, who did not even bother to reply but strode past him to his own house. But later in the day his uncle Hamzah, the mighty, came to the Ka'aba after a hunting expedition, with his bow hanging from his shoulder. He was, Ibn Ishaq says, 'the strongest man of Quraysh and the most unyielding'.[25] He always liked to finish a day in the field by making the ritual circumambulations and then chatting to anybody who happened to be at the Ka'aba. But on this occasion a woman took him aside and told him how offensively Abu Jahl had spoken to Muhammad earlier. Hamzah was not a Muslim, but when he heard this he saw the light in a blaze of pure rage. He set off at a run to find Abu Jahl and hit him with all his might with his bow across the back: 'Will you insult him when I follow his religion?' he bellowed. 'Hit me back if you can!' Abu Jahl hastily restrained his companions and told them to leave Hamzah alone 'for by al-Llah, I insulted his nephew deeply', he admitted.[26] Hamzah's conversion impressed the Quraysh; for obvious reasons they felt it was better to leave the Prophet alone.

But the most frequent cause of conversion was the Qu'ran itself. During the pilgrimage to the Ka'aba of 616, when pilgrims came to Mecca from all over Arabia, Abu Jahl posted his colleagues at all the gates of the city to warn them against Muhammad. One pilgrim, a poet called al-Tufayl ibn Amr of the western tribe of Daws, was so alarmed by what he heard that he stuffed his ears with cotton to make sure that he would not hear the Prophet's enchantment. But when he arrived at the Ka'aba and saw Muhammad standing in prayer before the shrine, he suddenly felt ridiculous. 'God bless my soul,' he said, 'here am I, an intelligent man, a poet, knowing perfectly well the difference between good and evil, so what is to prevent me from listening to what this man is saying? If it is good I shall accept it; if it is bad I shall reject it.' He followed Muhammad, who explained the religion to him and then recited some of the Qu'ran. Tufayl was astonished: 'By al-Llah, I have never heard anything finer or more just!' he exclaimed.[27] He went back to his tribe and during the next few years converted about seventy families in his own tribe.

The extreme beauty of the Qu'ran seems to have penetrated people's reserves. Tufayl had voluntarily removed the barriers of fear when he had taken the cotton from his ears. Others, however, were able to remain untouched and to keep the barricades in place. One day, the Quraysh decided to try a new tack and they sent Utba ibn Rab'ia of Abd Shams to make a deal with Muhammad: if he promised to keep quiet they would give him anything he wanted: money, position – even the kingship. If this is true, it is a mark of their desperation: money was almost a sacred value to many of the Quraysh and they had an inbuilt loathing of supreme authority and institutions like kingship. Muhammad waited until Utba had finished speaking and then said: 'Now, listen to me.' Utba sat back, put his hands behind him and, leaning on them, listened attentively while Muhammad began to recite Sura 41, which describes a barrier that some of the Quraysh were putting up in their hearts to prevent the divine message from entering their souls:

> Most of them have turned away and do not give ear.
> They say, 'Our hearts are veiled from that thou callest us to,
> and in our ears is a heaviness,
> and between us and thee there is a veil.'[28]

The Qu'ran often speaks of the veil which makes the hardened heart proof against the imperative power of its message. Utba was not yet ready to lower his reserves. When Muhammad prostrated himself at the end of the recitation, he did not join him but when he returned to his friends in the Senate they saw at once that he had had a powerful experience. Utba found it very difficult to describe what had happened to him, when he had listened to the beauty of the words. He could only say what it had *not* been like. It was different from any kind of inspiration that the Arabs had known before: it was not like poetry, the incantations of a magician or the unintelligent oracles of the *kahin*. It is interesting that none of Muhammad's opponents accused him of faking the revelations: something strange was obviously going on that they could not explain. Finally Utba warned the Quraysh: 'Take my advice and do as I do, and leave this man entirely alone, for, by God, the words which I have heard will be blazed abroad.'[29]

At one level one can say that Muhammad had discovered an entirely new literary form, which some people were ready for but which others found shocking and disturbing. It was so new and so powerful in its effect that its very existence seemed a miracle, beyond the reach of normal human attainment. Muhammad's enemies are challenged to produce another work like it; its unique character was proof of its divine origin and its verses were 'signs' providing a sacramental encounter with God.[30] Muslims still experience a mysterious presence when they recite the Qu'ran or sit in front of the texts from the holy book that decorate the walls of their mosques. We have seen that it is as central to Muslim spirituality as Jesus, the Word of God, in Christianity. Later, some Muslims would claim that it was the utterance in normal human speech of the 'Uncreated Word', like the Logos in the Prologue to St John's Gospel. The Qu'ran, therefore, is more than an imparting of privileged information, it is a symbol similar to the symbols of the Torah, the Person of Christ or the sacraments, which people in other traditions have cultivated as 'signs' of the divine in our midst.

The idea of a text, a work of art or a piece of music yielding a 'Real Presence' or an experience of transcendence has recently inspired Western critics like George Steiner and Peter Fuller. When Ibn Ishaq and the other early biographers speak of Islam 'entering the heart' of somebody who listened attentively to the Qu'ran, breaking down his reserves of prejudice or fear, he is perhaps suggesting something similar to the aesthetic experience described by Steiner in his book *Real Presences: Is there anything* in *what we say?* Those of us who find it difficult to see any beauty in the Qu'ran have probably experienced in our own traditions what Steiner calls 'the indiscretion of serious art and literature and music', which 'queries the last privacies of our existence'. Such art, Steiner argues, tells us in effect: 'change your life'. It is an encounter with a transcendent dimension that breaks into 'the small house of our cautionary being'. Once we have listened to the summons of such art, this house is no longer 'habitable in quite the same way as it was before'.[31] Steiner does not believe in God and he suggests that for many people art represents the only possibility of transcendence in a sceptical world. Obviously there are important differences between his theory and the experience of the Muslims who felt that their lives had been irrevocably changed by the beauty of the Qu'ran , but the testimonies of these first encounters with the sacred book of Islam does suggest a similar unsettling of sensibility, an awakening and a disturbing glimpse of enrichment that penetrates cautionary barricades. Steiner's book met with considerable acclaim when it was published, which suggests that it reflected the experience of many of his readers and his theory may give us some inkling of the remarkable effect of this classic work of Arabic literature. Muhammad as poet and prophet, and the Qu'ran as text and theophany must be one of the most striking instances of the kinship of the religious and the artistic experience.

Without this invasion or 'annunciation', as Steiner calls it, it is most unlikely that the early Muslim community would have been able to make the frightening break with the past, violate deep sanctities and overcome inherent prejudice. The beauty of the Qu'ran had resonated with something deeply buried within them and also pointed beyond itself, like the 'signs' it described. It was able to reach these privacies and encourage the Muslims to change their lives at a level that was far deeper than the rational. Muslims today would claim that the miracle of the Qu'ran consists in its ability to continue to have this effect on people today, even on those who are not native Arabic speakers. Thus the distinguished Iranian scholar Sayyid Hossein Nasr points out that the Qu'ran still demands that Muslims change their lives. The fragmentary, incoherent verses – especially of the earlier suras – demonstrate human language crushed under the weight of the divine Word: it also reveals an incoherence in the individual. In order to discover the inner, symbolic meaning of the Qu'ran, the Muslim must integrate his or her life. Reading or listening to the Qu'ran is not a cerebral experience to get information or to receive a clear directive, but a spiritual discipline. The process of *ta'wil* (symbolic interpretation) is a search for an inner meaning that demands that the individual also penetrate the depths of his or her own being. *Ta'wil* literally means to take something back to its beginning or origin and the Qu'ran also demands that when Muslims encounter the sacred text they too go from the external (*zahir*) to the secret, interior (*batin*) of their being to discover its Ground and Origin.[32]

Naturally a Western person will have a completely different experience. Not only is the beauty of the Arabic inaccessible in translation, but it demands an approach that is foreign to many of us. To confine oneself to a cerebral external reading without being nudged by the quality of the Arabic to look for the ineffable that lies beyond speech is likely to be a desolating experience, particularly if the reading is undertaken in a hostile spirit or from a vantage point of imagined superiority – as, for example, we found in Gibbon: this is not the receptive, creative spirit that will yield any kind of aesthetic experience.

Towards the end of 616 the Qu'ran made its most surprising convert. Deciding that it was time to kill Muhammad, Umar ibn al-Khattab strode through the streets of Mecca, sword in hand, to a house at the foot of Mount Safa where he knew that the Prophet was spending the afternoon. He did not know that his sister Fatimah and her husband Sa'id (the son of Zayd the *hanif*) had become Muslims and that, thinking that Umar was safely out of the way, they had invited Khabbab ibn al-Aratt, the Muslim blacksmith, to come and recite the most recent sura to them. But on his way to Mount Safa another secret Muslim of his clan accosted Umar and to deflect him from his purpose told him to go back home to see what was happening in his own house. Umar went back at a run and heard the words of the Qu'ran issuing from his own window as he turned into his street. 'What was that balderdash?' he roared as he entered the house. Khabbab hastily retired to an upstairs room, as Umar burst in upon Fatimah and Sa'id and beat his sister, knocking her to the ground. But as soon as he saw her blood he must have felt ashamed; at any rate a change came into his face. He picked up the manuscript that Khabbab had dropped in his haste and began to read the opening verses of Sura 20, being one of the few Quraysh who could read and write fluently. 'How fine and noble is this speech!' he said wonderingly, and this Muslim Saul of Tarsus was felled not by a vision of Jesus, the Word, but by the beauty of the Qu'ran which reached through his passionate hatred and prejudice to an inner receptivity that he had not been aware of. Immediately, Umar grabbed his sword again, ran through the streets of Mecca to Mount Safa and burst into the house where Muhammad was. Obviously thinking that attack was the best means of defence, Muhammad seized him by his cloak: 'What has brought you, son of Khattab?' he cried. Umar replied: 'O apostle of God, I have come to you to believe in God and his apostle and what he has brought from God.'[33] Muhammad gave thanks so loudly that everybody in the large house (who had hidden in terror at Umar's approach) realised what had happened.

But Ibn Ishaq has recorded another version of Umar's conversion which is worth quoting. Umar had been a great drinker in his unregenerate days and enjoyed nothing better than carousing with his friends in the market. One evening none of his drinking companions turned up, so Umar thought he might as well pass the time by making the circumambulations around the Ka'aba instead. When he arrived, he saw Muhammad standing close to the shrine reciting the Qu'ran quietly to himself and decided that he would like to hear the words. So he crept under the damask cloth that covered the great granite cube and edged his way round the shrine until he was standing in front of Muhammad. As he said: 'there was nothing between us but the cover of the Ka'aba' – all his defences but one were down. There the magic of the Arabic did its work: 'When I heard the Qu'ran my heart was softened and I wept, and Islam entered into me.'[34]

Umar was never a man for half-measures. The next morning he decided to break the news to his uncle Abu Jahl – going straight to the lion's den. 'The best of welcomes, nephew!' Abu Jahl cried cheerily as he opened the door, 'what has brought you?' Umar tells us: 'I answered that I had come to tell him that I believed in God and His apostle Muhammad and regarded as true what he had brought. He slammed the door in my face and said, "God damn you and damn what you have brought."'[35] As one might imagine, Umar's conversion was the last straw, especially since he absolutely refused to make the *salat* in private but prostrated himself before the Ka'aba in front of everybody. Abu Jahl and Abu Sufyan could not bear to watch him but there was nothing they could do because Umar was protected by his clan, Adi.

Abu Jahl now tried to starve Muhammad into submission and imposed a boycott on the clans of Hashim and al-Muttalib, managing to get all the other clans to sign a treaty to unite against the Muslim threat. Nobody could intermarry or trade with anybody in the two outlawed clans and this meant that nobody was supposed to sell them any food. For the sake of security, all members of Hashim and al-Muttalib, Muslim and non-Muslim alike, moved into Abu Talib's street, which became a little ghetto. When Muhammad, Khadija and their household arrived there, Abu Lahab and his family moved out and took up official residence in the district of Abd Shams. The ban lasted for two years. Abu Talib and the members of Hashim and al-Muttalib who had not become Muslims refused, as a matter of pure tribal principle, to abandon their kinsmen. But the ban was not popular, especially among people in the other clans who had relatives in Hashim and al-Muttalib and could not in conscience let them starve to death. Muslims like Abu Bakr and Umar (who were, of course, members of other clans) used to send food and supplies regularly into the ghetto, as did other relatives and friends. One Hishim ibn Amr, who had several relatives in Hashim, often used to bring a camel, laden with provisions, by night to Abu Talib's street, give the beast a thwack on its hindquarters and send it lumbering off down the alley. On one occasion Hakim ibn Hizam, Khadija's nephew, was stopped by Abu Jahl en route to the ghetto with a bag of flour in his hands. Soon the two were arguing fiercely and a bystander joined in, taking Hakim's side: was Abu

Jahl seriously going to stop a man taking food to his own aunt? When Abu Jahl still refused to let Hakim go, the angry passer-by gave him a huge blow with a camel's jaw which knocked him to the ground.

During the four sacred months, when violence was forbidden in Mecca, Muhammad and the Muslims could leave the ghetto and he went regularly to the Ka'aba. There he was the butt of fresh insults. Abu Lahab's wife, who fancied herself as a poet, liked to shout insulting verses at the Prophet when he passed by. On one occasion she hurled an armful of prickly firewood in his path. It was probably at this time that Sura 111 was revealed:

> Perish the hands of Abu Lahab, and perish he!
> His wealth avails him not, neither what he has earned;
> he shall roast at a flaming fire
> and his wife, the carrier of the firewood,
> upon her neck a rope of palm-fibre.

People who have been brought up on the Sermon on the Mount may find it rather disedifying that Muhammad did not turn the other cheek. But in the Gospels Jesus himself often cursed his enemies in good round terms. He prophesied a terrible fate for the towns of Bethsaid and Korozaim, which had not listened to his words, and in the Gospel of St Matthew he is said to have abused the Pharisees and Sadducees in a diatribe which was positively libellous.

At this time, too, a new intransigence creeps into the Qu'ran. Constantly it foretells a catastrophe for the city of Mecca, which had refused to listen to the Word of God. It seems that the Muslims' knowledge of the Jewish scriptures was beginning to expand during this hard period. The Qu'ran starts to tell new stories about the previous prophets to console the Muslims which reflect the excitement of discovery: such stories frequently begin with questions like 'Have you received the story of Moses?' or 'Have you caught the story of Pharaoh?' Moses was the most popular prophet at the time of the ban: the Qu'ran points out again and again that he had warned Pharaoh to obey the Word of God but the Egyptians had failed to listen and had been punished. But other prophets – Joseph, Noah, Jonah, Jacob, Jesus – had also warned their people that they must live in the right way, creating a just and benevolent society, if they wanted to avert an imminent catastrophe. The Qu'ran also included some non-Biblical prophets, men of note like Hood, Shuaib and Salih, whom God had sent to the ancient Arab peoples of Ad, Midian and Thamood with the same message. Muhammad's knowledge of scripture was still limited, however. The prophetic figures venerated by the Arabs in their own traditions were put side by side with the prophets of the Bible as though they were equal in status: indeed, as we have seen, the Qu'ran sees all rightly guided religions as coming from God. Muhammad did not know the chronology in which the scriptural prophets appeared: he seems, for example, to have thought that Mariam, the mother of Jesus, was the same as Mariam, the sister of Moses in the Jewish scriptures. The stories of the prophets reflect the situation of Muhammad and the first Muslims far more than the original Biblical version. Thus the story of Noah gives us a very clear idea of the difficulties Muhammad had experienced with the Senate of Mecca and the various objections it made to his prophethood:

> And We sent Noah to his people;
> and he said, 'O my people, serve God!
> You have no god other than He.
> Will you not be godfearing?'
> Said the Council of the unbelievers
> of his people, 'This is naught but
> a mortal like yourselves, who desires
> to gain superiority over you. And
> if God willed, He would have sent down
> angels. We never heard of this among
> our fathers, the ancients.
> He is naught but a man bedevilled.'[36]

But, as we have seen, the Qu'ran sees all such stories as 'signs', symbolic accounts of God's dealings with man rather than accurate historical accounts, and tries to pierce through the events of these old stories, as the Arabs knew them, to the kernel of the message.

After Noah has been rejected by his people, al-Llah commands him to build the Ark and drowns all those who did not heed his warning. At this time, the Day of Judgement *does* become a fearsome event in the Qu'ran: the just are separated from the unjust in the great symbolic scenarios, which are 'a *sign* for him who fears the chastisement in the world to come'.[37] But the Qu'ran makes it clear that this chastisement is not arbitrary: the cities and peoples who refused to heed the prophets' warnings brought their destruction on their own heads.[38] The city of Mecca would now experience a catastrophe because the Quraysh refused to amend their lives and create the kind of society that was in accordance with the true order.

But the message of the Qu'ran was not all doom and destruction at this time. Constantly it urges the Muslims to be patient and to endure their present sufferings with fortitude and dignity. They should not seize the opportunity for a personal vendetta against their enemies. The stories of the prophets of the past also consoled them by pointing out that their faith was not a monstrous 'innovation'; even though they seemed to be turning their backs on their fathers, they had their own spiritual lineage that reached back to Adam, the first Prophet, who had instructed mankind on the correct way to live. By this time, it was clear to Muhammad that he was diametrically opposed to the Quraysh, even to those who were less intransigent than Abu Jahl. Shortly after the imposition of the Ban, a small delegation had approached Muhammad hoping to find a peaceful solution. It was led by the venerable Walid of Makhzum, who was too near to death to be personally threatened by Muhammad, and consisted of three other leading men of the clans of Sahm, Asad and Jumah. These clans had all been members of the old Hilf al-Fudul and the delegates were probably concerned that the Ban would give Abu Jahl too much power in Mecca. They would have recognised Muhammad's potential ability and felt that he might be able to revive the fortunes of the weaker clans.

The delegation suggested a compromise: the Muslims could worship al-Llah in their religion, and the others could go on worshipping al-Lat, al-Uzza and Manat. But Muhammad had already thought this through. He answered the delegation with Sura 109 – the Sura of Rejection – which announced the parting of the ways:

> Say: 'O unbelievers,
> I serve not what you serve
> and you are not serving what I serve,
> nor am I serving what you have served,
> neither are you serving what I serve.
>
> To you your religion, and to me my religion!'

After the Ban had been enforced for two years, the situation suddenly improved for Muhammad and it looked as though his firmness had paid off. The Ban had become increasingly unpopular; expecting people to watch their blood relations starving went against too many Arab traditions and there had been a regular, illegal stream of food and provisions into the ghetto. Finally four Quraysh, who were closely related to members of Hashim and al-Muttalib, planned a campaign to end the Ban. Hishim ibn Amr, who had sent his food-laden camel down Abu Talib's street so frequently, began to rustle up support and managed to find four other like-minded people to force the issue with Abu Jahl. Three of these – al-Mu'tim ibn Adi, Abu al-Bakhtar ibn Hisham and Sama ibn al-Arwad – belonged to clans of the old Hilf and were probably worried about the ascendancy that Makhzum, Abu Jahl's clan, had gained in Mecca during the Ban. But the fourth man – al-Zuhayr ibn Abi Ummayya, who was related to Abu Talib – was a Makhzumite himself and it was agreed that he should open the proceedings.

On the appointed day, Zuhayr donned a long white robe and solemnly made the circumambulations around the Ka'aba. At the end, he stepped forward and publicly addressed all the elders of the city. How could they decently sit and watch Hashim and al-Muttalib suffering in this way? Abu Jahl protested angrily, but the other four men spoke up in support of Zuhayr's motion. Finally Mu'tim strode to the Ka'aba to find the document which the clans had signed at the start of the Ban, and the people were said to have been deeply impressed when it was discovered that the parchment had been eaten by worms, except for a small piece containing the opening formula: 'In thy name, O al-Llah!' They insisted that the Ban be revoked.

There must have been great rejoicing in the Muslim community; it seemed as though better times had begun. The exiled community in Abyssinia heard the news and Uthman ibn Ma'zum led about thirty families home to Mecca, leaving the rest behind with Abu Talib's son Ja'far. Muhammad and Khadija were delighted to be reunited with their daughter Ruqayyah and her husband Uthman ibn Affan. But the emigrants had returned too soon. The Ban had inevitably entailed some hardships, despite the illegal stream of provisions, and early in 619 a death made Muhammad's position in Mecca impossible.

7 · *Hijra*: A New Direction

His biographers sometimes call 619 Muhammad's Year of Sadness. Shortly after the end of the Ban, Khadija died: she had been in her sixties and her health may have been irreparably damaged by the food shortages. She had been Muhammad's closest companion and after her death nobody would replace her. Not even the faithful Abu Bakr or the passionate Umar would be able to provide Muhammad with the same intimate support, and the loss must have affected him profoundly. But not long afterwards a second death had more practical consequences. Abu Talib became gravely ill and it was clear that he would not recover. Before he died the Quraysh made a final bid for peace. Even though they had put such pressure on him, they knew that Abu Talib had behaved like a true Arab *sayyid* in giving such unswerving support to his clansmen, and now Abu Jahl led a deputation to his bedside to ask him to effect a reconciliation: if Muhammad would acknowledge their religion, they would leave him alone. But Muhammad had already thought this issue through two years earlier and told the Quraysh that al-Llah was the *only* God. They were furious and went away defiantly claiming that al-Llah Himself would judge between them and Muhammad.

After they had left, Muhammad was astonished when Abu Talib told him that he had been right to reject this compromise and he begged his uncle to go one step further and make his own surrender to al-Llah. But Abu Talib gently told him that if he made such a declaration of faith he would be doing it only to please him. He would die, as he had lived, in the faith of his fathers. At the last moment, however, Abbas noticed that the dying man's lips were moving and he told Muhammad that he seemed to be reciting the *shahada*. But Muhammad shook his head: he knew that Abu Talib had not entered Islam.

The new chief of Hashim was Abu Lahab, which was obviously very serious for Muhammad, but at first Abu Lahab did give him some measure of protection. This would have been expected of him, now that he was chief, but it was not nearly as effective as the protection of Abu Talib, because everybody knew that it was grudgingly given, and they took advantage of Muhammad's new vulnerability. His neighbours started to play very nasty tricks with a sheep's uterus: they used to thwack Muhammad with this disgusting object while he was at prayer and one joker even popped it into the family cooking-pot. One day, while Muhammad was walking in the city, a young Qurayshi threw dirt all over him. His daughter burst into tears when he returned home in this state and wept as she washed it off. 'Don't cry, my little girl,' Muhammad comforted her, 'for God will protect your father.' But he added grimly to himself: 'Quraysh never treated me thus while Abu Talib was alive.'[1]

Muhammad's new weakness may have affected the position of other Muslims. Abu Bakr, for example, had been practically ruined by the Ban: his capital had been reduced from 40,000 to 5,000 dirhams. He lived in the district of the clan of Jumah and ever since he had converted to Islam he had been on bad terms with its chief, the elderly, obese Ummayah ibn Khalaf. Ummayah had liked to expose his Muslim slave Bilal to the sun during the early period of persecution, but now he felt able to do the same to Abu Bakr, a respected merchant. He tied him and his young cousin Talhah together and left them in the broiling heat in this ignominious position. This demonstrated that Taym, their clan, was no longer willing or able to protect Abu Bakr, so he realised that there was no future for him in Mecca. With Muhammad's blessing, he left the city and set off to join the emigrant community in Abyssinia. But on the road he fell in with Ibn Dughumma, the chief of the small group of nomadic tribes (known as the Ahabish) who were the allies of the Quraysh. Ibn Dughumma was horrified when he heard that Abu Bakr had practically been thrown out of Mecca and suggested that they return forthwith and that he himself should take Abu Bakr under his protection. Abu Bakr was glad to agree, and the Quraysh, who were anxious to cultivate Ibn Dughumma, had to accept the situation, but they asked the Bedouin to ensure that Abu Bakr did not pray or recite the Qu'ran in public. He was a charismatic man, they explained, and was likely to lure the young people away from the faith of their fathers. Ibn Dughumma agreed to these terms and Abu Bakr promised that he would worship only in the privacy of his own home.

But others refused to lie low. Uthman ibn Ma'zum, the ascetic, was a member of Makhzum and enjoyed the powerful and effective protection of Walid, but he found it intolerable to be safe while others were suffering. So he went to Walid and, to the old man's obvious perplexity, renounced his protection. It seemed a splendid opportunity for voluntary penance, but was more characteristic of Christian than Muslim piety. During the Roman persecutions, some Christian zealots had denounced themselves voluntarily to the authorities in order to achieve martyrdom, but Muhammad did not approve of such excess. It also went against Arab tradition: life had always been hard enough in Arabia without taking on extra risk and suffering. A few days later, Uthman attended a poetry reading given by Labid ibn Rabi'a, the greatest Arab poet of the day. The Quraysh were honoured that Labid had visited their city and were mortified when Uthman started to heckle. When Labid recited: 'Everything but al-Llah is vain,' Uthman shouted, 'True!' but when Labid went on, 'And everything lovely must inevitably cease,' Uthman yelled, 'You lie! the joys of paradise will never cease!' This was unpardonable behaviour to an honoured guest and Labid was deeply offended. 'O men of Quraysh,' he said, 'your friends never used to be annoyed thus. Since when has this sort of thing happened among you?' 'Take no notice of what he said,' cried somebody in the audience, 'this is one of the louts with Muhammad. They have abandoned our religion.' But Uthman then became so offensive that this same man got up and gave him a black eye. Walid, a civilised old man who must have been looking at this outrageous scene with dismay, called: 'O nephew, your eye need not have suffered this had you remained in my sure protection.' But Uthman aggressively turned the other cheek and challenged the audience to black his other eye.[2] Muhammad made a point of dissociating himself from this distasteful incident.[3] He would have disapproved of such discourtesy and must have felt that the last thing he needed was this kind of provocation.

But then came the crisis. Egged on by Abu Jahl, Abu Lahab asked Muhammad whether his father Abd al-Muttalib, who had loved Muhammad and had been so proud of him when he was a child, was in hell. This was a trick question. Muhammad had adopted the Jewish–Christian idea that only those who professed the true faith could be saved. He had at his fingertips none of the nice liberal answers that monotheists have devised in recent years to get round this one. If he said that the old paganism could save people like Abd al-Muttalib, the Quraysh would naturally reply that in that case there was no need to abolish it. But if he admitted that Abd al-Muttalib was not saved, then Abu Lahab could withdraw his protection from one who had denigrated the memory of a beloved ancestor.

Muhammad had to find a new protector and it was a mark of his desperation that he attempted to find one in Taif, the city of al-Lat. Taif was a merchant city like Mecca, though not nearly so successful. But it was in a more fertile part of Arabia and as Muhammad approached the walled city on the hill, he would have walked through attractive gardens, orchards and cornfields. Several members of the clan of Abd Shams and Hashim, his own clan, had summer villas there, so Muhammad may have had contacts in the city. But it was a risky business as the Thaqif, the guardians of the ancient shrine, would have been very offended by Muhammad's condemnation of the cult of al-Lat. He visited three brothers and asked them to accept his religion and give him protection, but was insultingly rebuffed. Indeed the three Thaqif were so incensed by

Muhammad's effrontery in daring to propose such an arrangement that they had their slaves chase him through the streets.

To escape from the mob, Muhammad dived for shelter into the orchard which belonged to Utba ibn Rabi'a and his brother Shayba, who were sitting in the garden at that time and saw the whole thing. They were in the forefront of the opposition to Muhammad in Mecca but were fair-minded men and would have been distressed to see a Qurayshi in such ignominious flight. They sent a slave boy to him with a plate of grapes. Cowering in the orchard, Muhammad felt that he had come to the end of his own resources. He must have missed Khadija deeply at this moment: this was the kind of pain she had always been able to treat and he must have acutely felt the want of her advice. It was customary for Arabs to 'take refuge with' a god or *jinni* in an emergency, but now Muhammad 'took refuge with' God:

> O al-Llah, to Thee I complain of my weakness, little resource, and lowliness before men. O Most Merciful, Thou art the Lord of the weak and Thou art my Lord. To whom wilt Thou confide me? To one afar who will misuse me? Or to an enemy to whom Thou hast given power over me? If Thou art not angry with me, I care not. Thy favour is more wide for me. I take refuge in the light of Thy countenance by which the darkness is illumined, and the things of this world and the next are rightly ordered, lest Thy anger descend upon me or Thy wrath light upon me. It is for Thee to be satisfied until Thou art well pleased. There is no power and no might save in Thee.[4]

It is unusual for Ibn Ishaq to give such an intimate account of Muhammad's state of mind and this suggests that it represented a crisis in his spiritual development. He could no longer rely on human companionship but had to realise that there was no god, no security, no true 'protector' but al-Llah.

Almost immediately God seemed to answer his prayer with a 'sign' when Addas, the slave boy, arrived with the plate of grapes. He was a Christian from Nineveh in modern Iraq and was astonished to see this Arab blessing the platter 'in the name of God' before he ate. Muhammad for his part was astonished and delighted to hear that Addas came from Nineveh, the city of the prophet Jonah, and he told Addas that he was a prophet too and therefore the 'brother' of Jonah. Addas was so overcome that he kissed Muhammad's head, hands and feet, to the disgust of Utba and Shayba who had been watching the whole incident: it was yet another example of Muhammad's uncanny power over the young. But Muhammad felt less isolated after this contact with one of the People of the Book and the reminder of all the people in the great world outside Arabia who would understand his prophetic claim, even though the Arabs of the Hijaz could not. On his way home, it is said that he was further consoled by a crowd of *jinn* who overheard him reciting the Qu'ran and were astounded by its beauty.[5]

But 'taking refuge with al-Llah' did not mean that Muhammad could dispense with human protection. The Qu'ran makes it clear that Muslims are expected to use every human effort to look after themselves and not lazily leave everything to God: 'Verily God will not change the state of a people, unless they change the state of their own selves.'[6] It is a verse that Muslims engaged in a political struggle today like to quote. Before Muhammad entered the city, he sent word to three chiefs of other clans, asking them to accept him as a confederate. Once the Quraysh knew that he had been willing to defect to Taif, his position in the city would be even more dangerous. The first two chiefs he approached – Akhnas ibn Shariq of Zuhrah and Suhayl ibn Amr of Amir – both refused on points of tribal principle,[7] but the third – Mu'tim, chief of Nawfal, who had campaigned to annul the Ban – took Muhammad under his protection and he was able to enter the city.

This could not be a long-term solution, however, and at about this time Muhammad began to preach to the Bedouin pilgrims who came for the annual *hajj*, hoping to find a more permanent protector among them. He was beginning to expand his mission to include other Arabs. But at first the Bedouin were hostile and insulting, and displayed no interest in Muhammad's religion. It was a desolate period, but perhaps because Muhammad had been pushed beyond his original preconceptions and had come to the end of his own natural resources he had the greatest mystical experience in his life in the year 620.

He had been visiting his cousin Umm Hani, the sister of Ali and Ja'far, and, as she lived near the Ka'aba, he rose in the middle of the night and went to recite the Qu'ran there. Eventually he decided to sleep for a while in the *hijr*, an enclosed area to the north-west of the shrine. Then it seemed to him that he was woken by Gabriel, lifted on to a heavenly steed called Buruq and flown miraculously through the night to Jerusalem, which the Qu'ran calls *al-masjid al-aqsa*: the Further Mosque.[8] After this Night Flight (*'isra*), Muhammad and Gabriel alighted on the Temple Mount and were greeted by Abraham, Moses, Jesus and a crowd of other prophets. They prayed together and brought Muhammad three goblets containing water, milk and wine. Muhammad chose to drink the milk, as a symbol of the middle course that Islam has tried to steer between extreme asceticism on the one hand and hedonism on the other. Then a ladder (*miraj*) was brought and Muhammad and Gabriel climbed to the first of the seven heavens and began the ascent to the Throne of God. At each stage he saw one of the great prophets: Adam presided over the First Heaven, where Muhammad was shown a vision of hell; Jesus and John the

Baptist were in the Second Heaven; Joseph in the Third; Enoch in the Fourth; Aaron and Moses in the Fifth and Sixth and, finally, Abraham in the Seventh at the threshold of the divine sphere.

Ibn Ishaq leaves the supreme vision in reverent obscurity, but he quotes a tradition that gives a practical reason for this experience, even though this seems to have been a personal experience for Muhammad himself because it contained no revelation for inclusion in the Qu'ran. When he reached the divine throne, God told Muhammad that the Muslims must make *salat* fifty times a day, but on his way down Moses told Muhammad to go back and get the number reduced. Moses kept sending Muhammad back until the number of prescribed prayers was reduced to five, which he still felt was excessive, but Muhammad was too ashamed to ask for a further reduction. After Muhammad's death Muslims did pray five times a day and this tradition shows that religion was not meant to be a crushing burden, but a moderate discipline which everybody could manage.[9]

This religious experience has been immensely important in the evolution of Islamic spirituality. It is celebrated each year on 27 Rajab, the seventh lunar month, and over the centuries mystics, philosophers and poets have speculated on its significance. It has even entered the Western tradition, because Muslim accounts of the *miraj*, Muhammad's ascent to heaven, affected Dante's account of his imaginative journey through hell, purgatory and heaven in *The Divine Comedy*, even though with typical Western schizophrenia, as we have seen, he put the Prophet himself in one of the lowest circles of hell. The Sufis were particularly interested in the experience and believed that Muhammad's supreme vision had been described in the Qu'ran in Sura 53:

> Indeed he saw Him another time
> by the Lote-Tree of the Boundary
> nigh which is the Garden of the Refuge,
> where there covered the Lote Tree that which covered;
> his eye swerved not, nor swept astray.
> Indeed, he saw one of the greatest signs of his Lord.[10]

As in the Hindu tradition, the Lote Tree marks the limit of human knowledge. The Qu'ran makes it clear that Muhammad saw only one of the 'signs' of God, not God Himself, and later mystics emphasised the paradox of this vision, in which Muhammad both saw and did not see the Divine Essence.[11]

The Sufis depicted Muhammad as a hero, blazing a new trail to God in this experience, which is so close to the experiences of other mystics in other widely separated traditions. In the thirteenth-century Persian account by the great poet Farid ud-Din Attar, we are very close in spirit to John of the Cross, who also stressed the importance of leaving all our human concepts and experiences behind, going beyond what the Qu'ran called the Lote Tree, the boundary of normal mundane knowledge. Attar shows that Muhammad ultimately had to leave everybody behind: even Gabriel could not accompany the Prophet on the last stage of his journey. Having gone beyond normal sense perception and beyond logic and reason in his flight, Muhammad entered a new realm of experience, but he still had to be prepared to leave himself behind.

> He heard a call, a message from the Friend.
> A call came from the Essence of the All:
> 'Leave soul and body, transitory one!
> You, O My goal and purpose, enter now
> And see My Essence face to face, My friend!'
> In awe, he lost his speech and lost himself –
> Muhammad did not know Muhammad here,
> Saw not himself – He saw the Soul of Souls,
> The Face of Him who made the universe.[12]

It is an experience common to all the major mystical traditions, an expression of the belief that no man can see God and live. But having died to himself and faced the experience of extinction, Muhammad was restored to an enhanced being. Later he brought this experience back and expanded the human capacity for the divine. The *miraj* became a paradigm of the mystical strain of Islam: Sufis always spoke of an annihilation (*'fana*) in God which was followed by its revival (*baqa*) and an enhanced self-realisation.

Some Muslims have always insisted that Muḥammad made the journey to God's Throne in body, but Ibn Ishaq quotes a tradition from Aisha which makes it clear that the Night Journey and Ascension were purely spiritual experiences. However we choose to interpret it, mystical experience is a fact of human life and seems to be markedly similar in most traditions. The Buddhists would claim that such intimations of the ultimate and expansion of consciousness are purely natural states rather than an encounter with the Other. It seems that, pushed to a state of extremity, the human consciousness produces a particular scenario or mythical landscape to describe this encounter – rather as, in an entirely different context, people who are at a physical extremity and are near to death all seem to picture the experience in a certain way: going down a long passage, being met at a gate by somebody who tells them to return and so forth. In all religions some men and women have a particular talent for this type of activity and have cultivated these experiences by means of certain disciplines and techniques that, again, are remarkably similar. The *miraj* of Muhammad, as described by Muslim writers, is very close to the experience of Throne Mysticism in the Jewish tradition, which flourished from the second to the tenth century CE. The adepts would prepare themselves for their mystical flight and journey to God's Throne by special disciplines. They would fast, read special hymns that induced a certain receptivity, and use special physical techniques. Often it seems that they would put their heads between their knees as some of the Muslim traditions say Muhammad did; in other traditions, breathing exercises have been most important. Then they would experience a perilous ascent to God's Throne and, like the Muslims, they described the supreme vision in paradoxical ways that emphasise its essential ineffability. Mystics in this tradition also regarded its founders as heroes who had discovered a new path to God and risked personal danger while doing so.

Some aspects of the *'isra* and the *miraj* are very close to mystical initiations when people are making a painful passage from one mode of life to another. It is, for example, uncannily similar to the experience of the young matron Perpetua, a Christian martyr who died in Carthage during the persecution of Severus in 203. The *Acts of Perpetua and Felicitas*, which were edited by a redactor just after her death, are believed by most scholars to be genuine. They tell us that while Perpetua was waiting for her trial in prison, her companions urged her to ask God for a vision which would reveal to them whether they really were going to die. They had asked Perpetua because she was known to have special mystical talents, and she promised that she would have an answer for them the next day. She probably subconsciously put herself into a receptive frame of mind, rather as analysands today produce revealing dreams for their therapists.[13] Sure enough, that night Perpetua dreamed that she saw a ladder (like Muhammad's *miraj*) reaching up to heaven; the ascent was very dangerous and she was afraid at one moment that she would not make it to the top, but encouraged by her companions she persevered and found herself in a huge and beautiful garden. There a shepherd was milking a sheep and he gave her some of the curds; when Perpetua awoke she found that she was 'still chewing something indefinable and sweet'. Now she knew that she was certainly going to die and she urged her friends in prison 'to have no more hope in the world'.[14] She had several more dreams which she imparted to her companions, which show that she was subconsciously coming to terms with her own approaching death and was preparing herself not only for the passage to eternal life but for martyrdom, which was regarded as the ultimate religious experience in early Christianity. Muhammad was not going to die, but he was about to begin a new phase of his mission that required a severance from the past which was a kind of death. The vision was, however, consoling: he takes his milk not, like Perpetua, from the Good Shepherd but from the great prophets of the past in a vision which expresses his sense of continuity with the earlier revelations.

The *miraj* itself also resembles the initiatory experience of a shaman, which, according to the late American scholar Joseph Campbell, still 'occurs all the way from Siberia right through the Americas down to Tierra del Fuego'. He explains that in his early youth the shaman has 'an overwhelming psychological experience that turns him totally inward. It's a kind of schizophrenic crack-up. The whole unconscious opens up, and the shaman falls into it.'[15] The Bushmen, for example, induce this experience in a great marathon dance: one shaman described what happened when he fell into a trance and collapsed:

> When I emerge, I am already climbing, I'm climbing threads, the threads that lie over there in the south. I climb one and leave it, then I climb another one. Then I leave it and climb another. . . . And when you arrive at God's place you make yourself small. You have become small. You come in small to God's place. You do what you have to do there. Then you return to where everyone is . . . and finally you enter the body again.[16]

He has passed through a form of personal extinction and penetrated regions where others cannot go, bringing news from the realm of mythological imagery, from the seat of power.

As it has come down to us, the Night Journey shows that Muhammad was beginning to see that he might be more than just a humble Warner of the Quraysh, but he was still searching for a new human protector. During the *hajj* he used to make a point of visiting the pilgrims while they were camping for the three appointed days in the valley of Mina, going from one tent to another. In this way he met a group of six Arab pagans from Yathrib during the *hajj* of 620. They had camped in the gully of 'Aqaba in the part of the valley which was closest to Mecca. Muhammad sat with them, told them about his mission and recited the Qu'ran, but this time instead of meeting with hostility and rejection he found that the Arabs were attentive and excited. When he had finished they turned to one another and said that this must be the prophet that the Jews of Yathrib were always talking about. For years they had taunted their pagan neighbours with tales of a prophet who would destroy them, just as the ancient Arab tribes of Ad and Iram had been wiped out. If Muhammad was indeed this prophet it was important to stop the Jews getting to him first. They also saw at once that Muhammad could solve the apparently insuperable problems of Yathrib.

At this point, Yathrib was not yet a city like Mecca. It was an oasis, a fertile island of about twenty square miles which was surrounded by volcanic hills, rocks and uncultivable stony ground. It was not a commercial centre but an agricultural settlement in which the various tribal groups lived cheek by jowl in a state of deadly hostility in their hamlets and farms. The area had originally been cultivated by pioneering Jewish settlers. We do not know where these Jews came from. They may have been refugees from Palestine who had fled into Arabia after the Romans had put down the rebellion of 135 CE or they may have been Arab tribes who had converted to Judaism. A third possibility is that various unattached Arabs had affiliated themselves to a group of Hebrews and had adopted their religion. By the early seventh century, there were three main Jewish tribes in Yathrib – the Bani Qurayzah, the Bani Nadir and the smaller and less important Bani Qaynuqa. The Jews preserved a separate religious identity but otherwise they were almost indistinguishable from their pagan Arab neighbours. They had Arab not Hebrew names, observed the conventions of the tribal system and were frequently as bitterly hostile to one another as to any of the Arab tribes.

During the sixth century, the Bani Qaylah had emigrated from South Arabia and settled in the oasis alongside the Jews. These newcomers formed themselves into two related stems – the Aws and the Khasraj – who became two distinct tribes, consisting of a number of different clans. At first the Aws and the Khasraj were weaker than the Jews but gradually they acquired their own land, built their own fortresses and became their equals. By the early seventh century the Aws and the Khasraj were in a slightly stronger position than the Jews but they had started to fight one another.

The transition from the nomadic to the settled life had caused a crisis in Yathrib which was even more acutely felt than the malaise in Mecca. Tribal customs which had worked very well in the steppes were no longer appropriate. In the desert the nomads had defended their ancestral lands jealously, and this had been quite feasible when they were separated from one another by vast distances. But when they were all crammed into a small oasis, with each tribe jealously guarding its few meagre acres, the system broke down. One group would make a raid (*ghazu*) on enemy territory in the time-honoured way, and this had to be avenged. Gradually the various tribes of Yathrib became caught up in a cycle of violence; the constant warfare was ruining the land, destroying the crops and undermining the source of Yathrib's wealth and power. The Jewish tribes had become deeply involved in the conflict, and allied themselves in various configurations to either the Aws or the Khasraj. By 617 there was a stalemate. No one group could gain ascendancy and both sides and their allies were exhausted by the conflict. The civil war had culminated that year in the battle of Bu'ath, which gave a nominal victory to the Aws and their Jewish confederates, the Bani Nadir, but they were quite unable to capitalise upon their victory and make it effective. Everybody was beginning to realise that, despite their entrenched Arab suspicion of kingship, a supreme authority was the only hope for Yathrib. Abdallah ibn Ubbay, one of the chiefs of Khasraj, had refused to fight at the battle of Bu'ath, because he could see that it was hopeless. He had thus acquired a reputation for an impartiality of sorts and people were beginning to see him as a possible king or supreme chief. But naturally many people were wary of this solution. The Aws, as one might expect, were deeply reluctant to hand the supreme power over to a member of Khasraj, and the less powerful clans of Khasraj were equally unwilling to let Ibn Ubbay have the ascendancy.

When Muhammad presented himself to the six pilgrims from Yathrib during the *hajj* of 620, they immediately saw that as the Prophet of al-Llah he would be a much more impartial leader than Ibn Ubbay. They were not shocked by his monotheistic message. They had lived for so long beside the Jews that they were used to the idea that there was only one God and were quite willing to relegate the old goddesses to the level of *jinn* and angels. For a very long time they had felt inferior to the Jews because they had no scriptures of their own and were 'a people without knowledge',[17] so they thrilled to Muhammad's claim that he was a prophet for the Arabs and had brought them an Arabic Qu'ran. They made their surrender to God at once, with great hopes for Yathrib: 'We have left our people, for no tribe is so divided by hatred and rancour as they. Perhaps God will unite them through you. So let us go to them and invite them to this religion of yours; and if God unites them in it, then no man will be mightier than you.'[18] They agreed that they would report back to Muhammad in a year's time. It was essential for Muhammad to gain wider support in the oasis if he was to move there with his companions. He anticipated no trouble from the Jews, because he had always believed that his message was at one with theirs, but these pilgrims were all from the smaller tribes of Khasraj. They would have to attract some of the Aws to the faith, if Muhammad were going to unite Yathrib.

For some years now the Muslim cause seemed to have stagnated, but this was a sign that things could change for the better. Muhammad had also made some major changes in his household that year. He needed a wife and longed for a female presence in his life, so it was suggested that he should marry Sawdah, the cousin and sister-in-law of Suhayl, chief of Amir. She and her husband Sakran, Suhayl's brother, had emigrated to Abyssinia in 616 and Sakran had died shortly after they had returned to Mecca. Sawdah agreed to the match and Hatib ibn Amr, another of Suhayl's brothers, gave her in marriage to the Prophet.

Abu Bakr was also anxious to forge a closer link with Muhammad, whom he had served so loyally for all these years at great personal cost. His little daughter Aisha was only six years old in 620 and she had already been promised in marriage to the son of Mu'tim, chief of Nawfal, Muhammad's new protector. But Mu'tim was quite ready to forgo the match because his wife was afraid that their son would become a Muslim, and Aisha was formally betrothed to Muhammad in a ceremony at which the little girl was not present. In later years she recalled that the first inkling she had of her new status was when her mother explained that she could no longer play in the streets like the other children, but should invite her friends to play with her in the family house.

Muhammad's harem of wives has excited a lot of lurid and prurient speculation in the West as well as a good deal of ill-concealed envy, as we saw in Chapter 1 when I showed that Muhammad was frequently accused of lust. Later the Qu'ran decreed that a Muslim could have only four wives but Muhammad, as the Prophet, was allowed many more. Few people in Arabia at that time saw monogamy as a particularly desirable norm and in later years, when Muhammad was becoming a great Arab *sayyid*, his large harem was a mark of his status. In a tribal society, polygamy tends to be the norm. The Bible is not at all squeamish about the sexual exploits of King David or the enormous harem of King Solomon, which makes Muhammad's look quite pathetic. Like Muhammad, they both lived at a time when their people were making the transition from tribal to urban life. But it would be quite wrong to imagine Muhammad basking decadently in a garden of earthly delights; indeed his many wives were sometimes, as we shall see, rather a mixed blessing. We should simply notice two things. First, neither Sawdah nor Aisha were chosen for their sexual charms. Aisha was only a little girl, and at thirty Sawdah was past her first youth and was beginning to run to fat. We hear little more about her and this indicates that the marriage was more of a practical arrangement than a love-match. She could take care of Muhammad's household and she also gained in status, at least among the Muslim community, by becoming the wife of the Prophet. Second, both marriages had a political dimension: Muhammad was forging important links of kinship. He still had hopes of Suhayl, who was a deeply religious man, and the marriage with Sawdah made him a relative by marriage. It was also important to establish a closer tie with Abu Bakr: Muhammad was beginning to form an alternative kind of clan, which was not based on kinship but on ideology, yet the blood-tie was still felt to be very important.

Abu Bakr must have been glad of this link with Muhammad, because at about this time he had once more become isolated in Mecca. He had built a little mosque by the door of his house, which scandalised the clan of Jumah. 'He was', says Ibn Ishaq, 'a tender-hearted man and when he read the Qu'ran he was moved to tears. Youths, slaves, and women used to stand by him when he recited the Qu'ran, astonished by his demeanor.'[19] When he had been taken under the protection of Ibn al-Dughumma, the Quraysh had stipulated that there was to be no more of this public prayer, so now a delegation went to the Bedouin chief and asked indignantly:

> Have you given this fellow protection so that he can injure us? Lo, he prays and recites what Muhammad has produced and his heart becomes soft and he weeps. And he has a striking appearance so that we fear he may seduce our youths and women and weak ones. Go to him and tell him to go to his own house and do what he likes there.[20]

But Abu Bakr refused to give up his mosque: he probably felt that he could compromise no more and that enough was enough. So he became the butt of insults once more: people threw dirt at him in the streets and the chiefs of the Quraysh contemptuously told him that he had brought this filth on his own head.

During the *hajj* of 621, the six converts from Yathrib returned to Mecca, as arranged, bringing seven others with them, two of whom were members of Aws. Again they met Muhammad in the gully of 'Aqaba and made a formal promise to worship only al-Llah and to observe the commandments. Later one of them said:

> We gave allegiance to the apostle that we would associate nothing with God, not steal, not commit fornication, not kill our offspring, not slander our neighbours; we should not disobey [Muhammad] in what was right; if we fulfilled this paradise would be ours; if we committed any of those sins it was for God to punish or forgive us as He pleased.[21]

At this meeting, which became known as First 'Aqaba, religion was stressed more than politics. The old paganism had failed to solve the crisis in Yathrib and people were ready for a new ideology. Muhammad's religious requirements would help Muslims to cultivate a respect for other people as individuals with certain inalienable rights; this new morality would replace the old collective ideal of the tribe, which had made the group more important than its members. This new individualism would be a possible basis for a new kind of society, because it would help the people of Yathrib to realise that one person's gain did not necessarily mean another person's loss, as it had in the desert, where there were not enough of the essentials to go round.

When the pilgrims returned to Yathrib, Muhammad sent Mu'sab ibn Umayr, an extremely able Muslim who had recently returned from Abyssinia, back with them to instruct the people of the oasis and to recite the Qu'ran. The tribal hatred was now so engrained that neither the Aws nor the Khasraj could bear to hear a member of the enemy tribe reading the holy book or leading the prayers, so the recitation had to be performed by an impartial outsider. At first the leading men of Aws were extremely hostile to the new religion and one day Sa'd ibn Muadh, chief of one of its leading clans, was horrified to hear that Mus'ab was sitting openly in a garden in his territory, preaching to his clansmen. But Mus'ab was the guest of his first cousin, Asad ibn Zurara, one of the first six converts, and this meant that it was improper for Sa'd to insult the Meccan visitor. So he sent Usayd ibn al-Hudayr, his second in command, to drive Mus'ab off their land. Usayd seized his lance and strode off to the garden. When he found the earnest little circle sitting round Mu'sab, he glowered furiously and demanded to know what the Muslim meant by coming to deceive their weaker comrades. Mu'sab replied: 'Won't you sit down and listen? If you like what you hear you can accept it, and if you don't like it you can leave it alone.' Usayd agreed that that seemed fair enough, so he stuck his lance in the ground and sat down to listen to the Qu'ran. As usual the beauty of the words broke through his reserves, and his clansmen noticed that the expression on his face changed completely and became peaceful and luminous. At the end of the recitation, he cried: 'What a wonderful and beautiful discourse this is! What does one do if one wants to enter this religion?' Usayd told him to purify his garments, proclaim his faith in the one God and prostrate himself in reverence. As soon as Usayd had fulfilled these requirements, he set off at a run to find Sa'd.

As soon as Sa'd saw him, he knew by the expression on his face that Usayd had failed him. He seized his lance, shouting angrily: 'By al-Llah, I can see that you have been utterly ineffective!' and strode off to the garden. Exactly the same thing happened; Mu'sab asked him to sit and listen, Sa'd stuck his lance in the ground, and was overcome in his turn by the beauty of the Qu'ran. This conversion was decisive. Sa'd summoned his people round him and asked them why they accepted his leadership. They replied: '[You are] our chief, the most active in our interests, the best in judgement and the most fortunate in leadership.' Sa'd then told them to trust him no less implicitly in this matter, adding: 'I will not speak to a man or woman among you until you believe in God and his apostle.'[22] As a result the whole clan converted to Islam en masse. The story is obviously stylised and has been romanticised over the years, but Sa'd would prove to be one of the most fervent of the Muslims of Yathrib and his conversion probably did make a strong impression on people who were longing for a new strong leadership and a solution to their seemingly insoluble problems.

It was not long before there were Muslims in nearly every family in the oasis. There was a small pocket of pagan resistance in the clan of Aws, which was inspired by the poet and chief Abu Qays ibn al-Aslat. Poets had always been crucial in defining and celebrating the identity of the tribe and they could ruin a person's reputation as efficiently and thoroughly as the media can today. Adverse poetic propaganda could be as devastating in Arabia as a major military defeat and we should bear this fact in mind when we come to consider Muhammad's hostility to poets who ridiculed him. During this year of trial in Yathrib, Abu Qays urged the Arabs in his clan to remain true to their authentic Arabian form of monotheism and not to accept a Qu'ran that was tainted by its foreign associations. He addresses al-Llah, whom the people of Yathrib had already realised was the only God:

> Lord of mankind, serious things have happened.
> The difficult and the simple are involved.
> Lord of mankind, if we have erred
> Guide us to the good path.
> Were it not for our Lord we should be Jews
> And the religion of Jews is not convenient.
> Were it not for our Lord we should be Christians
> Along with the monks of Mount Jalil [Galilee].
> But when we were created we were created
> Hanifs; our religion is from all generations.
> We bring the sacrificial camels walking in fetters
> Covered with cloths but their shoulders bare.[23]

It was not surprising that Abu Qays should have seen the new Meccan faith as an associate of the People of the Book, because since First 'Aqaba Muhammad had introduced some important Jewish practices. He was obviously reaching out eagerly to the Jews in the oasis, and must have been looking forward to working and praying with the people of this older revelation, after such a long period of isolation. He instructed Mu'sab to hold a special meeting for Muslims on Friday afternoons, at the time when the Jews would be preparing for their Sabbath; this linked the new service with the Jewish festival, while at the same time keeping a tactful distance. Next he prescribed a fast for Muslims on the Jewish Yom Kippur (the Day of Atonement), which was held on the 10th of the Jewish month of Tishri: the Muslim fast was accordingly called 'Ashura', which in Arabised Aramaic means 'the tenth'. Muslims were now to pray in the middle of the day, as the Jews did; hitherto they had only made the *salat* in the morning and evening, rising also during the night to keep vigils. Muslims were now told that they could marry Jewish women and eat Jewish food. They did not observe all the Jewish dietary laws, however, but only a modified version, which was remarkably similar to that which was given in the Acts of the Apostles to the gentile converts to Christianity.[24] Above all Muslims were now told to pray facing Jerusalem, as the

Jews and Christians did. Muhammad's Night Journey to Jerusalem had shown that this ancient holy city was central to the Muslim faith too and in adopting Jerusalem as the *qibla* or direction of prayer it was a constant reminder and demonstration of the new religion's connection with the older revelations. Muslims now turned towards Jerusalem three times a day in prayer; their physical posture would teach them a new spiritual orientation and teach them at a fundamental level that they had the same aims as the People of the Book.

The Qu'ran also adopted the Aramaic name that the Jews gave to Yathrib: *medinta*, which simply meant 'the city'. In Arabic this became *al-Madinat*, which gives us our 'Medina'. Five years earlier, when Muhammad had been looking for a new home for some of his companions, he had appealed to the Monophysite Christians in Abyssinia but that venture, for reasons that we do not entirely understand, seems to have been a disappointment. Now Muhammad himself had discovered that he could not continue to live in Mecca, but it would have been unthinkable for the apostle to the Arabs to leave Arabia. This time he would urge the whole Muslim community to emigrate with him to the newly named oasis of Medina, and he was appealing to the Jewish tribes there for help and support.

In 622 a large party of pilgrims left Medina for Mecca at the time of the *hajj*. Some of these were still pagans, but seventy-three of the men and two of the women were Muslims and they represented the most influential families in Medina. During the journey there was an incident that proved to be strangely prescient. Al-Bara ibn Ma'rar, one of the chiefs of Khasraj, diffidently suggested to the other Muslim pilgrims that for the duration of the *hajj* they should change the *qibla*. They were all straining forward eagerly towards Mecca, where al-Llah had his most important shrine and where most of them were about to meet their Prophet for the first time. It somehow seemed perverse to turn their backs on Mecca when they prayed in order to face Jerusalem. The others felt that Bara was wrong, because as far as they knew Muhammad's *qibla* was Jerusalem and that was good enough for them. Bara stuck to his guns and made Mecca his *qibla* during the journey. But he remained uneasy about this, so after they had arrived he went immediately to the Ka'aba in search of Muhammad and asked his opinion. Muhammad's reply was ambiguous: 'You had a *qibla*, if you had but kept to it.'[25] But he himself still prayed facing Jerusalem and Bara obediently did the same. Later his clansmen remembered Bara's insight. He died shortly after he returned to Medina and it was believed that the intuitions of men who are near to death should be taken very seriously.

During the ritual sojourn in the valley of Mina, there was another meeting in the gully of 'Aqaba, but this time it took place at dead of night. The pledge that they made this year later became known as the Pledge of War: 'We pledged ourselves to war in complete obedience to the apostle, in weal or woe, in ease and hardship and evil circumstances; that we would not wrong anyone; that we would speak the truth at all times; and that in God's service we would fear the censure of none.'[26] The Pledge of War did not mean that Islam had suddenly become an aggressive and martial religion; it was simply required by the step Muhammad was about to take. He was urging his Companions to make a *hijra* or Emigration from Mecca to Medina, but the *hijra* was not just a geographical change. The Muslims of Mecca were about to abandon the Quraysh and accept the permanent protection of a tribe to whom they were not related by blood.[27] It was an unprecedented move and was in its own way as offensive to Arab sensibilities as the denigration of the pagan goddesses. There had always been a system of 'confederation' whereby an individual or a whole clan could become honorary members of another tribe and accept their protection. But this was never a permanent severance; the bonds of blood were a sacred value in Arabia and the basis of society. The very word *hijra* shows that this painful separation was uppermost in the minds of the people who made the decision to migrate to Medina. The first stem of the root-word *HJR*, *hajara-hu*, has been translated: 'he cut himself off from friendly or loving communion or intercourse . . . he ceased . . . to associate with them'.[28] For their part the Muslims of Medina had to promise that they would give protection (*awliya*) and help (*nasr*) on a permanent basis to people who were not kin to them. Henceforth they would be known as the Ansar, the people who gave help (*nasr*) to the Prophet and his Companions. 'Ansar' is usually translated 'the Helpers', but this gives a rather feeble impression of what was involved: *nasr* meant that you had to be ready to back up your 'help' and support with force if necessary. That is why the Muslims of Medina made the Pledge of War.

The Pledge was made secretly. Not only was Muhammad about to take an unheard-of decision for himself and his Meccan Companions, but he was in great danger. Ibn Ishaq stresses the positive aspects of the *hijra* and makes it appear to be a voluntary decision. But the Qu'ran speaks of the Muslims having been 'expelled' or 'driven out' of Mecca.[29] Muhammad seemed to have been aware that people were plotting against his life.[30] Perhaps Mu'tim had given him protection on his return from Taif only on condition that he stopped proselytising. The Qu'ran never speaks of the advantages of the *hijra* but suggests that the Muslims were being compelled to leave against their will. At the meeting during the *hajj* of 622 there was a sense of danger and of bridges being irretrievably burned. The meeting had to be kept secret; the Ansar did not even mention it to their pagan companions on the pilgrimage, in case they gossiped about the projected *hijra* in Mecca and gave the Quraysh an inkling of what was afoot.

On the night of the Pledge, the Ansar left their pagan companions sleeping in their tents and stole 'softly like sandgrouse' to the gully of 'Aqaba, where they met Muhammad accompanied by Abbas.[31] Abbas had not yet converted to Islam but he loved his nephew and the early sources show that he wanted to make sure that Muhammad would be entirely safe in Medina. He began the proceedings by warning the Ansar to think very carefully before pledging 'help' and protection to the Muslims of Quraysh: 'If you think that you can be faithful to what you have promised him and protect him from his opponents, then assume the burden you have undertaken. But if you think that you will betray and abandon him after he has gone out with you, then leave him now.'[32] But the Helpers were ready to stand by their decision. Bara took Muhammad by the hand, as the representative of the Aws and the Khasraj, and swore that the Muslims would give the Prophet exactly the same protection as they gave to their own women and children. But while Bara was speaking, another Helper interrupted: the people of Medina had made other alliances and treaties and if they protected the Meccan Muslims they might have to break some of them. What would happen if Muhammad later abandoned Medina and left its people vulnerable to former allies who would take their revenge? Muhammad smiled and replied: 'I am of you and you are of me. I will war against them that war against you and be at peace with those at peace with you.'[33] Then, as both sides were satisfied, the Helpers made the Pledge of War.

After they had returned to Medina, Muhammad began to persuade the Muslims in Mecca to make the *hijra*. It was an irrevocable and frightening step. Nobody knew how it would work out, because nothing quite like it had ever happened before in Arabia. Muhammad did not command Muslims to emigrate. Anybody who was reluctant or felt it to be beyond his strength was allowed to stay behind. Some important Muslims stayed in Mecca and were never charged with apostasy or cowardice. But during July and August 622 about seventy Muslims set off with their families for Medina, where they were lodged in the houses of the Helpers until they could set up their own homes. The Quraysh do not seem to have made a great effort to detain them, though some women and children were held forcibly and one man was carried back in triumph tied to his camel. But the Muslims were careful not to draw attention to themselves and often agreed to meet up outside the city. They travelled in small, unobtrusive groups. Umar left with his family, Uthman ibn Affan with his wife Ruqayyah, and other members of the Prophet's family went on ahead with Zayd and Hamzah. Muhammad and Abu Bakr stayed behind until everybody had left. But this huge defection soon left disturbing gaps in the city, symbolising the open wound that Muhammad had inflicted on the tribe of Quraysh, so prosperous and united only ten years earlier. Muhammad's cousin Abdallah ibn Jahsh had made the *hijra* with his family and sisters: after they had gone the large Jahsh house in the middle of Mecca was entirely empty. It looked a desolate and portentous sight to Utba ibn Rabi'a, 'with its doors blowing to and fro, empty of inhabitants'.[34]

Then in August Muhammad's protector Mu'tim died. Once again the Prophet's life was in danger. There was a special meeting about him in the Senate from which Abu Lahab carefully absented himself. Some chiefs just wanted to get Muhammad out of the city, but others realised that it could be very dangerous to allow Muhammad to join the other Emigrants. All those who had made the *hijra* were desperate and unprincipled traitors who had broken the sacred bonds of kinship. They would now stop at nothing, and with Muhammad at their head they could threaten the security of Mecca. Abu Jahl eventually came up with a plan which would remove Muhammad without causing a blood-feud. Each clan would choose a strong and well-connected young man as its representative and these youths would all kill Muhammad *together*. This would mean that all the clans were implicated, so that Hashim would have to be content with the blood-money. They would not be able to fight the whole of Quraysh.

The band of young men was soon recruited. They gathered together outside Muhammad's house, but they were disturbed to hear the voices of Sawdah and the Prophet's daughters coming through the windows. It would be shameful to kill a man in the presence of his women, and they decided to wait until he left the house in the morning. One of the conspirators looked through the window and saw Muhammad lying on his bed, wrapped in his cloak. They did not realise that, alerted, it is said, by the angel Gabriel, Muhammad had made his escape through a back window and had left Ali, who had delayed his *hijra* to help Muhammad tidy up his affairs, lying apparently asleep wearing his clothes. When Ali strolled out of the house the next morning, clad in Muhammad's cloak, the young men realised that they had been tricked. The Quraysh offered a reward of a hundred she-camels to anybody who could bring Muhammad back, dead or alive.

Meanwhile, Muhammad and Abu Bakr were hiding in a cave in one of the mountains outside the city. They stayed there for three days. From time to time their supporters slipped out of the city to bring them news and provisions. At one point, tradition has it, a search party actually passed the cave, but did not even bother to look inside: an enormous spider's web covered the entrance, in front of it an acacia tree had sprung up miraculously overnight and in exactly the place where a man would have to put his foot in order to climb into the cave there was a rock-dove, which had obviously been sitting on her eggs for some time. During these three days, Muhammad experienced a deep calm and a strong sense of God's presence. The Qu'ran refers to the experience of the *sakina*, which in Arabic means 'tranquillity' but in this context seems to have been influenced by the Hebrew *Shekinah*, the term for the divine presence on earth.

> God has helped him [Muhammad]
> already, when the unbelievers drove him forth,
> the second of two, when the two were in the Cave,
> when he said to his companion, 'Sorrow not; surely
> God is with us.' Then God sent down on him his *sakina*
> and confirmed him with legions you did not see.[35]

When it seemed safe, Muhammad and Abu Bakr climbed out of the cave, taking care not to disturb the rock-dove, and mounted the two camels that Abu Bakr had provided. Abu Bakr wanted to give the best camel to Muhammad, but he insisted on paying for her: this was his personal *hijra*, his offering to God, so it was important that he made the whole event entirely his own. He called the camel Qaswa and she remained his favourite mount for the rest of his life.

The journey on which they now embarked was extremely dangerous, because it was arguable that while on the road Muhammad was not yet under anybody's formal protection. Their guide took them by a very circuitous route, and they zigzagged back and forth to throw their pursuers off the scent. In the meantime, the Muslims in Medina were anxiously awaiting their arrival. Several of the Emigrants were living in Quba, the southernmost point of the oasis, and every day after the morning prayers they used to climb on to the volcanic rocks near by and scan the horizon. On the morning of 4 September 622 one of the Jews spotted the party and cried out to the Helpers: 'Sons of Qaylah! he is come, he is come!'[36] At once men, women and children surged out to meet the travellers and found them resting under a palm tree.

Muhammad and Abu Bakr stayed in Quba for three days, at the end of which Ali joined them. But the Muslims in the 'city' (as the most densely populated part of the oasis was called) were impatient to see him, so Muhammad set off to meet them and to decide where he was going to live. He was riding Qaswa, who was said to be under divine inspiration, and he gave her her head. Along the way, several people begged him to alight and stay in their houses, but Muhammad courteously refused until at last

Qaswa fell to her knees outside a date-store belonging to two orphan brothers and refused to budge. Muhammad got down, allowed his luggage to be carried into the nearest house and then began to negotiate with the brothers for the sale of their land. Once they had agreed on a proper price, he ordered work to be begun on a mosque, which would also be his family home. All the Muslims got to work, the Emigrants working alongside the Helpers. Not all the Quraysh were used to manual labour and Muhammad's elegant son-in-law Uthman ibn Affan seemed to find it particularly gruelling. As they worked, they sometimes sang verses composed for the occasion:

> O God, no good is but the good hereafter
> So help the Helpers and the Emigrants.[37]

Muhammad used to change the last line to 'So help the Emigrants and the Helpers'. This amendment ruined the rhyme and rhythm; it was a sort of playful demonstration of Muhammad's 'illiteracy': he was no natural poet and his obvious ineptitude showed just how miraculous the Qu'ran must be.

But the Emigrants and the Helpers needed a more formal bond than a song and a shared activity. A treaty was drawn up which, by a stroke of good fortune, has been preserved in the early sources, so we can see the blueprint of the first Islamic community. It stated that Muhammad was entering into a covenant with the Arab and Jewish tribes of Medina. All the different tribes of the oasis were to bury their old enmity and form, as it were, a new super-tribe. The Muslims and the Jews were to live peaceably with the pagans of Medina, as long as they did not make a separate treaty with Mecca in an attempt to get rid of the Prophet. Clause 20 of the Covenant states that 'No pagan is to give protection to any person of Quraysh, either his goods or his person, or take his part against any believer.'[38] God was the head of the community and the only source of security (*dhimma*).[39] As for the Muslims, they formed an entirely new kind of group. All the tribes were 'one community [*umma*] to the exclusion of all other men.'[40] Hitherto the tribe had been the basic unit of society; the *umma*, however, was a community which was based on religion rather than on kinship. This was unprecedented in Arabia. It had not been part of Muhammad's original mandate to form a theocracy – he would probably not have known what a theocracy was. But events had pushed him beyond his original preconceptions into an entirely new solution. For some years now, Islam had been a divisive force in society: Muhammad had been accused of stealing children away from their parents. But until the *hijra* nobody had dreamed of abandoning the tribe of Quraysh. Now the old tribal bonds had been abrogated and the Quraysh, the Aws and the Khasraj formed one *umma*. Islam was beginning to be a force for unity instead of division.

But inevitably the concept of the tribe affected the first Muslims' view of the *umma*. Tribal terms still shaped the way they saw the new community. Thus the Qu'ran:

> Those who believed and made the *hijra*
> and struggled with possessions and persons in the way of God,
> and those who gave their homes and 'helped' [that is, the Ansar]
> these are *awliya* [protectors] of one another.
> To those who believe but did not make the *hijra*
> it is not for you to give 'protection' [*walaya*]
> until they do make *hijra*.
> If they ask you for 'help' in respect for religion
> it is your duty to give 'help' [*nasr*]
> unless it is against a tribe with whom you have a treaty.[41]

To become a member, you had to make the *hijra*, leave your tribe and join the *umma*. Like the tribe, the *umma* was a world unto itself: 'one community to the exclusion of all men',[42] but it would make 'confederates' of other tribes in the conventional way. The unity of the *umma* was to reflect the divine unity, which Muslims were also commanded to build in their own personal lives. No tie of blood, no old tribal allegiance, must stand in the way or be allowed to split the unity of the *umma* into warring camps: no Muslim must fight against another, whatever his tribe. As yet, Muhammad was not the head of the *umma*. He had a very modest status in Medina, which was at the beginning far lower than that of Medinan chiefs like Sa'd ibn Muadh or Ibn Ubbay. The only special function he had was to be an impartial arbiter of disputes between Muslims.

It was a revolutionary solution, but in the early days everybody was ready to try it because the situation in Medina had been impossible and any change seemed preferable to the old incurable warfare. There was no opposition from the pagans. An Arab ascetic called Abu Amir (sometimes known as al-Rahib: the monk) did defect to Mecca after Muhammad had arrived, but after this any pagans who did not convert to Islam kept a low profile. Even Abu Qays converted to Islam and became a good and committed Muslim. The Jews were ready to accept the new system at first and some decided to convert to this new form of Arab monotheism. But Muhammad never asked them to accept his religion of al-Llah unless they particularly wished to convert. There is a passage in the Qu'ran which suggests that the Jews who did convert formed a sort of parallel community, and regarded themselves as Jews first and foremost.[43] They had received a perfectly authentic revelation of their own and, in Qu'ranic terms, there was no need for them to accept Islam. So at first everything looked hopeful and there was even a convert who was not an Arab at all. While the mosque was being built a Persian slave called Salman, owned by one of the Jews of the Bani Qurayzah, presented himself to Muhammad and told him his story. He had been born near Isfahan, had converted to Christianity and had travelled to Syria, where he had heard stories about the prophet who was to arise in Arabia. On his way to the Hijaz he had been taken prisoner and, providentially, brought to Medina. Salman would become a revered figure in Islam: he is usually seen as the forerunner of all the non-Arab Oriental peoples who put their talents at the service of Islam.

In April 623, about seven months after the *hijra*, the mosque was finished. It was built of brick, but in the northern wall facing Jerusalem a niche surrounded by stone marked the *qibla*, the direction of prayer. There was a large courtyard for the formal prayers. At first people used to turn up for prayer without a summons, but this was obviously unsatisfactory as everybody came at different times. Muhammad thought of using a ram's horn, like the Jews, or a wooden clapper, like the Oriental Christians, but one of the Emigrants had a dream: a man wearing a green cloak told him that the best way of summoning people to prayer was to have a man with a resonant voice call the people by crying 'al-Llahu Akbar!' (God is greater) three times to remind the Muslims that God is higher than any other good. The summons should continue thus: 'I bear witness that there is no God but al-Llah, I bear witness that Muhammad is the apostle of God. Come to prayer. Come to prayer. Come to divine service. Come to divine service. *al-Llahu Akbar. al-Llahu Akbar.* There is no god but al-Llah.' Muhammad liked the idea and appointed Bilal, Abu Bakr's freedman, as the obvious candidate. Every morning Bilal used to climb up to the top of the tallest house near the mosque, and sit on the rooftop waiting for dawn. When he saw it come, he used to stretch out his arms, before beginning the call, and say, 'O God, I praise Thee and ask Thy help for Quraysh that they may accept Thy religion.'[44]

Muhammad had no apartment of his own at the mosque, but two small buildings were attached to the eastern wall, one for Sawdah and one for Aisha. Later each of his wives would have her own room built on to the mosque and Muhammad would stay with each in turn. Once the mosque was ready, he sent Zayd to bring the women of his household, who were still in Mecca, to their new home. Zayd returned with Sawdah, Umm Kulthum and Fatimah, Muhammad's daughters (Zaynab had stayed behind with her pagan husband Abu al-As) and his own wife Umm Ayman. He was also accompanied by the last members of Abu Bakr's family to make the *hijra*: Abdallah, his son, Umm Ruman, his wife, and his daughters Asma and Aisha.

Once the women arrived, there were weddings. Muhammad decided that Zayd should have another wife who was nearer to his own age than Umm Ayman, and asked Abdallah ibn Jahsh on his behalf for the hand of his beautiful sister Zaynab, who was not at all pleased with the idea. The short, dark and snub-nosed Zayd was not a very attractive young man, and Zaynab had higher amibitions, as we shall see. But she agreed when she saw that it really was Muhammad's wish. Abu Bakr also married his daughter Asma to Muhammad's cousin Zubayr ibn al-Awwam, to bind him closer still to the Prophet's family.

Finally, about a month after she had arrived in Mecca, it was decided that it was time for the wedding of Muhammad with Aisha. She was still only nine years old, so there was no wedding feast and the ceremonial was kept to a minimum. Indeed, it was so low-key that on the day itself Aisha had no idea that she was going to be married and was playing with her friends on a see-saw. Abu Bakr had bought some fine red-striped cloth from Bahrein and this had been made into a wedding dress for her. Then they took her to her little apartment beside the mosque. There Muhammad was waiting for her, and he laughed and smiled while they decked her with jewellery and ornaments and combed her long hair. Eventually a bowl of milk was brought in and Muhammad and Aisha both drank from it. The marriage made little difference to Aisha's life. Tabari says that she was so young that she stayed in her parents' home and the marriage was consummated there later when she had reached puberty. Aisha went on playing with her girlfriends and her dolls. Sometimes Muhammad used to come to see her, and, Aisha says, the little girls 'would steal out of the house and he would go out after them and bring them back, for he was pleased for my sake to have them there'. Muhammad had enjoyed playing with his own daughters when they were small and he sometimes joined Aisha's games. One day, she remembered, 'the Prophet came in while I was playing with my dolls and he said, "O Aisha, whatever game is this?" I said: "It is Solomon's horses," and he laughed.'[45]

But Aisha became aware of a sadness in the *umma*. One day she found her father and his two freedmen, Amir and Bilal, lying on the ground sick with the fever that afflicted many of the Emigrants when they first arrived in Yathrib. All three were delirious and Bilal was lying by himself in a corner singing in his stentorian tones a song of homesickness for Mecca:

> Shall I ever spend a night again in Fakhkh
> With sweet herbs and thyme around me?
> Will the day dawn when I come down to the waters of Majanna,
> Shall I ever see Shama and Tafil again?[46]

Aisha ran straight to Muhammad. He was aware of the pain and dislocation that the Emigrants suffered. He reassured Aisha but added this prayer: 'O God make Medina as dear to us as Mecca, or even dearer.'[47] He was becoming aware of a more serious problem among the Helpers. Not all the new converts of Medina were totally committed; they had embraced Islam for the sake of expediency, not out of conviction. To them, conversion seemed to have become an irreversible trend and they did not want to get left behind, but for the time being they were just sitting on the fence, waiting to see what would happen to the new venture. These malcontents had gathered round Abdallah ibn Ubbay, who would probably have become the King of Medina if Muhammad had not arrived. Ibn Ubbay had become a Muslim, but he was obviously far from enthusiastic, and was hoping to hijack the movement if it ran into trouble. The second sura, the longest in the Qu'ran, was revealed during the first few months in Medina and shows Muhammad's awareness of the difficulty.[48] For the time being Muhammad was patient with Ibn Ubbay; he gave him an honoured place in the mosque and every Friday he was allowed to address the people during the weekly service. In return, he was usually polite to Muhammad, but sometimes his hostility came to the surface. After one unpleasant incident, one of the Helpers took Muhammad aside and begged: 'Don't be hard on him, for before God sent you to us we were making a diadem to crown him, and by God he thinks you have robbed him of a kingdom.'[49]

At first the Jews, like the malcontent Arabs, had been prepared to give Muhammad the benefit of the doubt, especially since he seemed so clearly inclined towards Judaism. But eventually they joined Ibn Ubbay and turned against Islam. They started to assemble in the mosque during services to 'listen to the stories of the Muslims and laugh and scoff at their religion.'[50] It was very easy for them, with their superior knowledge of scripture, to ridicule some of the Qu'ran's stories about the various prophets, which differed markedly from the Biblical version. They vociferously refused to accept Muhammad as a genuine prophet and jeeringly exclaimed how odd it was that a man who was supposed to have revelations from God could not even find his camel when it went missing.[51] These snide criticisms upset the Muslims so much that fighting often broke out and there were disreputable scenes in which the Jews were forcibly ejected from the mosque after some particularly vicious jibe. They had solid religious grounds for their rejection. They had been expecting a Messiah but believed that the era of prophecy was now over. No Jew or Christian at this time would claim to be a prophet any more than he would claim to be an angel or a patriarch. But there was also a precedent for the Jews of Medina to accept Muhammad, because

Judaism had a long tradition of welcoming 'Godfearers' into the synagogue. Such people did not observe the full Law of Moses but were regarded as friends and associates, and the Muslims would have seemed obvious candidates for such an alliance. But when the Jews realised how dramatically their own position had declined in Medina since Muhammad's arrival, they vehemently rejected him.

Muhammad's rejection by the Jews was probably the greatest disappointment of his life and one which challenged his whole religious position. But there were friendly Jews in Medina who taught him how to answer their fellows on their own terms by giving him important information about the scriptures. The Qu'ranic polemic against the Jews is well developed and shows how disturbing their criticism must have been, but with his enhanced knowledge Muhammad was able to rebut their damning comments. In their own scriptures, the Jews are called a faithless people, who had broken their covenant with God when they had relapsed into idolatry and worshipped the Golden Calf;[52] they had made an unwarranted 'innovation' when they had introduced the Oral Law;[53] time and again they had failed to listen to the warnings of their prophets.[54] Muhammad also learned about the chronology of Jewish history and discovered that the Jews and the Christians, whom he had previously thought belonged to one religion, in fact had serious disagreements. To outsiders like the Arabs there seemed little to choose between the two positions and it was natural to imagine that both of the People of the Book must have added some new, inauthentic elements to the original pure revelation. His quarrel with the Jews did not affect Muhammad's relations with Christianity. Sometimes indeed the Qu'ran sides with the Christians against the Jews, as when it answers the Jews' claim that they had crucified Jesus with the Docetist answer that Jesus had not really died at all on the Cross: what had seemed to die was only a simulacrum.[55] But the Qu'ran does find it scandalous that Christians should claim that God had sired a Son: it was not likely that Muhammad, who had suffered so much because of his refusal to accept that God had had daughters, would be sympathetic to this doctrine. Again and again, the Qu'ran asserts that this belief is an example of *zanna*, that idle, divisive speculation about things which nobody could possibly know but which had split the People of the Book into two warring camps.[56]

Nevertheless, Muhammad still held that his revelation was at one with the earlier revelations to the older prophets. Not all the Jews were hostile, and he insisted that despite their present troubles Muslims must emphasise the things they had in common with the People of the Book. It is also likely that Muhammad believed that not *all* Christians subscribed to the scandalous idea that God had had a Son. Muslims had a quarrel only with those Jews and Christians who were ill disposed to the Qu'ran or who had introduced unacceptable innovations into the pure religion:

> Dispute not with the People of the Book
> save in the fairer manner, except for
> those of them that do wrong; and say,
> 'We believe in what has been sent down
> to us, and what has been sent down to you;
> our God and your God is One, and to Him
> we have surrendered.'[57]

Even though the dispute with the three main Jewish tribes of Yathrib would grow much worse, this remained official Muslim policy.

In Medina Muhammad learned more about Abraham. With his new chronological knowledge of salvation history, he could see that it was important that Abraham had lived before either Moses or Jesus. It was therefore logical to assume that the followers of Moses and Jesus, who seemed to be locked in a fruitless debate, had both somehow introduced unhelpful innovations into the pure faith of Abraham, who had lived before either the Torah or the Gospel:

> Abraham in truth was not a Jew,
> neither a Christian; but one who surrendered himself [*muslīm*]
> and one of pure faith [*hanif*]; certainly he was never
> of the idolaters.
> Surely the people standing closest to Abraham
> are those who followed him, and this Prophet,
> and those who believe; and God is the Protector
> of the believers.[58]

In Mecca, Moses had been the favourite prophet of the Muslims; in Medina his place was taken by Abraham, and Muhammad had found a perfect answer to the jibes of the Jews. He and his Muslims were returning to the spirit of pure faith (*hanifiyyah*) of the man who had been the first *muslīm* to surrender to God. We do not know how far Muhammad had subscribed to the desire of some Arabs in the settled countries to return to Abraham's religion; there is no mention of the little Meccan *hanifiyyah* sect in the Qu'ran and little interest in Abraham before the Medinan suras. At this period, however, it seems that the Muslims called their faith the *hanifiyyah*, the pure religion followed by Abraham.

Muhammad had therefore found a way of rebutting the Jews without abandoning his central belief that faith meant surrender to God, not to a particular mundane expression of that faith. Indeed, his new appreciation of the importance of Abraham enabled him to deepen that perception. The Jews and the Christians who urged people to accept their particular revelations to the exclusion of all others were departing from the primordial revelation to Abraham and the pristine message of the earlier prophets who had all confirmed each other's insights:

> Say you: 'We believe in God, and
> in that which has been sent down on us
> and sent down on Abraham, Ishmael,
> Isaac and Jacob and the Tribes,
> and that which was given to Moses and Jesus
> and the Prophets, of their Lord; we
> make no division between any of them, and
> to Him we surrender.'[59]

It was surely 'idolatry' to prefer a human expression of the faith to God Himself. Revelations did not cancel out the messages of earlier prophets; they confirmed and continued them.

The mention of Ishmael, Abraham's elder son, is crucial in this list of great prophets. The friendly Arabian Jews told him the story of Ishmael for the first time and added some local legends of their own.[60] In the book of Genesis, Muhammad now learned, it was said that Abraham had had a son by his concubine Hagar whose name was Ishmael ('God has heard'). But when Sarah bore Isaac, she became jealous of Hagar and Ishmael and insisted that Abraham get rid of them. Abraham was grieved to lose his son, but God promised him that Ishmael would also be the father of a great nation. So Abraham sadly sent Hagar and his son into the wilderness and Ishmael grew up a wild man and a great warrior.[61] The Arabian Jews believed that Ishmael had become the ancestor of the Arabs and it was said that Abraham had brought Hagar and her son to the valley of Mecca and abandoned them there, and that God had taken care of them. Later, Abraham had visited Ishmael in Mecca and together they had built the Ka'aba, the first temple of God in Arabia. The Arabs were therefore sons of Abraham like the Jews.

This must have been music to Muhammad's ears. It gave a new significance to the Ka'aba, and showed that God had not forgotten the Arabs, who had been part of His plan since the earliest days. The Qu'ran shows Abraham and Ishmael praying that God would send a prophet to the Arabs after they had finished building His House.[62] Muhammad was bringing the Arabs the Book; now he would bring them a distinctively Arab faith, rooted in the sanctities of his ancestors.

Once it became clear that the enmity of most of the Jews was permanent, the new religion of al-Llah formally declared its independence of the older faith. In late January 624, during the month of Sha'ban, about eighteen months after the *hijra*, Muhammad was leading the Friday prayers in a mosque built in the territory of the clan of the late Bara ibn Mu'rar – a significant detail. Suddenly, inspired by a special revelation, Muhammad made the whole congregation turn round and pray facing Mecca instead of Jerusalem. God had given the Muslims a new focus and a new direction (*qibla*) for their prayer:

> We have seen thee turning thy face about
> in the heaven; now We will surely turn thee
> to a direction [*qibla*] which shall satisfy thee.
> Turn thy face towards the Holy Mosque; and
> wherever you are, turn your faces towards it.[63]

The change of the *qibla* has been called Muhammad's most creative religious gesture. In turning towards Mecca, Muslims were tacitly declaring that they belonged to none of the established communities, but were turning only towards God Himself. In prostrating themselves in the direction of the Ka'aba, which was independent of the two older revelations responsible for splitting up the one religion of God into warring sects, they were reverting to the primordial faith of the man who had built it:

> Those who have made division in their religion
> and become sects, thou art not of them in
> anything; their affair is unto God, then
> He will tell them what they have been doing. . . .
>
> Say: 'As for me, my Lord has guided me
> to a straight path, a right religion,
> the creed of Abraham, a man of pure faith [*hanif*];
> he was no idolater.'
> Say: 'My prayer, my ritual sacrifice,
> my living, my dying – all belongs to God,
> the Lord of all being.
> No associate has He. Even so I have been
> commanded, and I am the first of those
> that surrender.'
> Say: 'Shall I seek after a lord other
> than God, who is the Lord of all things?'[64]

To prefer a human system to God Himself was idolatry (*shirk*) and Muslims must make God, not a religious establishment or tradition, the central focus of their lives.

The Qu'ran was, of course, right that the Muslims would prefer this *qibla* to the *qibla* of Jerusalem. Emigrants and Helpers alike were devoted to the Ka'aba – it was no accident that Muhammad had first met the Helpers during the *hajj*. Now they did not have to feel that they were the poor relations of the two older religions, following lamely in their footsteps. They had their own orientation, which was independent of the religions that had unfortunate imperialistic associations for the Arabs. Their enthusiasm for Mecca was one more factor that would draw the Helpers and Emigrants together into a common *umma*, and the Emigrants would find that it assuaged the painful dislocation of the *hijra*.

The change of *qibla* was a sign of a proud new Muslim identity. Muslims were gradually assuming a common identity that was beginning to bond them even though they came from three separate tribes. They all rose at the same time when Bilal issued the call to prayer; all broke off their work together at midday and in the evening to make the *salat*. The alms reminded them of their common responsibility for the poor. Now, wherever they were, they would all prostrate themselves three times a day in the direction of Mecca, an orientation that all felt passionately attached to. But this new independence was made at a time when the Muslims were in an embattled position, surrounded by enemies on all sides. The Jews of Medina were very quick to interpret the change of *qibla* as an act of defiance. They became even more determined to get rid of Muhammad, and at this time too the community at Medina was expecting an attack from the powerful city of Mecca.

8 · Holy War

Muhammad has been a familiar figure up to this point. Having endured years of persecution and defeat, he has been a prophet unrecognised in his own country. It is an image which those of us who have been brought up in the Christian tradition can understand and respect. But after the *hijra* Muhammad became a spectacular success, politically as well as spiritually, and the Christian West has always distrusted this aspect of his career. Because he became a brilliant and charismatic political leader who not only transformed Arabia but changed the history of the world, his critics in Europe have dismissed him as an impostor who used religion as a means to power. Because the Christian world is dominated by the image of the crucified Jesus, who said that his kingdom was not of this world, we tend to see failure and humiliation as the hallmark of a religious leader. We do not expect our spiritual heroes to achieve a dazzling success in mundane terms.[1]

In particular we tend to find it scandalous and even wicked that Muhammad had to fight his way to peace, power and victory. Islam has been dubbed the religion of the sword, a faith which has abandoned true spirituality by sanctifying violence and intolerance. It is an image that has dogged Islam in the Christian West ever since the Middle Ages, even though Christians were fighting their own holy wars in the Middle East at this time. Today popular books and television programmes frequently sport titles like Rage of Islam, Sword of Islam, Sacred Rage or Holy Terror. But this is a distortion of the truth. Each religion has its own particular genius, a special insight that characterises its quest for an ultimate meaning and value. Christianity is supremely a religion of suffering and adversity and, in the West at least, it has always been at its best during periods of distress. The centuries of persecution in the early days of the Church reinforced the image of Christ crucified and made a profound impression on the Christian spirit. From the start, therefore, Christians felt that they had to reject 'the world',[2] so defiance or dissociation from the political establishment naturally became a virtue in the age of the martyrs. Suffering and dying for Christ became the supreme religious experience and it was a graphic demonstration of the Christians' rejection by the earthly powers. The Christian idea that man can be deified and transformed by suffering is inspiring and it has brought consolation to millions of desperate people. But it has also been abused: Christians have been told that they have a duty to endure oppression and injustice; that God supported a hierarchical order in which the rich man sat in his palace while the poor man sat at its gate; that suffering and persecution in this world will be rewarded in heaven. Even today Christian fundamentalists are being encouraged by certain sectors of the American establishment to preach such a gospel in Central and Southern America. But there are also Christians there who feel it their duty to live alongside the oppressed and the destitute and engage in a dedicated struggle for a just and decent society. It is in this light that we should consider the Islamic *jihad*, which Westerners usually translate as 'holy war'.

In the Christian tradition, therefore, there is a strong tendency to see political activity as extrinsic to the religious life: Christians have not generally seen earthly success as a spiritual triumph.[3] In Europe we have gradually evolved an ideal which separates Church and state and we usually blame Islam for 'confusing' two areas that are essentially distinct. But the Christian experience should not prejudice us against other cultural and religious traditions which have developed under different conditions. When Muhammad brought his revelation to his people, Arabia was outside the civilised world and its political and social order was disintegrating. Christianity, however, came to birth in the Roman empire, which imposed, however brutally, a certain peace and social security. Jesus and St Paul did not have to worry about the social and political order because it was already set up. Indeed, Paul's long missionary journeys would have been impossible outside the *pax Romana*: in Arabia an unprotected man could be killed with impunity on the road. Eventually Christianity became the official religion of the empire in the early fourth century, but the new Christian establishment did not feel that they had to create an entirely new political order: they simply baptised the old Roman law and institutions. Politics, therefore, remained a separate sphere.

Unlike Jesus, however, Muhammad did not have the luxury of being born 'when all the world was at peace'.[4] He was born into the bloodbath of seventh-century Arabia where the old values were being radically undermined and nothing adequate had yet appeared to take their place. At first Muhammad had insisted that he had no political function, even though, like the Hebrew prophets, he preached a message of social justice. But events which he could not have foreseen had impelled him to take up a new challenge when he was invited to emigrate to Medina. Perhaps he had already begun to conceive an ideal of Arab unity in which tribe would no longer fight tribe but would be joined in a new kind of community.

There was an urgent need for a new political solution and in the seventh century such a solution would inevitably be religious. But at the time of the *hijra* Muhammad had no definite vision and no concerted policy through which he hoped to achieve a fully articulated objective. He never formed those kind of grand schemes but responded to each new event as it occurred. This was essential. He was gradually moving towards the unknown and unprecedented and any clearly defined ideas and policies would inevitably belong in some sense to the old decaying order. Above all, God remained his first priority.

After the *hijra* to Medina, the Qu'ran changes as Muhammad begins to take more and more decisions of a political or social nature. The poetry of incoherence, the suras that stammer ineffable truths, are replaced by more practical verses, laying down new legislation or commenting on the current political situation. But this does not mean, as some of his Western critics have suggested, that Muhammad's pure vision had been contaminated by a lust for power. Whatever the Qu'ran is discussing, the transcendent point of reference is kept vividly before the mind. It has been said that there is not a single Qu'ranic concept that is not theocentric: it remains strikingly God-centred. At each point, the Qu'ran presents Muslims with the great challenge: are they going to surrender to God's will in faith or fall back on their own limited viewpoint? However mundane some of the statements may seem in translation, in the original Arabic a tone of grandeur is maintained. The music and word-order all help to elevate some of the more prosaic imagery – of the market, for example, when it speaks of striking a good bargain with God – and subsumes it into the divine order. Integration remains the chief experience: when Muslims listen to a short passage, they are reminded of the whole. The constantly repeated phrases and allusions, which can seem so tedious in translation, bring other passages to mind and help to concentrate the mind on the essential point. As Muhammad became more and more of a statesman, he was in the deepest sense still inspired and he was gradually evolving a solution that would bring peace to the Arabs.

But, even though he took on a political role later in his career, his social message was integral to his religious vision and was not something tacked on as an afterthought. When they were urged by the Qu'ran to contemplate God's 'signs' in the natural world, Muslims were cultivating a sense of divine order. Fish, birds, animals, flowers, mountains and winds do not have a choice about whether or not they submit to the divine plan: they express God's will for them in each moment of their existence. Without having to make a personal decision, they are thus natural *muslīms* who surrender to God's will and thereby achieve their potential. Man alone was given the gift and the terrible responsibility of free will. In a wonderful passage in the Qu'ran, God is shown offering freedom to all His other creatures, but they refuse it. Only man had the temerity to accept:

> We offered the trust to the heavens and the earth
> and the mountains, but they refused to carry it
> and were afraid of it; and man carried it. Surely
> he is sinful, very foolish.[5]

But God did not leave mankind without guidance. He sent innumerable prophets to every people on the face of the earth, so that they knew what He had intended for them. But ever since Adam, the first Prophet, people had refused to listen to these revelations of God's will. They had either failed to grasp the message or could not implement it in their daily lives. Consequently, time and again, their societies crashed around their ears because they were not constructed in the way things ought to be. The Qu'ran shows one people after another refusing to obey even the simplest commands of their prophets.[6] Instead, they perversely exploited the natural world for their own selfish purposes and made themselves the centre of the universe. Because they would not accept the divine blueprint for human behaviour, they destroyed the 'natural' order, just as the seas would cause havoc and chaos if they suddenly refused to keep within their due bounds. But the Quraysh had refused to listen to their prophet, so their society was doomed. Muhammad preached an imminent catastrophe not because he imagined God hurling a thunderbolt on Mecca in a fit of divine pique, but because the Quraysh were insisting on perverting the true order.

But all was not lost. God had given the people of Medina a chance to listen to their own Arabic Qu'ran and in the oasis Muhammad would manage to build a society constructed according to God's plan. Some of the prophets had been more successful than others: Abraham had managed to convince a significant number of people that there was only one God, and Moses and Jesus had both been able to persuade the People of the Book to implement the Torah and the Gospel. Muhammad would also persuade not only the people of Medina but ultimately most people in Arabia to join his new *umma*, and Muslims would come to see him as the most successful of the prophets. They date their era, not from the birth of Muhammad nor from the year of the first revelations (there was, after all, nothing new about these), but from the year of the *hijra*, because this was when Muslims began to incarnate the divine plan in human history.

This would involve them in an intensely dangerous struggle. Muhammad had arrived in Medina in September 622 as a refugee who had narrowly escaped death. He would continue to be in mortal danger for the next five years, and during this time the *umma* faced the possibility of extermination. In the West we often imagine Muhammad as a warlord, brandishing his sword in order to impose Islam on a reluctant world by force of arms. The reality was quite different. Muhammad and the first Muslims were fighting for their lives and they had also undertaken a project in which violence was inevitable. No radical social and political change has ever been achieved without bloodshed, and, because Muhammad was living in a period of confusion and disintegration, peace could be achieved only by the sword. Muslims look back on their Prophet's years in Medina as a Golden Age, but they were also years of sorrow, terror and bloodshed. The *umma* was able to put an end to the dangerous violence of Arabia only by means of a relentless effort.

The Qu'ran began to urge the Muslims of Medina to participate in a *jihad*. This would involve fighting and bloodshed, but the root *JHD* implies more than a 'holy war'. It signifies a physical, moral, spiritual and intellectual effort. There are plenty of Arabic words denoting armed combat, such as *harb* (war), *sira'a* (combat), *ma'araka* (battle) or *qital* (killing), which the Qu'ran could easily have used if war had been the Muslims' principal way of engaging in this effort. Instead it chooses a vaguer, richer word with a wide range of connotations. The *jihad* is not one of the five pillars of Islam. It is not the central prop of the religion, despite the common Western view. But it was and remains a duty for Muslims to commit themselves to a struggle on all fronts – moral, spiritual and political – to create a just and decent society, where the poor and vulnerable are not exploited, in the way that God had intended man to live. Fighting and warfare might sometimes be necessary, but it was only a minor part of the whole *jihad* or struggle. A well-known tradition (*hadith*) has Muhammad say on returning from a battle, 'We return from the little *jihad* to the greater *jihad*,' the more difficult and crucial effort to conquer the forces of evil in oneself and in one's own society in all the details of daily life.

As soon as the Muslims undertook the *hijra* they knew that they would have to be prepared to fight. The Helpers had made the Pledge of War at Second 'Aqaba and shortly after his arrival in Mecca Muhammad received a revelation giving the Emigrants permission to fight too:

> Leave is given to those who fight because
> they were wronged – surely God is able
>   to help them –
> who were expelled from their homes
> unjustly, because they said
> 'Our Lord is God.' Had God not driven back
> the people, some by the means of others,
> there had been destroyed cloisters and churches,

> oratories and mosques, wherein God's Name
> is much mentioned.

The Qu'ran was beginning to evolve a theology of the just war: it might sometimes be necessary to fight to preserve decent values. Unless religious people had sometimes been ready to ward off attack, all their places of worship (for example) would have been destroyed. God will give the Muslims victory only if they 'perform the prayer, and pay the alms', make just and honourable laws and create an equitable society.[7]

This revelation refers only to the Emigrants, who had been wronged by the Quraysh when they had been driven from their homes in Mecca: the Helpers were not yet given leave to participate in the fighting, because they had no official quarrel with Mecca. But the revelation should not be taken to imply that Muhammad was envisaging a full-scale war with Mecca at this early stage. That would have been pure madness. He had a much more modest offensive in mind: the *ghazu* or raid which had long been a sort of national sport in Arabia and an accepted way of making ends meet when times were hard. The Emigrants had very few opportunities of earning a living in Medina. They were mostly bankers, financiers and merchants and knew next to nothing about date-farming, even if there had been any land available for them to begin their own agricultural ventures. They were dependent on the Helpers for their livelihood and would become a drain on the *umma* unless they found an independent source of income. Not everybody could do what the brilliant young merchant Abd al-Rahman had done on arrival in Medina: he had simply asked his way to the market and had quickly created an income for himself by dint of successful buying and selling. There was very little opportunity for trade in Medina, and Mecca had the monopoly of large-scale business ventures.

The *ghazu* had been a rough and ready way of securing a fair circulation of the available wealth during the nomadic period. Raiders would invade the territory of an enemy tribe and capture their camels, cattle and other goods, taking care to avoid bloodshed and a consequent vendetta. Medina was ideally placed to attack the Meccan caravans, often guarded by only a few merchants, on their way to and from Syria, so in the year 623 Muhammad despatched two raiding parties of Emigrants to attack the caravans. He did not go himself at first but entrusted the expeditions to men like Hamzah or the experienced warrior Ubaydah ibn al-Harith. Nobody in Arabia would have been disedified by these raids, though they might have been surprised that the Muslims had the temerity to attack their powerful kinsmen. The early raids of 623 were not very successful. It was difficult to get accurate information about the movement of the caravans; no goods were seized and there was no fighting. But the

Meccans would have been rattled and irritated. They would have had to take precautions that had never been necessary before, and the Bedouin tribes along the Red Sea coast (the preferred trade route) would have been impressed by the Muslims' pluck. Even though the early raiders failed to attack the caravans, they made treaties with tribes at various strategic points along the road. In September 623 Muhammad himself decided to lead a *ghazu* against a large caravan led by Ummayah of Jumah (Abu Bakr's old tormentor). It consisted of 2,500 camels and, because the spoils looked so promising, about 200 Muslims volunteered to go along too. But, yet again, the caravan eluded the Muslims and there was no fighting.

In the winter months the Quraysh only sent their caravans south, into the Yemen and no longer had to pass Medina. But to show them that he meant business Muhammad sent a small raiding party of nine men under the leadership of his cousin Abdallah ibn Jahsh to attack one of the southbound caravans. It was the end of the sacred month of Rajab (January 624) and all fighting was strictly forbidden throughout Arabia. Muhammad gave Abdallah sealed instructions which were not to be opened until the expedition had been on the road for two days and he made him promise not to put any pressure on his companions: they were going closer to Mecca than any previous raiding expedition and it was likely to be dangerous.

Abdallah duly opened the letter two days later. The sources give different versions of the text. Ibn Ishaq says that the Muslims were told to go to Nakhlah, between Mecca and Taif, and simply spy on the caravan, but the ninth-century historian Muhammad ibn Umar al-Waqidi claims that the letter said: 'Go to the valley of Nakhlah and set an ambush for the Quraysh.'[8] This meant that the Muslim raiders would have to violate the sacred month. Muhammad probably had few scruples about this: these holy months were part of a pagan system that he was trying to overcome. To violate them was on a par with denigrating the goddesses. But two of the raiders may have wished to extricate themselves from the expedition, because they lost their camel at the next stopping place and told the other seven to go ahead without them. When Abdallah and his party arrived at Nakhlah, they found a small caravan camped nearby. What should they do? It was the last day of Rajab but if they waited until the next day, when fighting was permitted, the caravan would have reached the safety of the Meccan sanctuary. They decided to attack. Their first arrow killed one of the three merchants and the others immediately surrendered. Abdallah took the two men and their merchandise back with him to Medina.

But instead of greeting them as conquering heroes the people of Medina were horrified when they heard that the raid had violated the sacred month. As we have seen, the Arabs of Medina had not been disturbed by Muhammad's abolition of the cult of the goddesses. The Jews had prepared them for the monotheistic vision and they were quite ready to let that part of their pagan religion go. But they clearly felt passionate about the sacred months: they were not prepared to abandon this religious value. Muhammad, therefore, repudiated the raid and refused to accept any booty. While this might sound a rather cynical move, it seems that it was not a piece of cold-blooded, hypocritical expediency, although it was pragmatic. Muhammad would brook no compromise about the essentials: he had put all the Muslims in danger in Mecca by refusing a monolatrous solution to the conflict with the Quraysh. He was creating this reformed religion of al-Llah slowly, step by step, as events unfolded. He had no clear, detailed picture of the religion at the outset and, as he was working alone without the help of an established tradition, he often had to feel his way forward by means of trial and error. He had been quite ready to jettison the sacred months: they did not seem an essential religious value to him and we must remember that pagan practice and enthusiasms probably differed widely throughout Arabia. He was unlikely to have had any idea that the Medinans felt so strongly about this pagan practice and, when he saw the distress of the Helpers when the raiding-party returned, he realised that he had unwittingly trampled on their religious sensibilities. There was no point in holding obstinately to his course. If the people wanted to keep the sacred months they should be allowed to do so, because there was nothing in this practice that offended his religion of the one God.

Abdallah and his companions were deeply depressed when Muhammad repudiated the raid: it seemed that they had made the wrong decision and some believed that their very salvation was in jeopardy. Muhammad had a duty to console them and, yet again feeling his way forward, he used the incident to take his theology of the just war one step forward. Yes, it had been wrong to fight in the holy months, but there were worse crimes than that. To oppress people, as the Quraysh had persecuted the Muslims, violating a most sacred Arab value by ejecting them from their tribe, was far more serious. Sometimes a man of God had a duty to fight such manifest wrong.

> They will question thee concerning
> the holy month, and fighting in it.
> Say: 'Fighting in it is a heinous thing,
> but to bar people from God's way, disbelief in Him
> and the Holy Mosque, and to expel its people
> from it – that is more heinous in God's sight;
> and persecution is more heinous than slaying.[9]

This revelation eased the situation: the Jews continued to fulminate but the Helpers and the raiding-party were both reassured. Muhammad was able to divide the spoils among the Emigrants and he began negotiations with the Quraysh for an exchange of prisoners: he would release the two Meccan merchants in exchange for two Muslims who were still in Mecca but wanted to make the *hijra*. But Hakam ibn Kaysar, one of the Qurayshi captives, was so impressed by what he saw in Medina that he decided to remain and become a Muslim.

This incident is a good example of Muhammad's way of working. He was ready to die for his faith, but was also ready to compromise on inessentials. In the absence of a long-established ethical system, he would listen carefully to events and see them as a revelation of God's will – an important principle of historical monotheism. He had not expected the raid to cause such a storm of protest, but when it did he believed that God was showing him something important. The incident had caused him to formulate a principle which has been important in Islam. Muslims respect the pacifist message of Jesus (even though the Qu'ran points out that Christians can be very belligerent)[10] but they accept that force is sometimes necessary. If tyrants and loathsome regimes were not opposed militarily, evil would have swamped the whole world. Even the prophets had sometimes been compelled to fight and kill, as David, with God's help, had slain Goliath:

> Had God not driven back
> the people, some by the means of others,
> the earth had surely been corrupted; but God is bounteous
> unto all beings.[11]

Most Christians would agree with this conception of a just war, recognising that against a Hitler or a Ceausescu fighting and armed combat is the only effective way. Instead of being a pacifist religion that turns the other cheek, therefore, Islam fights tyranny and injustice. A Muslim may feel that he has a sacred duty to champion the weak and the oppressed. Today when Muslims call for a *jihad* against their enemies, they are usually responding to this Qu'ranic ideal.[12]

The Emigrants could now expect a blood-feud because the Quraysh would be bound to avenge the slaying at Nakhlah, but the Muslims were becoming more confident. A few weeks later during the month of Ramadan (March 624), Muhammad led a large army to the coast in order to intercept a Meccan caravan that Abu Sufyan was bringing back from Syria. This was one of the most important caravans of the year and 350 Muslims had volunteered, of whom 70 were Emigrants and the rest Helpers. The expedition rode to the Well of Badr near the Red Sea, where one of the great Arab fairs was held each year. Here they hoped to waylay the caravan. The expedition of Badr was to be one of the most crucial and formative events in the early history of Islam, but nobody was expecting it to be particularly important. It was just another *ghazu*, and several deeply committed Muslims stayed at home, including Muhammad's son-in-law, Uthman ibn Affan, whose wife Ruqayyah was dangerously ill.

Indeed, it looked as though the caravan would escape as usual. Abu Sufyan was a highly intelligent and capable man and he quickly got wind of the Muslim enterprise by questioning people on the road. Instead of taking the usual route across the Hijaz to Mecca, he turned sharp right towards the coast and despatched Damdam, a member of the local tribe of Ghifar, to ride to Mecca with all speed to get help. Damdam made a dramatic entrance. Abbas, Muhammad's uncle, remembered how the whole city had seemed to freeze in horror when they heard:

> the voice of Damdam crying out in the bottom of the *wadi*; as he stood upon his camel, having cut its nose, turned its saddle round, rent his shirt, while he was saying, 'O Quraysh, the transport camels! the transport camels! Muhammad and his companions are lying in wait for your property which is with Abu Sufyan. I do not think that you will overtake it. Help! Help!'[13]

The Quraysh were outraged. Did Muhammad think that he would be able to capture the biggest caravan of the year as easily as he had ambushed the little one at Nakhlah? All the leading men prepared themselves for battle. Even the elderly and corpulent Ummayah ibn Khalaf was crammed into his armour. Abu Lahab was allowed to stay behind, but Abbas rode out against his nephew, with Talib and Aqil (the two sons of Abu Talib who had not embraced Islam), and Hakim ibn Hizam, Khadija's nephew, joined the army. That evening about a thousand men marched out of Mecca and took the road to Badr.

When Muhammad heard this frightening news, he called a council of war. He was not the military leader of the *umma* and could not decide how best to meet this emergency without consulting the other chiefs. The Muslim volunteers had come out to take part in a *ghazu*, not a pitched battle. Should they retreat while there was still time, or stay and fight the Quraysh? Was there any hope of capturing the caravan before the army arrived? Abu Bakr and Umar made stirring speeches and the seventy Emigrants vowed that they would stay on at Badr, come what may, even though they would all find themselves fighting close relatives and former friends. Muhammad thanked them, and turned to the Helpers. At Second 'Aqaba they had only promised to defend Muhammad if he were attacked in Medina, but, speaking on their behalf, Sa'd ibn Muadh said:

We believe in you, we declare your truth and we witness that what you have brought us is the truth, and we have given you our word and agreement to hear and obey; so go where you wish and we are with you; and by God, if you were to ask us to cross this sea and you plunged into it, we would plunge into it with you; not a man would stay behind. We do not dislike the idea of meeting your enemy tomorrow. We are experienced in war, trustworthy in combat.[14]

These were brave words, but naturally the Muslims were still hoping that they would not have to fight, that God would deliver Abu Sufyan's caravan into their hands before the Meccan army arrived, so that they could retreat with honour. At the Well of Badr they captured two Meccan water-carriers who told them that they were not with the caravan but with the army. This news was so horrifying to the Muslims that the captors started to beat the prisoners, convinced that they must be lying. Muhammad put a stop to this and questioned the two men himself. When they told him which of the Quraysh had marched out against him, he told his men that Mecca had thrown the flower of the tribe into their hands.

In the meantime, Abu Sufyan had managed to elude the Muslim army. As soon as he had taken the caravan beyond Muhammad's reach, he sent word to the army: the caravan was safe and they should all go home. He may well have feared that Abu Jahl would make personal capital out of this expedition and gain the ascendancy in Mecca. He was also a shrewd, calculating man and, like Muhammad, he seems to have hoped for an ultimate reconciliation. But Abu Jahl would not hear of retreat. 'By al-Llah,' he said to his men, 'we will not go back until we have been to Badr. We will spend three days there, slaughter camels, and feast and drink wine, and the girls shall play for us. The Arabs will hear that we have come and will respect us in future.'[15] But not everybody was so eager, now that they had been reassured about the caravan. The clans of Zuhrah and Adi withdrew immediately, nervous of the power that a military and moral victory over Muhammad might give to Abu Jahl. Talib ibn Abi Talib took a contingent of Hashim home, because they could not bring themselves to fight their clansman. Abbas and Hakim, however, both stayed with the army.

As soon as they reached Badr and had settled in their camp, the Meccans despatched Umayr ibn Wahb of Jumah to take a look at Muhammad's army, which was hidden from them by a sand dune, to estimate the numbers. He was aghast when he saw the grim resolution on the faces of the Muslims and he advised the Quraysh not to fight, even though their army was more than twice the size of Muhammad's. He had 'seen camels carrying Death – the camels of Yathrib laden with certain death'. The Meccans had been looking forward to the engagement as a chivalric sport, but a glance at the Muslims convinced Umayr that not one of them would die before he had killed at least one of the Quraysh and, Umayr asked despairingly, 'if they kill of you a number equal to their own, what is the good of living after that?'[16] Arabs did not take unnecessary risks in warfare and always tried to avoid a large number of casualties: the incessant tribal warfare and the precarious nature of life in Arabia made them anxious to preserve as much manpower as possible. Other members of the Quraysh were understandably worried about fighting members of their own tribe and families. Hakim ibn Hizam, for example, was so impressed by Umayr's words that he went immediately to Utba ibn Rabi'a and begged him to try to prevent the battle. Utba had been the protector of the man who had been killed by the Muslims at Nakhlah and Hakim persuaded him to undertake the duty of revenge himself, so that honour could be satisfied. Utba saw the sense of this and rose to address the army: 'O people of Quraysh! by al-Llah you will gain naught by giving battle to Muhammad and his companions. If you fall upon him each one of you will always be looking with loathing on the face of another who has slain the son of his paternal or maternal uncle or some man of his paternal or maternal uncle.'[17] The Quraysh were not a warlike people. They were not impressive or experienced on the battlefield and had always preferred wily negotiation to a violent solution, but Abu Jahl was beyond reason. Utba was a coward! he retorted. He was simply afraid that he might kill his own son, who had gone over to Muhammad. No Arab could bear the charge of cowardice and, Ibn Ishaq says, after this 'war was kindled and all was marred and the folk held stubbornly on their evil course'.[18]

The Muslims had not wanted to fight either, but now that the die had been cast morale was high. Muhammad could not see the Meccan army and had no idea how big it was or he would probably have had second thoughts about staying to fight. He had positioned his men by the wells, which deprived the Quraysh of water and meant that they had to face east with the sun in their eyes. A shower of rain hardened the ground and made it easier for the Muslims to move but more difficult for the Meccans, who had to toil uphill.

As always in Arabia, the battle of Badr began with single combats, in which three leading Muslims, Hamzah, Ali and Ubaydah ibn al-Harith, fought three of the Quraysh: Utba, Shayba and al-Walid ibn Utba, who were avenging the dead man. All three of the Quraysh were killed and the Muslim Ubaydah ibn al-Harith received a mortal wound and was carried off the field. Then the fighting began in earnest. Despite their superior numbers, the Quraysh soon found to their astonishment that they were getting the worst of it. They fought in the old Arab style with careless bravado and each chief led his own men, so the army lacked a unified command. But the Muslims were strictly disciplined and desperate and had been carefully drilled by Muhammad. Suddenly he emerged as a good military tactician. He had lined them up in close formation and they began by bombarding the enemy with arrows, drawing their swords for hand-to-hand fighting only at the last moment. By midday the Quraysh, who had expected only to have to make a show of force, panicked and fled in disarray, leaving about fifty of their leading men, including Abu Jahl himself, dead on the field.

The Muslims were jubilant. They began to round up prisoners and, in the usual Arab fashion, started to kill them, but Muhammad put a stop to this. A revelation came down saying that the prisoners of war were to be ransomed. He also stopped the Muslims squabbling over the booty, and the 150 camels, ten horses and the pile of armour and equipment were divided up equally. Then the victorious army began the trek home with seventy prisoners of war, including Suhayl, the chief of Amir, Abbas and Muhammad's cousins Aqil and Nawfal. On the way home, Muhammad received a revelation for the prisoners themselves:

> O Prophet, say to the prisoners in your hands:
> 'If God knows of any good in your hearts
> He will give you better than what has been taken
> from you, and He will forgive you, surely
> God is All-forgiving, All-compassionate.'[19]

Even in the euphoria that followed his unexpected victory, Muhammad was looking forward to a final reconciliation.

The army was welcomed ecstatically when it marched into Medina, to the great discomfiture of the three main Jewish tribes and Ibn Ubbay's party. The moral effect of Badr cannot be overestimated. For years Muhammad had been the butt of scorn and insults, but after this spectacular and unsought success everybody in Arabia would have to take him seriously. In the history of the holy war in all three of the religions of historical monotheism, an unexpected victory or a sudden reversal of fortune seems like an act of God and always fills people with new confidence and conviction.[20] Like the Christian Crusaders in a similarly desperate situation, the Muslims had a kind of mass hallucination in which they saw legions of angels coming to their aid. With hindsight, everything seemed to have been arranged by God and they had been led to their victory almost in spite of themselves. They had not expected to fight a battle, they had been reluctant to fight and even their ignorance of the enemy's superior numbers seemed to be part of the divine plan.[21] God had seemed to inspire the Muslims during the battle. At one point Muhammad had hurled a handful of pebbles at the enemy in what was probably a traditional ritualistic gesture, but after the victory the Qu'ran depicted him and his companions as God's agents:

> You did not slay them, but God slew them;
> and when thou threwest, it was not
> thyself that threw, but God threw, and
> that He might confer on the believers
> a fair benefit; surely God is
> All-hearing, All-knowing.[22]

Until Badr, the Muslim cause had often seemed to be completely hopeless. But after this victory the Muslims were seized with an exhilarating confidence. It seemed that nothing would be able to stop them:

> If there be twenty of you, patient men,
> they will overcome two hundred; if there be
> a hundred of you, they will overcome
> a thousand disbelievers, for they are a people
> who understand not.
> Now God has lightened it for you, knowing
> that there is weakness in you. If there be
> a hundred of you, patient men, they will
> overcome two hundred; if there be of you
> a thousand, they will overcome two thousand
> by the leave of God; God is with the patient.[23]

But the emphasis was on patience, and constantly the early biographers dwell on the sobriety and earnestness that characterised the *jihad.* This was no hysterical fanaticism but a grim test of endurance. Muhammad and his wiser companions knew perfectly well that the victory had set them on a perilous course which might even destroy the *umma.* To retrieve their honour and prestige, on which their success was based, the Quraysh would have to retaliate. Although the Muslims had not intended it, God seemed to have plunged the *umma* into a full-scale war against the most powerful tribe in Arabia.

The idea of God intervening in history and taking part in a battle may seem extraordinary and distasteful, but such divine action is a crucial element in this monotheistic tradition. In Judaism and Christianity too, current events became theophanies and God was believed to reveal Himself in battles, political reverses and achievements. Certain events became moments of truth and were mythologised until they carried a symbolic significance which completely transformed the original happening. One can see such reflection and analysis of the deeper meaning of history as an imaginative attempt to find a pattern in the apparently meaningless flux of life. One of the most influential of all these reconstructed events was the drowning of Pharaoh and his army in the Red Sea: psalmists, prophets and sages all saw this as an irruption of the divine into history which became a type of salvation itself. Christians also meditated on this event, seeing it as a symbolic foreshadowing of Christ's passage from death to life; it also became a type of baptism, which marked a Christian's migration from despair and anomie to new life and hope. In the Qu'ran the crossing of the Red Sea was called a *furqan*, a word which denotes salvation and a separation of the just from the unjust; the Qu'ran itself was also called a *furqan*, which had transfigured the lives of the faithful at the same time as it had severed them dramatically from their kinsfolk:

> We gave Moses and Aaron the Salvation [*furqan*]
> and a Radiance and a Remembrance
> for the godfearing,
> such as fear God in the Unseen, trembling
> because of the Hour.
>
> And this [that is, the Qu'ran] is a blessed Remembrance
> that We have sent down.[24]

The evolving existence of the Qu'ran, which was constantly directing the *umma* and interpreting events, was a reminder of God's mysterious presence and involvement in the midst of their mundane affairs.

Now the battle of Badr also became a *furqan*, a sign of salvation. God had separated the just from the unjust in the Muslim victory, just as He had made a distinction between the Egyptians and the Israelites at the Red Sea:

> 'Let us flee from the Israelites,' the Egyptians cried. 'Yahweh is fighting for them against the Egyptians!' 'Stretch out your hand over the sea,' Yahweh said to Moses, 'that the waters may flow back on the Egyptians and their chariots and their horsemen.' Moses stretched out his hand over the sea and, as day broke, the sea returned to its bed. The fleeing Egyptians marched right into it, and Yahweh overthrew the Egyptians in the very middle of the sea and, as day broke, the sea returned to its bed. The returning waters overwhelmed the chariots and the horsemen of Pharaoh's whole army, which had followed the Israelites into the sea; not a single one of them was left. But the sons of Israel had marched through the sea on dry ground, walls of water to right and left of them. That day, Yahweh rescued Israel from the Egyptians, and Israel saw the Egyptians lying dead on the shore. Israel witnessed the great act that Yahweh had performed against the Egyptians, and the people venerated Yahweh; they put their faith in Yahweh and in Moses his servant.[25]

Muhammad had never read the Biblical account, but he understood its spirit well because his own religious vision had the same inner dynamic. On the day of Badr, al-Llah had rescued the *umma* from the Quraysh and the Muslims saw the Qurayshi leaders lying dead on the battlefield; the *umma* witnessed the great act that al-Llah had performed against the

Meccans and the people venerated al-Llah and Muhammad his servant. The difference was that, as so often in Muhammad's life, this was not a mythological recasting of an historical event but something which had actually happened before the Muslims' astonished eyes. Each year Jews commemorate this *furqan* at Passover; Muhammad, however, thought that it was the Yom Kippur fast that commemorated the victory at the Red Sea. As Tabari says:

When the Prophet (God's blessing be upon him) came to Medina, he observed the Jews fasting on the day of Ashura and questioned them; they informed him that it is the day on which God caused the drowning of the host of Pharaoh and delivered Moses and those of them who were with him. Muhammad remarked, We have more right than they, and both fasted himself and bade the people fast on that day.[26]

At that time Muhammad had been trying to model the religious life of the *umma* on Judaism, but a few weeks before Badr he had emancipated Islam from the customs of the older faith when he had changed the *qibla*. A few days after the victory, on 9 Ramadan, Muhammad declared that the fast of Ashura was no longer obligatory for Muslims; instead they would fast during Ramadan to commemorate their own special *furqan* of Badr. The fast of Ramadan, which was observed for the first time in March 625, became one of the five essential practices of Islam.

But Muhammad realised that there was a darker side to the new situation, because the *umma* had committed itself to a total war against the Quraysh. Mecca depended on its prestige, so the Quraysh would have to avenge the humiliation of Badr if they were to survive as a great Arab power. They had to avenge their fifty dead. The *umma* had, again almost in spite of itself, embarked on a new phase of the struggle (*jihad*). But unlike the Israelites, who had committed themselves to a holy war of extermination after the Red Sea, Muhammad had no wish to eliminate the Quraysh. Somehow he would have to win them over; to this end, even in the first flush of victory, he would treat the Qurayshi prisoners fairly. Immediately after the battle he had had two of the prisoners killed because they had mounted a formidable intellectual attack on him before the *hijra*: we have seen that Muhammad found this kind of critical challenge deeply threatening. But the rest of the captives were brought back safely to Medina and given decent lodging in the houses of the people who had taken them prisoner. Immediately the Qu'ran started to develop a humane policy towards prisoners of war. It decreed that they must not be ill-treated in any way and must be either released or returned for ransom. If there were no ransom forthcoming, the prisoner must be allowed to earn money to buy his freedom: his captor is urged to help him with the payments out of his own resources and the freeing of captives is praised as a virtuous and charitable act.[27] A later tradition (*hadith*) directs Muslims to treat their captives like members of their own family. It has Muhammad say: 'You must feed them as you feed yourselves, and clothe them as you clothe yourselves, and if you should set them on a hard task, you must help them in it yourselves.'[28] This Quranic and traditional legislation is, of course, in sad contrast to the treatment meted out to hostages taken by Muslims today. There is in fact nothing truly Islamic about such hostage-taking in the current struggle. Shiite Muslims who imprison and ill-treat their captives in Beirut and refuse to return them to their homes are not impelled to do this by 'Islam'; in fact, their behaviour offends against sacred and central precepts of their religion.

The prisoners taken at Badr were not unknown enemies but were the close relatives and friends of the Emigrants. As soon as Sawdah, Muhammad's wife, saw her cousin and brother-in-law Suhayl sitting ignominiously in a corner of the room with his hands tied behind his back, she could not contain herself. The old tribal instincts immediately came to the surface and the new Muslim ideology fell away in an instant. 'O Abu Yazid,' she cried scornfully to him, 'you surrendered too readily. You ought to have died a noble death.' But she was quickly recalled to the present by the stern rebuke of her husband, who had entered the room behind her: 'Sawdah! would you stir up trouble against God and his apostle?'[29] But Muhammad's own reflexive kinship feelings were also strong. He could not sleep that night thinking of his uncle and cousins lying miserably and uncomfortably in captivity and gave the order for their release. The humane and fair treatment paid off. Some of the prisoners were so impressed by life in the *umma* that they converted to Islam. Perhaps the most dramatic of these conversions was that of Umayr ibn Wahb (who had tried to persuade the Quraysh not to fight at Badr). When he had been returned to Mecca, his fellow clansman Safwan ibn Ummayah persuaded him to go back to Medina and assassinate Muhammad. He did go back but Muhammad caught him out and Umayr became a Muslim instead.

One of the captives was Muhammad's son-in-law Abu al-As, who had remained true to the old pagan religion. His wife Zaynab, the Prophet's daughter, who was still living in Mecca, sent his brother Amr to Medina with the ransom money she had raised herself and with a bracelet that had once belonged to Khadija. Muhammad immediately recognised it and turned quite pale with emotion. He begged the Muslims who were holding Abu al-As to let him go free without taking the ransom money and they were glad to agree. He had hoped that Abu al-As would convert to Islam but this did not happen, so he asked him to send Zaynab and their little girl Umamah to him in Medina. By this stage of the struggle it was becoming clear that marriages between pagans and Muslims were no longer practicable. Abu al-As sadly agreed, knowing that, even though Zaynab did not want to leave him, her position in Mecca would now be impossible.

The prospect of the reunion with Zaynab was comforting to Muhammad at this time, because when he had returned from Badr he had learned that his beautiful daughter Ruqayyah had died during his absence. Uthman was almost inconsolable, but was cheered when Muhammad offered him the hand of his other daughter Umm Kulthum. Muhammad visited Ruqayyah's grave with his youngest daughter Fatimah, drying her eyes with a corner of his cloak. Fatimah was now twenty years old and it was high time that she was married. Abu Bakr and Umar had both asked for her hand but Muhammad had his heart set on giving her to his young ward Ali, who had grown up with Fatimah like a brother. Ali was hesitant at first because of his extreme poverty: he had inherited nothing from his father Abu Talib. But Muhammad urged him to go ahead, and the couple were married a few weeks after Badr.

At about the same time, Muhammad decided to take another wife. Umar's daughter Hafsah had recently been widowed. Her husband, Kuhnays ibn Hudhafah, had married Hafsah when he had returned to Mecca from Abyssinia, but had died not long after Badr. Hafsah was now eighteen years old. She was beautiful and accomplished: like her father she was able to read and write but, also like her father, she had a quick temper which rather detracted from her charm. When Hafsah's mourning period was over, Umar had offered her to Uthman, not realising that Muhammad had decided that he should marry Umm Kulthum. Next he offered her to Abu Bakr, who remained silent when made this somewhat embarrassing offer. When Umar went to Muhammad to complain about the apparent discourtesy of his two close companions he was immediately mollified when the Prophet offered himself as a son-in-law. Abu Bakr hastened to repair the temporary rupture with Umar by claiming that he had been aware of Muhammad's intention to take Hafsah himself. The wedding was celebrated early in 625 and sealed the Prophet's political alliance with his two closest companions. He was now son-in-law to both.

Aisha was happy to welcome Hafsah. She would be jealous of the Prophet's later wives, but the ever-increasing bond between their two respective fathers would make the two girls friends. As Aisha was still only a young girl, it is likely that Hafsah became her leader in these early years. The two would ultimately make common cause with Sawdah, but at first they naturally enjoyed teasing the older woman. One day they decided to play a trick on her. They told her that the *dajjal*, the false prophet who was a bogy to many of the Muslims, had arrived. Sawdah was so frightened that she dived into the kitchen tent to hide from this terrifying figure. The two giggling girls rushed immediately to tell Muhammad the joke and he hurried off to rescue poor Sawdah, who emerged from her refuge looking dusty but so relieved that the *dajjal* had not in fact arrived that she did not bother to berate her two little 'sisters', as the wives of the Prophet called themselves.

But life was not always amusing for the young wives. One day, while Aisha was in her early teens, Muhammad asked her to watch over a prisoner-of-war. Aisha became distracted and the man escaped. When Muhammad returned and discovered what had happened, he was furious: 'May al-Llah cut off your hand!' he shouted angrily to Aisha, as he rushed out of her apartment to pursue the captive. Later, the prisoner recaptured, he returned home and found Aisha sitting glumly staring at her hands. What on earth was the matter with her, he asked? Had she been possessed by a *jinni*? Aisha replied that she was wondering which hand al-Llah was going to cut off. Feeling rebuked and ashamed, Muhammad immediately apologised to the little girl and told her that he would pray that al-Llah would bless anybody whom he had ever cursed.

Muhammad's standing had improved after Badr, but not all the Helpers were enthusiastic about his enhanced prestige. Despite the euphoria and pride in the victory, most thoughtful Muslims knew very well that it might not be so easy to defeat the Quraysh another time. So the year that followed Badr was a time of great anxiety, which was naturally increased when people heard that Mecca was calling upon the Bedouin tribes to support them in its struggle against Muhammad. Ibn Ubbay and the opposition party played on these fears, arguing that Islam had put Medina in deadly peril. Granted, the oasis had been on the brink of destruction before Muhammad had arrived but now the whole of Arabia was beginning to turn against it. These fears were entirely understandable. Ibn Ubbay declared that he was ready to obey the revelations, but refused to obey Muhammad personally because he seemed bent on plunging Medina into a dangerous war. But, as the Qu'ran pointed out, when revelations *did* come down endorsing Muhammad's decisions and confirming that the *jihad* was necessary, the opposition remained mutinous and sometimes looked scared to death.[30]

Ibn Ubbay was backed by the Jewish tribes, who had been horrified by Muhammad's new standing in Medina and saw Mecca as a natural ally. Immediately after the victory, for example, Ka'b ibn al-Ashraf, a Jewish poet of the Bani Nadir, went directly to Mecca and started to compose inflammatory verses, urging the Quraysh to march against Muhammad and avenge their dead.

O that the earth when they were killed
Had split asunder and engulfed its people,
That he who spread the report had been thrust through
or lived cowering, blind and deaf.[31]

Ka'b's verses made it very clear to the Quraysh that not all the people of Medina stood stoutly behind Muhammad. The Jewish tribes were formidable. They had sizeable armies and impressive fighting power and, in the event of a Meccan attack, might well be persuaded to join the Quraysh to get rid of the upstart. Poetry was central to the political life of Arabia and Ka'b's songs helped to rouse the Quraysh from the torpor of depression and grief into which they had been thrown by the defeat.

Abu Sufyan had become one of the most important men in Mecca after the catastrophe. Most of the other leaders had been killed and Muhammad's hostile uncle Abu Lahab had died shortly after Badr. Henceforth, Abu Sufyan would direct the struggle against Muhammad. In a special meeting of the Senate it was decided that the proceeds of the caravan that he had managed to bring back safely from Syria would be devoted to the war against Medina and, some ten weeks after Badr, Abu Sufyan himself led a *ghazu* as a token and a warning of what was to come. He led 200 men to the outskirts of Medina, where they camped in the fields, and by night he slipped into the territory of the Jewish Bani Nadir, Ka'b's tribe, and was entertained by its chief Sallam ibn Mishkan, who discussed the situation with him and, according to Ibn Ishaq, 'gave him secret information about the Muslims'. The next day he and his men devastated some fields, burned down some palm trees (an act which went deeply against all Arab principles and was always construed as a prelude to war) and killed two of the Helpers who were working on the land. As soon as he heard the news, Muhammad led a troop of Muslims in pursuit and the Quraysh promptly fled, throwing away their provisions to help them to make a quick getaway.

The Jewish tribes had obviously become a security risk. If a Meccan army were to camp south of Medina, where the two most powerful tribes had their territory, the Jewish armies could easily join the Quraysh, whom they plainly regarded as allies. If the Quraysh attacked the city from the north, which would be their best option, the Jewish tribes could attack the Muslims from the rear so that they were completely surrounded. Muhammad realised that he had to put a stop to this dissension. His Jewish converts informed him that the Bani Qaynuqa, the smallest of the three tribes, were particularly hostile to the *umma*. Before the *hijra* they had been the allies of Ibn Ubbay and after Badr they had decided to break their covenant with Muhammad and revive the old alliance in order to boost the opposition party and oust the Prophet. Their territory was nearer the centre of the 'city' of Medina: unlike the other two tribes, they were not farmers but smiths and craftsmen. Shortly after Badr and Ka'b's defection to Mecca, Muhammad visited them in their quarters and urged them to accept him as a prophet in the name of their common religious tradition. The Jews of Qaynuqa listened in mutinous silence and replied that they had no intention of remaining in the *umma*: 'O Muhammad, you seem to think that we are your people. Do not deceive yourself because you have encountered a people [at Badr] with no knowledge of war and got the better of them; for by God if we fight you, you will find that we are real men!'[32] After this threat, Muhammad withdrew and awaited developments.

A few days later there was an incident in the *souk* of the Qaynuqa. One of the Jewish goldsmiths played a trick on a Muslim woman who was trading there: he stealthily pinned her skirt to the back of her upper garments so that when she stood up she exposed herself. Feelings were at such a pitch between the Muslims and the Jews of Qaynuqa that when one of the Helpers leaped on the goldsmith with a cry of rage the fighting escalated horribly and a Jew and a Muslim were killed. Casualties were thus equal and Muhammad was called in, in his official capacity as judge of disputes, to restore the peace. But the Jews refused to accept his arbitration, barricaded themselves into their fortress and called upon their Arab allies to come to their aid. Qaynuqa had about 700 fighting men at their disposal and if their old Arab allies *had* answered their summons and brought their own forces out to meet Muhammad he would not have been able to defeat them. Ibn Ubbay was anxious to help Qaynuqa and consulted their other ally Ubadah ibn Samit. But Ubadah was a committed Muslim and he pointed out that this old alliance with the Jews had been cancelled out when they had all signed the treaty with Muhammad. Ibn Ubbay realised that he was powerless to help because the rest of the Arabs remained staunchly behind the Prophet. Qaynuqa had expected to lead a rebellion against Muhammad and the Emigrants, but instead, to their horror, they found themselves besieged by all the Arabs of Medina. For two weeks they waited for Ibn Ubbay to make good his promise but eventually they were forced to surrender unconditionally.

Immediately Ibn Ubbay went to Muhammad to ask that he treat them mercifully and, when the Prophet failed to reply, he grabbed him by the collar. Muhammad went white with anger, but Ibn Ubbay persisted: how could he be expected to desert his old confederates, who had so often helped him in the past? He knew that Muhammad would be well within his rights, according to the conventions of Arabia, to massacre the whole tribe but Muhammad granted the Qaynuqa their lives provided that they instantly left the oasis. Ibn Ubbay was told to escort them out of Medina.

Once they had understood that Ibn Ubbay no longer had any power to help them, the Qaynuqa seemed ready to leave. They had taken a gamble, which had not come off because they had completely underestimated the power that Muhammad had acquired; they had not realised that the old system had gone for ever, and still believed that their former Arab confederates were just waiting for the chance to restore it. They left the oasis apparently without protest knowing that they were lucky to have escaped with their lives. Tribes had often been expelled from the oasis during the wars in the pre-Islamic period: all Medinans were familiar with this punishment and the Qaynuqa would have expected to have to go. They took refuge with another Jewish group in the Wadi al-Qura and settled eventually on the Syrian border.

It is very difficult for us in the West to deal with Muhammad's relations with the Jews of Medina, because it raises too many shameful spectres from our own past. But Muhammad's struggle with the three main Jewish tribes of the oasis was quite different from the racial and religious hatred that fired the pogroms of Christian Europe for nearly a thousand years. The irrational terrors of Christians found final expression in Hitler's secular crusade against the Jews. Muhammad had no such fears or fantasies; he had no desire to make Medina *Judenrein*. His quarrel with Qaynuqa was purely political and was never extended to those smaller Jewish clans in Medina who remained true to the Covenant and lived side by side with the Muslims in peace.

This was a very dangerous time for the *umma*, whose members knew that they had to expect a massive attack from Mecca and simply could not afford to harbour an enemy within. The expulsion of Qaynuqa was a warning to other potential dissidents like Ibn Ubbay and the Bani Nadir. It showed that Muhammad was not a man to trifle with. A few months later, when the poet Ka'b had returned to Medina and was writing more defamatory verses to stir up sedition, Muhammad had him assassinated. Muhammad was always alarmed by hostile poets: their pronouncements were believed to have near-magical power, as we have seen. In Arabia a poet could be a deadly weapon and again Muhammad could not afford to allow him to inflame the disaffected parties in Medina or to inspire the Bedouin tribes who heard his verses to join Abu Sufyan's coalition against Medina. The Bani Nadir had been suitably chastened by the defeat of Qaynuqa and when Ka'b was assassinated they went to Muhammad to complain that he had put one of their chief men to death. Muhammad knew that they were just as hostile to him as Ka'b but that, for the time being, they were keeping quiet, and he told them that he could tolerate dissident thoughts and opinions but not seditious action. He then offered to make a special treaty with Nadir, in addition to the Covenant, to ensure their safety and silence. The Bani Nadir were glad to agree. As he waited for the Meccan attack, Muhammad had successfully muzzled the opposition at home.

Muhammad's adept handling of this crisis increased his status in Medina still more but he was certainly not yet regarded as the head of the *umma*. He could not have contained the joint threat of Qaynuqa and Ibn Ubbay without the support of Ubadah ibn Samit. Muhammad was given a fifth (*khums*) of the goods left behind by Qaynuqa. It was customary for a chief to receive a quarter of all such takings to use on behalf of his people: he was expected to distribute gifts, care for the poor and provide hospitality. The *khums* marked Muhammad off slightly from the other chiefs, but showed that he was now regarded as occupying a comparable position. While waiting anxiously for the Meccan offensive, Muhammad busily consolidated the prestige he had won at Badr. Whenever he heard that one of the nomadic tribes, urged on by Meccan propaganda, was preparing to invade Medinan territory, he would march aggressively to forestall the attack and the opposition tended to melt away as soon as the Muslim troops arrived. In the late summer he managed to inflict yet another humiliation on the Quraysh. Since Badr, the caravans had not been able to use the Red Sea route to Syria but Safwan ibn Ummayah decided to take the Najd road to the Iraq, travelling east of Medina. This route was inconvenient, because the watering places were far apart, but Safwan sent extra water-bearing camels in addition to those that carried a rich cargo of silver worth about 100,000 dirhams. Muhammad managed to get news of this caravan and sent Zayd to intercept it. Zayd and his men managed to catch it unawares while it was resting at the Well of Qarada: Muslim soldiers had acquired a fearful reputation since Badr and as soon as the Meccans saw them approaching they fled in terror, leaving the whole caravan behind.

The Quraysh intensified their preparations for an attack on Medina but they waited until after the winter. Eventually on 11 March 625, 3,000 men with 3,000 camels and about 200 horses left Mecca and began a leisurely journey towards Medina. The Quraysh had been joined by their Bedouin allies in the group of tribes known as the Ahabish, the Thaqif of Taif and the tribe of Abd Manat. On 21 March the army arrived outside Medina and camped on the plain in front of Mount Uhud to the north-west of the oasis. Muhammad and the Medinans had heard that the army was finally on its way only a week earlier. There was no time to get the crops in from the fields, but they managed to bring all the people in from the outlying areas of the settlement and barricade them into the 'city' with their camels, cattle, sheep and goats. As soon as the army arrived, the chiefs of Medina held a council of war. The most experienced urged extreme caution: everybody should stay inside the 'city' and refuse to go out to meet the enemy. It was very difficult to sustain a siege in Arabia and, when this plan had been adopted on previous occasions, the enemy had always been forced to leave without a fight. But some of the younger generation wanted action. They argued that at Badr Muhammad had defeated a huge army with only 350 men: surely God would help him again. They were supported by some of the farmers, who could not bear to think of the Quraysh eating their way through the crops that had been left outside the 'city'. These hotheads became so belligerent that eventually they carried the day and preparations for battle began.

But later the hawks got cold feet, especially after people like Sa'd ibn Muadh had told them that they were courting disaster. They told Muhammad that they were now ready to stay inside the 'city', but Muhammad quite properly stood by the decision to fight. 'Once a prophet has put on his armour,' he explained, 'it is not fitting he should take it off until the battle is fought.'[33] Any dithering at this point would have been fatal. So on the evening of 22 March, 6 Shawwab, Muhammad mounted his favourite horse and led about a thousand men towards Uhud, some twenty miles away, to meet an army three times bigger. The Jews refused to fight because it was their Sabbath, but the Muslims knew very well that they were praying for the success of Mecca. The army camped that night halfway between Medina and Uhud and in the morning Ibn Ubbay defected, taking three hundred men back to the city. He did not even bother to inform Muhammad of his decision, but explained to some of the Helpers that he wanted to dissociate himself from this absurd and suicidal campaign. 'He has disobeyed me, and obeyed the striplings and men of no judgement,' he said. 'I don't see why we should lose our lives in this ill-chosen spot.'[34] The decision was understandable if dishonourable, but Ibn Ubbay may have been playing a deeper game. In 617 he had withdrawn from the battle of Bu'ath because he had realised that a complete victory was impossible and this had stood him in good stead and had almost made him king of Medina. If Muhammad was defeated, as seemed highly likely, Ibn Ubbay would have separated himself from the disaster and would be there to pick up the pieces.

The Muslims faced the Quraysh the next morning, therefore, with a dangerously depleted army. Abu Sufyan stood in the centre of the front line, flanked on the right by Khalid, the son of the late Walid of Makhzum, and on the left by Ikrimah, the son of Abu Jahl. Before the fighting began, Abu Sufyan stepped forward and told the Aws and the Khasraj to abandon Muhammad and go home; Mecca had no real quarrel with them. But the Helpers yelled back defiantly that they would never leave their Prophet. Next Abu Amir, the Medinan monotheist who had defected to

Mecca after Muhammad had arrived in the oasis, stepped forward to address his people. 'O men of Aws,' he called to his tribe, 'I am Abu Amir.' 'Then God blind you, you impious rascal!' they shouted back. Abu Amir was shocked: he had boasted in Mecca that one word from him would win the Aws over to Quraysh. Now he went back muttering: 'Evil has befallen my people since I left them.'[35]

The armies began to advance towards each other. Behind the Meccan troops, Abu Sufyan's wife Hind walked with some of the other high-born women, beating tambourines and singing:

If you advance we hug you
Spread soft rugs beneath you
If you retreat we leave you
leave and no more love you.[36]

Hind had always hated Muhammad, but she had lost her father Utba ibn Rabi'a and two of her sons at Badr and she had vowed to eat the liver of Hamzah, who had slain Utba in single combat. The fighting began. It is difficult to tell what happened in any detail, because the sources are confused. At first the Muslims were able to hold their own. Muhammad had arranged his troops in the same close formation that had been so successful at Badr, and at one point it seemed as though they had put the enemy to flight. But then the Muslim archers disobeyed orders, broke ranks and were attacked from the rear by Khalid, who surged forward in a brilliant cavalry charge. The Muslims fled in ignominy. Muhammad tried to stop them but was knocked senseless by a blow to the head, and word spread that he had been killed.

In fact Muhammad was only stunned. He was carried into a grove and recovered quite quickly. But the Quraysh did not bother to check the report; as soon as they heard that he was dead, they seemed to have stopped fighting and failed to follow up their victory, so that the Muslims were able to retreat in reasonably good order. Twenty-two Meccans and sixty-five Muslims had been killed, but it was not a great victory for the Quraysh. They had failed to kill Muhammad and wipe out the *umma*. Only three of the Muslim dead – Hamzah, Abdallah ibn Jahsh and Mu'sab – were Emigrants and the rest were Helpers, with whom they were not anxious to fight. After the battle, they alienated some of the Bedouin allies by mutilating the corpses. One of the Quraysh split open Hamzah's belly, tore out the liver and brought it to Hind, who chewed a morsel of it to fulfil her vow. Then she started to chop off Hamzah's nose, ears and genitals, urging the other women to do the same with other bodies. They left the field wearing grisly bracelets, pendants and collars, to the disgust of the Bedouin and some of their own men, who felt that this had polluted their cause.

Before his army moved off, Abu Sufyan heard the disappointing news that Muhammad had not been killed after all. The struggle with Medina was not over. 'Next year at Badr!' he cried, as a final challenge, and on behalf of Muhammad one of the Companions cried: 'Yes, it is an appointment between us!'[37] The Muslims were in good enough shape, despite their heavy losses, to make a token chase. For three days, they followed the Meccan army and at night Muhammad made all his men spread out as far from one another as they could and each one lit a fire, so that it looked as though a vast army were camping there. The ruse deterred those of the Quraysh who wanted to return to Medina and have another shot at destroying the *umma.*

But this was a poor consolation. After Uhud most of the Muslims were deeply depressed: if Badr had been a sign of salvation, was the defeat of Uhud a sign that God had deserted Muhammad? The Qu'ran responded to these anxieties in the third sura, pointing out that it was wrong to think of the disaster as an act of God. The Muslims had only themselves to blame. They had been quarrelsome, rebellious and indisciplined throughout the campaign. Yet Uhud had been a sign in its own way: it had distinguished the true Muslims from the cowards who had deserted with Ibn Ubbay.

As one might expect, Ibn Ubbay and the Jews were all jubilant. Ibn Ubbay and his supporters loudly insisted that if his policy had been followed all those casualties would have been prevented. The Jews argued that Muhammad was simply an ambitious man, with no prophetic credentials: whoever heard of a true prophet suffering such a reverse? Umar wanted to kill these detractors, but Muhammad calmed him down. The Quraysh would never again inflict such a humiliation on the *umma*, he vowed, and one day they would worship at the Ka'aba again. But despite his quiet confidence Uhud had damaged his prestige and caused a rupture with Ibn Ubbay. Up to then the Muslim opposition had sat ineffectually on the fence, but after Uhud Ibn Ubbay went out of his way to find any and every opportunity of destroying Muhammad. On the Friday after the battle, Ibn Ubbay had been publicly shamed in the mosque. When he got up to speak two of the Helpers had grabbed him and told him that after his treachery he should keep his mouth shut. He strode from the mosque in a fury and refused to ask for Muhammad's prayers and forgiveness. After Uhud, his party was given a new name by the Qu'ran, which called Ibn Ubbay and his followers the *munafiqin*, which is usually translated the 'hypocrites'. But W. Montgomery Watt suggests that the 'Creepers' or the 'Mice' might be a more accurate rendering: at Uhud they had crept away to their holes like frightened little animals.[38]

There were also pressing practical problems that had to be solved. Each one of the sixty-five Muslims who had died at Uhud had left behind wives and families who had to be provided for and it seems that after the defeat the revelation came down to Muhammad that allowed the Muslims to take four wives:

> Give orphans their property, and do not
> exchange the corrupt for the good; and devour
> not their property with your property; surely
> that is a great crime.
> If you fear that you will not act justly
> towards the orphans, marry such women
> as seem good to you, two, three, four,
> but if you fear you will not be equitable,
> then only one, or what your right hands own;
> so it is likelier you will not be partial.[39]

Muhammad's Western critics tend to see this condoning of polygamy as a piece of pure male chauvinism. Popular films like *Harem* give an absurd and inflated picture of the sexual life of the Muslim sheikh which reveals more about Western fantasy than it does about the reality. But, seen in context, polygamy was not designed to improve the sex life of the boys – it was a piece of social legislation. The problem of orphans had exercised Muhammad since the beginning of his career and it had been exacerbated by the deaths at Uhud. The men who had died had left not only widows but daughters, sisters and other relatives who needed a new protector. Their new guardians might not be scrupulous about administering the property of these orphans: some might even keep these women unmarried so that they could hold on to their property. It was not unusual for a man to marry his women wards as a way of absorbing their property into his own estate.

There was probably a shortage of men in Arabia, which left a surplus of unmarried women who were often badly exploited. The Qu'ran is most concerned about this problem and resorted to polygamy as a way of dealing with it. This would enable all the girls who had been orphaned to be married, but it insisted that a man could take more than one wife only if he promised to administer their property equitably. It also stipulates that no orphan girl should be married to her guardian against her will, as though she were simply a moveable property.[40] The Qu'ran also makes provision for divorce. In the pre-Islamic period, when wives still lived in the paternal household, a woman or her male relatives had been able to terminate a relationship. In the Qu'ran, a man is empowered to refuse her request for divorce but there is a clause in favour of the woman. In Arabia it was customary for a man to give a *mahl*, a dowry, to his bride. This had usually been absorbed by the woman's male relatives, but in Islam the dowry was to be given directly to the woman herself. To this day, women are allowed to do whatever they choose with this money: give it to charity, build a swimming pool or start a business. But in the event of divorce, a man is not allowed to reclaim the *mahl*, so a woman's security is assured.[41]

Western critics often blame the Qu'ran for its treatment of women, which they see as inequitous, but in fact the emancipation of women was dear to the Prophet's heart. There are complaints that the Qu'ran preaches a double standard: the laws of inheritance, for example, decree that a woman can inherit only half of what her brothers (who have to provide the *mahl* to start a new family) will receive. Again, women are allowed to be witnesses in law, but their witness is only half as valuable as that of a man. In the context of the twentieth century – when, we should remember, we are still campaigning for equal rights for women – this Qu'ranic legislation does seem prohibitive. But in seventh-century Arabia it was revolutionary. We must remember what life had been like for women in the pre-Islamic period when female infanticide was the norm and when women had no rights at all. Like slaves, women were treated as an inferior species, who had no legal existence. In such a primitive world, what Muhammad achieved for women was extraordinary. The very idea that a woman could be a witness or could inherit anything at all in her own right was astonishing. We must also recall that in Christian Europe, women had to wait until the nineteenth century before they had anything similar: even then, the law remained heavily weighted towards men.

Again, we have to see the ruling about polygamy in context. In seventh-century Arabia, when a man could have as many wives as he chose, to prescribe only four was a limitation, not a licence to new oppression. Further, the Qu'ran immediately follows the verses giving Muslims the right to take four wives with a qualification which has been taken very seriously. Unless a man is confident that he can be scrupulously fair to all his wives, he must remain monogamous.[42] Muslim law has built on this: a man must spend absolutely the same amount of time with each one of his wives; besides treating each wife equally financially and legally, a man must not have the slightest preference for one but must esteem and love them all equally. It has been widely agreed in the Islamic world that mere human beings cannot fulfil this Qu'ranic requirement: it is impossible to show such impartiality and as a result Muhammad's qualification, which he need not have made, means that no Muslim should really have more than one wife. In countries where polygamy has been forbidden, the authorities have justified this innovation not on secular but on religious grounds.

In Medina after the defeat of Uhud, the Qu'ran was not, therefore, encouraging men to build up exotic harems. It was not only limiting the number of wives that Muslims should have, but was also asking them to make an act of faith in the future. The Qu'ran repeatedly forbids the practice of female infanticide: it became one of the basic commandments to which every convert had to assent. Instead of using this brutal method of birth control, the Qu'ran urges Muslims to trust in God in a society in which all vulnerable people – the aged, the orphans and babies – must be given full human rights and treated equitably.[43] In one of the most beautiful passages of the gospels, Jesus urges his disciples to consider the birds of the air and the lilies of the field and not to worry about the future: God would provide for all their needs.[44] In a rather similar way, the Qu'ran urged Muslims to find confidence in God's benevolence in the 'signs' of nature. They must also trust in God without resorting to the cruel and exploitative measures of the *Jahiliyah* and cultivate a joyful confidence that He will provide. They must marry needy women and have large families, trusting that God will ultimately enable them to survive:

> Marry the spouseless among you, and your
> slaves and handmaidens that are righteous;
> if they are poor, God will enrich them
> of his bounty; God is All-embracing
> All knowing.[45]

This was an act of faith that demanded considerable courage. Muhammad had himself given the Muslims an example of concern for the vulnerable women of the *umma*. After Uhud he had taken a fourth wife, providing a home for Zaynab bint Kuzaymah, the widow of Ubaydah ibn al-Harith, the martyr of Badr. She was also the daughter of the chief of the Bedouin tribe of Amir, and so the match forged a political alliance. An apartment was built for her beside the mosque and she joined her 'sisters' Sawdah, Aisha and Hafsah.

Muhammad was urging Muslims to have confidence in their future and, if they believed that they could behave equitably, take on new responsibilities at a time when Abu Sufyan was building a giant confederacy to destroy the *umma*. But, as usual, he was also taking more normal precautions. He realised that he must get the support of the Bedouin tribes to the east and north-east of Medina to prevent them joining the Meccan alliance. Muhammad sent raiding parties out to impress the Bedouin, but in the summer of 625 two incidents showed how vulnerable Medina had become.

Two Bedouin tribes of the Najd had asked Muhammad for instruction in Islam: some of their members had become Muslims and wanted to learn how to recite the Qu'ran, so Muhammad sent six of his ablest men on this mission. During their journey, they rested at the Well of Raji near Mecca and were attacked by one of the chiefs of Hudhayl. Three of the Muslims were killed and the other three taken prisoner. One of these was stoned to death when he tried to escape and the others were taken to Mecca to be sold to their Qurayshi enemies. Safwan ibn Ummayah bought one of the prisoners to avenge the death of his father, the old chief of Jumah who had died at Badr: both of the Muslims were taken outside the Sanctuary and crucified.

At about the same time, Abu Bara, chief of the Bedouin tribe of Amir and Muhammad's new father-in-law, likewise asked for missionaries to instruct his people in Islam. But this was also an appeal for help against warring factions in his own tribe. Forty Muslims were despatched and were nearly all massacred at the Well of Ma'unah just outside Amir's territory. One of Abu Bara's rivals in his tribe had persuaded some members of the neighbouring tribe of Sulaym to do the deed. Two of the Muslims, however, had been pasturing the camels near by and became aware of the catastrophe only when they saw the vultures hovering over the campsite. They rushed back to find their companions dead; one of the survivors was taken prisoner and the other managed to make his way back to Medina. On the road, however, he came across two members of the Bani Amir lying peacefully asleep under a tree. Assuming that Amir had been responsible for the massacre, he drew his sword and killed them, then hurried back to tell Muhammad what he had done. To his surprise, however, he was told that he had done wrong and that the *umma* would have to pay a blood-wite, the fee for blood spilt wrongfully, which had begun to be accepted by some of the tribes in place of an actual life. Muhammad believed that the Amiris should not have been killed. It was true that some members of Amir had been behind the massacre, but technically it had been committed by Sulaym. By paying blood-money to Abu Bara, who was horrified by what had happened, Muhammad hoped to win his whole tribe over to Islam. His poets began to write their own propaganda, mourning the martyrs of Raji and Ma'unah, and Muhammad's decent conduct to Abu Bara also made some of its former enemies think more kindly of the *umma*. Indeed, it is said that some of the Sulaymites who had committed the massacre had been so impressed by the faith and courage of the Muslims at the moment of death that they became converts themselves.

Muhammad began to raise the blood-price in Medina. One of the groups he approached was the Jewish tribe of Nadir, which was also allied to Abu Bara. He made his request at a meeting of their council, accompanied by Abu Bakr and Usayd ibn Hudayr, one of the Helpers. The Jews seemed agreeable and co-operative, and they asked the

Muslims to wait outside while they considered the request. But while they were waiting Muhammad suddenly slipped away from his friends and went back home. Later he told them that he had been warned by Gabriel that the Jews were plotting to kill him. In fact a divine revelation would not have been strictly necessary. Some members of Nadir would still have wanted to avenge the death of the poet Ka'b ibn al-Ashraf and the Muslim sources claim to know exactly who was about to drop a boulder on to Muhammad from a nearby roof-top.

Muhammad then sent one of the Helpers on his behalf to deliver an ultimatum. Muhammad ibn Maslama, a member of the tribe of Aws, which had been the allies of Nadir before the *hijra*, duly told them, 'The Messenger of God has sent me to you and he says, "By planning to slay me you have broken the treaty that I made with you."' They could no longer live in the city after this treachery. The Jews were astonished that a member of Aws could convey such a message: like Qaynuqa the previous year, they still seemed unable to accept that the old order had been permanently abolished. Ibn Maslama had to tell them bluntly: 'Hearts have changed and Islam has wiped out old alliances.'[46]

The Jews decided to try to negotiate with Muhammad, to see if they could find a compromise, but Ibn Ubbay saw this as an excellent chance to make another attempt to get rid of Muhammad. He told them that he would join forces with them if they were prepared to secede from the *umma*. So, like the Bani Qaynuqa before them, the Jews of Nadir withdrew to their fortress, watched the Muslims surrounding them and waited for Ibn Ubbay and his party to come and relieve them. But nothing happened. Yet again, Ibn Ubbay had misjudged the strength of Muhammad's position and thought that he had been more damaged by Uhud than he really was. After two weeks, when Nadir knew that they could not hold out much longer, Muhammad gave the order to cut down their palm trees. This unmistakable sign of war terrified the Jews and they surrendered, begging only that Muhammad should spare their lives. Muhammad agreed on condition that they left the oasis immediately, taking with them only those goods which they could carry away on their camels. The Nadir loaded all their possessions, even breaking down the lintels of their doors rather than leaving them for Muhammad, and left the oasis in a proud procession, as though they were going in triumph. The women dressed in all their jewels and finery, beating tambourines and singing to the accompaniment of pipes and drums. Weaving their way through Medina, they eventually took the northern road to Syria. Some of them stayed in the nearby Jewish settlement of Khaybar and from there they helped Abu Sufyan to build his confederacy, drumming up support among the northern tribes.

In the year after Uhud, Muhammad had managed to recoup some of the prestige he had lost, and the affair of the Bani Nadir was yet another defeat for Ibn Ubbay. The Prophet continued to put down any incipient raids and in April 626 he won a decisive moral victory. As he had left the field of Uhud, Abu Sufyan had challenged the Muslims to meet him once again at Badr, during the annual fair, so in April 626 Muhammad set out with 1,500 men and camped at Badr for a whole week. But Abu Sufyan never appeared. He had not expected Muhammad to keep the appointment and had set out with his army as a mere show, planning to turn back as soon as he heard that the Muslims had failed to leave Medina. It was a year of severe drought and there was not a blade of grass to feed the camels during the journey, so after a couple of days Abu Sufyan led his army home. He was bitterly reproached by his fellow citizens for failing to keep the tryst, particularly because the Bedouin had been full of admiration for the Muslims' courage and readiness to face a much larger Meccan army at Badr a second time. Not only was Muhammad's position improving in Medina, but the tide was just beginning to turn in his favour in the rest of Arabia.

Even though the Muslims knew that after the humiliation of Second Badr the Meccans had intensified their preparations for a new offensive against the *umma*, Muhammad still hoped for a final peaceful settlement. In January 626 his new wife Zaynab had died, just eight months after her wedding, and a few months later he approached Hind bint al-Mughira, the widow of his cousin Abu Salamah, and asked for her hand. Umm Salamah, as she is usually known, was also the sister of one of the leading members of the powerful Meccan clan of Makhzum, which could prove to be a useful connection. She was twenty-nine years old and still extremely beautiful; she also seems to have been an intelligent woman and a good companion to Muhammad. He often chose to take her along on major campaigns and on at least one occasion she was able to offer valuable advice. She was, however, reluctant to marry Muhammad at first. She was no longer young, she said, and had a jealous nature: she was not sure that she would be able to take life in the harem. Muhammad smilingly assured her that he was even older than she and that God would take care of her jealousy.

Umm Salamah had been correct to fear harem rivalry; Muhammad's marriage to her introduced a rift among his wives that reflected the various parties within the *umma* who were competing for political power. A Makhzumite, Umm Salamah represented the more aristocratic group of Emigrants, while Aisha and Hafsah, daughters of Muhammad's two closest companions, represented the more plebeian party in power. As new wives entered the harem they tended to join one of these two rival groups. Umm Salamah frequently looked for support to a third minor party, the *ahl al-bait* or the people of the household, who were members of Muhammad's immediate family and looked to Fatimah, a rather shy and timid woman, as their chief hope. These factions among Muhammad's wives reflect crucial factions in the *umma* that would become extremely serious after the Prophet's death and which, to some extent, still divide Muslims today. The *ahl al-bait*, who wanted Fatimah and Ali and their descendants to lead the Muslim world, would become the Shiah. It was not very long after Umm Salamah's wedding that a new wife entered the harem who would swell this group and frequently ally herself with the aristocratic party. Zaynab bint Jahsh, the Prophet's cousin, had been divorced by Zayd and married to Muhammad himself. The circumstances of this affair raised a few eyebrows and have been used by critics of Islam to denigrate its Prophet.

People such as Voltaire and Prideaux have seen the incident as a demonstration of Muhammad's insatiable sexual appetite and of his crafty manipulations of the revelations to further his own desires. They give a rather more lurid version of events than do Muslims. One afternoon Muhammad had gone to visit Zayd, who happened to be out. His wife Zaynab opened the door and because she was not expecting visitors was very lightly clad. Zaynab was now in her late thirties but was still said to be extremely beautiful and on this occasion Muhammad succumbed to her charms. He turned away hastily, muttering something that sounded like, 'Praise be to God who changes men's hearts.'[47] Zaynab had never wanted to marry Zayd and now she seized on Muhammad's admiration as a way out. She told Zayd so frequently and vehemently about the electrifying impression she had made on the Prophet, that life became impossible. Zayd went to Muhammad and offered to divorce his wife if Muhammad wanted her himself, but the Prophet sent him away, telling him to fear God and keep his wife. But there was now no hope for the marriage: Zaynab's nagging made Zayd so miserable that he divorced her anyway and the Prophet eventually decided to marry her.

There was criticism of the proposed match: some said that it was illegal as Zaynab had been married to Muhammad's adopted son, but Muhammad received a revelation telling him that the marriage was certainly not incestuous.[48] Zayd had been Muhammad's foster son and the relationship between them was artificial: in marrying Zaynab the Prophet was not violating the proscribed degrees. Muhammad happened to be with Aisha when this revelation came down and she said, rather tartly: 'truly thy Lord makes haste to do thy bidding.' Western people have generally shared this view, but the fact that this apparently critical tradition has been preserved shows that in general Muhammad's contemporaries took a rather more pragmatic view. They saw Muhammad as a man with passions and if al-Llah chose to give his Messenger a few extra privileges, who were they to criticise? Today Muslims deny that Muhammad married Zaynab out of lust and, indeed, it seems most unlikely that a woman of 39, who had been living on the brink of malnutrition all her life and exposed to the merciless sun of Arabia would inspire such a storm of emotion in anybody's breast, let alone that of a cousin who had known her since she was a child. But Muhammad had always been very close to the Jahsh family including Zaynab. He would, Muslims argue, have felt responsible for her after she had been divorced and was, as we know, concerned about unprotected women in the *umma*. If he had wanted Zaynab for her sexual charms, he could have married her himself years earlier. The incident also demonstrated the fact that a fostering or adoptive relationship was not a tie of blood and need be no bar to marriage.

Shortly after Zaynab's wedding celebrations and possibly connected with it, came the revelation known as the Verses of the Curtain, which decreed that Muhammad's wives must be secluded from the rest of the *umma*. Muslim traditions explain the introduction of the *hijab*, which is usually translated as 'the Veil', in various ways. Some say that it was Umar, who had aggressively chauvinist views, who urged Muhammad to seclude his wives from view by means of a curtain. There had recently been unpleasant incidents when the Hypocrites had insulted Muhammad's wives as they went out at night to relieve themselves. Others say that as Muhammad became more important and more aware of life in the civilised countries, he wanted to adopt the Persian and Byzantine custom of secluding women of the upper classes as a mark of his wives' new dignity. All, however, point out that sexual morality was lax in Arabia during the pre-Islamic period. There tended to be a great deal of indecent talk and innuendo and a great deal of flirting and propositioning. In traditional society, a sexual scandal can be extremely serious and arouse strong emotions in a community. Muhammad was probably well aware that Ibn Ubbay and his supporters would be delighted to damage the Muslim cause by pointing to a disgrace in his own family.

It is said that at Zaynab's wedding feast, some of the guests stayed too long and made a nuisance of themselves. This prompted a revelation which put some distance between Muhammad's family and the rest of the *umma*:

> Believers, do not enter the houses of the Prophet
> for a meal without waiting for the proper time,
> unless you are given leave. But if you are
> invited, enter; and when you have eaten,
> disperse. Do not engage in familiar talk,

> for this would annoy the Prophet and he would
> be ashamed to bid you go; but of the truth, al-Llah
> is not ashamed. If you ask his wives for anything,
> Speak to them from behind a curtain [*hijab*]
> This is more chaste for your hearts and their hearts.[49]

Muhammad, it will be remembered, had no room of his own at the mosque; he simply slept in the apartments of his wives. But as he became more important in Medina his home inevitably became a public place, as more and more people came to consult him about their personal or religious problems or asked him to arbitrate in a dispute. Some Muslims liked to approach him through his wives, in the hope of getting his ear. Aisha, for example, was known to have had several friendly chats with a particular young man, which people remembered later when a scandal broke out that threatened to split the *umma* down the middle. The *hijab* or curtain was not intended to be an oppressive measure. It was designed to prevent a scandalous situation developing which Muhammad's enemies could use to discredit him.

We should pause to consider the question of the *hijab*, and the Muslim institution of the veil. It is often seen in the West as a symbol of male oppression, but in the Qu'ran it was simply a piece of protocol that applied only to the Prophet's wives. Muslim women are required, like men, to dress modestly, but women are not told to veil themselves from view, nor to seclude themselves from men in a separate part of the house. These were later developments and did not become widespread in the Islamic empire until three or four generations after the death of Muhammad. It appears that the custom of veiling and secluding women came into the Muslim world from Persia and Byzantium, where women had long been treated in this way.

In fact the veil or curtain was not designed to degrade Muhammad's wives but was a symbol of their superior status. After Muhammad's death, his wives became very powerful people: they were respected authorities on religious matters and were frequently consulted about Muhammad's practice (*sunnah*) or opinions. Aisha became extremely important politically and in 656 led a revolution against Ali, the Fourth Caliph. It seems that later other women became jealous of the status of Muhammad's wives and demanded that they should be allowed to wear the veil too. Islamic culture was strongly egalitarian and it seemed incongruous that the Prophet's wives should be distinguished and honoured in this way. Thus many of the Muslim women who first took the veil saw it as a symbol of power and influence, not as a badge of male oppression. Certainly when the wives of the Crusaders saw the respect in which Muslim women were held, they took to wearing the veil in the hope of teaching their own menfolk to treat them better. It is always difficult to understand the symbols and practices of another culture. In Europe we are beginning to realise that we have often misinterpreted and undermined other traditional cultures in our former colonies and protectorates, and many Muslim women today, even those who have been brought up in the West, find it extremely offensive when Western feminists condemn their culture as misogynist. Most religions have been male affairs and have a patriarchal bias, but it is a mistake to see Islam as more at fault in this respect than any other tradition. In the Middle Ages the position was reversed: then the Muslims were horrified to see the way Western Christians treated their women in the Crusader states, and Christian scholars denounced Islam for giving too much power to menials like slaves and women. Today when some Muslim women resume traditional dress, it is not always because they have been brainwashed by a chauvinist religion, but because they find that a return to their own cultural roots is profoundly satisfying. It is often a rejection of the Western imperialist attitude which claims to understand their traditions better than they do themselves.

In January 627, shortly after the introduction of the *hijab* for the Prophet's wives, a painful incident showed how quickly any slur against his family could undermine Muhammad's position. He had led an expedition against the Bani al-Mustaliq, a branch of Khuza'ah, which was preparing to raid Medina. He took them by surprise at the Well of Muraysi on the Red Sea coast, north-west of Medina, put them to flight and made off with 2,000 camels, 5,000 sheep and goats and 200 of their women, including Juwayriyah bint al-Harith, the daughter of the chief. Aisha had been allowed to accompany the expedition and her heart sank as soon as she saw Juwayriyah – who had come to haggle with Muhammad about her ransom – simply because she was so pretty. 'By al-Llah I had scarcely seen her in the doorway of my room before I detested her,' she recalled later with disarming frankness. 'I knew he would see her as I saw her.'[50] Sure enough, Muhammad offered to marry her when she converted to Islam, and thus transformed an enemy tribe into an ally.

The Muslims camped at the Well of Muraysi for another couple of days. More of the Hypocrites had volunteered to join this raid than usual because it promised rich booty, and suddenly a trivial incident exposed the underlying tensions of the *umma*. A brawl had broken out between two of the local tribesmen, who had been hired to water the Muslims' horses, and each one called upon the traditional allies of their tribes: one on the Quraysh and the other on the Khasraj. Instantly Emigrants and Helpers responded to this tribal challenge and for a few minutes were at each others' throats – yet another indication of the strength of the old loyalties which could overthrow the new Islamic ideology so easily if Muslims were off guard. Umar and some of the other close companions of Muhammad quickly stepped in and stopped the fighting, but Ibn Ubbay was furious. What had the people of Medina come to that they allowed themselves to be ordered around by foreigners? 'They dispute our priority, they outnumber us in our own country and nothing so fits us and the vagabonds of Quraysh as the ancient saying "Feed a dog and it will devour you." By al-Llah when we return to Medina the stronger will drive out the weaker.'[51] One of the Helpers reported this threat to Muhammad and Umar instantly seized his sword. 'What? and say that Muhammad kills his Companions?' Muhammad asked mildly. But he gave the orders to march immediately, even though it meant travelling during the worst heat of the day – a thing he had never done before. During the journey home, Sura 13 – The Hypocrites – was revealed, but Muhammad kept it to himself until he got back to Medina.

During one of the halts, Aisha slipped away to relieve herself and when she returned to the camp, which was about to leave, she found that she had lost her necklace. She went back to hunt for it and while she was looking the men who were saddling her camel lifted her veiled howdah on to its back, thinking that she was still in it. Then the expedition moved off and when Aisha returned to the campsite she found it deserted. She was not particularly disturbed, because she knew that she would soon be missed, so she lay down to wait. Then Safwan ibn al-Mu'attal, the young man who had known Aisha quite well before the *hijab* had been introduced and who had fallen behind the rest, came by and recognised her. Aisha quickly veiled herself and he put her on the back of his own camel. Her absence had still not been discovered and when she suddenly arrived with Safwan tongues started to wag. The Hypocrites were quick to spread the scandal, stirring up latent tribal hostility against the Emigrants, who had brought all these wars upon them. The poet Hassan ibn Thabit, who had loyally celebrated Muhammad's triumphs since the *hijra*, began to lament the desertion of the old goddesses and described himself as surrounded by a sea of refugees in Medina. Even some of the Emigrants started to doubt Aisha's innocence, including her own cousin Mistah and Hamnah bint Jahsh, Zaynab's sister who was jealous on her behalf because Aisha was the Prophet's favourite. Zaynab, however, staunchly defended the girl.

Aisha had fallen ill when the party returned to Mecca and it was only gradually that she became aware of the gossip. She had noticed that Muhammad had been rather cold and distant with her and had asked to be moved to her parents' house where she could be looked after. Muhammad felt at a loss. It was particularly alarming to him that the revelations had suddenly stopped – a mark of his obvious distress and confusion. This time he could not turn to his usual companions for help. He clearly could not consult Abu Bakr about his own daughter and he did not ask Umar's opinion, probably because of Umar's well-known severity towards women. Instead he turned to the younger generation. When he asked Zayd's son Usamah what he thought of her, the boy spoke up for her warmly, as did the maidservant Buraya, who told Muhammad: 'I know only good of her. The only fault I have to find with Aisha is that when I am kneading the dough and tell her to watch it, the pet lamb comes and eats it!' But Ali was hostile and cynical: 'Women are plentiful,' he said dismissively, 'and you can always change one for another.'[52] Aisha never forgave him.

Ibn Ubbay continued to stir up trouble, delighted with this opportunity to discredit the Prophet. Muhammad had to call a meeting of the chiefs of Medina to ask for their support should he find it necessary to take action against one of their number who was trying to harm his family. He knew that some Muslims of Khasraj would be distressed if he proceeded against Ibn Ubbay without their permission. This meeting showed how fragile the new Muslim unity was. The issue revealed a deep fissure that still existed between Khasraj and Aws. Some of the chiefs of Aws, knowing very well that most of Aisha's enemies were members of Khasraj, urged that the stirrers of scandal should all be beheaded. Instantly a Khasrajite accused them of hypocrisy and the two tribes almost came to blows. A resolution to this crisis had to be found if the *umma* was to remain intact.

Finally, therefore, Muhammad went to confront Aisha herself. She was now recovered and seemed inconsolable. She had cried for two days and her parents had been no help at all. Umm Ruman, her mother, simply told her that all beautiful women had to expect this kind of trouble and Abu Bakr plainly did not know what to think: eventually he advised her to return to her hut at the mosque. When Muhammad arrived, her parents were with her and all three were weeping bitterly. But Aisha's tears dried like magic when the Prophet appeared. Muhammad urged her to confess her sin honestly, if she was guilty: God would forgive her. With great dignity, the fourteen-year-old girl looked steadily at her husband and parents as she made her reply. It was pointless for her to speak, she said. She would never admit to something that she had not done and if she protested her innocence, nobody would believe her. All she could do was to emulate that patriarch in the Qu'ran – desperately she searched her memory for his name but it eluded her – anyway, he had been the father of Joseph, and had said: 'My duty is to show becoming patience and God's aid is to be asked against what you describe.' Having said her last word, she went silently and lay down on her bed.

Muhammad must have been convinced, because when she had finished speaking he fell into the trance that often accompanied the revelations: he swooned and, even though it was a cold day, he perspired heavily. Abu Bakr put a leather cushion under his head and covered him with a mantle, while he and Umm Ruman waited in terror for God's comments. Aisha, however, who was in great danger, was icily calm: she was confident that God would not treat her unjustly. Finally Muhammad came to himself: 'Good news, Aisha!' he called. 'God has sent down word about your innocence.' Overcome with relief, her parents urged her to get up and to come to Muhammad. But Aisha simply replied: 'I shall neither come to him nor thank him. Nor will I thank the both of you who listened to the slander and did not deny it. I shall rise to give thanks to al-Llah alone.'[53] Accepting this rebuke, Muhammad went outside to confront the crowd that had gathered and recited the new verses that cleared Aisha, and condemned the slander as 'a manifest calumny'.[54]

The incident showed that Aisha had become a proud, fearless woman and she was able to regain her place in Muhammad's affections. Her dignified handling of the situation shows the confidence that Islam could give to a woman. None of the Prophet's wives seem to have been in the least cowed by their husband. They were quite ready to stand up to him and he always listened carefully to what they had to say. Frequently, however, the other wives complained that he favoured Aisha. Muhammad tried to keep to an impartial regime: he spent the night with each wife in turn and, when he went on an expedition, would draw lots to determine which of them was to accompany him. But he was only human and his real preference was clear to the whole *umma.* Muslims who liked to send him gifts used to send them to the mosque on the day that he was with Aisha, because they thought that this would please him. This was humiliating for the other wives and Umm Salamah went to Muhammad to get him to tell the Muslims to send gifts to all the apartments. But Muhammad begged her to stop nagging him about Aisha, pointing out that she was the only one of his present wives in whose company he received his revelations. Umm Salamah then sent Fatimah along, hoping that she would be more successful with her father. 'Dear little daughter,' Muhammad said gently, 'do you not love whom I love?' which threw Fatimah into complete confusion. Finally Zaynab came to protest and lost her temper, heaping abuse on Aisha. Muhammad turned to Aisha and told her to defend herself, which she did with such passion and eloquence that Zaynab was reduced to silence. Muhammad was amused: it was quite obvious to him, he said, that she was the true daughter of her father, Abu Bakr. But Aisha could not get away with everything. One day, jealous of the place that Khadija still held in Muhammad's affections, she called her a 'toothless old woman'. Muhammad was seriously displeased: nobody could be dearer to him than Khadija who had supported him when the rest of the world had rejected him.

In March 627, a few weeks after the scandal about Aisha had subsided, the Meccans and their Confederates were on the march with an army of 10,000. Muhammad could muster only about 3,000 men from Medina and his Bedouin allies, so there was no question of going out to meet the enemy as he had been forced to at Uhud, and all the Muslims barricaded themselves into their 'city'. Medina was not difficult to defend. It was surrounded on three sides by cliffs and plains of volcanic rock and it was relatively easy to man the roads that ran through this difficult terrain into the oasis. It was from the north that Medina was most vulnerable and Muhammad hit on an expedient which his contemporaries probably found extraordinary. The Quraysh and their allies seemed to be in no hurry but were grandly making their way north in easy stages, so the Muslims had plenty of time to make their preparations. They were able to gather in the crops from the outlying areas, so that the besieging army would find no fodder as they had last time, and then the whole *umma* set to work to build a huge trench or moat around the northern part of the oasis. Tradition has it that this plan was suggested by Salman, the Persian convert, who had recently been given his freedom. The trench did not need to be continuous, because in some places there were fortresses which gave adequate protection, but to get it finished in time required a mighty concerted effort. Each family group was responsible for a certain section of the trench and Muhammad worked alongside the others, singing the verses that they had sung while they had built the mosque after the *hijra*. Morale seems to have been high: some of his Companions recalled Muhammad looking extremely beautiful and vigorous as he laboured, joking and laughing with the other men. He led them in a new song:

> Lord but for Thee we had never been guided
> Never had given alms or prayed the prayer.
> Send then serenity upon us,
> Make firm our feet for the encounter:
> Those foes oppressed us, sought to prevent us
> But we refused.[55]

On 31 March 627 the Quraysh arrived with their army and stared nonplussed at the deep trench. The earth from the ditch had been used to build a huge escarpment, which effectively shielded the Muslims in their camp at the foot of Mount Sa'l and gave them a superior vantage point from which to hurl missiles. Indeed, as the Meccan army stared at the trench in bewilderment a shower of arrows warned them that they were sitting targets and they hastily withdrew until they were out of range. In a way that is almost comical, Salman's trench effectively stymied the whole massive offensive and the Qurayshi leaders simply did not know how to deal with it. Yet again, their army was led by Abu Sufyan and Ikrimah (son of Abu Jahl), and Khalid ibn al-Walid commanded the cavalry with Amr ibn al-As, the Qurayshite who had long been a dedicated enemy of Muhammad. But the cavalry, of which they had such hopes, was now completely useless, because the horses could not get over the trench. On the few occasions when one or two did manage to leap across it, their riders were instantly cut to pieces. To send the infantry across would mean that they would probably incur too many casualties, and they had no siege engines or ladders with them. In any case, the Quraysh despised manual labour and clearly considered the trench to be in the worst possible taste: it was unsporting, unArab and contradicted all the conventions of chivalric warfare. From time to time people like Ikrimah would try to lead a dashing charge but found themselves balked and literally brought up short:

> Some horsemen of the Quraysh . . . donned their armour and went forth on horseback to the stations of the Bani Kinana, saying, 'Prepare for fighting and then you will know who are true knights today.' They galloped forward until they stopped at the trench. When they saw it they exclaimed, 'This is a device which the Arabs have never employed!'[56]

They decided to try a more wily method and get the Jewish tribe of Qurayzah, in the south of the oasis, to let them into the city. At the beginning of the year, Huyay ibn Akhtab, chief of the exiled Jewish tribe of Nadir now living in Khaybar, had visited Abu Sufyan in Mecca and promised to support him in his struggle against Muhammad. He had gone with Safwan and some of the other Quraysh into the Ka'aba to swear an oath before God that they would not fail one another until they had destroyed the *umma*. Abu Sufyan thought he should take the opportunity to ask them their opinion of Muhammad's religious claims: 'You, O Jews, are the people of the first scripture and know the nature of our dispute with Muhammad. Is our religion the best or is his?' Huyay replied that the religion of the Quraysh was definitely the best. The Muslims were scandalised when they heard that Huyay had thus defended idolatry.[57] The Jews of Khaybar had sent a large army to Medina and had managed to rouse up the Arab tribes in the north against Medina, bribing them if necessary with the promise of half their date crop. So the tribes of Asad, Ghatafan and Sulaym had all sent contingents to Medina to join Abu Sufyan's confederacy. Now Huyay tried to persuade the Bani Qurayzah either to attack the Muslims themselves from the rear or to let about 2,000 of Nadir and Ghatafan into the settlement where they could begin their attack by slaughtering the women and children who were barricaded into the fortresses dotted all over the settlement. The Jews were hesitant: they knew what had happened to people like Qaynuqah and Nadir who had opposed Muhammad and some of them were beginning to wonder whether he might not be the long-awaited prophet after all. But, when they saw the huge army that the Quraysh had brought to Medina filling the plain in front of the city to the horizon, Ka'b ibn Asad, chief of Qurayzah, agreed to help the Confederacy.

Umar was the first to learn of Qurayzah's treachery and he reported it immediately to Muhammad, who was visibly distressed. He had always dreaded this possibility and knew that the Muslim army would not be able to sustain such an attack from all sides. He sent Sa'd ibn Muadh, who had been the chief Arab ally of Qurayzah before the *hijra*, to conduct an investigation in their territory and he reported that the Jews seemed defiant: 'Who is the Messenger of God?' they had asked. 'There is no pact between us and Muhammad nor any agreement.'[58] At one point it seems that a handful of them began their attack from the south-east of the oasis and surrounded one of the fortresses containing the Muslim women and children, but this effort petered out. Muhammad began his own diplomatic offensive among the Qurayzah, which tried to make the Jews lose heart and distrust the Quraysh. But for about three weeks it was quite uncertain which way the Jews would go. The Muslim army was becoming exhausted; it seems that the Hypocrites were also spreading alarm and dismay, urging the Helpers to abandon Muhammad to his tribe. Some of them even seem to have tried to escape from Medina and join Abu Sufyan. The Qu'ran makes it clear that the Muslims came to the brink of despair and some were close to losing faith:

> your eyes swerved
> and your hearts reached your throats, while you thought
> strange thoughts about God;
> there it was that the believers were tried,
> and shaken most mightily.[59]

Yet they were delivered from this Dark Night of fear. It is not clear what happened exactly, but it seems that the Jews of Qurayzah began to distrust the Meccans and insisted on taking Qurayshi hostages to ensure their fidelity: what would happen if the Meccans fled and left the Jews to the mercy of Muhammad? The Quraysh were also becoming exhausted. It was always difficult to maintain a siege in Arabia; they had no provisions, and men and horses were hungry. The Quraysh were not skilled or experienced soldiers and they were easily shaken by sudden reversals. It seems that their resolve snapped when the weather suddenly changed. Certainly the Qu'ran speaks of the drop in the temperature, the wind and the rain as an act of God. Abu Sufyan made his decision:

O Quraysh, we are not in a permanent camp; the horses and camels are dying; the Bani Qurayzah have broken their word to us and we have heard disquieting reports of them. You can see the violence of the wind which leaves us neither cooking pots, nor fire, nor tents to count on. Be off, for I am going![60]

So saying, he leaped on to his camel and beat it, not realising in his haste that it was still hobbled. He was followed by his own tribe and by the Bedouin, who had been chuntering and restless for some time, and they quickly dispersed. As the Confederacy beat an ignominious retreat, Khalid said to Abu Sufyan: 'Every man of sense now knows that Muhammad has not lied.'[61] When the Muslims peered over the top of the escarpment the next morning, the vast plain was entirely empty.

But what was Muhammad to do about the Jews of Qurayzah, who had brought the *umma* to the brink of extinction? He did not let his men rest but on the following morning, inspired it is said by Gabriel, Muhammad summoned the Muslim army to the village of Qurayzah. This is a grim and horrible story and has hideous overtones for most of us today. Huyay had joined Qurayzah in their quarters after the Quraysh and the confederates had left Medina, as he had promised. When they heard that Muhammad was advancing on their territory, the Qurayzah duly barricaded themselves into their fortreess and managed to hold out against the Muslims for twenty-five days. They knew that as unfaithful allies they could expect no mercy, and Huyay and Ka'b seem to have urged them to accept the inevitable. They put three possibilities before their people: they could either submit to Muhammad unconditionally (his extraordinary success argued that he might be a true prophet); or they could kill their women and children and attack the Muslim army: if they died they would not have to worry about their dependants and if they won they could easily find new wives; or they could take Muhammad unawares by attacking him on their Sabbath, when he would not be expecting them to act.

The Jews rejected all these options and asked Muhammad to let them leave the oasis on the same terms as the Bani Nadir. Muhammad refused: Nadir had proved to be even more dangerous to the *umma* after it had left Medina, so this time he was determined to exact total surrender. He allowed Qurayzah to consult one of their former allies: Abu Lubabah ibn Abd al-Mundhir, the chief of Auf. This part of the story is obscure. The Jews are said to have asked Abu Lubabah what Muhammad intended to do and he touched his throat, tacitly telling them that they had been sentenced to death. He was then so overcome by remorse that he bound himself to a pillar of the mosque for fifteen days until Muhammad released him. If he had told the Jews of their fate in this way, it does not seem to have affected their decision, so it has been suggested that he had perhaps indicated that he would honour his old allegiance to Qurayzah. The next day, the Qurayzah agreed to accept Muhammad's judgement and opened their gates to the Muslim army, presumably trusting in the support of their former confederates in the tribe of Aws.

Indeed, the Aws begged Muhammad to be merciful; had he not granted the Bani Qaynuqa their lives at the request of Ibn Ubbay, a Khasrajite? Muhammad asked them if they would accept the decision of one of their own leading men and they agreed. During the siege, Sa'd ibn Muadh had received a fatal wound, but he was carried to the territory of Qurayzah on a donkey. His fellow chiefs urged him to spare their former allies, but Sa'd would have realised that this could be the thin end of the wedge that would bring chaos back to Medina. Should an old loyalty take precedence over commitment to the *umma*? Sa'd judged that all the 700 men should be killed, their wives and children sold into slavery and their property divided among the Muslims. Muhammad cried aloud: 'You have judged according to the very sentence of al-Llah above the seven skies!'[62]

The next day Muhammad ordered another trench to be dug, this time in the *souk* of Medina. Some individuals were spared at the request of the Muslims, but the rest were tied together in groups and beheaded; their bodies were thrown into the trench. Only one woman was executed, for throwing a millstone on one of the Muslims during the siege of the tribe. Aisha remembered her vividly:

> She was actually with me and was talking with me and laughing immoderately as the apostle was killing her men in the market when suddenly an unseen voice called her name. 'Good heavens,' I cried, 'what is the matter?' 'I am to be killed,' she replied. 'What for?' I asked. 'Because of something I did,' she answered. She was taken away and beheaded. Aisha used to say, I shall never forget my wonder at her good spirits and her loud laughter when all the time she knew that she would be killed.[63]

It is probably impossible for us to dissociate this story from Nazi atrocities and it will inevitably alienate many people irrevocably from Muhammad. But Western scholars like Maxime Rodinson and W. Montgomery Watt argue that it is not correct to judge the incident by twentieth-century standards. This was a very primitive society – far more primitive than the Jewish society in which Jesus had lived and promulgated his gospel of mercy and love some 600 years earlier. At this stage the Arabs had no concept of a universal natural law, which is difficult – perhaps impossible – for people to attain unless there is a modicum of public order, such as that imposed by a great empire in the ancient world. At the time of Muhammad, Medina was probably more like the Jerusalem of King David, who was a mighty slayer of the enemies of God and who on one occasion massacred two hundred Philistines, castrated them and sent the grisly pile of foreskins to their king. Many of the psalms attributed to David were in fact composed centuries later – some as late as 550 BCE – but they still describe in gruesome detail the horrible things the Israelites hoped to do to their enemies. In the early seventh century, an Arab chief would not be expected to show any mercy to traitors like Qurayzah.

The Muslim *umma* had narrowly escaped extermination at the siege and emotions were naturally running high. Qurayzah had nearly destroyed Medina. If Muhammad had let them go they would at once have swelled the Jewish opposition at Khaybar and have organised another offensive against Medina: the next time the Muslims might not be so lucky and the bloody struggle for survival would continue indefinitely with more suffering and more deaths. The summary executions would have impressed Muhammad's enemies. Nobody seems to have been shocked by the massacre and the Qurayzah themselves seem to have accepted its inevitability. The executions sent a grim message to the Jews at Khaybar, and the Arab tribes would have noted that Muhammad was not afraid of any friends or allies of Qurayzah avenging their deaths in a blood-feud. It was a symbol of the extraordinary power that Muhammad had achieved after the siege, when he had become the leader of the most powerful group in Arabia.

The massacre of Qurayzah is a reminder of the desperate conditions of Arabia during Muhammad's lifetime. Of course we are right to condemn it without reserve, but it was not as great a crime as it would be today. Muhammad was not working within a world empire which imposed widespread order nor within one of the established religious traditions. He had nothing like the Ten Commandments (though even Moses is said to have commanded the Israelites to massacre the entire population of Canaan shortly after he had told them: 'Thou shalt not kill.'). All Muhammad had was the old tribal morality, which had permitted this expedient to preserve the group. The problem was compounded by the fact that Muhammad's victory had made him the most powerful chief in Arabia at the head of a group that was not a conventional tribe. He had just begun to transcend tribalism and was in a no man's land between two stages of social development.

But it is important to note that this tragic beginning did not permanently colour the Muslim attitude to Jews. Once the Muslims had established their own world empire and were evolving a more sophisticated and humane ethic in their own Holy Law, they would establish a system of toleration such as had long prevailed in the civilised parts of the Middle East. In that part of the Oikumene various religious groups had long lived side by side. Anti-Semitism is a vice of Western Christianity not of Islam, and we should bear that in mind if we feel tempted to make generalisations about this horrible incident in Medina. Even in Muhammad's own time, smaller Jewish groups remained in Medina after 627 and were allowed to live in peace with no further reprisals. It appears that the second part of the Covenant of Medina, which deals with the Jewish population of the settlement, was composed after this date. In the Islamic empire Jews like Christians had full religious liberty; the Jews lived there in peace until the creation of the State of Israel in our own century. The Jews of Islam never suffered like the Jews of Christendom. The anti-Semitic myths of Europe were introduced into the Middle East at the end of the last century by Christian missionaries and were usually scorned by the populace. But in recent years some Muslims have turned to passages of the Qu'ran which refer to the rebellious Jewish tribes of Medina and tend to ignore the far more numerous verses which speak positively of the Jews and their great prophets. This is an entirely new development in a history of 1,200 years of good relations between Jews and Muslims.[64]

The Qu'ran teaches that war is always abominable. Muslims must never open hostilities, for the only just war is a war of self-defence, but, once they have undertaken a war, Muslims must fight with absolute commitment in order to bring the fighting to an end as soon as possible.[65] If the enemy proposes a truce or shows an inclination towards peace, Muslims are commanded by the Qu'ran to end hostilities immediately, provided that the terms of peace are not immoral or dishonourable.[66] But the Qu'ran is also emphatic that it is a sacred duty to bring armed conflict to a speedy close and face the enemy steadfastly. Any wavering or indecision which could mean that the conflict drags on indefinitely must be avoided.[67]

The purpose of any war must be to restore peace and harmony as soon as possible. Much as we may shudder at the horrible spectacle in the *souk* of Medina in May 627, it has been argued that, purely politically, it was the right decision. It was the last of such atrocities, because it marked the beginning of the end of the worst phase of the *jihad*. Muhammad had defeated one of the largest Arab armies that had ever united against a single enemy at the Battle of the Trench; he had quashed the opposition of three powerful Jewish tribes and shown that he would brook no further treachery or plotting against the *umma*. He had proved that he was now the most powerful man in Arabia, who had brought to a speedy, peremptory end a bloody conflict that could have dragged on for years.

The word 'Islam' comes from a root which means peace and reconciliation. After the massacre of Qurayzah we shall see a marked change in the policy of the *jihad*. Now that he was no longer fighting for his life, Muhammad could begin to impose the *pax Islamica* upon Arabia. The following year he would insist on a policy of peace and reconciliation which almost alienated his closest and most loyal companions.

9 · Holy Peace

Muhammad's victory over the Quraysh at the siege of Medina was a magnificent triumph. Five years earlier, he had arrived in the oasis as a weary, travel-worn refugee who had been hounded almost to death by the people of Mecca. Now he had reversed that state of affairs, proving before the whole of Arabia that Mecca's day was over. They had utterly failed to get rid of Muhammad and the *umma* and would never recover the prestige on which their power and their whole way of life had been based. Mecca was now a doomed city and Muhammad, as even Khalid ibn al-Walid had acknowledged when the Quraysh had raised the siege, was the coming man. The old tribal system, the ideology of *hilm* and the aggressive capitalism of the Quraysh had proved ineffective before the moral and political power of Islam. The bloody phase of the *jihad* was now over. Muhammad had always wanted to win the Quraysh over to his side rather than destroy them completely, and after the siege he had to begin the process of reconciliation without, and this was essential, showing any sign of weakness or indecision.

At this time Muhammad's conception of his mission appears to have changed yet again. Since his victory at Badr, he had begun to see that Arab unity was no longer an impossibility. Now his defeat of the Quraysh and his summary treatment of the Bani Qurayzah had impressed the Bedouin tribes, many of which were now ready to abandon the Quraysh and enter an alliance with the *umma* at Medina. Muhammad was now looking further than Mecca. He needed to win over the city because it had become central to his religious vision, but he was beginning to consider the area north of Medina as offering an opportunity for the expansion of Islam. This does not mean that he had any dreams of world conquest but simply that he wanted to bring his Arabic Qu'ran to the northern tribes and also, perhaps, to the Arabs of Syria and the Iraq who had been absorbed into the Byzantine polity and religious system. There is a tradition, which is not mentioned by the earliest sources, that at about this time Muhammad despatched letters and rich gifts to the emperors of Byzantium and Persia, to the Negus of Abyssinia and the Muqawqis of Egypt inviting them to enter Islam. This is almost certainly apocryphal because there is no evidence that Muhammad saw Islam as a universal religion which would supersede the revelations of the People of the Book. It was still a religion for the sons of Ishmael, as Judaism was a religion for the sons of Jacob. For about a hundred years after the death of their prophet, Muslims continued to see Islam as simply a religion for Arabs, but there may have been some truth in the legend of these embassies to neighbouring rulers. It expresses Muhammad's new confidence and his larger vision. He was no longer just the leader of a persecuted sect, no longer just one among several other chiefs of Medina, but one of the most important *sayyids* of Arabia. He may also have wanted to forestall any Meccan requests for foreign aid in this last phase of the struggle. In the letters that have come down to us, Muhammad simply asked these rulers to accept him as a prophet. Muhammad now believed that al-Llah had sent him as a prophet to *all* the Arabs. At the same time as he wrote to the emperors, the Negus and Muqawqis, it is said that he also wrote to the two northern Arab tribes of Ghassan and Hanifah, which were largely Christian. He would not have expected them to abandon their Christianity, but to enter the *umma* on rather the same basis as the remaining Jewish clans in Medina.

In the year 627–8 Muhammad began to build up his own confederacy, inviting the tribes to become his allies in the same way as the Ahabish had become the confederates of the Quraysh. Individuals among the Bedouin had converted to Islam and some had actually made the *hijra* to Medina, and though the alliances that he was making in this year were often strictly political, he hoped that this would eventually lead to a religious commitment. It was essential that he continued to present an image of strength and decisiveness. During this year too he despatched various expeditions against tribes which were members of the Meccan Confederacy like Asad and Thalabah, who may have come a little closer to Medina than usual during this year of abnormally severe drought. The *ghazu* would have been giving a 'hands off' message. He also despatched a raid against the tribe of Sa'd, which was contemplating an alliance with the Jews of Khaybar. The Bedouin were beginning to see that it was dangerous to be friendly to the *umma*'s enemies, and its strength would have increased their respect for Muhammad and his religion.

Muhammad had no plans to attack Mecca that year, but he was trying to weaken the Meccan monopoly of trade. As more converts made the *hijra* and the population of Medina increased, it became essential for the *umma* to establish its own trade with Syria and bring imports into the oasis. He sent expeditions to the north, possibly to attract some of the Syrian trade to Medina, as well as to spread his religious message. Abd al-Rahman, for example, took a caravan to Dumat al-Jandal on the road to Syria, where a great fair was held each year. Medina had been gradually effecting an economic blockade of Mecca since Badr, when the Red Sea route had become impossible for the Quraysh. During the year after the siege of Medina, Muhammad sought to tighten this blockade and at the same time to secure trading opportunities for the Muslims. Zayd was sent to trade in Syria, but his caravan was attacked and he himself left for dead, though he managed to drag himself back to Medina. Shortly afterwards Zayd had better luck with a *ghazu* which attacked a Meccan caravan on its way back from Syria. One of the Qurayshi merchants with this caravan happened to be Muhammad's pagan son-in-law Abu al-As. He escaped and crept into Medina by night to visit his former wife Zaynab. Next morning, at the early prayers in the mosque, Zaynab announced that she had given her protection to Abu al-As ibn al-Rabi. Muhammad, who had known nothing of this, supported his daughter's right to grant this man protection, though he privately warned her not to sleep with him.

Zaynab told Muhammad that Abu al-As was terribly unhappy to have lost the merchandise because he had acquired it on behalf of various people in Mecca who had entrusted their goods to him. Muhammad immediately asked the raiders who had captured the caravan to return these goods to Abu al-As and they obeyed scrupulously, even going so far as to give him back some old water-skins, bottles and useless pieces of wood. This paid off. Abu al-As went back to Mecca, distributed the merchandise to its owners and then made the *hijra*, submitted to Islam and was reunited with Zaynab. He had been prepared to give up a beloved wife and daughter in his zeal for the pagan religion, but now his people were doomed: he had to accept the inevitable. Some people in Mecca were beginning to feel the same way and Muhammad must have been aware of this. They had marched against Medina in honour of the old gods; at Uhud their war cry had been 'O al-Uzza! O Hubal!', but these deities had been powerless against Muhammad's religion of al-Llah. Yet others, like Safwan, Ikrimah and Suhayl, chief of Amir, remained committed to the struggle against Muhammad.

Muhammad must have heard about this change of heart from converts like Abu al-As and his own spies (he now had quite a highly developed intelligence system). But it was difficult to know exactly how to approach Mecca, since, as we shall see, he had no intention of leading a military offensive against the holy city. He had, as usual, no clearly defined plan, but he must have been exercised with the problem at a subconscious level because in March 628 during the traditional month for the *hajj* pilgrimage a solution or rather a vision of reconciliation and victory surfaced in a dream. He had seen himself with the shaven head of the pilgrim, wearing the traditional pilgrim costume, standing in the Ka'aba, holding its key in his hand. It seemed to fill him with an assurance of victory which was later expressed in these words of God in the Qu'ran:

> 'You shall enter the Holy Mosque,
> if God wills, in security, your
> heads shaved, your hair cut short,
> not fearing.'[1]

The next morning he announced that he was going to make the pilgrimage to the Ka'aba and invited his Companions to accompany him. It is easy to imagine the fear, wonder and uncertain joy that filled the Muslims when they heard this extraordinary invitation. Muhammad made it clear that this would not be a military expedition. The Muslims would wear the traditional white robe of the pilgrims and they would not bear arms. It was extremely dangerous, of course, and the Bedouin confederates of the *umma* declined the invitation, but about a thousand of the Emigrants and Helpers agreed to go with Muhammad. Even Ibn Ubbay and some of his supporters went along, which shows that they had been greatly chastened by the Muslim victory, against all the odds, the previous year and by the fate of the Bani Qurayzah. Muhammad decided to take his wife Umm Salamah with him, and the two women who had been present at Second 'Aqaba were also permitted to take part in the pilgrimage.

The pilgrims hastily began their preparations and gathered together seventy camels, which, according to the ancient ritual, had to be sacrificed in the sacred precinct. Muhammad dressed in the traditional pilgrim garb, which consisted of two pieces of unstitched cloth, one of which was draped round the waist, the other round the shoulders: it is still worn by pilgrims who make the *hajj* to Mecca today. Umar argued that the Quraysh would be bound to attack the Muslim pilgrims and urged that the pilgrims ride fully armed in case of an assault. But Muhammad was adamant: 'I will not carry arms,' he said firmly. 'I had come forth for no other end than to make the Pilgrimage.'[2] He was still filled with the confidence and assurance of his dream that he would somehow be reunited with the Ka'aba 'without fear', even though, as we shall see, he had no detailed notion of how this would come about. But he was adamant that he was not going out to fight on this occasion, so each pilgrim simply carried a short sword suitable only for hunting, which he was to keep in its sheath.

At the first stop, Muhammad consecrated one of the camels in the traditional way, making special marks on it, hanging ceremonial garlands around its neck and turning it in the direction of Mecca. He then uttered the ancient cry of the pilgrims as they approached the Ka'aba, '*Labbayk al-Llahuma Labbayk!*' which means 'Here I am, O God, at your service!' Some of the pilgrims followed suit, but others decided to postpone making the formal consecration until later, because there were certain ritual restrictions about hunting game during the pilgrimage.

Muhammad knew perfectly well that he had put the Quraysh in an extremely difficult position. As the guardians of Mecca, it would be scandalous if they forbade a thousand Arab pilgrims, who were punctiliously observing the ancient rituals, to enter the Meccan sanctuary, but it would be an enormous moral triumph for Muhammad if he did enter the holy city in this way and would simply confirm their humiliation at his hands. Suhayl, Ikrimah and Safwan and their supporters were determined to prevent him from entering the city, even if this did mean that they shocked the Bedouin tribes. But Abu Sufyan seems to have remained curiously silent. He was a man of outstanding intelligence and he probably realised that the game was up and that Muhammad could no longer be dealt with by conventional methods.

But he seems to have been the only person in the Senate to have taken this view. Khalid ibn al-Walid was sent with a troop of 200 cavalry to prevent the Muslims from entering the city and when the pilgrims had reached the Well of Usfan, about twenty-five miles north-east of Mecca, their scout brought them the news that Khalid was only eight miles away. Muhammad replied confidently: 'Alas, Quraysh, war has devoured them! What harm would they have suffered if they had left me and the rest of the Arabs to go our own ways? . . . By al-Llah, I will not cease to fight for the mission with which God has entrusted me until he makes it victorious or I perish.'[3] He asked the pilgrims to find a local guide who could lead them to the Sanctuary, the sacred region round Mecca where all fighting and violence was forbidden. A member of the clan of Aslam volunteered and took them by a very rugged track which was beyond Khalid's reach. When they reached the easy ground and arrived at the outermost point of the Sanctuary, Muhammad reminded the pilgrims of the religious nature of their expedition. They were about to enter a holy place and he urged them to make a spiritual transition and put their sins behind them, saying: 'We ask God's forgiveness and we repent towards Him.'[4] Then he ordered them to take the road towards Hudaybiyah at the edge of the Sanctuary, telling them to make their camels kick up the sand so that Khalid and his men would realise that they were now out of danger.

Muhammad's dream had probably led him to expect that the Quraysh would give in to pressure and allow the Muslim pilgrims to enter the city, but Khalid's armed force showed that they were ready to kill his unarmed company rather than admit them to the Ka'aba. As usual, he responded to the situation imaginatively as it developed, even though he can have had no idea how things would turn out. When they reached Hudaybiyah, Muhammad's camel Qaswa, who seems to have made a speciality of this, suddenly fell to her knees and refused to get up. The pilgrims crowded round her shouting 'Hal! hal!' in the usual way, but Qaswa would not budge and the men berated her stubbornness. But Muhammad said that this was not her nature and reminded them of the defeat of the Abyssinians in the Year of the Elephant, when the great beast had knelt before the Ka'aba: 'the One who restrained the elephant from Mecca is keeping [Qaswa] back. Today whatever condition Quraysh make in which they ask me to show kindness to kindred, I will agree to.'[5] Reconciliation, not war, was to characterise this expedition and he told the pilgrims to dismount. When they objected that there was no water, Muhammad is said to have given an arrow to one of the Companions, who struck it into one of the dry water-holes and the water bubbled up immediately.

The camels drank their fill and lay down, and the pilgrims, who were probably disappointed that they were not being asked to do something more heroic, sat down beside them. What transpired was indeed a 'sit-in', an eloquent demonstration that would have made a powerful impression on the Bedouin. All eyes were on Muhammad at this time; news travelled quickly from tribe to tribe and the nomads would have been horrified to hear that the Quraysh had been ready to attack a troop of peaceful Arab pilgrims and had forbidden them access to the Ka'aba, which was a sacred right for all Arabs. Sitting patiently at the edge of the Sanctuary, in full pilgrim dress, Muhammad was demonstrating that in this matter the Muslims were more in line with Arab tradition than the guardians of the Ka'aba. Soon after they had arrived, a delegation came from the tribe of Khuza'ah, which was led by Budayl ibn Warqa, one of its chiefs who had been visiting Mecca and had heard the news. When Budayl asked him why he had come, Muhammad replied that the Muslims had come not to do battle but to visit the holy places: if necessary, they would fight, poorly equipped as they were, for their right to visit the Ka'aba, but they wanted to give the Quraysh time to make up their minds what they wanted to do. Budayl was horrified that peaceful pilgrims had been refused entrance in this way, and he promised that the Khuza'ah would supply the Muslims with food and information as long as they were in Hudaybiyah.

He returned immediately to Mecca and objected angrily to the Qurayshi policy, which violated all the traditions which the Arabs held to be most holy. Ikrimah refused even to listen to what Muhammad had said, but Safwan asked to hear the message. When Budayl had stressed Muhammad's peaceful intentions, some of the Quraysh were incredulous: 'He may not have come wanting war,' they said, 'but by al-Llah he shall never come in here against our will, nor shall the Arabs ever say that we have allowed it.'[6] Rather than let him in, they vowed that they would stand between Muhammad and the Ka'aba and fight until their last man had been killed. But, as a way of causing division in the Muslim ranks, they sent word to Ibn Ubbay and invited him to perform the rights at the

Ka'aba, because they knew him to be a friend of Mecca. To their surprise, however, Ibn Ubbay sent word that he could not think of making the circumambulations before Muhammad. Whatever his past opinion – and he would oppose Muhammad again in the future – at Hudaybiyah Ibn Ubbay proved himself to be a good Muslim.

Other members of the Quraysh, including Safwan and Suhayl, thought that they should try to negotiate with Muhammad. Urwah ibn Mas'ud of Taif, a confederate who was visiting Mecca, offered to act as a go-between, arguing that it would only be counter-productive to refuse Muhammad's reasonable request, especially as he had publicly declared that he was ready to make concessions. The Quraysh accepted Urwah's offer, but first they sent one of their Bedouin allies, al-Hulays ibn Alqama, chief of the tribe of al-Harith, who was the leading man of the whole Ahabish. He was a devout pagan, and as soon as Muhammad saw him coming he said to his fellow pilgrims: 'Here is one of the pious folk, so send the sacrificial camels to meet him.' When Hulays saw the seventy camels trotting towards him, all beautifully decked in their garlands and bearing the special marks of consecration, he felt that he had seen enough. He did not even bother to interrogate Muhammad but went straight back to the Quraysh to tell them that these really were *bona fide* pilgrims and must, as of right, be admitted to the Ka'aba. But Safwan and his colleagues were furious at this unwelcome report. They told Hulays to sit down and shut up: he was only an ignorant Bedouin. This was a grave mistake, as Hulays immediately let them know when he rose with dignity and said:

> You men of Quraysh, it was not for this that we made an alliance and agreement with you. Is a man who comes to do honour to the house of al-Llah to be excluded from it? By Him who holds my life in his hand, either you let Muhammad do what he has come to do or I shall take away [my] troops to the last man.[7]

The Quraysh hastily apologised and asked Hulays to bear with them until they had been able to arrive at a compromise that would satisfy everybody.

Next they sent Urwah ibn Mas'ud to Hudaybiyah. He sat with Muhammad and warned him that the Quraysh were arming to the teeth: how could he possibly hope to sustain an attack when he was backed by a motley group of people who all belonged to different tribes, some of whom had fought each other bitterly in the past. Abu Bakr was so incensed that he shouted, 'Suck at al-Lat's nipples!' and Urwah told him that it was just as well that he happened to be in his debt, because otherwise he would have been forced to pay him back for that insult. To attract Muhammad's attention, he took hold of his beard in the traditional Arab gesture of familiarity, but another Muslim slapped his hand away.

Urwah left the camp greatly impressed by the Muslims' intense devotion to Muhammad. As Ibn Ishaq says, he had seen that 'Whenever he performed his ablutions, they rose to get the water he had used; if he spat they ran to it; if a hair of his head fell they ran to pick it up.' Urwah was a well-travelled merchant, and he reported back to the Quraysh that not even the emperors of Byzantium and Persia were held in such reverence. 'I have seen a people who will never abandon him for any reason, so form your own opinion,' he told them.[8]

Muhammad decided to send his own envoy into Mecca. First he sent one of the Helpers, thinking that this would be less inflammatory, but the Quraysh hamstrung the man's camel and would have killed him had not Hulays' troops come to his defence. Next Muhammad asked Umar, but even he was wary and hesitant: none of his clansmen was strong enough to protect him, and he suggested that Uthman ibn Affan should go instead. Uthman had many aristocratic connections in the city, so the Quraysh listened to his message but were unimpressed. They told him that as he was there he could perform the *tawwaf* round the Ka'aba if he liked, but, like Ibn Ubbay, Uthman refused to perform the ritual before Muhammad. The Quraysh then kept him as a hostage and sent word to the Muslim camp that he had been killed.

When Muhammad heard this news, he vowed that he would not leave Hudaybiyah until he had confronted the enemy. It was a moment of crisis and it looked as though the whole expedition, which had seemed a literally inspired idea, had misfired horribly. At this moment of extremity, he is said to have fallen into a tranced state, very similar to the swoon that came over him when he was receiving a revelation, except that he did not lose consciousness. He must have searched his soul deeply and desperately for a solution. Then he summoned the Muslims and asked them to swear a special oath of fealty to him. One by one the thousand pilgrims came to take his hand and swear the oath that would become known as the *bay'at al-ridwan*, the Pledge of Good Pleasure. The sources give conflicting versions of the content of this oath. Some say that the Muslims vowed to fight the Quraysh to the death, but theirs is the minority view. More traditions claim that the Muslims simply swore that they would not run away, but Waqidi says that each Muslim grasped Muhammad's hand and vowed to follow what was 'in his soul', to obey Muhammad implicitly during this crisis.[9] Everybody swore the oath, including Ibn Ubbay and the Hypocrites who had joined the pilgrimage.

It is tempting to follow Waqidi here. When Muhammad had entered that state of intense concentration, he must have resolved at some deep and possibly instinctual level to take a course of action that he knew would not only seem intolerable but which could even cause a rebellion among his followers. It would seem a complete reversal of his previous policy towards the Quraysh. As yet it was a hunch rather than a clearly articulated and rational policy. He was listening to the deep logic of the events that were unfolding at Hudaybiyah in a way that he had not expected when he had led his pilgrims out of Medina. Shortly after everybody had taken the oath, word came that Uthman was not dead after all. Then Muhammad saw Suhayl approaching the camp with two companions and knew that the arrival of this envoy meant that the Quraysh had decided to negotiate. He sat with Suhayl for a long time, and after an intense discussion terms were agreed that filled his companions with dismay.

Muhammad promised that he would return to Medina without visiting the Ka'aba on this occasion, which meant that none of the Arab tribes would be able to say that he had forced the hands of the Quraysh. But the next year, at the same time, the Muslims would return to Mecca as pilgrims once again and this time the Quraysh would vacate the city for three days so that they could perform the rites of the *umra* or the Lesser Pilgrimage around the Ka'aba in peace. There would be a truce for ten years between Mecca and Medina, on condition that Muhammad promised to return to Mecca any member of the Quraysh who became a Muslim and made the *hijra* without the consent of his guardians. But the Quraysh would not have to return any Muslim who defected to them. Finally, the Bedouin tribes were released from former obligations and could choose to form an alliance with either Mecca or Medina. The Qu'ran had stipulated that Muslims were always to agree to any conditions that the enemy proposed, if there was a chance of a truce. But these terms seemed dishonourable to the Muslims. Muhammad appeared to be throwing away the advantage he had gained during this expedition by tamely agreeing to withdraw without forcing the pilgrimage issue. The truce with Mecca meant that the Muslims could no longer raid the caravans of the Quraysh: how were the Emigrants going to earn a living and why was Muhammad abandoning the economic blockade that had so successfully begun to strangle the Meccan trade monopoly? Above all, why on earth had Muhammad agreed to return any new converts to Mecca, when the Quraysh did not have to reciprocate and return Muslim apostates and defectors to Medina? Muhammad seemed to have abandoned the *jihad*, in which so many Muslims had died and others had risked everything, and calmly handed the advantage to Mecca. As Ibn Ishaq says, 'The apostle's companions had gone out without any doubt of occupying Mecca because of the vision which the apostle had seen, and when they saw the negotiations for peace and a withdrawal going on and what the apostle had taken on himself they felt depressed almost to the point of death.'[10]

Worse, mutiny was in the air. The treaty was more than Umar could stand and he jumped up immediately and went to Abu Bakr. 'Are we not Muslims and they polytheists?' he demanded. 'Why should we agree to what is demeaning to our religion?'[11] Abu Bakr was also shaken but he told Umar that he still had faith in Muhammad. Later Umar said that if he could have found a hundred companions to follow him he would have defected from the *umma*. But Muhammad could see further than anybody else at Hudaybiyah; even though the pilgrimage had not turned out as he expected, it had been an inspiration that had put him on the road to peace. He was about to try something entirely new which was beyond the grasp of even his most loyal and trusty Companions, let alone the rank and file who were sitting in stunned silence trying to take in this sudden reversal. Muhammad, however, knew at some deep level exactly what he was about, even though he was groping his way towards it in the dark. As long as he was barred from the Ka'aba the Bedouin tribes would hesitate to join him. He had to prove that his Muslims were as devoted to the most sacred place in Arabia as they. By making peace with Mecca he had gained access to the Sanctuary, which was a vital weapon in the propaganda war, and he had wrung from the Quraysh the important acknowledgement that Mecca and Medina were now equals. This was especially apparent in the clause which allowed the nomadic tribes to abandon their old alliance with the Quraysh and become confederates of the *umma*: the tribe of Khuza'ah, to which Muhammad had become related by marriage,[12] instantly took advantage of the new situation and joined Muhammad. After defeating the Quraysh at Medina, the obvious thing would have been to press on and destroy them militarily, but Muhammad had never wanted this. By abandoning the economic blockade, he was hoping to woo the Quraysh and win them over peacefully. Muhammad was moving towards an unprecedented political and religious solution for the Arabs, and that meant that he could never do the expected and obvious thing, because that tied him to the unhappy *status quo*.

When he sat down with Suhayl to sign the treaty, Muhammad knew that he had stretched the loyalty of his Muslims almost beyond what they could bear. Would they remain true to the Pledge of Good Pleasure or did he have a mutiny on his hands? Matters became even more strained when the Muslims heard the actual wording of the treaty. Muhammad summoned Ali to write to his dictation and when he began with the *bismallah*, the special Muslim opening formula – 'In the name of al-Llah, the Compassionate [*al-Rahman*], the Merciful [*al-Rahim*]' – Suhayl immediately objected. The Quraysh had always hated these divine titles and he was not going to put his name to them now that Muhammad seemed ready to come to heel: 'I do not recognise this: but write, "In thy name, O al-Llah!"' To the utter horror of the Muslims, Muhammad immediately agreed and told Ali to change the wording. But worse was to come. Muhammad continued: 'This is what Muhammad, the apostle of God, has agreed with Suhayl ibn Amr.' Again Suhayl had an objection: 'If I witnessed that you were God's apostle, I would not have fought you,' he said, reasonably enough. 'Write down your own name and the name of your father.' Ali had already written the words 'the apostle of God' and said that he simply could not bring himself to excise them, so Muhammad asked him to point to the words on the parchment and struck them out himself. He continued: 'This is what Muhammad ibn Abdallah has agreed with Suhayl ibn Amr.'[13]

As if the situation were not difficult enough, Suhayl's son Abu Jandal suddenly burst on to the scene just as the treaty was being signed. He had converted to Islam and Suhayl had imprisoned him in his own house to stop him joining Muhammad, but he had escaped and now arrived triumphantly dragging his fetters behind him. Suhayl leaped to his feet, smashed his fist into his son's face and grabbed his chains. 'Muhammad!' he demanded, 'the agreement between us was concluded before this man came to you.' The Muslims gazed incredulously: surely Muhammad was not going to betray Abu Jandal and meekly hand him over to his father to face a life of humiliation and degradation? But Muhammad remained grimly true to the treaty and refused to allow Abu Jandal to make the *hijra* without his father's permission. As Suhayl dragged him roughly back to Mecca, Abu Jandal shrieked at the top of his voice, 'Am I to be returned to the polytheists that they may entice me from my religion, O Muslims?' As Ibn Ishaq says with classic understatement: 'That increased the people's dejection.' It was small comfort when Muhammad called after him, 'O Abu Jandal, be patient and control yourself, for God will provide relief and a means of escape for you and those of you who are helpless. We have made peace with them and we and they have invoked al-Llah in our agreement and we cannot deal falsely with them!'[14]

As far as Umar was concerned, this was the last straw. Immediately he rose to his feet and dared to challenge the man he had obeyed implicitly for twelve years: Was he not God's messenger? Were the Muslims not right and their enemies wrong? Why had they made such a dishonourable peace? Had Muhammad promised them or had he not when they had left Medina a few days earlier that they would worship once again at the Ka'aba? Muhammad admitted that he had made this promise, then added: 'but did I tell you that we should do it this year?' Umar was forced to agree that he had not, so Muhammad said: 'I *am* God's Messenger. I will not go against His commandments and He will not make me the loser.'[15] Even though he was still distressed and perplexed, Umar subsided and agreed to put his hand to the treaty, with Ali, Abu Bakr, Abd al-Rahman and Abdallah ibn Suhayl (Abu Jandal's brother) and Muhammad ibn Maslama.

But the pilgrims were still mutinous and there was a dangerous moment when they seemed on the point of rebellion. After the treaty had been witnessed, Muhammad cried aloud that they would now observe the rites of the pilgrimage right there in Hudaybiyah, even though they had not reached the Ka'aba. Every man would shave his head and they should sacrifice the seventy consecrated camels. There was absolute silence. Unmoving, the pilgrims stared bitterly at Muhammad. In despair, he retreated to his tent, knowing that if he lost their obedience and support at this crucial moment all was lost. What should he do? he asked Umm Salamah, who had been watching the scene from his red-leather tent. She had judged the situation perfectly: Muhammad should go out to the people once more, she told him, and refuse to speak to anyone until he had sacrificed his own camel in front of the whole pilgrim body. It was exactly the right decision. The dramatic and spectacular blood-letting immediately broke the tension. Muhammad left his tent, looking neither to right nor to left, strode over to the camel he had consecrated and performed the ritual sacrifice. It was a holy action, familiar to all the Arab pilgrims, but it was also an act of defiance and independence because Muhammad was breaking with tradition in sacrificing the camel outside Mecca itself. It released some spring of recognition in the silent crowd, broke through the torpor of depression and incomprehension and provided a catharsis. Immediately the men leaped to their feet and raced over to the other camels, probably intensely relieved to be able to *do* something at last. They sacrificed the animals, crying aloud the ancient Arab formula, 'In thy name, O al-Llah!' and adding the Muslim slogan, 'al-Llahu Akbar!' When Muhammad called one of the Helpers to him and asked him to shave his head, the Muslims nearly fell over one another in their eagerness to do the same, and set about each other's heads with such a frenzy of enthusiasm that Umm Salamah said later that she was afraid they would inflict mortal wounds in their zeal. Tradition has it that just as they started to leave Hudaybiyah a sudden wind lifted the mound of black hair and carried it into Mecca as a sign that God had accepted their sacrifice.

The pilgrims started home in a lighter mood, but some bitterness remained and Muhammad knew that he would have to make it up to them by devising a new expedition that would not jeopardise the treaty. He may also have had lingering doubts of his own, because he had almost certainly expected to be allowed to enter Mecca in triumph without signing that difficult pact. During the journey he seemed distant and preoccupied and

Umar was afraid that his rebelliousness and defiance had permanently damaged their friendship. He dreaded a revelation coming down to condemn his temerity, and when Muhammad barely replied to a remark of his he feared the worst. Suddenly a messenger arrived, summoning him to ride ahead to join Muhammad, and Umar's heart sank. But to his intense relief he found the Prophet looking radiant, as though a huge weight of anxiety had fallen from his shoulders. 'A sura has descended upon me,' the Prophet announced, 'which is dearer to me than anything under the sun.'[16] Sura 48 – the Sura of Victory (*al-fat'h*) – revealed the full significance of the events of Hudaybiyah and is a necessary complement and qualification of the theology of the just war. When Western critics accuse Islam of being an inherently aggressive religion because of the *jihad*, they should take into account Muhammad's theology of peace, which was revealed to him once he had fought his way through to the point where he could begin to impose the *pax Islamica* on war-torn Arabia.

In previous chapters we have seen that Muhammad may not always have expressed himself in such accessible imagery as Jesus but that his message was not as dissimilar as Christians tend to imagine. The difference is that Muhammad was trying to implement his teaching in more practical terms that were immediately related to a particular political or social situation. In fact we know very little about Jesus' political attitude. It has been suggested in recent years that he was crucified by the Romans for an attempted rebellion: some Biblical scholars have seen the account of his overturning the tables of the moneylenders in the Temple as a truncated version of a coup, by means of which he and his followers took over the Temple for a period of three days. However that may be, Jesus certainly also seems to have preached a pacifist message, turning the other cheek, refusing to defend himself even verbally and condemning those who lived by the sword. His apparent defeat and humiliation bewildered his disciples, and most of them deserted him in his hour of need. At Hudaybiyah Muhammad responded imaginatively to an unexpected situation and also turned the other cheek to the Quraysh, accepting an apparent humiliation which almost caused his closest companions to abandon him. In the Victory Sura, however, the deeper meaning of this apparent reversal was explained to the Muslims, just as after Jesus' death writers like St Paul would explain the underlying significance of the scandal of the Cross.

The sura begins with a luminous assurance that Muhammad had not been defeated at Hudaybiyah, despite appearances to the contrary:

> Surely We have given thee
> a manifest victory [*fat'h*]
> that God may forgive thee thy former and thy latter sins,

and complete His blessing upon thee and guide thee
on a straight path,
and that God may help thee
with mighty help.[17]

At Badr God had revealed His presence in the midst of a battle, which had been a sign and a salvation, but God had also been present in the apparent humiliation of Hudaybiyah, when He had sent down His *sakina*, the spirit of peace and tranquillity:

It is He who sent down the *sakina*
into the hearts of the believers, that
they might add faith to their faith.[18]

God had sent down His *sakina* once before, when Abu Bakr and Muhammad had hidden for three days in the Cave outside Mecca, despised and rejected by their kinsmen and facing the possibility of imminent, pointless death. The *sakina*, it will also be recalled, seems to have been related to the Hebrew *Shekinah*, the term for God's presence in the world. Badr and Hudaybiyah, therefore, were both 'signs' of salvation that revealed that God was mysteriously present in current historical events. He was just as active in peace as in war and could make what looked like a defeat into a manifest victory.

The sura goes on to say that when the pilgrims had undertaken the perilous enterprise of the unarmed pilgrimage to Mecca, they had made an act of faith which the Bedouin who had refused to accompany Muhammad had not been ready for.[19] They had made another act of faith and trust when they had pledged fealty to Muhammad under the acacia tree. The Quraysh could have wiped them out, but they had promised to obey Muhammad even though he had led them into the darkness of the shadow of humiliation; the consequent treaty was also a 'sign' which the Muslims had to interpret, looking beyond the externals to the inner meaning.[20] At Badr the victory had been a *furqan* which had separated the just from the unjust in battle; the victory (*fat'h*) of Hudaybiyah had distinguished believer from unbeliever by the spirit of peace:

When the unbelievers set in their hearts
fierceness, the fierceness of pagandom,
then God sent His *sakina* upon
His Messenger and the believers, and
fastened to them the word of godfearing.[21]

Muhammad had been gripped by an imperative which was a politically creative act. He had intuitively penetrated to a deeper understanding of the dynamics of change in Arabia, and events would vindicate his insight. From this point, now that he had saved the *umma* from the threat of extinction, the *jihad* would become an effort of peace that demanded all his patience and ingenuity. Badr and Hudaybiyah are, therefore, two sides of a single coin and both were essential to the Qu'ranic vision. Sometimes it would be necessary to fight in order to preserve decent values, and while the war lasted the Muslims must fight with absolute dedication and show no sign of weakness, lest hostilities drag on interminably, causing more bloodshed and more pointless fighting. But there was also a time for peace, even if this meant an immediate loss of face, because this could also be best in the long term. It is not true that Islam preaches a total intransigence and inspires a mindless fanaticism. Instead the Qu'ran evolves a complementary theology of war and peace, which most Christians would not find difficult to accept.

But Hudaybiyah did demand faith, as the Qu'ran had explained. If Muhammad's religious vision had not been paramount, he would not have been able to carry his followers with him. If the majority had wanted a quick political triumph they would not have been prepared to make this act of trust. The Victory Sura closes with a serene vision of a community characterised primarily by a religious spirit which is manifestly in the tradition of the two earlier revelations of Judaism and Christianity:

> Muhammad is the Messenger of God,
> and those who are with him are hard
> against the unbelievers, merciful
> one to another. Thou seest them
> bowing, prostrating, seeking bounty
> from God and good pleasure. Their
> mark is on their faces, the trace of
> prostration. That is their likeness
> in the Torah, and their likeness
> in the Gospel: as a seed that puts
> forth its shoot, and strengthens it,
> and it grows stout and rises straight
> upon its stalk, pleasing the sowers,
> that through them He may enrage
> the unbelievers. God has promised
> those of them who believe and do deeds
> of righteousness, forgiveness and
> a mighty wage.[22]

It might be objected that this piety has an aggressive edge and seems designed to 'enrage' the unbelievers. But all three traditions of historical monotheism share this intransigence and a refusal to compromise on religious essentials. Even the peaceable Jesus said that he had come to bring not peace but the sword,[23] and the Gospels give us a much fiercer portrait than we sometimes find in popular piety.

If the *umma* was to continue to flourish and take its place alongside the earlier revelations, however, it had to grow and attract new converts. Here Muhammad's new policy of conciliation was immediately seen to be productive, because the truce created a more relaxed atmosphere which encouraged discussion between Muslim and pagan and a free exchange of views. Commenting on the 'manifest victory' of Hudaybiyah, Ibn Ishaq says:

> No previous victory in Islam was greater than this. There was nothing but battle when men met; but when there was an armistice and war was abolished and men met in safety and consulted together none talked about Islam intelligently without entering it. In these two years [628–30] double as many or more than double as many entered Islam as ever before.[24]

At Hudaybiyah Muhammad had shown that Islam had its roots in the most sacred traditions of the Arabs and his meteoric rise to pre-eminence in Arabia proved that his religion worked. The Arabs were not fanatics but their difficult years in the desert had made them deeply pragmatic. When they considered the practical success of the *umma* they began to think that this might be the change for which people had been searching for so long.

But by the treaty of Hudaybiyah Muhammad was bound to return any converts who made the *hijra* to Mecca. He now tried to find a way to extricate himself from this. The treaty, for example, had not said anything about returning women converts, so when Uthman's half-sister emigrated to Medina shortly after Hudaybiyah Muhammad refused to send her back. After this test case, women were allowed to make the *hijra*, but if they came without their guardians' consent Muhammad would send their dowries back to the Quraysh. At about the same time, an extremely determined male convert appeared in Medina. Abu Basir ibn Asid, a confederate of the clan of Zuhrah, managed to give his guardians and protectors the slip and made the *hijra*. The Quraysh despatched an envoy, who took a freedman with him as a companion, to bring Abu Basir back and Muhammad regretfully explained to him that he had no option but to return him to Mecca. But Abu Basir was not going to give up so easily. When the three travellers were resting in Dhu al-Hulayfa, about eight miles south of Medina, he got hold of the envoy's sword and killed him. The freedman ran back in horror to Medina and flung himself at Muhammad's feet, stammering out the terrible news as Abu Basir himself arrived in the mosque. Abu Basir told Muhammad that his obligation was over, because honour had been satisfied when the Prophet had delivered him back to the Quraysh; because he had not been able to make the *hijra* he was not technically a Muslim, so Muhammad was not guilty of the envoy's blood. But Muhammad still refused to accept him into the *umma* and tried to hand him over to the poor freedman, who, appalled at the idea of travelling 200 miles alone with Abu Basir, hastily excused himself and fled for his life. Muhammad then told Abu Basir that, even though he could not stay in Medina, he was now free to go wherever he wished. As he left, Muhammad said ambiguously: 'What a firebrand! He would have kindled a fire had there been others with him.'[25]

Abu Basir understood the hint implied in the last words and went off to camp at al-Isa on the Red Sea coast near the trade route which the Quraysh had been able to use again since the armistice. News of the incident travelled to Mecca, including Muhammad's gnomic comment, and was eagerly seized upon by people like Abu Jandal ibn Suhayl, who were longing to make the *hijra*. Since Hudaybiyah the vigilance of their guardians had relaxed, so about seventy young men found it quite easy to escape from Mecca and make their way not to Muhammad at Medina but to Abu Basir at al-Isa. There was nothing in the treaty of Hudaybiyah to forbid this and none of the young men were members of the *umma*. They became highwaymen and attacked every single Meccan caravan that passed along the trade route to Syria. Muhammad was not responsible for them and could not be held to have broken the treaty, but the Quraysh discovered that in effect the old economic boycott had been partly restored. Since their defeat, the prestige of the Quraysh had declined so much that they could no longer command the support of the Bedouin in the area if they sent an army to finish the young highwaymen. Eventually they were forced to ask Muhammad to remove this threat by receiving the young men into the *umma*. Muhammad was delighted to send for them, but the summons came too late for Abu Basir himself, who had just died.

Muhammad had been able to get round the terms of the treaty on a technicality. This was a recognised ploy in Arabia. We shall see the Quraysh trying something similar in their struggle with Muhammad just over a year later. As a skilful Arab politician, Muhammad knew how to use the rules of the tribal system to his own advantage and this can be offputting to a modern Western person who, quite understandably, regards the tribal ethic as cruel and arbitrary and finds it distasteful that Muhammad should have been willing to have anything to do with it. We have long outgrown the tribal or communal ethic, though it had been the only way to secure a modicum of peace and order in more primitive times. It had worked well in Arabia for centuries, but now its time was over. Yet Muhammad, like all his contemporaries, was deeply rooted in the tribal system and accepted its basic principles. It was the only kind of polity and system of social security that he could imagine and, during this period of transition, it would have been impossible to make a radical change. In the affair of Abu Basir, Muhammad had used a fine point of tribal law to strengthen the *umma*, which was seeking to reform the crumbling system and correct some of its worst abuses.

In the social legislation of the Qu'ran, therefore, Muhammad does not break with tribalism completely. The Qu'ran sees revenge as a mark of virtue and a social and religious duty. Muslims must retaliate exactly, eye for eye, tooth for tooth.[26] It is difficult for people who have been brought up on the Sermon on the Mount to accept this. We find it abominable that a sacred book should recommend that a thief should have his hand chopped off, and we cannot understand why Muhammad does not outlaw revenge and preach a message of forgiveness. But we must remember that Jesus was not head of state, as Muhammad had become after Hudaybiyah. He did not have to concern himself with the maintenance of public order, a job carried out by the religious establishment that he is said to have reviled and by the officials of Rome. If he had been responsible for social legislation, he would in all probability have been forced to resort to similarly draconian methods because in most pre-modern societies the law has had to be enforced with a severity and brutality which seems horrific to us today. Even in Britain until relatively recently we did not merely mutilate a thief: we either killed him for quite trivial offences or sent him off to the colonies as a slave. It is certainly regrettable that some Islamic countries, though by no means all, have preserved these old punishments but it is unfair to stigmatise the Qu'ran and the Islamic tradition as brutal. It has been pointed out that future Islamic rulers could not afford to allow the Qu'ranic legislation to stand on its own because it was too lenient to be effective in a larger community; they had to back it up with new legislation to ensure a modicum of social security.[27]

Muhammad had seen the *umma* as a sort of super-tribe and he continued the old methods of keeping order. There was no police force in Medina or in Arabia; from time immemorial the next of kin had always been responsible for punishing offenders and for creating a deterrent that would as far as possible inhibit violence. The Qu'ran preserves this system and tells relatives that they have a duty to revenge a murder.[28]

This vengeance was to be strictly limited: *only* an eye could be required for an eye, a tooth for a tooth, otherwise the new victim, who had been punished excessively, would 'be helped'; that is, his own next of kin would give him *nasr* and start a new round of hostilities and a vicious cycle of unstoppable violence would begin. Indeed the Qu'ran shows that it is an act of virtue to be satisfied with *less* than was due. It recalls the rules that God had sent down to the Hebrew prophets in the Torah, which had been endorsed later by the sages and rabbis and goes one step further:

And therein We prescribed for them
'A life for a life, an eye for an eye,
a nose for a nose, an ear for an ear,
a tooth for a tooth, and for wounds
retaliation'; but whosoever forgoes it
as a freewill offering, that shall be for him
an expiation.[29]

When Jesus had referred to these words in the Torah, he had told his followers to love their enemies: he was a witty man and this paradox contains a deep but complex religious insight which is not always easy to interpret. Muhammad did not go as far as Jesus. When he urged Muslims to forgive one another and forgo retaliation, he was probably urging them to be satisfied with a blood-wite instead of taking another life. But this ideal of forgiveness, in however limited a form, was an innovation in Arabia and a moral advance on the old system.

It is often said that, where Christianity is a religion of love, Islam is a religion of social justice. Loving your neighbour is seen by Christians as the test of true religion; the Qu'ranic definition of the religious spirit is less ambitious but arguably more practicable:

True piety is this:
to believe in God, and the Last Day,
the angels, the Book, and the Prophets,
to give of one's substance, however cherished,
to kinsmen and orphans,
the needy, the traveller, beggars,
and to ransom the slave,
to perform the prayer, to pay the alms [*zakat*].[30]

In the *umma* society was to be organised on egalitarian principles: the same duties were required of everybody and there was to be no elite or hierarchy of priests and monks. Almsgiving would seek to close the gulf between rich and poor, and to free a slave was a virtuous deed.[31] In principle everybody in the *umma* would be treated in the same way: if love could neither prevail nor be enforced, justice and equality could be legislated for. It does seem as though the Qu'ran and, later, Islamic Holy Law (*shari'a*) did help Muslims to cultivate a deeply egalitarian spirit.[32] Not long after Muhammad's death, an important Bedouin chief called Jabalah ibn al-Ayham became a Muslim. One day a lowly member of the *umma* struck him on the cheek. Islamic principle did not require Jabalah to turn the other cheek, and he fully expected that an extremely severe punishment would be imposed on the offender because of his high rank. Instead he was simply told that he had permission to strike his assailant once on the face, to avenge the insult exactly and fairly. Jabalah was so outraged that he abandoned Islam and returned to Christianity.

It is possible to see the egalitarian ideal of Islam as a practical way of fostering brotherly love by reducing all men to the same social and political level. Just after the *hijra*, Muhammad is said to have introduced the practice of 'brothering', whereby each Emigrant was bonded to one of the Helpers and told to regard him as a brother. It was an attempt to weld the three tribal groups into a united community, a practical illustration of the new religious kinship which was to transcend the ties of blood. In all three religions of the monotheistic tradition the ideal of community is a supreme and sacred value. It is fundamental to both Judaism and Christianity that, where two or three are gathered together, God is in their midst. St Paul wrote that the Christian community constituted the Body of Christ and we shall see that the *umma* has acquired an almost sacramental importance in Muslim piety. Muhammad was fostering the individualism that was beginning to appear in Arabia: thus the Qu'ran decrees that the relatives of a dead man can punish only his murderer, not just any member of the offender's tribe, as in the old system.[33] But the communal ideal has remained crucial too and the sense of the brotherhood of all Muslims has gone very deep in Islam.

Muhammad had based his moral system on *muruwah*, the old tribal humanism of the Arabs, which was concerned with the common good, co-operation and caring for the poor and vulnerable. Muhammad's chief innovation was to extend these principles to include all Muslims, to the entire *umma* rather than to just the members of a single tribe. In helping his companions to cultivate a sense that all Muslims – whether they belonged to Aws, Khasraj or Quraysh – were now brothers he laid the foundations for a distinctively Islamic polity in the future. That is one of the reasons why it has been difficult for Muslims to adapt to the Western ideal of the nation state, which divides the *umma* up again into potentially hostile 'tribes' or separate groups.[34]

Indeed Muhammad himself set a high standard of 'brothering' in his own behaviour. The man who was becoming increasingly fearsome to his enemies was deeply loved within the *umma*, which despite the constant danger it faced seems to have been a very happy community. Muhammad refused to put a gulf of formality between himself and the other Muslims. He hated to be addressed with pompous, honorific titles, and was often seen sitting unaffectedly on the ground in the mosque, frequently choosing to sit with the poorest members of the community. Children were especially drawn to him. He was for ever picking them up and hugging and kissing them. When he had been away on an expedition, it was customary for the children of the *umma* to go out to meet him when the raiding party returned and they would lead him into the oasis in a triumphant procession. If he heard a baby crying in the mosque during Friday prayers, he nearly always brought the prayers to an end earlier than he had intended: he could not bear to think of the distress of the baby's mother.

The laws formulated in the Qu'ran sound ruthless to us today, but the Prophet himself was known to be lenient. One tradition recalls an occasion when Muhammad had passed sentence on a poor man who had committed a minor crime: for his penance he was told to give alms. The man replied that he had neither food nor goods to give away. Just at that moment a large basket of dates was carried into the mosque as a gift to the Prophet. 'Here you are,' Muhammad said, and told the man to distribute the dates among the poor. The criminal replied that he honestly did not know of anyone in the settlement who was worse off than himself. Muhammad laughed and told him that to eat the dates would be his penance.

The cultivation of kindness and compassion had been central to the Islamic message from the beginning. The law may have seemed a blunt instrument at this period, but the process of refinement (*tazaqqa*) of the Muslim outlook had begun. Again, Muhammad set an example. There is a tradition that one day he saw a freedman engaged in a particularly back-breaking task. He went up to him stealthily from behind and put his hands over his eyes, as children do. The freedman replied that it could only be the Prophet who would think of lightening his day with such an affectionate action.

Over the centuries in the West, we have tended to think of Muhammad as a grim figure, a cruel warrior and a callous politician. But he was a man of great kindness and sensibility. He loved animals, for example, and if he saw a cat asleep on his cloak he would not dream of disturbing it. It has been said that one of the tests of a society is its attitude towards animals. All religions encourage an attitude of love and respect for the natural world, and Muhammad was trying to teach Muslims this. During the *Jahiliyah* the Arabs had treated animals very cruelly: they used to cut off lumps of flesh to eat while the beasts were still alive and put painful rings round the necks of camels. Muhammad forbade any painful branding or organised animal fights. One tradition has him telling a story in which a man who gave water to a dog on a thirsty day was sent to Paradise and a woman who starved her cat to death was sent to hell. The preservation of these traditions shows how important the values had become in the Muslim world and how quickly the community had advanced towards a more humane and compassionate vision.

Now the Jews were to be integrated into this more humane Arabia.

Shortly after Hudaybiyah, Muhammad sent a message to Abyssinia, inviting the Muslims there to join him in Medina to help in the struggle. Then he turned his attention to the north again. The Jewish settlement of Khaybar, which had played such a dangerous role during the siege of Medina, had been chastened by the fate of the Bani Qurayzah but it was still stirring up hostility among the northern tribes. Muhammad wanted to make sure that Khaybar would never threaten the security of the *umma* again, so not long after his return from Hudaybiyah he set off to Khaybar with a force of about 600 men. This time, as the booty looked promising, his Bedouin allies were keen to go along, but Muhammad would not let them: he wanted to reward the Muslims who had felt balked and frustrated by Hudaybiyah and give them some outlet for their thwarted need for action. But Khaybar was an extremely strong settlement and was thought to be impregnable. Like Medina, it was surrounded by plains of volcanic rock and its date-farms and orchards were defended by seven large fortresses. The Quraysh hardly dared to believe the news that Muhammad had set out on this foolhardy expedition: it seemed that, with such a small army, he was courting disaster.

But yet again Muhammad's chief ally was the chronic disunity which always seemed to accompany the decline of the tribal system in Arabia. Unlike the *umma*, Khaybar was deeply divided within itself. Each of the tribes in the settlement was autonomous and they found it impossible to unite against the common foe. They sent a message to their confederates, the Ghatafan, but they never turned up. Some said that they heard a mysterious voice summoning them back to their own territory, but Muhammad may have bribed them to keep away with the promise of a substantial portion of Medina's date-harvest. The Muslims arrived in Khaybar at night, and in the morning the workers who came out with their spades and baskets found themselves face to face with a grimly silent army. 'Muhammad and his force!' they cried and fled back to the settlement. '*al-Llahu Akbar*!' cried Muhammad. 'Khaybar is destroyed.'

But in fact the siege of Khaybar lasted a whole month. The Muslims systematically surrounded each fort in turn, bombarding it with arrows until it surrendered, and then taking booty and hostages. Eventually the Jews approached Muhammad with an offer of peace, when it was quite clear that they could not possibly win. In accordance with the Qu'ranic precept, Muhammad accepted the terms, which were not particularly humiliating to Khaybar. It was exactly the sort of deal that Arabs in the settled areas frequently made with the Bedouin, who were usually better soldiers. In return for half their date-crop, Muhammad would give the Jews of Khaybar military protection and they became vassals of Medina, having exchanged their old Bedouin protectors for Muhammad. When the Jews of Fadak, a small but rich oasis to the north-east of Khaybar, heard about this treaty, they decided to forestall a possible Muslim attack and surrendered to Muhammad on the same terms. To seal the agreement, Muhammad married the beautiful seventeen-year-old Safiyah (the daughter of his old enemy Huyay), who had been widowed during the campaign. She is said to have foreseen the Jewish defeat by Medina in a dream and was quite willing to convert to Islam. The marriage was celebrated during the first half of the journey home.

When they returned to Medina, the Muslims from Abyssinia had arrived and Muhammad embraced his cousin Ja'far, whom he had last seen as a young man of twenty-seven thirteen years earlier. He kissed him on the forehead, saying that he did not know which delighted him more, the victory of Khaybar or this reunion. He had also to greet yet another wife. Earlier that year he had received the news that his cousin and brother-in-law Ubaydallah ibn Jahsh had died in Abyssinia. Ubaydallah, it will be recalled, had been a monotheist before the coming of Muhammad, and in Abyssinia, to the distress of the Muslim community there, he had apostasised from Islam and become a Christian. Muhammad had decided to marry his wife Ramlah, who is usually known by her *kunya* Umm Habibah, and, when the mourning period was over, the marriage had been performed by proxy before the Negus. This was obviously no love-match but a shrewd political move, because Umm Habibah was the daughter of Abu Sufyan. An apartment had been prepared for her beside the mosque and when she arrived in Medina she moved straight in, whereas Safiyah stayed in a nearby house until her own hut was ready.

Aisha was mortified when she heard about this new wife. Umm Habibah was no threat to her but the Jewish girl was extremely lovely. When Muhammad asked her what she thought of Safiyah, Aisha was brazen and offhand. She could not understand what all the fuss was about, she replied; one Jewess was much like another. 'Don't say that,' Muhammad replied, 'for she has entered Islam and has made good her surrender.' Safiyah had a difficult time in the harem at first because the other wives were quick to taunt her about her father Huyay. One day she went in tears to Muhammad, who comforted her: she was to tell the others, 'My father is Aaron and my uncle is Moses.'[35] But eventually she and Aisha became good friends, and the three young wives – Aisha, Hafsah and Safiyah – formed a trio distinct from the others.

The rest of the year was spent in routine raids, some of which were undertaken at the request of his new Jewish allies in the north. Then in the sacred month of the Dhu al-Hijja in March 629 it was time for Muhammad to lead the Lesser Pilgrimage to the Ka'aba, in accordance with the treaty of Hudaybiyah. This time 2,600 pilgrims accompanied him and, when they approached the Meccan Sanctuary, the Quraysh evacuated the city as they had promised so that the Muslim pilgrims could visit the holy places undisturbed. The chiefs stood together on the top of the mountain Abu Qubays and watched the whole extraordinary scene in a trance of horror. The huge crowd of pilgrims in their white garments filed slowly into their holy city, led by Muhammad riding on Qaswa, and the valley resounded with their cry: 'Here I am at your service, O God!' When he reached the Ka'aba, Muhammad dismounted and kissed the Black Stone, embracing and stroking it, and then began to make the circumambulations followed by the whole pilgrim body. To complete the ancient ritual of this Lesser Pilgrimage, which unlike the *hajj* did not include a visit to Mount Arafat and the valley of Mina, the pilgrims ran seven times between the hills of Safa and Marwah.

It must have been a very strange experience for Muhammad and the Emigrants to return to this deserted city, and it must also have been appalling to the Quraysh to watch Bilal, the black Abyssinian who had been a mere slave in their city, climb on top of the Ka'aba and give out the call to prayer three times a day. Abbas, Muhammad's uncle, came into the city to visit his nephew and offered him his sister Maymunah, who had recently been widowed, as a wife. Muhammad accepted, possibly to entice Abbas to enter his religion at last, and he invited the Quraysh to his wedding feast. This was pushing things too far, and Suhayl came down from Abu Qubays to tell Muhammad that his three days were up and he should leave the city immediately. Sa'd ibn Ubadah, one of the Helpers who was with Muhammad at this time, was furious at the apparent discourtesy but Muhammad quickly silenced him: 'O Sa'd, no ill words to those who have come to visit us in our camp.'[36] To the astonishment of the Quraysh, the whole crowd of pilgrims had left the city by nightfall, disciplined in a way that seemed inconceivable to the Meccans, whose disunity and indiscipline had contributed to their own downfall.

Some of the younger members of the Quraysh had seen the writing on the wall during this pilgrimage, which had been an immense moral triumph for Muhammad and was discussed eagerly throughout Arabia. From this moment the city was doomed. More and more Bedouin became Muhammad's confederates and many of the younger citizens of Mecca made the *hijra*. Two of these conversions were particularly significant. Amr ibn al-As and Khalid ibn al-Walid had become the most important warriors in the city after Badr but now they could see that there was no longer any future for them in Mecca. As Khalid said: 'The way has become clear. The man is certainly a prophet, and by al-Llah I'm going to be a Muslim'[37] Divine aid seemed the only possible explanation for Muhammad's extraordinary success. Khalid and Amr are said to have made the *hijra* together and to have been received joyfully at Medina. Khalid was worried that his past record would count against him. A leading officer at both Uhud and the Battle of the Trench, he had been responsible for the deaths of many Muslims and was afraid of a vendetta. But Muhammad assured him that the act of *islām* wiped out old debts and represented an entirely new start. This was an essential principle of the *umma*. Not only did it signify a new spiritual birth but it was the only way Islam could impose peace in Arabia.

It was a triumphant year for Muhammad, but also a year of sorrow. Shortly after the Lesser Pilgrimage, his daughter Zaynab died and, later, he lost two members of his family in an expedition to the Syrian border. During the last years of his life, the Prophet increasingly turned his attention to the north. We are not entirely sure of his reasons, but the political situation outside Arabia had changed dramatically. Persia and Byzantium had for decades been engaged in an exhausting war. During Muhammad's early career, Persia had been in the ascendant and had invaded Syria and besieged Constantinople. This must have concerned the Quraysh and caused them to question their position of neutrality. But recently the tide had turned in favour of Byzantium and in 625, the year of Uhud, Heraclius had driven the Persians back and begun to invade their own territory. If Muhammad could have replaced the Christian empire with the Arabs in the north, he might have been able to challenge both the Byzantines and the Sassanids. In these last years, therefore, he seems to have been making a bid to make his presence felt on the border and to draw the Christian tribes of the north into the *umma*, on the same sort of basis as the Jewish settlements.

At all events he sent Zayd and Ja'far to the Syrian border at the head of a huge army of 3,000 men. The expedition remains something of a mystery and much essential information is missing. It seems that as they marched, the Muslims learned that Heraclius was nearby with about 100,000 men. They decided to press on, however. At the village of Mu'ta near the Dead Sea in what is now Jordan, they were attacked by a detachment of Byzantines. Zayd, Ja'far and ten other Muslims were killed and Khalid, who had also accompanied the expedition, decided to take the army home.

When Muhammad heard the news he went directly to the families of Zayd and Ja'far, whose wife Asma recalled that she was baking bread when Muhammad arrived and knew by the expression on his face that something terrible had happened. Muhammad asked to see Ja'far's two sons, knelt down beside them, hugged them close and wept. Asma began to cry aloud and lament in the traditional Arab fashion, and the women hurried to her. As he left, Muhammad asked them to make sure that they looked after the family and brought them food during the next few days. As he walked through the streets back to the mosque, Zayd's little daughter ran out of their house and threw herself into his arms. Muhammad picked her up and stood there, holding her and sobbing convulsively.

We do not know exactly why Khalid had decided to bring the army home, since it had incurred relatively light casualties, but when they arrived in Medina they were booed and hissed, so Muhammad had to take them under his powerful protection. About a month later, honour was satisfied when Amr ibn al-As led another expedition to attack the northern tribes which seemed to be massing on the borders and easily put them to flight.

But there was one great personal joy for Muhammad that year. The Muqawqis of Egypt is said to have sent Muhammad a beautiful curly-haired Egyptian slave girl, a Coptic Christian called Maryam, and Muhammad took her as his concubine. He used to visit her daily, spending more and more time with her, probably finding it a relief to escape from the jealous atmosphere of the harem. Nobody would have found this odd. The Torah had made provision for concubinage, when the Israelites were at a similar stage of changing from the nomadic to the settled life. Abraham himself, of course, had taken Hagar as his concubine, and Ishmael, the father of the Arabs, had been the child of that union. So it must have seemed propitious when Maryam became pregnant, and, when his son was born the following year, Muhammad called him Ibrahim.

But, as one might expect, his wives were extremely jealous of the little nobody who was carrying the Prophet's child. Aisha and Hafsah organised a protest and a rebellion in the harem. It is difficult to understand this strange incident, which caused a major crisis and may have involved more than meets the eye. The story as it stands is attributed to Umar, who had militant views about women, believed they should be seen and not heard and felt that the wives of the Emigrants were picking up bad habits from the women of Medina. Muhammad, however, was much softer and more lenient with his women and one day Umar was horrified to hear the most unholy racket issuing from the Prophet's apartments. The wives were squabbling over some booty that had recently been acquired and were insisting that Muhammad give a bigger share to his own family than to the rest of the *umma*. Umar called to Muhammad, asking his permission to come in, and immediately silence fell. When he entered he found the Prophet helpless with laughter: as soon as they had heard Umar's voice, the women had scuttled in terror behind the *hijab*. Umar grimly remarked that it would be better if his wives had a similar respect for the Prophet and yelled to the women who were cowering behind the curtain: 'O enemies of yourselves, are you afraid of me and not of the Messenger of God?' 'Absolutely,' one of the wives replied, 'for you are rougher and harsher than God's Messenger.'[38]

Umar had already been worried that his daughter Hafsah was getting out of hand and had told her that she must control her jealousy and accept the fact, for example, that she was not as attractive as Aisha. But Hafsah had become so vociferous about Maryam that at one point Muhammad had wearily promised that he would not see her again, but then found that nothing had improved. Egged on by Aisha and Hafsah, the wives sneered jubilantly at Maryam and continued squabbling and feuding with one another. Finally the atmosphere became so unpleasant that Muhammad withdrew from all his wives for a month.

But, as in most of these harem tales, this quarrel seems to reflect a problem in the rest of the *umma*. After the victory of Khaybar, the Muslims enjoyed a new prosperity: Aisha said that before Khaybar she never knew what it was to have eaten her fill of dates. But the new wealth had created problems. Some of the farmers were anxious to put their feet up and enjoy it, others started to intrigue for a greater share of the booty that came from expeditions, and it appears that Muhammad's own family had begun to ask for special gifts that should have gone to the poor. Muhammad was extremely concerned about the morally weakening effects of affluence, particularly in the harem. This issue figures in Umar's version of the story of Muhammad's separation from his wives. All the Muslims were appalled to hear that Muhammad had withdrawn from his harem. Nobody could talk about anything else and a crowd gathered outside the mosque, looking nervously at the little room on the roof where Muhammad was sitting by himself. Umar recalled that somebody rushed round to his house with the news and beat so urgently on the door that he thought that at least the northern tribes had besieged the city. It was much worse than that, the visitor cried: Muhammad has put away all his wives!

This was no mere domestic crisis. Muhammad's marriages were political alliances which had been carefully planned. His relationship with Abu Bakr and Umar could have been damaged if he divorced their daughters. Now everything had been put in jeopardy because of the squabbles of a few women. The agitation may also have been caused by internal conflicts in Medina which had affected Muhammad's wives but which we know nothing about. Umar rushed round to the mosque immediately to see what he could do, but at first Muhammad refused to see him. When Umar was eventually admitted, he remembered looking round the miserable little room, which had nothing in it but three untanned hides. Muhammad was lying gloomily on a mat without even a blanket, and the weave of the rushes had been impressed on his cheek. To his immense relief, Umar learned that Muhammad was not going to divorce the women and gradually wrung a smile out of the Prophet by sharing some tales of his own difficulties with the women since they had all emigrated to Medina, where the men did not seem able to keep their wives in order. When the Prophet had finally relaxed, Umar sat down beside him on the ground and asked why on earth al-Llah could not give his Messenger a few home comforts; after all, the emperors of Byzantium and Persia lived in extreme opulence. But Muhammad rebuked him: they had had their happiness in this world.

It is a difficult story for us today. It has so many unacceptably chauvinist elements. It may have been more about the growing materialism in the *umma* than about sexual jealousy. Muhammad kept apart from his wives for a month and they were given a choice: they could either accept his terms and live a decent Islamic life or he would give them an amicable divorce. It is noteworthy that in the Verses of the Choice, as they are called, there is no mention of Maryam or the women's jealousy; instead the emphasis is on the attitude to luxury and material goods:

> O Prophet, say to thy wives: 'If you desire
> the present life and its adornment, come now,
> I will make you provision, and set you free
> with kindliness.
> But if you desire God and his Messenger
> and the Last Abode, surely God has prepared
> for those amongst you such as do good
> a mighty wage.'[39]

The women agreed to these conditions and from that point Muhammad's wives became even more important in the *umma*. The Qu'ran gave them the title 'Mothers of the Faithful' and decreed that they should not marry again after Muhammad's death, not because he was jealous of future spouses, but because such marriages could breed dynasties and cabals that would split the *umma*.

Indeed, just after the Verses of the Choice the Qu'ran gives a much more positive picture of the relationship between the sexes in the *umma*, showing men and women sharing the duties and privileges of Islam side by side in an egalitarian society:

> Men and women who have surrendered,
> believing men and believing women,
> obedient men and obedient women,
> truthful men and truthful women,
> enduring men and enduring women,

humble men and humble women,
men and women who give in charity,
men who fast and women who fast,
men and women who guard their private parts,
men and women who remember God oft –
for them God has prepared forgiveness
and a mighty wage.[40]

Later Muslims may sometimes have retreated from this Qu'ranic vision of equality, but Western feminists who denounce Islam for its misogyny should perhaps reflect that the Christian tradition has also been extremely negative to women. The New Testament in the main offers a positive message to women, but in fact over the centuries the Gospel has been anything but good news for 'the second sex'.[41] Christian misogyny was peculiarly neurotic because it was based on a rejection of sexuality which is unique among the world religions and certainly not found in either Judaism or Islam. It is not fair to blame Muhammad and Islam for their misogyny. If Muslim women today reject some of the freedoms that we feel we have offered them, this is not due to perversity but because the Western view of women and the relations between the sexes is confused. We preach equality and liberation, but at the same time exploit and degrade women in advertising, pornography and much popular entertainment in a way that Muslims find alien and offensive.

Inevitably we hear more about the strains and factions among Muhammad's wives than about daily life in the harem, but it would be a mistake to imagine that there was no love or happiness there. When Muhammad had recited the Verses of the Choice to Aisha, he had told her to think very carefully before she made her decision; he advised her to ask her parents for their opinion. But Aisha waved that suggestion aside. She did not even have to think: she chose al-Llah and His Messenger. She was extremely jealous and sometimes used to spy on Muhammad to make sure he wasn't seeing other women. Maryam's pregnancy must have been especially painful: all the other wives had had children by their previous husbands but Aisha was childless. There is a pathetic story where she asks Muhammad to give her a *kunya* like the others, and he gave her the *kunya* Umm Abdallah, because she had a special relationship with her little nephew of that name. But it would be quite wrong to imagine that her life was unbearably unhappy. Muhammad was an indulgent husband: he was far kinder to Aisha than her father had been: Abu Bakr had been known to strike his daughters. He may have insisted that his wives lived frugally but Aisha tells us that Muhammad always helped them with the household chores and he did everything for himself: he mended and patched his clothes, cobbled his own shoes and looked after the goats. He was trying to educate his Muslims to adopt a more respectful attitude to women, and the fact that these traditions were preserved at a time when most people in most religions would think it shocking that a great prophet should bother with the housework shows that his message was received, even though Muslims like Abu Bakr and Umar found it impossible to change their ways.

Nobody was ever able to replace Khadija, but with Aisha it seems that Muhammad was able to unbend. One day, for example, he challenged her to a race. When he won, he cried out triumphantly that now they were equal: when Aisha had been a little girl in Mecca, she had once run away from him and he had been unable to catch her. But there were also more intimate scenes. Aisha liked to anoint Muhammad's hair with his favourite perfume, wash in the same bowl as he and drink from the same cup. She also loved looking after him when he was ill, though she was not above teasing him if she thought that he was pampering himself too much. One day, when the two were sitting together, Muhammad busily mending a pair of sandals, she saw his face light up at a passing thought. She watched him for a moment and gave him a compliment on his bright, happy expression. Muhammad got up and kissed her on the forehead, saying: 'O Aisha, may al-Llah reward you well. I am not the source of joy to you that you are to me.'[42]

But Aisha had a serious side to her and was extremely intelligent. There is a tradition that when Muhammad had to be absent from Medina, he used to tell the Muslims that they should consult Aisha if they had any religious problems. After his death she was an important authority about the Prophet's life and religious practice, which is again astonishing, particularly when one recalls that caliphs like Abu Bakr, Umar and Ali did not share their Prophet's respect for women. 2,210 such traditions (*ahadith*) are attributed to Aisha, though al-Bukhari and Muslim, who made the great collections of *Hadith* during the ninth century, threw most of these out. They accepted only 174 of the traditions which were said to have been given to Aisha directly by the Prophet himself. She was also very important in the turbulent politics of the early Islamic empire and led a revolt against Ali during his caliphate. Women were not crushed by Islam, as people tend to imagine in the West. Some found that it enabled them to fulfil a potential that would have been inconceivable in the days of the *Jahiliyah*.

At the end of the year, the Meccans broke the Treaty of Hudaybiyah and were newly vulnerable. The tribe of Bakr had remained confederates of the Quraysh but they had for decades been the sworn enemy of the Khuza'ah, which had joined Muhammad's confederacy. In November 629 one of the clans of Bakr had attacked the Khuza'ah by night in their own territory in a surprise attack and it appears that some of the Quraysh had aided and abetted this assault: they had given weapons to Bakr and it is said that Safwan had even taken part in the fighting. Khuza'ah promptly retaliated and there was even fighting between the two tribes in the Meccan Sanctuary, so the Khuza'ah appealed to Muhammad and he agreed to come to their aid.

Immediately some of the Quraysh had second thoughts when they realised that they had handed Muhammad a perfect excuse to attack Mecca. Safwan and Ikrimah remained hawkish and defiant, but even Suhayl, whose mother had been a member of Khuza'ah, was for disowning Bakr. Muhammad had his own informants and remarked to his Companions that they could soon expect to see Abu Sufyan in Medina. Since his defeat at the Battle of the Trench, Abu Sufyan had probably begun to realise that it was pointless to continue this feud with Muhammad, who had just become his son-in-law as a result of his marriage to Umm Habibah. Sure enough, shortly after the breach of the armistice, Abu Sufyan arrived in Medina to ask for peace – an event that would have been unthinkable two years earlier.

There are various stories about Abu Sufyan's peace initiative in Medina. He is said to have visited his daughter Umm Habibah to ask her to use her influence with Muhammad, but she would not even let him sit down on Muhammad's rug. This is unlikely to be true, because Muhammad did not enjoy this kind of veneration and reverence during his lifetime. Next, Abu Sufyan is supposed to have asked the advice of Abu Bakr, Umar, Uthman and Ali, which is slightly suspicious because it has him approaching the first four caliphs of Islam in exactly the right order. But Abu Sufyan did play an extremely important role at this time. He could not quite bring himself to make the surrender of *islām* but he realised that Muhammad's final victory was inevitable and that the Quraysh should try to get the best terms they could. He and Suhayl were trying to extricate the Meccans from the dispute by disclaiming responsibility for Bakr, using the same kind of technicality that Muhammad had employed a year earlier in the affair of Abu Basir. But the Quraysh were now too weak to pull it off and it was suggested to Abu Sufyan by Ali that he should ask Muhammad if he would agree to honour him as the protector of any Meccans who wanted to surrender to Muhammad. This would enable them to save face and preserve their lives in the event of a Muslim conquest of the city, because they would have to submit not to Muhammad directly but to one of their own men.

Abu Sufyan agreed to think this over and left for Mecca, where he probably did a good deal to prepare his fellow tribesmen to accept the inevitable. After his departure, Muhammad began to prepare for a new expedition, summoning the *umma* and their allies to join the Muslim army. The destination of the expedition was kept a closely guarded secret for security reasons, but naturally there was a great deal of excited speculation. On 10 Ramadan, January 630, Muhammad set out at the head of the largest army ever to leave Medina. Nearly all the men in the *umma* had volunteered and along the road their Bedouin allies joined the expedition, bringing the numbers up to 10,000 men. But still nobody knew for sure where they were headed. Certainly they could have been going to Mecca, but it was also possible that they were going to attack some of the southern tribes or the city of Taif, which had remained hostile to Islam. That possibility occurred to the southern tribe of Hawazin when they heard that Muhammad's army was heading in their direction and they started to assemble their own massive army at Taif, the city of al-Lat and a centre of paganism. In Mecca the Quraysh naturally expected the worst. Abbas begged them to try to forestall the catastrophe: 'Alas Quraysh, if the apostle enters Mecca by force before they come and ask for protection, that will be the end of Quraysh for ever.'[43] He set out by night to join Muhammad and on the road overtook Abu Sufyan and Budayl, chief of Khuza'ah, who were also headed for the Muslim camp. The three men spent the night there and in the morning Muhammad asked Abu Sufyan if he was ready to make *islām*. Abu Sufyan said that he could assent to the first part of the Muslim proclamation of faith: 'There is no god but al-Llah' – the pagan deities had been shown to be useless – but he still had doubts about Muhammad's prophethood. Yet he was shocked and impressed when he saw all the members of the massive army prostrating themselves in the direction of Mecca during the morning prayer, and when he watched the various tribes marching past on their way to his city he knew that the Quraysh would have to surrender.

He hurried back to Mecca and summoned the people by crying at the top of his voice: 'O Quraysh, this is Muhammad who has come to you with a force you cannot resist.' He then offered them the option suggested by Ali. Anybody who wanted to surrender should put himself under his protection and Muhammad would honour this: they should either go to his house or stay in their own homes when the Muslim army arrived. His wife Hind was beside herself with rage. Seizing Abu Sufyan by his moustaches, she cried to the people: 'Kill this fat greasy bladder of lard! What a rotten protector of his people!'[44] But Abu Sufyan begged them not to listen to her: the time for such defiance was over. He had seen an army that Mecca could not resist. The Quraysh, pragmatic to the last, were certainly not about to create an Arabian Masada, so they went off to their houses and barricaded themselves indoors as a token of their submission.

But a few wanted to fight. Ikrimah, Safwan and Suhayl gathered on

Abu Qays with a small force and attacked Khalid's section of the army as it entered the city. They were quickly beaten and Ikrimah and Safwan fled from Mecca, but Suhayl decided to surrender and went to his own house. The rest of the Muslim army entered the city without striking a single blow. Muhammad's red tent had been pitched near the Ka'aba and there he joined Umm Salamah and Maymunah, the two wives who had accompanied him, with Ali and Fatimah. Shortly after they had settled, Ali's sister Umm Hani, who had been married to a pagan and had never made the *hijra*, arrived to plead for the lives of two of her relatives who had taken part in the fighting against Khalid. Even though Ali and Fatimah wanted them executed, Muhammad immediately promised that they would be safe under her protection. He had no desire to begin bloody reprisals. Nobody was made to accept Islam nor do they seem to have felt under any pressure to do so. Muhammad did not want to coerce the people but to effect a reconciliation.

He had come to Mecca not to persecute the Quraysh but to abolish the religion which had failed them. After he had slept for a while, he rose, performed the ritual ablutions and offered the prayer. Then, mounted on Qaswa, he rode round the Ka'aba seven times, touching the Black Stone each time and crying 'al-Llahu Akbar!' The shout was taken up by his 10,000 soldiers and soon the whole city resounded with the words that symbolised the final victory of Islam. Next Muhammad turned his attention to the 360 idols around the shrine: crowded on to their roofs and balconies, the Quraysh watched him smash each idol while he recited the verse:

> the truth has come, and falsehood has vanished away;
> surely falsehood
> is certain to vanish.[45]

Inside the Ka'aba the walls had been decorated with pictures of the pagan deities and Muhammad ordered them all to be obliterated, though it is said that he allowed frescoes of Jesus and Mary to remain. Eventually Islam would forbid the use of all imagery in its worship because it distracts the mind from God by allowing it to dwell on purely human symbols of the divine.

Some of the Meccans had ventured forth from their houses and had made their way to the Ka'aba, where they waited for Muhammad to leave the shrine. He stood in front of the house of al-Llah and begged them to accept the new order, the unity of the *umma*, and to lay aside the haughty pride and self-sufficiency of paganism which could create only division and injustice. He ended with a verse of the Qu'ran, which Muslims later interpreted as a condemnation of racism, a vice from which Islam has been relatively free:

O Quraysh, God has taken from you the haughtiness of paganism and its veneration of ancestors. Man springs from Adam, and Adam sprang from dust:

> O mankind, We have created you
> male and female, and appointed you
> races and tribes, that you may know
> one another. Surely the noblest
> among you in the sight of God is
> the most godfearing of you. God is
> All-knowing, All-wise.[46]

Finally Muhammad issued a general amnesty. Only about ten people were put on the Black List. They included Ikrimah (but not Safwan, for some reason), people who had spread anti-Muslim propaganda and people who had injured the Prophet's family. But any of these people who asked forgiveness seem to have been spared.

It was a wise policy. Muhammad knew, for example, that Suhayl was now at large and told his followers to treat him courteously. 'No black looks for Suhayl if you meet him!' he ordered. 'Let him come out freely, for by my life he is a man of intelligence and honour, not one to be blind to the truth of Islam!'[47] After his speech at the Ka'aba, Muhammad withdrew to Mount Safa and invited the people of Mecca to swear fealty to him and accept his political suzerainty. One by one the Quraysh filed up to Muhammad, as he stood flanked by Umar and Abu Bakr. One of the women who stood before him was veiled and when she spoke Muhammad recognised her: it was Hind, Abu Sufyan's wife, who was on the condemned list for mutilating the body of Hamzah. 'You are Hind bint Utba?' he asked. 'I am,' she replied defiantly. 'Forgive me what is past and God will forgive you.' Muhammad continued his catechism. Would she undertake not to commit adultery or steal? Would she promise not to commit infanticide by killing her children? To this Hind replied: 'I brought them up when they were little, but you killed them on the day of Badr when they were grown up, so you are the one to know about them!'[48] Hind decided to make *islām* and told Muhammad: 'Messenger of al-Llah, you cannot proceed against me now for I am a professing Muslim.' The Prophet smiled and said: 'Of course, you are free.'[49] Soon she saw her husband and her sons given important office in the *umma* as a reward for Abu Sufyan's co-operation. Eventually his descendants became the founders of the Ummayad dynasty.

Relatives of Safwan and Ikrimah begged for their lives and Muhammad promised that they could enter the city freely, provided that they accepted his leadership. Both decided to return and Ikrimah was the first to accept Islam. In return, Muhammad greeted him affectionately and forbade anybody to vilify his father Abu Jahl. Safwan and Suhayl both swore fealty to Muhammad but could not yet make the Muslim profession of faith. One of the condemned men on the Black List has been immortalised by Salman Rushdie in *The Satanic Verses*, though his fictional version which presents Muhammad as cold, cruel and vengeful, is very different from the real story. Abdallah ibn Sa'id, the foster-brother of Uthman ibn Affan, had made the *hijra* in 622 but seems to have lost faith in Muhammad's inspiration. He had become his amanuensis and, either as a joke or as a test, had made slight alterations in the text of the Qu'ran. When Muhammad had recited, '*alimun sami'un*' (al-Llah is knowing and hearing), Abdallah had written, '*alimun hakinum*' (al-Llah is knowing and wise). After Muhammad had failed to notice these details, Abdallah had apostasised and defected to Mecca, where the Quraysh had made capital of his story. The Qu'ran had told Muhammad himself that there would be fatal consequences if he tried to alter the sacred text to suit himself and its insistence on this point probably reflects Muhammad's consciousness of the difficulty of preserving the integrity of his message: natural mistakes could so easily be made. When he knew that he had been condemned to death, Abdallah fled to Uthman, who protected him until the upheaval of the conquest was over. Then he brought him to Muhammad and asked for mercy. It is said that Muhammad was silent for a long time before he lifted the sentence of death and that he later berated his Companions for not taking this silence as an opportunity to kill Abdallah. But after he had been removed from the Black List Abdallah became a Muslim once more and held high office in the Islamic empire after Muhammad's death.

The conquest of Mecca had been the final victory (*fat'h*) for which the earlier victories of Badr and Hudaybiyah had been a preparation. The word *fat'h* literally means 'opening' and became the official term for the conquest of a city which opened a new door for Islam. By conquering Mecca, Muhammad had vindicated his prophetic claim. But this conquest had been achieved without bloodshed and Muhammad's peaceful policy paid off. Within a few years, paganism was quite dead in Mecca and some of Muhammad's most committed enemies like Ikrimah and Suhayl became devout and fervent Muslims.

There was not much time for Muhammad to enjoy his victory, however, because he heard that the army of Hawazin had assembled at Taif. Shortly after the conquest, Muhammad had sent Khalid to Nakhlah to destroy the effigy of al-Uzza there and later Ali would be sent to smash the shrine of Manat at Hudhayl. The Thaqif and their allies were determined that al-Lat should not meet the same fate and 20,000 men had come to fight in her defence. It was a perilous moment in which everything could have been lost, but the newly conquered Quraysh were prepared to fight alongside Muhammad and the Muslims: Taif and Hawazin were their old enemies. Overnight, Muhammad, the conqueror of Mecca, had become the champion of the city. The armies met for battle in the valley of Hunayn at the end of January 630, about a fortnight after the conquest. There the Muslims were almost routed but at the last moment they made a fresh assault and put the enemy to flight. Some hid in the hills and others took refuge in the walled city of Taif. Muhammad attempted to besiege the city but soon realised that he would not conquer it this time and withdrew.

The division of the booty after the battle of Hunayn was a tremendous affair in which some of the tensions within the *umma* came out into the open. In order to win over his former adversaries like Abu Sufyan, Safwan and Suhayl Muhammad gave them the lion's share. Safwan was so overcome that he instantly made his Islamic surrender. 'I bear witness that no soul could have such goodness as this, if it were not the soul of the Prophet,' he cried. 'I bear witness that there is no god but al-Llah and that you are His Messenger.'[50] Suhayl also became a Muslim. He had always been a religious man and he became the most zealous of all the new converts. Naturally, however, Muhammad's own faithful followers were offended by this apparent favouritism. In particular the Helpers saw it as a sign that since Muhammad had been reunited with the Quraysh he would abandon them and forget that the Aws and Khasraj had taken him in when he had just been a discredited refugee. Muhammad saved the situation by making a moving speech in which he acknowledged all that the people of Medina had done for him. He promised that Medina would be his home until the end of his life and tears trickled down the cheeks of the Helpers as he made his final prayer:

> Are you disturbed in your minds because of the good things of this life by which I win over a people that they may become Muslims while I entrust you to your Islam? Are you not satisfied that men should take away flocks and herds while you take back with you the apostle of God? By Him in whose hand is the soul of Muhammad, but for the *hijra* [of the Emigrants who had followed him] I should be one of the Helpers myself. If all men went one way and the Helpers another I should take the way of the Helpers. God have mercy on the Helpers, their sons and their sons' sons.[51]

For the time being, at least, the Helpers were satisfied, but after dividing the spoils, receiving the submission and allegiance of Hawazin and gathering together his army, Muhammad made the Lesser Pilgrimage and returned home to Medina.

The old tribal system had depended upon each group preserving the balance of power: the ethics of the vendetta had tried to ensure that, if a member of one tribe was killed, the offending tribe would be weakened to exactly the same extent. But Muhammad had now become too powerful to be contained by the system and this brought a measure of peace to Arabia. The nomadic tribes had the choice of allying themselves with Muhammad or becoming fair game for the increasingly large *umma* and its allies. During the next two years delegations from tribe after tribe arrived in Medina. They had to promise to smash their idols, to furnish troops on demand, not to attack the *umma* and its other confederates and to pay the *zakat*. Some of the nomads became sincere believers but others remained true to the old religion in their hearts, and Muhammad was perfectly aware of this. Again, he made no effort to enforce strict theological orthodoxy, hoping that the political submission would eventually lead to the religious surrender of *islām*. Almost single-handedly Muhammad had managed to impose the *pax Islamica*.

But fighting and warlike expeditions were part of the Arab way of life and the habit of aggression was inbred. Muhammad realised that if the new peace were not to disintegrate, he would have to try and preserve an outward momentum. As more and more tribes became members or confederates of the *umma* and thus out of bounds to Muslim raiders, he tried to channel their energy into an attack on the northern tribes, which had remained hostile. Something similar happened in Christian Europe during the eleventh century, when the Church was trying to stop the knights and barons attacking one another and attempted, by various means, to promote what they called the Peace of God. Eventually in 1095 at the Council of Clermont, Pope Urban II urged the Christians to unite against their common foe in the Holy Land and called the First Crusade against the Muslim infidel: there would be the Peace of God in the West and the War of God in the Middle East.

In October 630 Muhammad announced a new expedition and this time, contrary to his usual custom, he let it be known that they would be going to the Byzantine frontier so that the men could make suitable preparations for the long journey. We do not know exactly why Muhammad insisted on making this expedition, which was extremely unpopular. It was hot, the date-harvest was ready for the picking and the Muslims had a healthy fear of the Byzantine army. It is not likely that Muhammad was already beginning to plan the conquest of Syria and Palestine. He may simply have wanted to avenge the defeat of Mu'ta or to establish himself more securely in the northern part of Arabia. Most of the Muslims began to prepare for the expedition, but a significant number grumbled, dragged their feet and some even refused to go. The Hypocrites were reluctant, as one would expect; some of the new Bedouin allies asked to be excused; other Muslims wanted to stay at home, farm their dates and make money; but some of the people who objected were impeccable Muslims. Even Ali stayed behind in Medina, though the sources loyally claim that Muhammad had asked him to look after the family during his absence. Eventually some 30,000 men set out on the gruelling march north. About ninety people stayed at home, however; they may have been plotting against the Prophet: people naturally felt aggrieved when they saw people like Abu Sufyan receiving honours and rich gifts, while the original Helpers and Emigrants seem to have been forgotten. It frequently happens in any party that the original supporters become a problem, holding fast to the early idealism of the movement and looking askance at those who are forced, perhaps through unworthy opportunistic motives, to become latter-day disciples. Muhammad had sensibly created a climate which helped his old enemies to think more favourably of Islam, but this meant that he had a problem at home. The disaffection became obvious even among those who had joined the expedition. There was constant grumbling in Ibn Ubbay's camp; some people deliberately dropped behind and others muttered darkly about the folly of exposing themselves to the powerful Byzantine army. When Muhammad asked what the mutterers were talking about, they airily replied: 'We were just chatting and joking, O apostle.' As the Qu'ran shows, Muhammad was not fooled.[52]

But eventually the army arrived at Tabuk, about 250 miles north-west of Medina, and Muhammad managed to remain there for some ten days. It was no mean feat to stay with such a large army on the doorstep of Byzantium, and the Bedouin in the area would have been impressed. While he was there he made pacts with the local rulers. The Christian King Yuhunna of Eilat in modern Israel paid tribute to him, as did three Jewish settlements at Jarba and Adhruh in what is now Jordan and Maqna on the Red Sea coast. Khalid was also despatched with a small force to bring the ruler of Dumat al-Jandal to heel, and he likewise arrived to make peace with Muhammad.

It was a modest but significant success and Muhammad felt buoyant and confident on the way home. He was determined to put down the opposition in his own camp, after making such a promising beginning for the Medinan state in the outside world. But the grumbling and dissension continued on the homeward march; at one point there seems to have been a plot to push Muhammad over a cliff. Finally, however, he arrived safely at a point a short distance from Medina. Before leaving the oasis he had been asked to consecrate a new mosque which had been built in Qu'ba and he had promised to do this on his return. Now he seems to have had reason to believe that the mosque was a centre of disaffection: the Qu'ran even hints that the people who built it had re-established connections with some of Muhammad's old enemies who had not yet been reconciled to his success.[53] So, before entering Medina, Muhammad sent two men into Qu'ba to set fire to the mosque. The next morning he held an inquiry into the conduct of the people who had stayed behind in Medina. Most hastily apologised and offered plausible excuses, but three were sent to Coventry for nearly two months.

This seems to have finished the Muslim opposition. Not long after his return from Tabuk Muhammad stood by the grave of his old adversary Ibn Ubbay as a mark of respect and reconciliation. It was also the end of the pagan opposition. In January 631 the city of Taif, the last pagan stronghold, was forced to surrender just one year after Muhammad had abandoned his siege. Since the Hawazin had become Muhammad's allies after Hunayn, they had been increasingly isolated and harried until their position was impossible. The delegates from Taif begged Muhammad for special terms. They were merchants who travelled a good deal and they wanted permission to sleep with women who were not their wives on business trips; they also wanted to drink the wine from their vineyards and, above all, they begged to be able to keep the shrine of al-Lat for a few more years. Or, finally, for just one more year. Muhammad refused all their pleas. The only concession he granted was that they would not have to destroy al-Lat themselves and incur the wrath of their people. So Muhammad sent Abu Sufyan to Taif to destroy the goddess on his behalf.

It was a symbolic moment. Abu Sufyan had fought Muhammad for five years and had marched into battle with the name of al-Lat on his lips. It was a sure sign that paganism was doomed. It had served the Arabs well but it had failed to help them to adjust to the settled life and the new demands of the seventh century. The inner dynamics of social change were now on Muhammad's side. Muhammad's was an extraordinary achievement. He had not relied simply on divine inspiration but, according to the Qu'ranic principle, he had used all his natural resources and considerable personal genius to carry the day. But in 631 he was an old man and his health was beginning to fail: would the *umma* survive his death?

10 · Death of the Prophet?

When Muhammad had made the *hijra* in 622 the little Islamic community had taken its first step forward to political power: ten years later it dominated almost the whole of Arabia and had laid the foundations for a new Arab polity which would enable Muslims to govern a huge empire for over a thousand years. This political success had involved continuous strain and effort and the tumultuous years at Medina had shown how difficult and dangerous it could be to undertake the reconstruction of human society according to God's plan. Muhammad experienced the strain of translating the ineffable Word of God into human language, which had sometimes seemed to crack and splinter under the divine impact. The struggle to incarnate the Word of God in human society had also taken Muslims to the limits of their endurance and perception, so that they had sometimes been on the brink of despair and sometimes on the point of abandoning Muhammad altogether. But his success proved to be the best argument for his extraordinary and controversial policies. When Muhammad had made the decision to fight at Badr, to expel or massacre the Jewish tribes or to make the treaty at Hudaybiyah, he had not been inspired directly by God but had had to ask for help and advice and use his own native wit. The Qu'ran did not expect Muslims to abandon their natural common sense or to sit back and wait for God to save them by means of a miracle. Islam was a practical and realistic faith, which saw human intelligence and divine inspiration working harmoniously side by side. By the year 632 it seemed as though God's will was really about to be done in Arabia. Unlike so many of the earlier prophets, Muhammad had not only brought individual men and women a new personal vision of hope, but he had undertaken the task of redeeming human history and creating a just society which would enable men and women to fulfil their true potential. The political success of the *umma* had almost become a sacrament for the Muslims: it was an outward sign of God's invisible presence in their midst. Political activity would continue to be a sacred responsibility and the later success of the Muslim empire a 'sign' that mankind as a whole could be redeemed.

Instead of wandering in unworldly fashion round the hills of Galilee preaching and healing, like the Jesus of the Gospels, Muhammad had had to engage in a grim political effort to reform his society, and his followers were pledged to continue this struggle. Instead of devoting all their efforts to restructuring their own personal lives within the context of the *pax Romana*, like the early Christians, Muhammad and his companions had undertaken the redemption of their society, without which there could be no moral or spiritual advance. The Qu'ran is clear that the eternal fate of the individual is of paramount importance and takes precedence over the social duties of Muslims. History and political activity is never an end in itself but is overshadowed and qualified by a transcendent divine order: the eternal fate of the individual is more important than social reform, as the constant Qu'ranic symbolism of Judgement, Hell and Heaven makes clear. In this the Qu'ran responds to the new spirit of individualism which was beginning to make itself felt in Arabia, and its social legislation reflects this concern. Despite the decline of the tribal system, old communal ideals were still normative and Muhammad could not ignore this fact and produce a full-blown individualism to satisfy our present Western liberal ideals – but he had made a start. Yet the salvation of the individual could not be achieved if the endless cycle of bloodshed and exploitation continued in Arabia: a corrupt or disintegrating society inevitably breeds immorality, malaise and despair in all but the truly heroic, so the conditions of seventh-century Arabia demanded a social as well as an individual plan of salvation.

Muhammad had managed to create a community in Medina which was strong and independent of the surrounding chaos. Other tribal groups were beginning to join it, though they were not as yet all committed to his religious vision. In order to survive, the *umma* had to be strong and powerful, yet Muhammad's chief aim had not been political strength but to create a *good* society.

Muhammad's success seemed to vindicate the Qu'ranic claim that societies which refused this order were bound to perish. But the struggle was not over. When the Muslims had returned from Tabuk, some had put away their swords, but Muhammad is said to have told them that the fighting was not over and that they should prepare for a new effort. The challenge of realising God's will in human history would never end: there would always be new dangers and problems to overcome. Sometimes Muslims would have to fight; at other times they could live in peace. But they had embarked on the project of redeeming history as well as the individual, to make what *ought* to happen a living reality in the world. To the present day, Muslims have taken this vocation very seriously.

The grudging submission of Taif showed that many of the Arabs were reluctant to embrace the new order. The Bedouin allies had only a superficial loyalty to Muhammad, yet he had a core of dedicated Muslims who may not always have understood fully what he was trying to do yet who would later show that they had grasped the essential message. Abu Bakr, Umar and Uthman ibn Affan had become members of their Prophet's family by marriage and this had reaffirmed their spiritual kinship with him. They understood that religion was a priority: first the Arabs had to reform themselves by practising the 'pillars' of Islam which taught them to put God at the centre of their lives and look after the vulnerable members of society.

The fourth close disciple of Muhammad was his ward Ali, who was younger than the others and sometimes impatient of the older men. But by 632 he was one of the only members of Muhammad's immediate household left. Umm Kulthum had died during the expedition to Tabuk and this meant that Fatimah (Ali's wife) was the only surviving child of Khadija. Muhammad was devoted to Ali's two sons Hasan and Husayn. He used to let them climb on his back and ride him like a horse. But Muhammad also had a new baby son by his concubine Maryam the Egyptian. He used to love carrying little Ibrahim around Medina. Aisha, however, refused to be impressed. 'Don't you think he is like me?' he would ask. 'I see no likeness,' retorted Aisha. 'Look how plump he is and see his beautiful complexion!' enthused the Prophet. 'Anyone fed on sheep's milk is bound to be plump and fair,' Aisha replied tartly,[1] probably annoyed that special milk was delivered to Ibrahim's foster-mother every day. Despite this care, the baby fell ill at the beginning of 632 and it was clear that he would not recover. Muhammad was with his son when he died and, weeping bitterly, took him into his arms at the last moment. He comforted himself that it would not be long before they were reunited.

Muhammad became increasingly conscious of his approaching death during the tenth year after the *hijra*. He always liked to make a retreat during Ramadan if he was able to spend it in Medina and this year he asked his Companions to make a longer retreat than usual, confiding to Fatimah that he thought his time had come. So in the Dhu al-Hijja, the traditional month for the *hajj*, Muhammad announced that he would lead the pilgrimage himself that year. It would be the first time that these ancient rites around the Ka'aba and the shrines around Mount Arafat had been performed only by the worshippers of the One God, and Muhammad was determined to root his new religion into the sacred traditions of the Arabs. He set out at the end of February 632 with all his wives and a huge crowd of pilgrims, arriving outside Mecca on 5 Dhu al-Hijja, 3 March. He began to utter the ancient cry of the pilgrims: 'Here I am at your service, O God.' Then he began to lead them through the old pagan rituals, so dear to the hearts of the Arabs, giving them a new significance at the same time as he was assuring an essential and creative continuity with the past.

Every Muslim should try to make the *hajj* at least once in a lifetime, provided that his or her circumstances permit. To an outsider these rites seem bizarre – as do any alien religious or social rituals – but they are still able to inspire an intense religious experience and Muslims often find that the *hajj* is the climax of their spiritual lives, both as individuals and as members of the *umma*. The communal and personal aspects of Islamic spirituality are perfectly enshrined in the rites and practices of the *hajj*. Today many of the thousands of pilgrims who assemble each year in Mecca to make the pilgrimage together are not Arabs, but they have been able to make these ancient Arabian rituals their own. As they converge on the Ka'aba, clad in the traditional pilgrim dress that obliterates all distinctions of race or class, they feel that they have been liberated from the egotistic limitations of their daily lives and have been caught up into a community that has one focus and one orientation. The circumambulations around the Ka'aba recently inspired the late Iranian philosopher Ali Shariati:

> As you circumambulate and move closer to the Ka'aba, you feel like a small stream merging with a big river. Carried by a wave you lose touch with the ground. Suddenly, you are floating, carried on by the flood. As you approach the centre, the pressure of the crowd squeezes you so hard that you are given a new life. You are now part of the People; you are now a Man, alive and eternal. . . . The Ka'aba is the world's sun whose face attracts you into its orbit. You have become part of this universal system. Circumambulating around Allah, you will soon forget yourself. . . . You have been transformed into a particle that is gradually melting and disappearing. This is absolute love at its peak.[2]

Jews and Christians have also emphasised the spirituality of the community: St Paul's extended image of the Body of Christ also argues that the unity of the Church and the communion of its members is a revelation of the highest love. The *hajj* offers each individual Muslim the experience of personal integration in the context of the *umma*, with God at its centre.

In one sense the *hajj* gives Muslims an image of the ideal community, in attitude and orientation. In most religions, peace and harmony are important pilgrimage themes and once the pilgrims have entered the Sanctuary all violence of any kind is forbidden: pilgrims may not even kill an insect or speak an impatient word. Hence the outrage throughout the Muslim world when the *hajj* of 1987 was violated by Iranian pilgrims who instigated a riot in which 402 people were killed and 649 injured.

The Qu'ran constantly speaks of the Return to God which all creatures must inevitably make, and the *hajj* is a powerful expression of the Muslims' voluntary journey back to God, from whence they came. The pilgrim cry, which they all shout in unison, reminds them that as individuals and as *umma* they have dedicated themselves wholly to God's service and for the days of the *hajj* they are able to live this commitment more intensely than usual, turning their back on all other concerns. When Muhammad had led his pilgrim body of Emigrants, Helpers and Bedouin to the Ka'aba in 632 they must all have felt that this was a return journey in a profound sense. Most pilgrimages to holy places are seen as some kind of approach to the roots of one's being or to the beginning of the world, and the Emigrants must have felt a special sense of homecoming. But Muhammad was reminding all the Arabs that they were returning to their roots because Abraham and Ishmael, the fathers of the Arabs, were said to have built the shrine. Today also Muslims experience a sense of returning to the roots of their Muslim identity. They naturally remember Muhammad, but the rites of the pilgrimage are primarily designed to recall Abraham and Ishmael, the fathers of all true believers. Thus when they run seven times between Safa and Marwah, they remember how Hagar ran frantically backwards and forwards in search of water for the little Ishmael, after Abraham had left them in the desert. Later they go even further back to their common origins when they stand on the slopes of Mount Arafat, sixteen miles outside Mecca, and recall the original covenant God made with Adam, the first prophet and founder of the human race. At Mina they throw stones at the three pillars as a reminder of the constant struggle with temptation that the *jihad* in God's service requires. Then they sacrifice a sheep or a goat in memory of Abraham's animal sacrifice after he had offered his own son to God. All over the world, Muslims who have not made the *hajj* that year perform this rite at the appointed time, so that the whole *umma* demonstrates its readiness to sacrifice everything, even the things that are dearest to them, in God's service.

Today the mosque of Namira stands near Mount Arafat on the spot where Muhammad is believed to have preached his Farewell Sermon to the pilgrims of 632. He reminded them to deal justly with one another, to treat women as kindly as possible, and to abandon all the blood-feuds for offences committed in the pagan period. The *umma* was one: 'Know that every Muslim is a Muslim's brother, and that the Muslims are brethren. It is only lawful to take from a brother what he gives you willingly, so wrong not yourselves. O God, have I not told you?'[3] This commandment may sound minimal compared with the Sermon on the Mount or St Paul's hymn to charity, but Muhammad was a realist and knew that what he was asking was revolutionary. Instead of being members of distinct tribes, the

Arab Muslims were now one community, just as the God of the Ka'aba was One.

When he returned to Medina after the Farewell Pilgrimage, Muhammad began to experience incapacitating headaches. Aisha remembered that one day she was lying in her apartment with a headache herself. 'O my head!' she moaned when Muhammad came in. 'Nay, Aisha,' he replied, 'it is O *my* head.' But at this stage he was still able to tease her gently. How would Aisha like to die before he did? It would give him the chance to take her into his arms at the graveside and give her a lovely funeral. Aisha replied with her usual asperity: after the funeral he would go straight off to sleep with one of his other wives! 'Nay, Aisha,' Muhammad said as he left the apartment, 'it is O *my* head.'[4]

The pain got worse and he also seems to have suffered from fainting fits, but he never retired permanently to bed. He would often wrap a cloth round his aching temples and go to the mosque to lead the prayers or to address the people. But one morning he seemed to pray for a specially long time in honour of the Muslims who had died at Uhud and added: 'God has given one of his servants the choice between this world and that which is with God and he has chosen the latter.' But the only person who seems to have understood this reference to Muhammad's death was Abu Bakr, who began to weep bitterly. 'Gently, gently, Abu Bakr,' Muhammad said tenderly.[5] But eventually the Prophet collapsed in Maymunah's hut. His wives hung lovingly over him and noticed that he kept asking: Where shall I be tomorrow? Where shall I be tomorrow?' Realising that he wanted to know when he could be with Aisha, they unanimously agreed that he should be moved to her hut and be nursed there.

Muhammad lay there quietly with his head in Aisha's lap, but people seemed to have considered it a mere temporary indisposition, because he still attended the public prayers in the mosque. The *umma* appears to have found the idea of his death so unbearable and frightening that it failed to read the signs correctly, though Abu Bakr warned Aisha that Muhammad was not long for this world. What he had achieved in Arabia was unique and unprecedented, so life without him in the new order seemed inconceivable. People snatched at any straw of hope, as when Muhammad staggered to the mosque one day to reassure them that Usamah, Zayd's young son, was quite able and experienced enough to lead an expedition to the north. When he got too ill, he asked Abu Bakr to lead the prayers for him, and even Aisha seems to have resisted this decision. Eventually Muhammad had to speak to them sharply to get them to obey him. Aisha later said that she had objected not because she felt that her father was unworthy of this honour, but because she was afraid that people would hate him for doing Muhammad's job. But still Muhammad gave them grounds for hope, because he would sometimes attend the prayers even though he was too ill to recite them himself, sitting quietly beside Abu Bakr.

On 12 Rabi (8 June 632) Abu Bakr noticed during prayers that the attention of the people was wavering and that they were looking towards the entrance of the mosque. He knew at once that Muhammad must have come in because nothing else would have distracted the congregation in this way. Muhammad looked much better; indeed, somebody said that they had never seen him looking so radiant, and a wave of joy and relief filled the mosque. Abu Bakr instantly made ready to stand down, but Muhammad put his hands on his shoulders and pushed him gently back to the head of the congregation and sat down beside him until the service was over. Afterwards he went back to Aisha's hut and lay quietly with his head in her lap. He seemed so much better that Abu Bakr asked leave to visit a wife he had recently married, who still lived on the other side of Medina. During the afternoon, Ali and Abbas both looked in and spread the good news that the Prophet seemed to be on the mend, and when Abd al-Rahman dropped in to visit, Muhammad noticed that he was holding a toothpick and made it clear that he wanted to use it. Aisha softened it for him and noticed that he used the implement more vigorously than ever before. But not long afterwards Aisha felt that he was lying more heavily in her lap and that he seemed to be losing consciousness. Still she did not realise what was happening. As she said later, 'It was due to my ignorance and extreme youth that the apostle died in my arms.' She heard him murmur the words, 'Nay, the most Exalted Companion in paradise,'[6] and then discovered that he had gone. Carefully she laid his head on the pillow and began to beat her breast, slap her face and cry aloud in the time-honoured Arab way.

When the people heard the women lamenting the dead, they hurried ashen-faced to the mosque. The news travelled quickly through the oasis and Abu Bakr hurried back to the 'city'. He took one look at Muhammad, kissed his face and bade him farewell. Then he went into the mosque, where he found Umar addressing the crowds. Umar absolutely refused to believe that Muhammad was dead: his soul had just left his body temporarily, he argued, and he would certainly return to his people. He would be the last of them all to die. There must have been an hysterical note in Umar's compulsive harangue, because Abu Bakr murmured, 'Gently, Umar,' but Umar could not stop talking. All that Abu Bakr could do was to step forward quietly, and the expression on his face and his composure must have impressed the people, because they gradually stopped listening to Umar's tirade and clustered round him.

Abu Bakr reminded them that Muhammad had dedicated his whole life to preaching the unity of God. The Qu'ran had warned them incessantly that they must not give to any mere creature the honour due to God alone. Constantly Muhammad had warned them against honouring him in the same way as the Christians honoured Jesus; he was only a mere mortal like themselves. To refuse to admit that Muhammad had died, therefore, was to deny the basic truth about Muhammad. But as long as the Muslims remained true to the belief that God alone was worthy of worship, Muhammad would live on. 'O men, if anyone worships Muhammad, Muhammad is dead,' he ended eloquently. 'If anyone worships God, God is alive, immortal.'[7] Finally, he quoted the verse that had been revealed to Muhammad after the battle of Uhud, when so many of the Muslims had been overwhelmed by the rumour that the Prophet had been killed:

> Muhammad is naught but a Messenger; Messengers
> have passed away before him. Why, if he should die
> or is slain, will you turn upon your heels?
> If any man should turn about on his heels, he will
> not harm God in any way; and God will recompense
> the thankful.[8]

These verses made such an impression on the people that it was as though they had never heard them before. Umar was completely devastated: 'By God, when I heard Abu Bakr recite those words I was dumbfounded, so that my legs would not bear me and I fell to the ground knowing that the apostle was indeed dead.'[9]

The shock of Muhammad's death was one of the gravest crises that the Muslim community had ever had to face. Until this moment, Muhammad had guided their every step, so how would they continue without him? Were they supposed to continue? Some of the Bedouin tribes, whose commitment had been merely political, broke away from the *umma* thinking that the death of Muhammad had abrogated their pact. There was a real danger that Arabia would lapse into its old tribal divisions. Some of the more committed Muslims may also have wondered whether Muhammad's death meant the end of the Muhammadan venture,[10] and those who wanted to appoint a successor split immediately into rival camps; these probably reflected the divisions in the community that had worried Muhammad during his last years.

Most of the Emigrants supported the claim of Abu Bakr, who had been Muhammad's close friend from the very beginning of his mission. Umar also supported this claim. But the Helpers naturally wanted Sa'd ibn Ubadah, one of their own number, to be the first Caliph or Representative of Muhammad; and the Prophet's immediate family believed that he would have wanted Ali to succeed him. Abu Bakr eventually carried the day, largely because his calm grasp of the crisis had impressed the whole *umma*. After he had been elected, Abu Bakr addressed the community, laying down the principles that should henceforth apply to all Muslim rulers:

I have been given authority over you but I am not the best of you. If I do well, help me, and if I do ill, then put me right. Truth consists in loyalty and falsehood in treachery. The weak among you shall be strong in my eyes until I secure his right if God will; and the strong among you shall be weak in my eyes until I wrest the right from him. If a people refrain from fighting in the way of God, God will smite them with disgrace. Wickedness is never widespread in a people but God brings calamity upon them all. Obey me as long as I obey God and His apostle, and if I disobey them you owe me no obedience. Arise to prayer. God have mercy on you.[11]

At first Ali held aloof from Abu Bakr, but later he made his submission. Abu Bakr died after only two years and was succeeded by Umar, then by Uthman; finally in 656 Ali became the Fourth Caliph. They were known as the *rashidun*, the Rightly Guided caliphs, because they governed in accordance with Muhammad's principles. Ali in particular emphasised that a Muslim ruler must not be tyrannical. He was, under God, on a par with his subjects and must take care to lighten the burden of the poor and destitute. That is the only way for a regime to survive:

So if your subjects complain of burden, of blight, of the cutting off of irrigation water, of lack of rain, or of the transformation of the earth through its being inundated by a flood or ruined by drought, lighten their burden to the extent you wish your affair to be rectified. And let not anything by which you have lightened their burden weigh heavily against you, for it is a store which they will return to you by bringing about prosperity in your land and establishing your rule . . . Truly the destruction of the earth only results from the destitution of its inhabitants, and its inhabitants become destitute only when rulers concern themselves with amassing wealth, when they have misgivings about the endurance of their own rule and when they profit little from warning examples.[12]

A ruler must not separate himself from his people in splendid isolation. He must share their burdens, be available to listen to their problems and take their advice.

Not all Muslim rulers have lived up to these high standards. Indeed, the fact that Muslims look back to the period of the *rashidun* as a Golden Age shows that later caliphs and sultans did not adhere with the same passion to the principles of egalitarianism and justice. But sometimes a Muslim would be able to build an empire by showing that he was living and ruling by these principles. As we have seen, at the time of the Crusades both

Nur ad-Din and Saladin went out of their way to give to the poor, reform taxation on Islamic lines and to be accessible to the people. In our own day we have seen Muslims bringing down rulers like the Shah of Iran and President Sadat of Egypt because their governments were unIslamic.[13] The ideals that had inspired Muhammad and the *rashidun* have continued to be a powerful force in Muslim society, and a ruler ignores them at his peril.

Christianity has had a passion for theological discussion, and the major divisions in Christendom have been brought about by doctrinal disputes. Like Judaism, Islam has no similar concept of theological 'heresy'. Its most formative disputes and most crucial divisions have been caused by political differences. The unity of the *umma*, which had been so important to Muhammad, was broken when a split developed between the main body of the Muslims, known as the Sunnah, and the *Shiah-i Ali*, the party of Ali, who believed that only one of Ali's descendants should govern the *umma*. As a minority party, the Shiah developed a piety of protest which was typified by Muhammad's grandson Husayn, who had refused to accept the Ummayad caliphate and was cruelly killed with his small band of companions at the battle of Kerbala by the Caliph Yazid. The intense disputes between the various Shiite and Sunni groups about who should lead the Muslim community and what kind of society it should be have been as formative and important as the great Christological debates in Christianity. This in itself shows that the political reality of the *umma* has been a sacred value in Islam. There are no doctrinal differences between Shiites and Sunnis, though each has developed a distinctive type of piety. We have seen that the Qu'ran regards such theological divisions as disedifying and futile. But politics has been important in Islam not simply because Muslim rulers have used it to further their own political power, but because the Islamic venture has been a dynamic attempt to redeem history from the disintegration and chaos that must ensue if society is not governed by just and equitable laws. The political effort is not extrinsic to a Muslim's personal spiritual life, but the *umma* is of sacramental importance. It could be considered to hold rather the same place as a particular theological option (Catholic, Protestant, Methodist, Baptist) has in the spiritual lives of each Christian.

After Muhammad's death, the continuing success of the Muslim venture vindicated the political effort, and seemed to demonstrate that if a society was reorganised according to God's will it would prevail. The Arab armies had quickly established an empire which spread from the Himalayas to the Pyrenees. Originally this was inspired less by the Qu'ran than by Arab imperialism. There was no attempt to force the new religion on their new subjects. Islam continued to be seen as the religion of the

Arabs, just as Judaism was the religion of the sons of Israel; there was even a brief period in about 700 when conversions were forbidden by law. But about a hundred years after Muhammad's death the caliphs did begin to encourage conversions and people began to flock into Islam, proving that the Qu'ran answered a religious need for the people of the Middle East and North Africa. It was able to assimilate the wisdom of other ancient cultures and quickly established its own distinctive cultural tradition. Islam was not a threatening divisive force but proved able to integrate society.

Muslim jurists developed a theology of the *jihad* to meet the new conditions. They taught that, because there was only one God, the whole world should be united in one polity and it was the duty of all Muslims to engage in a continued struggle to make the world accept the divine principles and create a just society. The *umma*, the House of Islam, was the sacred area where the will of God had been imposed; the rest of the world, the House of War, was the profane area which should be made to surrender to God's rule. Until this had been achieved, Islam must engage in a perpetual warlike effort. But this martial theology was laid aside in practice and became a dead letter once it was clear that the Islamic empire had reached the limits of its expansion about a hundred years after Muhammad's death, and Muslims developed normal diplomatic and economic links with their neighbours in the House of War. There was no pressure on Jews, Christians or Zoroastrians to convert to Islam; Muslims continued to uphold the old religious pluralism of the Middle East and learned to coexist with members of other religions, which, according to the Qu'ran, were perfectly valid earlier revelations.

The rise and fall of the various dynasties and empires, the further expansion of Islam into India and Indonesia, and the development of new and different moods and ways of interpreting the Qu'ran can all be seen as a continuation of the Islamic dialogue with history. Muslims continued to respond creatively to the challenge of modernity until relatively recently. They were able to respond to catastrophes like the Mongol devastations in the thirteenth century and rise again to new power and achievement. The Qu'ran continued to give people of many different races and times the means of surmounting disaster and finding the courage to carry on. Sometimes the new effort would be a specifically spiritual response. Thus the great mystic Jalal ad-Din Rumi produced the *Mathnawi*, which is perhaps the greatest classic of the Sufi tradition, a few years after the destruction of Baghdad, the capital of the Islamic empire, by the Mongol hordes. The Sufis show how deeply the political and social element of Islam affects Muslim spirituality. Devotion to the *umma* has always been an important component of the mystic vocation. As Louis Massignon, the great expert on Sufi mysticism, has explained: 'The mystic call is as a rule the result of an inner rebellion of the conscience against social injustices, not only those of others but primarily and particularly against one's own faults: with a desire intensified by inner purification to find God at any price.'[14] The Sufi vocation is primarily ascetic: they engage in a campaign of spiritual effort which they call the 'greater *jihad*' (as opposed to the 'lesser *jihad*' of physical combat). To the present day, however, an intense spirituality modulates easily into political activism in the Muslim world. Sufis have been in the forefront of many reform movements or in the van of opposition to anything that threatens the *umma*, whether this is an external enemy like the Mongol army or a ruler who is failing to govern in accordance with Islamic principles. Sufis do not withdraw from the world like Christian monks: the world is the theatre of their campaign to find God.

This spirituality is based on the example of the Prophet himself, who did not retire from the world but worked incessantly to reorganise his society. Instead of waiting for utopia or a messianic fulfilment, Muhammad had tried to create his own ideal society himself at Medina. From the first, Muslims modelled themselves on the pattern of his own life: his *hijra* had been a prelude to a political campaign and from the time of the Kharaji sect, who broke away from the main *umma* during the seventh century, to the group known as the *takfir wa'l hijra* in Sadat's Egypt, Muslims who want to reform the *umma* have withdrawn from what they see as a corrupt society and waged war against the establishment. Abu Bakr had told Muslims that it was their duty to depose him if he failed to rule correctly, and Muslims take this very seriously. The welfare of the *umma* is so integral to their spiritual lives that they do not regard a retreat from the world as the highest spiritual duty. They must engage in the *jihad*, not in a spirit of atavistic or fanatical rage, but in a spirit of self-sacrifice, courage and endurance. As the late Ali Shariati explained to the people of Iran during the rule of the Shah, death to self was not the solitary discipline of monasticism, but the dedicated struggle to defend the people of God, even if this meant suffering and death:

> . . . Your monasticism is not in a monastery, but in society; self-sacrifice, sincerity, self-negation, bearing bondages, deprivations, tortures, anguishes and accepting dangers in the arenas of clashes and for the sake of the people that you reach God. The Prophet has said, 'Every religion has a kind of monasticism and the monasticism of my religion is the *jihad*.'[15]

Each religion has its own special emphasis, but this social concern is important to the spirituality of all three monotheistic traditions. If Christians find the Muslims' conception of their essentially political vocation strange, they should reflect that their doctrinal concern and passion for abstruse theological formulations of ineffable truths seem equally bizarre to Muslims and Jews.

One of the chief ways in which Muslims have built this deep sense of brotherhood and solidarity has been through devotion to the Prophet Muhammad. Muslims have continued to emphasise that Muhammad is merely an ordinary man like themselves, but over the centuries they have added a qualification. Yes, Muhammad is a man like other men, but he is 'like a precious gem among stones'.[16] Where ordinary stones are opaque and heavy, a jewel is translucent, shot through with the transfiguring element of light. Muhammad's life has become a 'sign' like the other signs that the Qu'ran urges Muslims to see in the natural world. His prophetic career was a symbol, a theophany, which not only shows God's activity in the world, but illustrates the perfect human surrender to God. The development of the ideal of Muhammadan sanctity has been an imaginative attempt to penetrate the meaning of his life and apply it to the circumstances of daily life. Christians also developed an image of Jesus the man, who is also the Logos, the blueprint of God's plan for creation. Unlike the devotion to Jesus, however, the Muslim devotion to Muhammad is not to the personal, historical character but to a symbol or sacrament which, like the symbolism of great art, illuminates life and gives it a new meaning by pointing to another dimension of reality beyond itself.

Muhammad is therefore seen symbolically as the Perfect Man, the human archetype and the image of a perfect receptivity to God. Hence the imaginative importance of the belief in Muhammad's illiteracy, because it displays his total openness to the Divine Word: this, like his Night Journey, is seen as a perfect example of that *'fana* or annihilation in God of which the Sufis speak. Just as Christians have developed the practice of the imitation of Christ, Muslims seek to imitate Muhammad in their daily lives in order to approximate as closely as possible to this perfection and so to come as close as they can to God Himself. As one might expect, this process of imitation has been more practical and concrete than the imitation of Christ. During the eighth and ninth centuries, Muslim scholars began a process of research to compile the great collections of Muhammad's sayings (*hadith*: traditions) and customary practice (*sunnah*). They travelled throughout the Islamic empire to discover as many authentic accounts of things that Muhammad had said or done on certain occasions, and these, with the Qu'ran, formed the basis of the Islamic Holy Law (*shari'a*). They also became the basis of each Muslim's daily life and spirituality. The *sunnah* taught Muslims to imitate the way Muhammad spoke, ate, loved, washed and worshipped so that in the smallest details of their lives they are reproducing his life on earth and in a real but symbolic sense bringing him to life once more.

Christians do not have anything equivalent to either the Torah or the *shari'a* and tend to think that this minute observance must be burdensome and prohibitive. It is a type of spirituality that has been given a very bad press in the New Testament, where Paul inveighs against the Torah as part of his polemic against the Jewish Christians who wanted to keep the religion of Jesus a strict sect of Judaism. But neither Muslims nor Jews regard the Law as a burden. Muslims see the *sunnah* as a type of sacrament: they help them to develop that God-consciousness prescribed by the Qu'ran in the interstices of their daily lives. By modelling themselves as closely as possible on the Prophet, they are not only internalising him at a very deep level but they are also trying to cultivate the inner attitude of Muhammad and draw close to the God that they find in the depths of their beings. Some of the *hadith* are actually sayings of God Himself which have been put on to the lips of the Prophet. These *hadith qudsi*, sacred traditions, emphasise that God is not a metaphysical Being 'out there' but is in some sense mysteriously identified with the ground of their being. This famous tradition lists the stages whereby one apprehends this inner presence: you must begin by observing the commandments and then progress to voluntary acts of piety:

> My servant draws near to me by means of nothing dearer to me than that which I have established as a duty for him. And my servant continues drawing nearer to me through supererogatory acts until I love him: and when I love him, I become his ear through which he hears, his eye with which he sees, his hand with which he grasps, and his foot with which he walks.[17]

The external actions, like the physical elements of the Christian sacraments, are the outward signs of this inward grace and must be observed and guarded with reverence. This concern means that Muslims all over the world share a particular lifestyle and whatever their other differences have acquired a very clear Muslim identity which instantly draws them together. The way they pray or wash, their table manners or personal hygiene follow a common, distinctive pattern. Muslims from China, Indonesia and the various parts of the Middle East will for example perform the prostrations of *salat* in exactly the same way, taking precisely the same number of seconds.

Muslims who revere Muhammad in this symbolic manner will not be particularly interested in the quest for the historical Muhammad, any more than Christians who have made a similar imaginative commitment to Christ will be disturbed by current research into Jesus' mundane life. But the Salman Rushdie affair has shown that what is perceived as an attack on the Prophet has violated a sacred area of the Muslim psyche throughout the world. It was always a capital offence in the Islamic empire to denigrate Muhammad or his religion, but it has particular power to wound Muslims today because of the humiliation of the *umma* at the hands of the Western world. During the eighteenth century, the Islamic empire began to decline, and this time it found it particularly difficult to rise again to new life. Its decline and fall coincided with the rise of the West with a type of society which had never been achieved in the world before and which was, therefore, difficult to combat. This has not just been a political humiliation but has touched the core of the Muslim identity. If Islam is, for the first time in its history, no longer successful how can its claims be true? The Qu'ranic social prescriptions had hitherto proved infallible, but if Muslim society fell apart even though the *umma* was doing its best to implement the divine plan something had gone radically wrong with Islamic history.

Again, it must be emphasised that the success of the *umma* has a central and quasi-sacramental importance in the personal religious life of each Muslim. It has produced a religious crisis in the Islamic world similar in gravity to that experienced in Europe when the scientific discoveries of Lyell and Darwin seemed to undermine the foundations of the Christian faith. The despair of a poem like Matthew Arnold's 'Dover Beach' and the desolation of Alfred Lord Tennyson's *In Memoriam* may give us some insight into the dread and dismay that some Muslims are experiencing today. How to explain the apparent impotence of Islam before the West and its triumphant secularism? The essence of the social teaching of the Qu'ran had been that a society founded on the right principles could not fail, because it was in harmony with the way things ought to be. The success of the *umma* under Muhammad and his successors had proved that such a society worked; its success had sacramental value. Christianity has usually been at its best during times of adversity; Islam has the opposite problem.

At the very beginning of this book, when we were considering the Western view of Muhammad, we looked briefly at the rage and despair of the martyrs of Cordova in the ninth century. In the Islamic world today, many people are turning to a new radical form of Islam that is sometimes fuelled by a similar dread. Like the Cordovans, many Muslims are trying to discover a new identity and to return to their own roots. This has been a theme in the so-called fundamentalist movements in recent years. Not only have Muslims felt humiliated and degraded before the external power of the West, but they have felt disoriented and lost because their own traditions seem to be swamped by the dominant Western culture. The secularism which we have cultivated carefully in the West has sprung from our own traditions, but in the Islamic countries it seems alien and foreign – of negative rather than positive import. A generation of people has grown up in the Islamic world at home neither in the East nor in the West, and the answer that many people have found has been a return to their Islamic roots. Just as Muhammad sought to embed his religion in the sacred traditions of Arabia when he redefined the meaning of the *hajj*, radical Muslims have sought to root themselves more securely in their Islamic past.

Another theme of the new fundamentalism has been an attempt to get Islamic history back on the right tack and to make the *umma* effective and strong once again. The Iranian revolution was not just an atavistic return to the past, but was an attempt to impose decent values in Iran again. The ideal of the Islamic state in Pakistan and Iran roused deep hopes that seemed strange to Westerners, who have developed a secular ideal of government, but both represented a profound religious and cultural imperative and a chance to make Islam work effectively once more. The history of both efforts shows how problematic and fraught with insuperable difficulties such an attempt to incarnate God's Word is proving to be in the twentieth century. Whereas in the past Muslims were able to rise again after their various disasters and crises – the death of the Prophet, the Mongol devastations and so forth – this time it is proving to be a great deal harder, and a certain frantic despair has entered the religion.

The phenomenon of Islamic fundamentalism is complex; it has sprung from great pain and enshrines a desperate need on the part of many Muslim people to take their destiny into their own hands again, in the time-honoured Islamic way. Some of these new radical forms of Islam do not seem healthy, but seem full of the insecurity and dismay that fuelled the suicidal cult of the martyrs of Cordova, who were fired by many of the same needs and fears. We have seen that at the time of the Suez crisis the Islamic scholar Wilfred Cantwell Smith wrote that a healthy and functioning Islam was crucial because it had helped Muslim people to cultivate decent values and ideals which we in the West also share because they spring from a common tradition. Since Suez, the West has alienated the people of the Middle East even more and has discredited the liberal secularism that it is so anxious to spread. We in the West have never been able to cope with Islam: our ideas of it have been crude and dismissive and today we seem to belie our own avowed commitment to tolerance and compassion by our contempt for the pain and inchoate distress in the Muslim world. Islam is not going to disappear or wither away; it would have been better if it had remained healthy and strong. We can only hope that it is not too late.

People in the Islamic world have many problems in the late twentieth century, but, as Wilfred Cantwell Smith pointed out in 1956, the West also has a problem. The 'fundamental weakness' of both Western civilisation and Christianity in the modern world:

> is their inability to recognise that they share the planet not with inferiors but with equals. Unless Western civilisation intellectually and socially, politically and economically, and the Christian church theologically, can learn to treat other men with fundamental respect, these two in their turn will have failed to come to terms with the actualities of the twentieth century. The problems raised in this are, of course, as profound as anything that we have touched on for Islam.[18]

The reality is that Islam and the West share a common tradition. From the time of the Prophet Muhammad, Muslims have recognised this, but the West cannot accept it. Today some Muslims are beginning to turn against the cultures of the People of the Book, which have humiliated and despised them. They have even begun to Islamise their new hatred. The beloved figure of the Prophet Muhammad became central to one of the latest clashes between Islam and the West during the Salman Rushdie affair. If Muslims need to understand our Western traditions and institutions more thoroughly today, we in the West need to divest ourselves of some of our old prejudice. Perhaps one place to start is with the figure of Muhammad: a complex, passionate man who sometimes did things that it is difficult for us to accept, but who had genius of a profound order and founded a religion and a cultural tradition that was not based on the sword – despite the Western myth – and whose name 'Islam' signifies peace and reconciliation.

Notes

All quotations from the Qu'ran are taken from the translation of Arthur J. Arberry, *The Koran Interpreted* (Oxford, 1964), unless otherwise stated.

Quotations from the Jewish and Christian Scriptures are taken from the Jerusalem Bible.

Chapter 1: MUHAMMAD THE ENEMY

1. John of Joinville, *The Life of St Louis*, trans. René Hague and ed. Natalis de Wailly (London, 1955), p. 36.
2. Paul Alvaro, *Indiculus Luminosus*, quoted in R. W. Southern, *Western Views of Islam in the Middle Ages* (London, 1962), p. 21.
3. Perfectus was probably a Latin version of the Arab name al-Kamil (the Complete One); other martyrs were called Servus Dei, which must be a translation of Abdallah (the Slave of God).
4. Paul Alvaro, *Vita Eulogii*, quoted in Norman Daniel, *The Arabs and Medieval Europe* (London and Beirut, 1975), p. 29.
5. II Thessalonians 1:4–8. The author was not St Paul; the letter was written years after Paul's death.
6. Revelation 19:19.
7. *Gesta Francorum or The Deeds of the Franks and Other Pilgrims to Jerusalem*, trans. Rosalind Hill (London, 1962), p. 22.
8. Southern, *Western Views of Islam*, p. 29.
9. Quoted in Daniel, *The Arabs and Medieval Europe*, p. 156.
10. *The Comedy of Dante Alighieri*, Cantica I: Hell, trans. Dorothy L. Sayers (London, 1949), Canto XXVIII:22–7, p. 246.
11. *Gesta Regum*, quoted in Southern, *Western Views of Islam*, p. 35.
12. *Chronicon*, in ibid., p. 36.
13. Quoted in Benjamin Kedar, *Crusade and Mission: European Approaches to the Muslims* (Princeton, 1984), p. 99.
14. Ibid., p. 101.
15. Quoted in Régine Pernoud, *The Crusaders*, trans. Enid Grant (Edinburgh and London, 1963), p. 221.
16. Ibid.
17. Kedar, *Crusade and Mission*, pp. 125–6.
18. Quoted in Pernoud, *The Crusaders*, pp. 222–3.
19. Umberto Eco, 'Dreaming of the Middle Ages', in *Travels in Hyper-Reality*, trans. William Weaver (London, 1987), p. 64.
20. Quoted in Southern, *Western Views of Islam*, pp. 79–80.
21. Daniel, *The Arabs and Medieval Europe*, p. 302.
22. Norman Daniel, *Islam and the West: The Making of an Image* (Edinburgh, 1960), pp. 284–5.

23. Quoted in Edward W. Said, *Orientalism: Western Conceptions of the Orient* (New York and London, 1985 edn), p. 66.
24. Humphry Prideaux, *The True Nature of Imposture, Fully Displayed in the Life of Mahomet* (7th edn, London, 1708), p. 80.
25. Daniel, *Islam and the West*, p. 297.
26. Ibid., p. 300.
27. Ibid., p. 290.
28. *The Decline and Fall of the Roman Empire*, ed. Dero E. Saunders, abridged in one volume (London, 1980), pp. 657–8.
29. *On Heroes and Hero-Worship* (London, 1841), p. 63.
30. Quoted in Said, *Orientalism*, p. 172.
31. Ibid.
32. Ibid., p. 171.
33. *Histoire générale*, quoted in ibid., p. 149.
34. M. Baudricourt, *La Guerre et le gouvernement de l'Algérie* (Paris, 1853), p. 160.
35. Quoted in Said, *Orientalism*, p. 38.
36. *Holy War: The Crusades and Their Impact on Today's World* (London, 1988).
37. Rana Kabbani, *Letter to Christendom* (London, 1989), p. 54.
38. Fay Weldon, *Sacred Cows* (London, 1989), pp. 6, 12.
39. Conor Cruise O'Brien, *The Times*, 11 May 1989.
40. *Islam in Modern History* (Princeton and London, 1957), pp. 304–5.

Chapter 2: MUHAMMAD THE MAN OF AL-LLAH

1. After the revelations, Muhammad is said to have thickened the 'l' sound of 'al-Llah' so that it became *al-Llah* to distinguish thc Islamic from the pagan concept of God. This usage is more correct than the familiar 'Allah'.

Chapter 3: JAHILIYAH

1. Zoroastrianism was preached by the prophet Zarathustra in Iran in the seventh and sixth centuries BCE at about the same time as Jeremiah and Isaiah were preaching in Jerusalem. It is a dualistic faith which sees an eternal struggle between two supreme powers, a Good and an Evil principle.
2. A. J. Toynbee, *A Study of History* (London, 1951), vol. III, pp. 7–22.
3. W. Montgomery Watt, *Muhammad's Mecca: History in the Qu'ran* (Edinburgh, 1988).
4. It seems, however, that some of the pagans of Yathrib had effigies of Manat in their homes.
5. See the genealogical table of the Quraysh on p. 18.
6. Muhammad is traditionally believed to have been born in the Year of the Elephant, but Western scholars put the Abyssinian invasion about ten years earlier, in 560.
7. Quoted by Muhammad ibn Ishaq, *Sirat Rasul Allah* 38, in A. Guillaume (trans. and ed.), *The Life of Muhammad* (London, 1955), p. 21.
8. Sura 29:61–3.
9. Sura 10:22–4; see also 29:65, 31:31, 17:69.
10. *Sira* 143, in Guillaume (trans. and ed.), *The Life of Muhammad*, p. 99.
11. Ibid., 145, p. 100.

Chapter 4: REVELATION

1. Sura 93:6–8.
2. Today many Muslims believe that Muhammad was the archetypal Perfect Man and that he was therefore incapable of 'error'. I discuss this in more detail in Chapter 9.
3. Muhammad ibn Ishaq, *Sirat Rasul Allah* 150, in A. Guillaume (trans. and ed.), *The Life of Muhammad* (London, 1955), p. 104.
4. Sura 61:6. See also Tor Andrae, *Muhammad: The Man and His Faith*, trans. Théophil Menzel (London, 1936), pp. 44–5.
5. Ibn Ishaq, *Sira* 136, in Guillaume (trans. and ed.), *The Life of Muhammad*, p. 94.
6. Ibid., 134, p. 93. Ad and Iram were ancient Arab peoples, whose destruction was mentioned in the Qu'ran.
7. *Kitab at-Tabaqat al-Kabir*, quoted in Andrae, *Mohammad*, pp. 43–4.
8. The translation of Hilf al-Fudul as the League of the Virtuous or Chivalrous has been disputed.
9. Ibn Ishaq, *Sira* 104–5, in Guillaume (trans. and ed.), *The Life of Muhammad*, p. 71.
10. Abu Bakr Ahmad at-Baihaqi (d.1066), *Dala'il an nubuwwa*, 1.12, quoted in Annemarie Schimmel, *And Muhammad Is His Messenger: The Veneration of the Prophet in Islamic Piety* (Chapel Hill and London, 1985), p. 68.
11. Ibn Ishaq, *Sira* 116–17, in Guillaume (trans. and ed.), *The Life of Muhammad*, p. 81.
12. Thus Andrae, *Mohammed*, pp. 50–1.
13. Ibn Ishaq, *Sira* 121, in Guillaume (trans. and ed.), *The Life of Muhammad*, p. 83.
14. Ibid., 120, p. 82.
15. Ibid., 155, p. 111.
16. Some of the Arabs in this story are almost always referred to by their *kunyas* in the sources, eg. Abu Talib, Abu Sufyan and Umm Salamah.
17. Ibn Ishaq, *Sira* 124–5, in Guillaume (trans. and ed.), *The Life of Muhammad*, pp. 85–6.
18. Sura 28:86.
19. Muhammad ibn Isma'il al-Bukhari, quoted in Martin Lings, *Muhammad: His Life Based on the Earliest Sources* (London, 1983), pp. 43–4.
20. Sura 96:1.
21. Ibn Ishaq, *Sira* 153, in Guillaume (trans. and ed.), *A Life of Muhammad*, p. 106.
22. Isaiah 6:1–9.
23. Jeremiah 20:7–9.
24. Andrae, *Mohammad*, p. 59.
25. Ibn Ishaq, *Sira* 153, in Guillaume (trans. and ed.), *The Life of Muhammad*, p. 106.
26. Ibid., 154, p. 107. *Namus* was the Greek *nomos*, Law, that is the Law of Moses or the Torah revealed to the people of Israel. This word used by Waraqa was new to the Arabs. Muslims identified it with Gabriel. Waraqa meant that this was one of the great revelations that God periodically made to men.
27. Sura 35:22.
28. See, for example, Sura 6:160ff.
29. Sura 3:76.
30. Sura 61:6.
31. Sura 81:19–24.
32. Ibn Ishaq, *Sira* 151, in Guillaume (trans. and ed.), *The Life of Muhammad*, p. 105.
33. Jalal al-Din Suyuti, *al-itqan fi'ulum al-aq'ran*, quoted in Maxime Rodinson, *Mohammed*, trans. Anne Carter (London, 1971), p. 74.

34. Bukhari, Hadith 1.3, quoted in Lings, *Muhammad*, pp. 44–5.
35. Sura 75:17–19.
36. Arberry translates the last two words of the sura 'declare it' but the Arabic really means something like: 'give glory to God.'

Chapter 5: THE WARNER

1. Sura 42:7.
2. Sura 88:21–2.
3. Sura 74:1–5, 8–10. Some authorities think that this, not Sura 96, was the first part of the Qu'ran to be revealed.
4. Sura 80:24–32.
5. Sura 51:19, 70:24. In the early days *zakat* was established as a principle, but did not become a regular tax until after Muhammad's death.
6. W. Montgomery Watt, *Muhammad at Mecca* (Oxford, 1953), Excursus D 'Tazakka', pp. 165–9.
7. Sura 92:18, 9:103, 63:9, 102:1.
8. Sura 4:2,5,10, 6:152, 17:34, 51:19, 70:24.
9. Sura 96:6–8.
10. Sura 104:1–3.
11. Sura 70:11–14.
12. Sura 105.
13. Sura 80:11.
14. Sura 106.
15. Sura 55:1–12.
16. Sura 36:33–40.
17. Sura 36:41–4.
18. Isaiah 55:8–9.
19. Sura 2:158–9.
20. Sura 6:96–9.
21. Sura 10:69, 21:26–30.
22. Sura 8:2–4.
23. Sura 2:89, 27:14.
24. Muhammad ibn Sa'd, *Kitab at-Tabaqat al-Kabir*, 8:102, quoted in Martin Lings, *Muhammad: His Life Based on the Earliest Sources* (London, 1983), p. 51.
25. Muhammad ibn Ishaq, *Sirat Rasul Allah* 162, in A. Guillaume (trans. and ed.), *The Life of Muhammad* (London, 1955), p. 116.
26. Ibid., 161, p. 115.
27. Ibn Sa'd, *Tabaqat*, 3:1,37, quoted in Lings, *Muhammad*, p. 47.
28. Quoted in Watt, *Muhammad at Mecca*, p. 87.
29. Ibn Ishaq, *Sira* 166, in Guillaume (trans. and ed.), *The Life of Muhammad*, p. 117.
30. Sura 26:214.
31. Sura 17:28–31.
32. Abu Ja'fah at-Tabari, *Tariq ar-Rasul wa'l-Muluk* 1171, in Guillaume (trans. and ed.), *The Life of Muhammad*, pp. 117–18.
33. Sura 83:13.
34. Sura 37:15.
35. Sura 37:12–19.
36. Sura 45:23.
37. Sura 83:9–14.
38. Sura 36:77–83.

Chapter 6: THE SATANIC VERSES

1. Muhammad ibn Ishaq, *Sirat RasulAllah* 166–7, in A. Guillaume (trans. and ed.), *The Life of Muhammad* (London, 1955), p. 118.
2. See Sura 38:4–8.
3. See, for example, Sura 46:8.
4. Sura 17:75–7.
5. Quoted in W. Montgomery Watt, *Muhammad at Mecca* (Oxford, 1953), p. 100.
6. *Tafsir*, xvii, 119–21, quoted in Watt, *Muhammad at Mecca*, p. 102.
7. *Tariq ar-Rasul wa'al Muluk* 1192, quoted in Guillaume (trans. and ed.), *The Life of Muhammad*, p. 165.
8. Sura 53:19–20.
9. Sura 53:26, though even here the angels' intercession is minimised.
10. Tabari, *Tariq* 1192, quoted in Guillaume (trans. and ed.), *The Life of Muhammad*, p. 166.
11. See Sura 7:9–15.
12. William O. Beeman, 'Images of the Great Satan: Representations of the United States in the Iranian Revolution', in Nikki R. Keddie (ed.), *Religion and Politics in Iran: Shi'ism from Quietism to Revolution* (New Haven, 1983), pp. 191–217.
13. *Tariq* 1192, quoted in Guillaume (trans. and ed.), *The Life of Muhammad*, p. 166.
14. Sura 53:19–26.
15. Sura 22:51.
16. Sura 2:100; cf. 13:37, 16:101, 17:41, 17:86.
17. See Sura 69:44–7.
18. Sura 29:17, 10:18, 39:43.
19. Sura 25:17ff., 16:86, 10:28.
20. Sura 36:74.
21. Ibn Ishaq, *Sira* 167–8, in Guillaume (trans. and ed.), *The Life of Muhammad*, p. 119.
22. Ibid.
23. Ibid., 206–7, p. 145.
24. Sur 19:16–22.
25. Quoted in Ibn Ishaq, *Sira* 183–4, in Guillaume (trans. and ed.), *The Life of Muhammad*, pp. 130–1.
26. Ibid., 185, p. 131.
27. Ibid., p. 132.
28. Sura 41:1–6.
29. Ibn Ishaq, *Sira* 186–7, in Guillaume (trans. and ed.), *The Life of Muhammad*, pp. 132–3.
30. Sura 52:34, 2:23, 10:38.
31. George Steiner, *Real Presences: Is There Anything* in *What We Say?* (London, 1989), pp. 142–3.
32. Seyyed Hossein Nasr, *Ideals and Realities of Islam* (London, 1966), pp. 47–8.
33. Ibn Ishaq, *Sira* 227, in Guillaume (trans. and ed.), *The Life of Muhammad*, p. 157.
34. Ibid., 228, p. 158.
35. Ibid., 230, p. 159.
36. Sura 23:22–4.
37. Sura 11:105.
38. Sura 11:102–3.

Chapter 7: HIJRA: A NEW DIRECTION

1. Quoted in Muhammad ibn Ishaq, *Sirat Rasul Allah* 278, in A. Guillaume (trans. and ed.), *The Life of Muhammad* (London, 1955), p. 191
2. Ibid., 244, pp. 169–70.
3. Muhammad ibn Isma'il al-Bukhari, *Ahadith*, 63:26, quoted in Martin Lings, *Muhammad: His Life Based on the Earliest Sources* (London, 1983), p. 94.
4. Ibn Ishaq, *Sira* 280, in Guillaume (trans. and ed.), *The Life of Muhammad*, p. 193.
5. Sura 46:28–32.
6. Sura 13:12.
7. Neither refused Muhammad protection specifically because of his religion. Akhnas refused because even though he was regarded as the chief of the clan he was actually one of its confederates and was not empowered, therefore, to grant protection to outsiders. Suhayl replied that he could not give Muhammad protection because he came from the wrong branch of Quraysh.
8. Sura 17:1.
9. Ibn Ishaq, *Sira* 271, in Guillaume (trans. and ed.), *The Life of Muhammad*, p. 186.
10. Sura 53:13–18.
11. See Annemarie Schimmel, *And Muhammad Is His Messenger: The Veneration of the Prophet in Islamic Piety* (Chapel Hill and London, 1985), pp. 161–75.
12. *Ilahinama*, quoted in ibid., pp. 167–8.
13. In *The Making of Late Antiquity* (Cambridge, Mass., and London, 1978), Peter Brown shows that trance and ecstasy were normative in early Christianity. The dream had particular importance in the religious life of the age – pagan as well as Christian. 'It was a paradigm of the open frontier between human and divine: when a man was asleep and his bodily senses were stilled, the frontier lay wide open between himself and the gods' (p. 65).
14. *Acts of Perpetua and Felicitas*, IV, quoted in Peter Dronke, *Women Writers of the Middle Ages: A Critical Study of Texts from Perpetua (d.203) to Marguerite Porete (d.1310)* (Cambridge, 1984), p. 2.
15. *The Power of Myth* (with Bill Moyers) (New York, 1988), p. 85.
16. Ibid., p. 87.
17. Ibn Ishaq, *Sira* 134, in Guillaume (trans. and ed.), *The Life of Muhammad*, p. 93.
18. Ibid., 287, p. 198.
19. Ibid., 246, p. 171.
20. Ibid.
21. Quoted in Ibn Ishaq, *Sira* 289, in Guillaume (trans. and ed.), *The Life of Muhammad*, p. 199. The command that forbade Muslims to 'slay their children' prohibited the custom of female infanticide, which had been common in pre-Islamic Arabia.
22. Ibid., 291–2, pp. 200–1.
23. Quoted in ibid., 293, p. 201.
24. Sura 5:5–7. Muslims are forbidden to eat pork, carrion, the flesh of strangled animals and those who have died of natural causes, the blood of an animal and meat that has been sacrificed to idols. Cf. Acts of the Apostles 15:19–21,29.
25. Ibn Ishaq, *Sira* 295, in Guillaume (trans. and ed.), *The Life of Muhammad*, p. 202.
26. Ibid., 304–5, p. 208.
27. Some of the Muslims had relatives in Medina: Muhammad himself had Medinan connections through his mother Amina. But the *hijra* demanded that Muslims abandon the whole tribe and blood-group for another to whom they were not related.

28. W. Montgomery Watt, *Muhammad's Mecca: History in the Qu'ran* (Edinburgh, 1988), p. 25.
29. Sura 60:1,9,47–13.
30. Sura 8:30, 28:19, 27:48–51.
31. Western scholars question the historical role of Abbas at Second 'Aqaba. They point out that Abbas was the founder of the Abbasid dynasty and that this and other flattering references were an attempt to whitewash his reputation. As we shall see, Abbas seems to have fought against Muhammad and did not convert to Islam until almost the last moment.
32. Ibn Ishaq, *Sira* 296, in Guillaume (trans. and ed.), *The Life of Muhammad*, p. 203.
33. Ibid., 297, p. 204.
34. Ibid., 316, p. 215.
35. Sura 9:40.
36. Ibn Ishaq, *Sira* 334, in Guillaume (trans. and ed.), *The Life of Muhammad*, p. 227.
37. Ibid., 337, p. 229.
38. Ibid., 342, p. 232.
39. Ibid.
40. Ibid., 341, pp. 231–2.
41. Sura 8:72. This translation is by W. Montgomery Watt in *Muhammad's Mecca*, p. 20.
42. Ibn Ishaq, *Sira* 341, in Guillaume (trans. and ed.), *The Life of Muhammad*, p. 232.
43. Sura 3:109.
44. Ibn Ishaq, *Sira* 247, in Guillaume (trans. and ed.), *The Life of Muhammad*, p. 236.
45. Muhammad ibn Sa'd, *Kitab at-Tabaqat al-Kabir*, VIII, 42, quoted in Lings, *Muhammad*, pp. 133–4.
46. Ibn Ishaq, *Sira* 414, in Guillaume (trans. and ed.), *The Life of Muhammad*, p. 280. Fakhkh is a place outside Mecca; Majanna was the market place in the lower part of the city; Shama and Tafil are two Meccan mountains.
47. Ibid.
48. Sura 2:6–14.
49. Ibn Ishaq, *Sira* 413, in Guillaume (trans. and ed.), *The Life of Muhammad*, p. 279.
50. Ibid., 362, p. 246.
51. Ibid., 361, p. 246.
52. Sura 2:25, 4:153, 5:15.
53. Sura 3:72, 3:87. The Jews are also accused of distorting the meaning of texts to suit themselves (4:48, 5:16). Later Muslims have used these verses to argue that the Jewish scriptures are corrupt. The text, however, says that the Jews have 'altered words from their proper meanings'.
54. Sura 2:79, 5:82.
55. See, for example, 4:156–7. This is not an attack on Jesus or against Christianity but is part of the polemic against the Jews. The idea that Jesus had not really suffered and died on the Cross was a feature of various Oriental Christian docetist sects and of Manichaeism, which seems to have penetrated Arabia.
56. See Sura 2:110.
57. Sura 29:46.
58. Sura 3:58–62.
59. Sura 2:129–32.
60. See D. Sidersky, *Les Origines des légendes musulmans dans le Coran et dans les vies des prophètes* (Paris, 1933), pp. 51–3.
61. Genesis 21:8–21.
62. Sura 2:122–4.

63. Sura 2:39. See also 2:140–6.
64. Sura 6:160, 162–3.

Chapter 8: HOLY WAR

1. These remarks apply only to Western Christianity. The Eastern Orthodox Church did not cultivate the image of the vulnerable Christ but Christ Pantocrater, Emperor of the Universe. The Emperor of Byzantium was his representative on earth and his splendid court was modelled on Christ's court in heaven.
2. This attitude is already present in the New Testament: I John 2:12–17.
3. Even the Puritans saw worldly prosperity as a *reward* rather than a spiritual achievement in itself.
4. *The Roman Martyrology*: entry for Christmas day.
5. Sura 33:72.
6. See, for example, Sura 11:28–125.
7. Sura 22:40–3.
8. Tor Andrae, *Muhammad: The Man and His Faith*, trans. Theophil Menzel (London, 1936), p. 197.
9. Sura 2:213–15.
10. Sura 5:17, but in 5:85 the Qu'ran suggests that the Christians are far more charitable than the Jews.
11. Sura 22:252.
12. I have discussed the modern *jihad* more fully in *Holy War: The Crusades and Their Impact on Today's World* (London, 1988), pp. 223–84.
13. Quoted in Muhammad ibn Ishaq, *Sirat Rasul Allah* 430, in A. Guillaume (trans. and ed.), *The Life of Muhammad* (London, 1955), p. 291.
14. Ibid., 435, p. 294.
15. Ibid., 438, p. 296.
16. Ibid., 441, p. 298.
17. Ibid.
18. Ibid., 442, p. 298.
19. Sura 8:70.
20. Armstrong, *Holy War*, throughout.
21. Sura 8:45.
22. Sura 8:17.
23. Sura 8:66–7.
24. Sura 21:49.
25. Exodus 14:25–31.
26. *Tariq ar-Rasul wa 'l-Muluk* 1281, quoted in W. Montgomery Watt, *Muhammad at Medina* (Oxford, 1956), p. 205.
27. See Sura 47:5, 24:34, 2:178.
28. Quoted in Muhammad Zafrulla Khan, *Islam: Its Meaning for Modern Man* (London, 1962), p. 182.
29. Ibn Ishaq, *Sira* 459, in Guillaume (trans. and ed.), *The Life of Muhammad*, p. 309.
30. Sura 47:22.
31. Ibn Ishaq, *Sira* 543, in Guillaume (trans. and ed.), *The Life of Muhammad*, p. 361.
32. Ibid., 545, p. 363.
33. Muhammad ibn Umar al-Waqidi, *Kitab al-Maghazi* 214, quoted in Martin Lings, *Muhammad: His Life Based on the Earliest Sources* (London, 1983), p. 176.
34. Ibn Ishaq, *Sira* 559, in Guillaume (trans. and ed.), *The Life of Muhammad*, p. 372.
35. Ibid., 562, p. 374.
36. Ibid.

37. Ibid., 583, p. 386.
38. *Muhammad at Medina*, p. 184.
39. Sura 4.:3.
40. Sura 4:23.
41. Sura 2:225–40; 65:1–70.
42. Sura 4:3.
43. Sura 6:152.
44. Matthew 6:26.
45. Sura 24:33.
46. Quoted in Maxime Rodinson, *Mohammed*, trans. Anne Carter (London, 1961), p. 192. Source not given.
47. Muhammad ibn Sa'ad, *Kitab at-Tabaqat al-Kabir*, VIII, 71–2, quoted in Ling's, *Muhammad*, p. 213.
48. Sura 33:36–40.
49. Sura 33:53.
50. Ibn Ishaq, *Sira* 729, p. 493.
51. Ibid., 726, p. 491.
52. Ibid., 735, p. 496.
53. Ibid.; 735, p. 496, and *Ahadith* of Ahmad ibn Hanilal VI:60, 197 and Muhammad ibn al-Bukhari, III:108, 296; quoted in Nabia Abbot, *Aishah, the Beloved of Muhammad* (Chicago, 1942), p. 36. The patriarch whose name Aisha could not remember was, of course, Jacob. See Qu'ran, Sura 12:18.
54. Sura 24:11.
55. Waqidi, *Kitab al-Maghazi*, 448–9; Ibn Sa'd, *Tabaqat*, 2:51, quoted in Lings, *Muhammad*, p. 218.
56. Ibn Ishaq, *Sira* 677, p. 454.
57. See Sura 4:54.
58. Ibn Ishaq, *Sira* 675, p. 453.
59. Sura 33:10–11.
60. Ibn Ishaq, *Sira* 683, p. 460.
61. Waqidi, *Kitab*, 488–90, quoted in Lings, *Muhammad*, p. 227.
62. Ibn Ishaq, *Sira* 689, p. 464.
63. Ibid., 689, pp. 464–5.
64. See Bernard Lewis in *Semites and Anti-Semites, An Inquiry into Conflict and Prejudice* (London, 1986), pp. 117–39, 164–259.
65. Sura 2:191,251.
66. Sura 8:62–3.
67. Sura 3:147–8.
68. Watt, *Muhammad at Medina*, pp. 215–17; Rodinson, *Mohammed*, p. 214.

Chapter 9: HOLY PEACE

1. Sura 48:27.
2. Muhammad ibn Umar al-Waqidi, *Kitab al-Maghazi* 587, quoted in Martin Lings, *Muhammad: His Life Based on the Earliest Sources* (London, 1983), p. 247.
3. Muhammad ibn Ishaq, *Sirat Rasul Allah* 741, in A. Guillaume (trans. and ed.), *The Life of Muhammad* (London, 1955), p. 500.
4. Ibid.
5. Ibid.
6. Ibid., 743, p. 501.
7. Ibid., p. 502.
8. Ibid., p. 745, p. 503.

9. W. Montgomery Watt, *Muhammad at Medina* (Oxford, 1956), p. 50.
10. Ibn Ishaq, *Sira* 748, in Guillaume (trans. and ed.), *The Life of Muhammad*, p. 505.
11. Ibid., 747, p. 504.
12. By his marriage to Juwayriyah, daughter of the chief of al-Mustaliq of Khuza'ah, after the attack on al-Mustaliq in January 627.
13. Ibn Ishaq, *Sira* 747, in Guillaume (trans. and ed.), *The Life of Muhammad*, p. 504.
14. Ibid., 748, p. 505.
15. Quoted in Lings, *Muhammad*, p. 254. Source not given.
16. Ibid., p. 255.
17. Sura 48:1.
18. Sura 48:2.
19. Sura 48:10–17.
20. Sura 48:20.
21. Sura 48:26–7.
22. Sura 48:29.
23. Matthew 10:34–6.
24. Ibn Ishaq, *Sira* 751, in Guillaume (trans. and ed.), *The Life of Muhammad*, p. 507.
25. Ibid., 752, p. 507.
26. Sura 2:174–5.
27. Marshall G. S. Hodgson, *The Venture of Islam: Conscience and History in a World Civilization* (Chicago, 1974), vol. I, p. 339.
28. Sura 17:35.
29. Sura 5:49. Cf. 16:127, 42:37.
30. Sura 2:172.
31. Sura 2:172. Muhammad has been blamed for not abolishing slavery, but this is an anachronistic judgement. The institution is also taken for granted by New Testament writers. But Muhammad did in fact reduce slavery in Arabia by imposing the *pax Islamica*, which cut down on raids and violence in the peninsula.
32. It is also true that the egalitarian spirit was deeply embedded in the culture of the Middle East and that Islam was in part a response to this.
33. Watt, *Muhammad at Medina*, p. 268.
34. William and Fidelity Lancaster, 'The Gulf Crisis and Arab Disenchantment', *Middle East International*, 385, 12 October 1990. For Arab views about division between Muslims.
35. Muhammad ibn Sa'd, *Kitab at-Tabaqat al-Kabir* VII, 147, quoted in Lings, *Muhammad*, p. 271.
36. Quoted in Lings, *Muhammad*, p. 282. Source not given.
37. Ibn Ishaq, *Sira* 717, in Guillaume (trans. and ed.), *The Life of Muhammad*, p. 485.
38. Muhammad ibn Isma'il al-Bukhari, *Ahadith* LXIII, 6 quoted in Lings, *Muhammad*, p. 275.
39. Sura 33:28–9.
40. Sura 33:35.
41. I have discussed this in more detail in *The Gospel According to Woman: Christianity's Creation of the Sex War in the West* (London, 1986).
42. Tradition of Abu Na'im al-Isfahani, *dala'il an nubuwwa*, II, 45 quoted in Nabia Abbott, *Aishah, the Beloved of Muhammad* (Chicago, 1942), p. 67.
43. Ibn Ishaq, *Sira* 812, in Guillaume (trans. and ed.), *The Life of Muhammad*, p. 546.
44. Ibid., 815, p. 548.
45. Sura 17:82.
46. Ibn Ishaq, *Sira* 821, in Guillaume (trans. and ed.), *The Life of Muhammad*, p. 553. The verse from the Qu'ran is Sura 49:13.
47. Quoted in Lings, *Muhammad*, p. 304. Source not given.

48. Abu Ja'far at-Tabari, *Tariq ar-Rasul wa 'l-Muluk* 1642, in Guillaume (trans. and ed.), *The Life of Muhammad*, p. 553.
49. Muhammad Zafrulla Khan, *Islam: Its Meaning for Modern Man* (London, 1962), p. 60.
50. Quoted in Lings, *Muhammad*, p. 311. Source not given.
51. Ibn Ishaq, *Sira* 886, in Guillaume (trans. and ed.), *The Life of Muhammad*, pp. 596–7.
52. Sura 9:66.
53. Sura 9:108. It has been suggested that the rebellious Muslims were in touch with Abu Amir, the monotheist known as 'the Monk' who had defected to Mecca after Muhammad had arrived in Medina.

Chapter 10: DEATH OF THE PROPHET?

1. Quoted in Martin Lings, *Muhammad: His Life Based on the Earliest Sources* (London 1983), p. 317. No source given.
2. Ali Shariati, *Hajj*, trans. Laleh Bakhtiar (Tehran, 1988), pp. 54–6.
3. Muhammad ibn Ishaq, *Sirat Rasul Allah* 969, in A. Guillaume (trans. and ed.), *The Life of Muhammad* (London, 1955), p. 651.
4. Ibid., 1,000, p. 678.
5. Ibid., 1,006, p. 679.
6. Ibid., 1,011, p. 682.
7. Ibid., 1,012, p. 683.
8. Sura 3:138.
9. Ibn Ishaq, *Sira* 1013, in Guillaume (trans. and ed.), *The Life of Muhammad*, p. 683.
10. Wilfred Cantwell Smith, Islam and Modern History (Princeton and London, 1957), p. 32, suggests this, but warns that not many Muslims would endorse it.
11. Ibn Ishaq, *Sira* 1,017, in Guillaume (trans. and ed.), *The Life of Muhammad*, p. 687.
12. Instructions given by Ali to Malik al-Ashtar, when he was appointed governor of Egypt, in William C. Chittick (trans. and ed.), *A Shi'ite Anthology* (London, 1980), p. 75.
13. I have discussed this in *Holy War: The Crusades and Their Impact on Today's World* (London, 1988), pp. 223–84.
14. *Encyclopaedia of Islam* (1st edn, Leiden, 1913), entry under 'Tasawwuf', quoted also in Malise Ruthven, *Islam and the World* (London, 1984), p. 230.
15. Shariati, *Hajj*, p. 54.
16. Seyyid Hossein Nasr, *Ideals and Realities of Islam* (London, 1966), p. 88.
17. Seyyid Hossein Nasr, 'The Significance of the *Sunnah* and *Hadith* in Islamic Spirituality', in *Islamic Spirituality: Foundation*, which he also edited (London, 1987), pp. 107–8.
18. Smith, *Islam and Modern History*, p. 305.

Select Bibliography

Abbott, Nabia, *Aishah, the Beloved of Muhammad* (Chicago, 1942).
Alighieri, Dante, *The Divine Comedy*, Cantica I: *Hell*, trans. Dorothy L. Sayers (London, 1949).
Andrae, Tor, *Muhammad: The Man and His Faith*, trans. Theophil Menzel (London, 1936).
Arberry, Arthur J., *The Koran Interpreted* (Oxford, 1964).
——, *Sufism: An Account of the Mystics of Islam* (London, 1950).
Armstrong, Karen, *The Gospel According to Woman: Christianity's Creation of the Sex War in the West* (London and New York, 1986).
——, *Holy War: The Crusades and Their Impact on Today's World* (London, 1988; New York, 1991).
Baudricourt, M., *La Guerre et le gouvernement de l'Algérie* (Paris, 1853).
Bell, Richard, *The Origin of Islam in Its Christian Environment* (London, 1926).
——, *Qu'ran, Translated with a Critical Re-arrangement of Its Suras*, 2 vols (Edinburgh, 1937–9).
Boulares, Habib, *Islam: The Fear and the Hope*, trans. Lewis Ware (London, 1990).
Brown, Peter, *The Making of Late Antiquity* (Cambridge, Mass., and London, 1978).
Campbell, Joseph (with Bill Moyers), *The Power of Myth* (New York and London, 1988).
Carlyle, Thomas, *On Heroes and Hero-Worship* (London, 1841).
Chittick, William C. (ed. and trans.), *A Shi'ite Anthology* (London, 1980).
Corbin, Henri, *Creative Imagination in the Sufism of Ibn Arabi*, trans. Ralph Manheim (London, 1970).
——, *Spiritual Body and Celestial Earth: From Mazdean Iran to Shi'ite Iran*, trans. Nancy Pearson (London, 1990).
Crone, Patricia, and Cook, Michael, *Hagarism: The Making of the Islamic World* (Cambridge, 1977).
Cupitt, Don, *Taking Leave of God* (London, 1980).
Dan, Joseph, 'The Religious Experience of the *Merkavah*', in Arthur Green (ed.), *Jewish Spirituality*, 2 vols (London, 1986), vol. I.
Daniel, Norman, *Islam and the West: The Making of an Image* (Edinburgh, 1960).
——, *The Arabs and Medieval Europe* (London and Beirut, 1975).
Deshti, Ali, *Twenty-three Years*, trans. F. R. C. Bagley (London, 1985).
Dronke, Peter, *Women Writers of the Middle Ages: A Critical Study of Texts from Perpetua (d.203) to Marguerite Porete (d.1310)* (Cambridge, 1984).
Eco, Umberto, *Travels in Hyper-Reality* (London, 1987).
Eliade, Mircea, *The Sacred and the Profane: The Nature of Religion*, trans. Willard R. Trask (New York, 1959).
Frend, W. H. C., *Martyrdom and Persecution in the Early Church: A Study of a Conflict from the Maccabees to Donatus* (Oxford, 1965).
Fuller, Peter, *Images of God: The Consolations of Lost Illusions* (London, 1982).

Gabrieli, Francesco, *Muhammad and the Conquests of Islam*, trans. Virginia Luling and Rosamund Linell (London, 1968).
Gibbon, Edward, *The Decline and Fall of the Roman Empire*, ed. Dero E. Saunders, abridged in one volume (London, 1980).
Gilsenan, Michael, *Recognizing Islam, Religion and Society in the Modern Middle East*, (London & New York, 1982).
Green, Arthur (ed.), *Jewish Spirituality*, 2 vols (London, 1986–8).
Guillaume, A. (trans. and ed.), *The Life of Muhammad: A Translation of Ishaq's Sirat Rasul Allah* (London, 1955).
Heschel, Abraham J., *The Prophets*, 2 vols (New York, 1962).
Hill, Rosalind (trans. and ed.), *Gesta Francorum or The Deeds of the Franks and the Other Pilgrims to Jerusalem* (London, 1962).
Hodgson, Marshall G. S., *The Venture of Islam: Conscience and History in a World Civilization*, 3 vols (Chicago, 1974).
Iqbal, Sir Mohammad, *Six Lectures on the Reconstruction of Religious Thought in Islam* (Lahore, 1930).
John of Joinville, *The Life of St Louis*, trans. René Hague and Natalis de Wailly (London, 1955).
Kabbani, Rana, *Europe's Myths of the Orient* (London, 1986).
——, *Letter to Christendom* (London, 1989).
Kedar, Benjamin, *Crusade and Mission: European Approaches towards the Muslims* (Princeton, 1984).
Keddie, Nikki R. (ed.), *Religion and Politics in Iran: Shiism from Quietism to Revolution* (New Haven and London, 1983).
Kepel, Gilles, *The Prophet and Pharaoh: Muslim Extremism in Egypt*, trans. Jon Rothschild (London, 1985).
Khan, Muhammad Zafrulla, *Islam: Its Meaning for Modern Man* (London, 1962).
Leaman, Oliver, *An Introduction to Medieval Islamic Philosophy* (Cambridge, 1985).
Lewis, Bernard, *The Arabs in History* (London, 1950).
——, *Islam from the Prophet Mohammad to the Capture of Constantinople*, 2 vols, vol I: *Politics and War*, vol. II: *Religion and Society* (New York and London, 1976).
——, *The Muslim Discovery of Europe* (New York and London, 1982).
——, *The Jews of Islam* (New York and London, 1982).
——, *Semites and Anti-Semites: An Inquiry into Conflict and Prejudice* (London, 1986).
Liebeschuetz, J. H. W. G., *Continuity and Change in Roman Religion* (Cambridge, 1979).
Lings, Martin, *Muhammad: His Life Based on the Earliest Sources* (London, 1983).
Mansfield, Peter, *The Arabs* (3rd edn, London, 1985).
Massignon, Louis, *La Passion d'Hallaj*, 2 vols (Paris, 1922).
Nasr, Sayyid Hossein, *Muhammad: Man of Allah* (London, 1982).
——, (ed.), *Islamic Spirituality: Foundation* (London, 1987).
——, *Ideals and Realities of Islam* (London, 1966).
Nicholson, R. A., *The Mystics of Islam* (London, 1914).
——, *Eastern Poetry and Prose* (Cambridge, 1922).
Parrinder, Geoffrey, *Sex in the World's Religions* (London, 1980).
Pernoud, Régine, *The Crusaders*, trans. Enid Grant (Edinburgh and London, 1963).
Prideaux, Humphry, *The True Nature of Imposture, Fitly Displayed in the Life of Mahomet* (7th edn, London, 1708).
Rodinson, Maxime, *Mohammed*, trans. Anne Carter (London, 1971).
——, *Europe and the Mystique of Islam*, trans. Roger Veinous (London, 1988).
Ruthven, Malise, *Islam in the World* (London, 1984).
——, *A Satanic Affair: Salman Rushdie and the Rage of Islam* (London, 1990).

Said, Edward W., *Orientalism: Western Conceptions of the Orient* (New York and London, 1978).
——, *Covering Islam: How the Media and the Experts Determine How We See the Rest of the World* (New York and London, 1981).
Sardar, Ziauddin, and Davies, Merryl Wyn, *Distorted Imagination: Lessons from the Rushdie Affair* (London, 1990).
Saunders, J. J., *A History of Medieval Islam* (London and Boston, 1965).
Schimmel, Annemarie, *And Muhammad Is His Messenger: The Veneration of the Prophet in Islamic Piety* (Chapel Hill and London, 1985).
Scholem, Gershom G., *Major Trends in Jewish Mysticism* (2nd edn, London, 1955).
Schuon, Frithjof, *Understanding Islam* (London, 1963).
Shariati, Ali, *Hajj*, trans. Laleh Bakhtiar (Tehran, 1988).
——, *What Is To Be Done?: The Enlightened Thinkers and an Islamic Renaissance*, ed. Farhang Rajaee (Houston, 1986).
Sidersky, D., *Les Origines des légendes musulmans dans le Coran et dans les vies des prophètes* (Paris, 1933).
Smith, Wilfred Cantwell, *Islam in Modern History* (Princeton and London, 1957).
——, *Towards a World Theology* (London, 1981).
Southern, R. W., *Western Views of Islam in the Middle Ages* (Cambridge, Mass., 1962).
Steiner, George, *Real Presences: Is There Anything* in *What We Say?* (London, 1989).
Torrey, C. C, *The Commercial–Theological Terms in the Koran* (Leiden, 1892).
Toynbee, A. J., *A Study of History* (London, 1951).
Trimingham, J. Spencer, *Christianity Among the Arabs in Pre-Islamic Times* (London, 1979).
Von Grunebaum, G. E., *Classical Islam: A History 600–1258*, trans. Katherine Watson (London, 1970).
Watt, W. Montgomery, *Muhammad at Mecca* (Oxford, 1953).
——, *Muhammad at Medina* (Oxford, 1956).
——, *Islam and the Integration of Society* (London, 1961).
——, *Muhammad's Mecca: History in the Qu'ran* (Edinburgh, 1988).
Weldon, Fay, *Sacred Cows* (London, 1989).
Wensinck, A. J., *The Muslim Creed: Its Genesis and Historical Development* (Cambridge, 1932).

Index